Archetypes

PUBLISHED WITH GENEROUS SUPPORT FROM:
ARNE V. SCHLESCHS FOND
BESTLES FOND
THE DREYER FOUNDATION
LEMVIGH-MÜLLER FONDEN
NEW CARLSBERG FOUNDATION
POLITIKEN-FONDEN

Arche

ESSENTIAL WORKS OF
DANISH DESIGN / MICHAEL SHERIDAN

STRANDBERG PUBLISHING

types

PROLOGUE
Living History / 6

Kitchen and Table

KAY BOJESEN 1938/1951–53
Grand Prix / 24

GRETHE MEYER / IBI TRIER MØRCH 1957–59
Stub / 44

HANNE VALEUR 1962
K-60 / 58

ARNE JACOBSEN 1964–67
Cylinda-line / 76

GRETHE MEYER 1966–71
Hvidpot / 92

GRETHE MEYER 1970–76
Ildpot / 116

OLE PALSBY 1976–77
Eva Trio / 132

Table and Chair

ARNE JACOBSEN 1954–55
FH 3207 / 150

VILHELM WOHLERT 1957–58
Louisiana Chair / 162

POUL HENNINGSEN 1955–58
PH 5 / 174

BØRGE MOGENSEN 1964–66
Fredericia 6286 / 188

Contents

Living Rooms

MOGENS KOCH 1942
Le Klint 105 / 204

GRETHE MEYER / BØRGE MOGENSEN 1952–57
Boligens Byggeskabe / 218

BØRGE MOGENSEN 1956–63
Fredericia 2254 / 234

MOGENS KOCH 1938/1960
MK-49 / 246

KIM NAVER 1967–69
Cotil 1828 / 256

KNUD HOLSCHER 1973–76/1981–82
String-line / 270

Terrace and Garden

MOGENS KOCH 1933/1938/1960
MK-16 / 292

BØRGE MOGENSEN 1964–69
SM 50 / 304

KARSTEN RAVN / LARS LUNDQUIST 1969–73
RL Grill Series / 316

EPILOGUE
Design for Life / 336

NOTES / 342

BIBLIOGRAPHY / 350

INDEX / 352

CREDITS / 354

ACKNOWLEDGMENTS / 355

Scattered throughout history of Danish design there exists a special class of things that were designed many decades ago and yet remain contemporary, by virtue of their basic functions, unequaled utility and modest forms. This book examines twenty of those objects or series of objects in unprecedented detail, in the hope of promoting a general appreciation of their excellence and a deeper understanding of the people who designed them. In every case, the designer or designers purged their creative work of artistic signature or personal flourish. Instead, they pursued the distilled or essential form of the object through a union of purpose, materials and production technique. On the basis of that essential character, these designs can be classified as **archetypes**.

The idea of the archetype can be traced to ancient Greece and has been subject to many interpretations. Plato and his followers used the term *eidos* (meaning both Idea and Form) to discuss an imaginary example of a thing that represented its fundamental character. On that basis, modern philosophers employed the term "archetype" (from the Greek *archétypon*) to refer to the original thing from which later examples are derived. In the field of psychology, Carl Jung used the term to describe figures that reoccur in the subconscious mind and provide tools for interpreting behavior. In literature and then cinema, the term describes a type of character that embodies certain traits. Another interpretation of the archetype — the one employed in this book — is the object that incorporates lessons from earlier examples to arrive at a nearly ideal example of the type.

Mogens Koch. Drawing
for pleated paper lantern.
Ink on paper, August 1942.

This book pursues a middle ground between the typical types of design books: the monograph focused on a single designer and the historical overview. As the monograph is focused on the biography and personality of the designer, the objects generally illustrate the arc of the subject's career. By necessity, an overview of a particular era or design movement uses exemplary objects to illustrate general developments and high points. While both types of books are illuminating, the objects are often presented with only one or two illustrations, and detailed information may be limited by the format. By combining detailed descriptions of twenty objects with biographical information about their designers, it becomes possible to gain insight into each object while also recognizing its significance to the designer's production. A focus on practical concerns reveals that these historical artifacts remain entirely suited to modern living.

The reader will naturally wonder how the objects were selected, especially as they represent a narrow range of designers, several of whom appear in multiple chapters. Moreover, a wide range of well-known objects representing recognized masters of Danish design have been omitted. In fact, the physical definition of an archetype — a thing that has found its essential form and peak of utility through a process of evolution — provided the basis for the selection of objects. In the history of Danish Design, the fundamental process of evolution was the progression from handmade objects for a few to factory-made items for the many. That fact is generally recognized, with the exhibitions of the Copenhagen Cabinetmakers' Guild (established 1554) as the most commonly cited example.

Beginning in the 1927, as cabinetmakers struggled to maintain their trade, the Guild initiated a program that paired master artisans with architects for the purpose of creating and exhibiting new designs.[1] Over the next forty years, those events provided the basis for the renewal of the Danish furniture tradition, by exhibiting pieces designed by Kaare Klint and his former students, including Mogens Koch, Ole Wanscher, Orla Mølgaard-Nielsen and Rigmor Andersen. Equally or more importantly, the exhibitions served as the incubator for the Danish furniture industry by giving young designers, such as Finn Juhl, Hans J. Wegner and Børge Mogensen, the opportunity to create experimental models, many of which were transformed into factory-made versions.

PROLOGUE

Living History

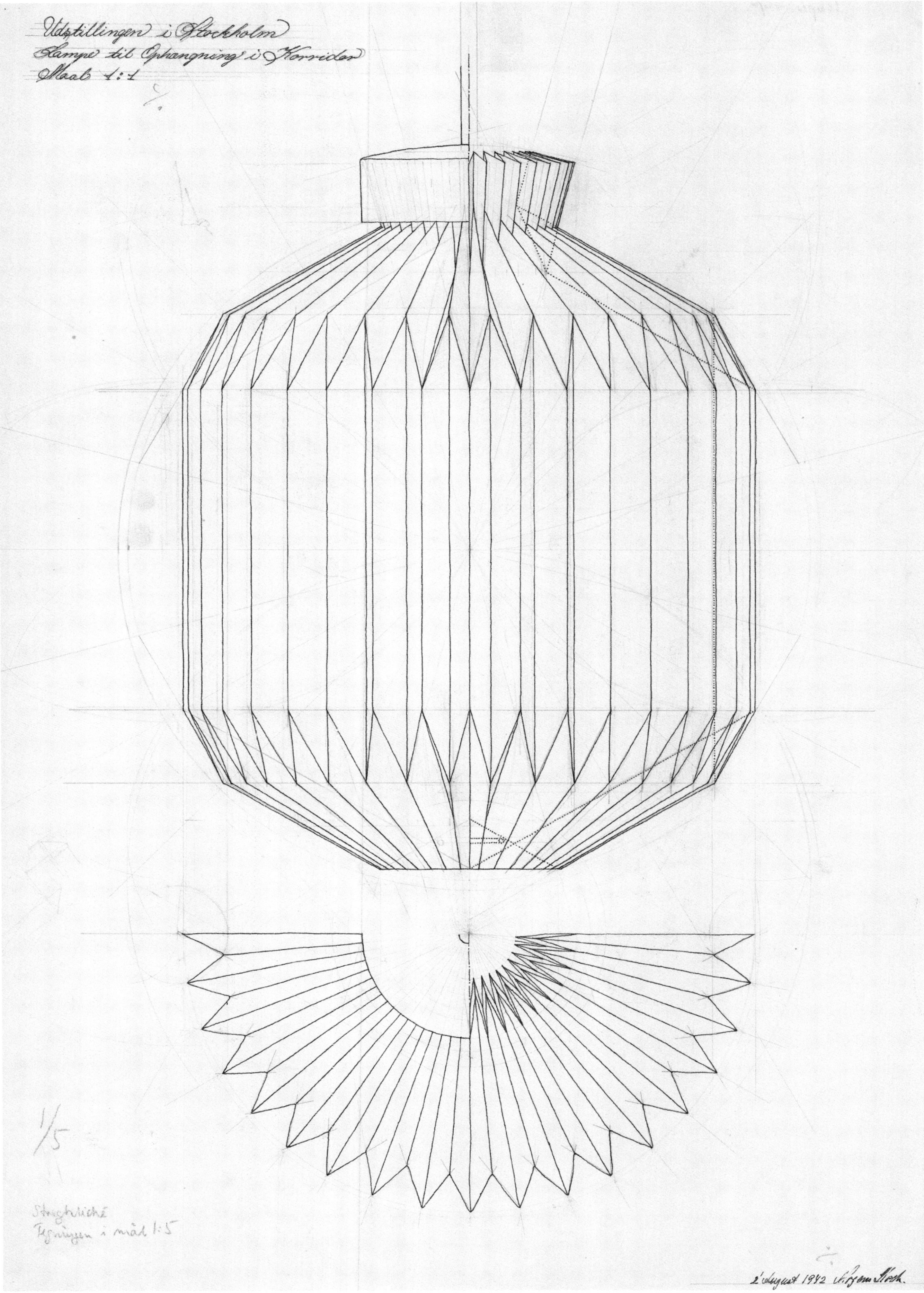

Udstillingen i Stockholm
Lampe til Ophængning i Korridor
Maal 1:1

1/5

Størrelsen
Tegningen i maal 1:5

2' August 1942 Jørgen Utzon

Following the working definition of the archetype, the objects featured in this book are limited to things designed for mass production. A number of the objects were initially handcrafted, but each of them was conceived with the factory in mind. All twenty of the objects represent what Grethe Meyer described as "a compromise between practical demands, possibilities of production and aesthetic design."[2] In that case, *compromise* does not signal a retreat from excellence, but a union of those three factors into an indivisible whole. That union was the ideal to which each of the designers aspired.

The requirement of industrial design eliminates a vast amount of furniture designed by major talents, most notably pieces designed by Kaare Klint and Poul Kjærholm. Both architects pursued the ideal of the archetype by emphasizing the character of their materials and using geometry to discipline their forms. Klint's insistence on perfect craftsmanship ensured that nearly all of his furniture was made by cabinetmakers.[3] However, a number of his former students applied his principles to industrial design and created a string of archetypes in a range of fields, as described throughout the book. Poul Kjærholm's mature work was based on steel, but the perfection of his furniture is utterly dependent on handicraft. Indeed, he was Klint's most direct successor.[4]

The second standard of selection was the pursuit of forms that do not display a personal style and which are almost anonymous. The working definition of the archetype contradicts the ideal of the designer as an individual artist, because the object is the result of an evolutionary process that incorporates lessons from works by other designers. The aesthetic talents of the people who designed the archetypes in this book are undeniable. And yet, they worked to avoid an artistic signature, even as they knew that their works would be marketed as "designed by Mogens Koch" or "designed by Grethe Meyer." In that regard, they were following the modest example of the artisan, by designing objects that were rooted in tradition and making incremental improvements or refinements.

As such, we can recognize an artisanal approach to industrial design that eschewed artistic expression in favor of geometry, which is not a style but instead a universal language of form. Each of the designers had a deep understanding of their working materials. Indeed, several of them were trained in handicraft before they became industrial designers. Regardless of their training, every one of them understood their creations as links in a long chain of cultural development that stretches deep into the past and might be sustained with industrial methods. Whether silversmith or weaver, cabinetmaker or architect, they understood that the age of handcraft had passed into history and that the values and standards of the workshop would only survive if they were transferred to the factory.

The standard of anonymous form naturally eliminates factory-made furniture by designers whose work was rooted in personal expression. The obvious examples are chairs designed by Finn Juhl and by Hans J. Wegner, both of whom achieved celebrity status on the basis of their sculptural forms. Juhl pursued a literal interpretation of the traditional Danish concept of *møbelkunst* (furniture art) and compared his work to Surrealist sculpture.[5] Wegner's treatment of wood was so distinct that his finest works bear an unmistakable artistic signature.[6] Juhl served as a guiding light for younger designers who rejected Kaare Klint's teachings of modesty and evolution, which they regarded as an infringement on creative freedom. Several of them became leading lights in the Danish furniture industry.[7]

Finn Juhl. BO 59 lounge chair, 1946. Teak and wool upholstery. Bovirke. / Hans J. Wegner. CH 27 lounge chair, 1952. Oak and rattan. Carl Hansen & Søn. ← Installation view of 1933 Copenhagen Cabinetmakers' Guild exhibition. Display of furniture designed by Kaare Klint and produced by Rud. Rasmussens Snedkerier. In the foreground, two sizes of the Red Chair (Models 3758 and 3949) designed in 1927/28. At right, folding deck chair (Model 4699) and folding table (Model 4701). On the floor, rugs designed by Mogens Koch and woven by Ea Koch.

The third standard of selection contained within the definition of an archetype is absolute fitness to purpose. Indeed, utility is the fundamental requirement if a useful object is to be considered a nearly ideal example of its type. Moreover, it is the continuing utility of an object that ensures its contemporary character. For example, Bang & Olufsen televisions of the 1980s were designed with a primary focus on the consumer's experience, but they cannot be considered contemporary, because the technology has become obsolete. By contrast, the objects in this book are so simple and serve such basic needs that they will always remain useful. As the designers rejected personal expression, they used the purpose of a thing as the basis of its design.

That approach requires patience and discipline on the part of the designer and of the other participants in the process. What is often overlooked in books on design is the role of the producer in supporting the research, study and testing necessary to arrive at a completely resolved design. Many of the designers represented in this book worked with companies that were willing to make the investments of time and money required to develop products that are not only beautiful but also truly practical and extremely durable. For the most part, those companies were privately held, highly specialized businesses that were operated by directors who stood behind their wares. The fact that they did so ensured a level of quality in design and use that is even more uncommon today than it was decades ago.

The requirement for absolute utility excludes many mass-produced objects with extremely simple forms, especially in the fields of tableware and cookware. Starting around 1950, a number of manufacturers engaged sculptors to create new designs that would update their public image and appeal to the market in the United States, where a magazine editor had invented the concept of "Danish Modern."[8] The most successful artist-designers were Henning Koppel, who was hired by the Georg Jensen silver smithy in 1945, and Jens H. Quistgaard, who worked for an American company founded to promote his designs: Dansk Designs.[9] While both Koppel and Quistgaard had a gift for graceful forms, the practical aspect of their designs often suffered due to their inherently artistic approach.

This selection of Danish domestic archetypes is certainly incomplete. However, a wider range of objects might have overwhelmed both author and reader without advancing the understanding of archetypal design. Instead, this book examines a single example of several useful objects that are commonly found in the home: flatware and tableware, upright chairs with or without arms, lamps for various types of lighting, multi-purpose textile and so forth. The glaring omission is a sofa. While there are several archetypal examples, television and then streaming have led to several types with very different forms. While models based on the chair remain in production, low, heavily padded sofas that resemble a bed are extremely popular. As a result, there is no single type equally useful to everyone, and it is impossible to present only one example.

The objects were selected on the basis of excellence rather than commercial status. Eight of them have been in continuous production since they were introduced, while the others were discontinued decades ago. During the research for this book, six of the objects were revived, although one was later discontinued. In fact, the commercial success or failure of these objects is unrelated to their useful qualities. Just as commercial status was irrelevant to the selection of objects, the identity of the designer was also irrelevant. They assured their inclusion in this book while creating their archetypal objects decades ago. As it happened, fifteen of the twenty archetypes are the work of former students or employees of Kaare Klint, the architect and educator who provided the theoretical basis for so much of modern Danish design. A summary of his principles serves as a useful prelude for the detailed descriptions of the selected objects.

Jens H. Quistgaard. Fjord flatware, 1953. Stainless steel and teak. Dansk Designs.
/ Jens H. Quistgaard. Købenstyle pot, 1954. Enameled steel. Dansk Designs.
← Poul Kjærholm. PK 20 lounge chair, 1968. Chrome-plated steel and cowhide. Produced by E. Kold Christensen.

Kaare Klint was the second son of the painter, engineer and architect Peder Vilhelm Jensen-Klint who is best remembered for his monumental Grundtvig Church, which was constructed entirely of yellow brick over a period of nineteen years (1921–40) and finished by the son. Born in 1888, Kaare Klint had an eclectic education that included studies with the painter and designer Johan Rohde, instruction in furniture design and interior decoration from the Arts and Crafts master Jens Møller-Jensen and architectural training from his father. In 1913, Kaare Klint won a second prize in a competition for factory-made furniture, which attracted the attention of the architect Carl Petersen, a former student of Jensen-Klint who became a mentor to the young man.

During 1914–15, Klint worked for Petersen and designed furniture for the Faaborg Museum, which is located on the island of Funen and devoted to the work of the Funen Painters, who were most active during 1885–1925.[10] The completion of the museum, in 1910, initiated a revival of neoclassical architecture in Denmark and led to Petersen's appointment as a professor at the School of Architecture within the Royal Danish Academy. In 1923, with Petersen's support, Klint was employed as a lecturer at the School and charged with establishing a department of furniture design and interior architecture.[11] He would spend the rest of his life teaching at the Academy, where he was appointed professor in 1944, and designing furniture and interior architecture for a combination of private clients and public institutions.

Klint operated the Department of Furniture Design as an extension of his practice by assigning projects that paralleled his own work for clients and provided the students with practical challenges. His designs and the students' assignments were based on a careful study of practical concerns, which might include the contents of a storage unit or the seating arrangements around a table. The fundamental tool in that research was the precise measurement of objects and people, in order to identify typical dimensions that would satisfy the purpose of the furniture using the least amount of space. Assessing the state of Danish furniture in 1948, Mogens Koch provided a summary of Klint's teaching methods that emphasizes the dimensional surveys:

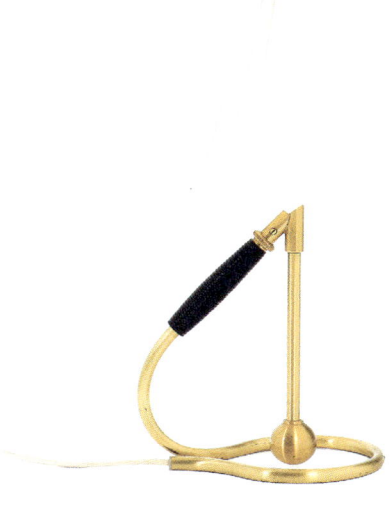

"Kaare Klint's furniture school at the Academy of Fine Arts, which was attended by architects as well as by carpenters who had first graduated from the School of Arts and Crafts, was fundamental to this development. The requirements for size were carefully examined in relation to the human dimensions, which of course must directly determine the proportions of the furniture. The requirements for storage furniture, such as wardrobes and cabinets for tableware and linen, books and paper, were carefully studied through measurements of garments, porcelain, glass, cutlery, tablecloths and book and paper formats, and everything was arranged the furniture in a way that economized on space. Finally, of course, the arrangement of furniture or the furnishing of rooms, with the many possible combination, was addressed."[12]

Klint's lessons can be distilled to five points that exerted a profound and lasting effect on his students and employees and filtered through the larger communities of artisans and architects:

Kaare Klint. Church Chair with arms, 1936. Beech and paper cord. Klint's simple ladderback chair was the only one of his designs to enter mass production. The version without arms was fitted with a shelf for a hymnal and a hat rack and used to furnish his Bethlehem Church as well as his father's Grundtvig Church, which the son completed in 1940. All of those chairs were produced by Fritz Hansen Eftf., which kept both versions of the chair in production for several decades. / Sideboard with removable trays (Model 4122), 1930. Cuban mahogany. Rud. Rasmussens Snedkerier. ← Kaare Klint. Table lamp (Model 306), 1944. Brass, leather and paper. Le Klint A/S. / The Spherical Bed (Model 5761), 1938. Cuban mahogany and ebony. Cotton bedspread woven by Lis Ahlmann. Rud. Rasmussens Snedkerier.

13

History as Resource Klint regarded the history of furniture as a treasury of useful solutions to age-old concerns that could be adapted to contemporary conditions and production methods. As a result, he found it wasteful when avant-garde architects announced the arrival of a new era based on technology and imagined a fresh start.

Utility by Design The starting point for the renewal of historical models was a precise assessment of current needs. The dimensional studies that Klint assigned to the students were a form of functional analysis, which revealed the requirements for a useful cabinet, sideboard or bookcase.

Geometric Form As Klint and his students renewed and refined historical models, they stripped away the decorative features that reflected earlier social structures and artistic ideals. Rather than search for a new style, they employed geometry to create anonymous forms that would emphasize the materials and construction.

Material Character Klint's aversion to decorative style was matched by his deep affinity for natural materials, which were treated as simply as possible. In that way, the piece of furniture would be characterized by the colors and textures of the materials, while the role of the designer would be relegated to the background.

Kaare Klint. Sketch for modular office furniture. Pencil on paper, 1917. Klint's sketch encapsulates his idea of using a module to reconcile the sizes of useful articles with the scale of the human body. → Arne Jacobsen. Study for sideboard to hold tableware for six persons. Pencil and watercolor on paper, 1926. Jacobsen's studies at the Royal Academy's School of Architecture included at least one semester in the Department of Furniture Design, where he absorbed Kaare Klint's ideal of using geometry as the basis of functional design.

Unity of All Things Klint's ideal was a harmonious union of furniture and interior space. The instrument of that harmony was a simple geometric module — typically a square or a rectangle — that allowed him to scale his design to the size of the room and could also be repeated in details and patterns.

Reviewing Klint's principles and teaching methods, it becomes clear that he was training his students to design archetypes, even if he did not use that word. Moreover, we can recognize his fundamental role in the larger arc of Danish design history, from handcrafted items to mass-produced objects that, nonetheless, preserved at least the values of the workshop. Despite his early interest in inexpensive furniture for the home, Klint's Church Chair would be the only one of his furniture designs to enter mass production. And yet, he succeeded in his ambition to create factory-made furniture, indirectly, through the work of his followers.

The clearest example of that success is found in the work of Mogens Koch, who employed Klint's teachings to create a handmade bookcase that serves as a module for larger assemblies and provided the basis for a factory-made variant. Summarizing that process of evolution also provides a glimpse at an archetype of Danish industrial design that might well have been included among the featured objects, were its creator not already amply represented.

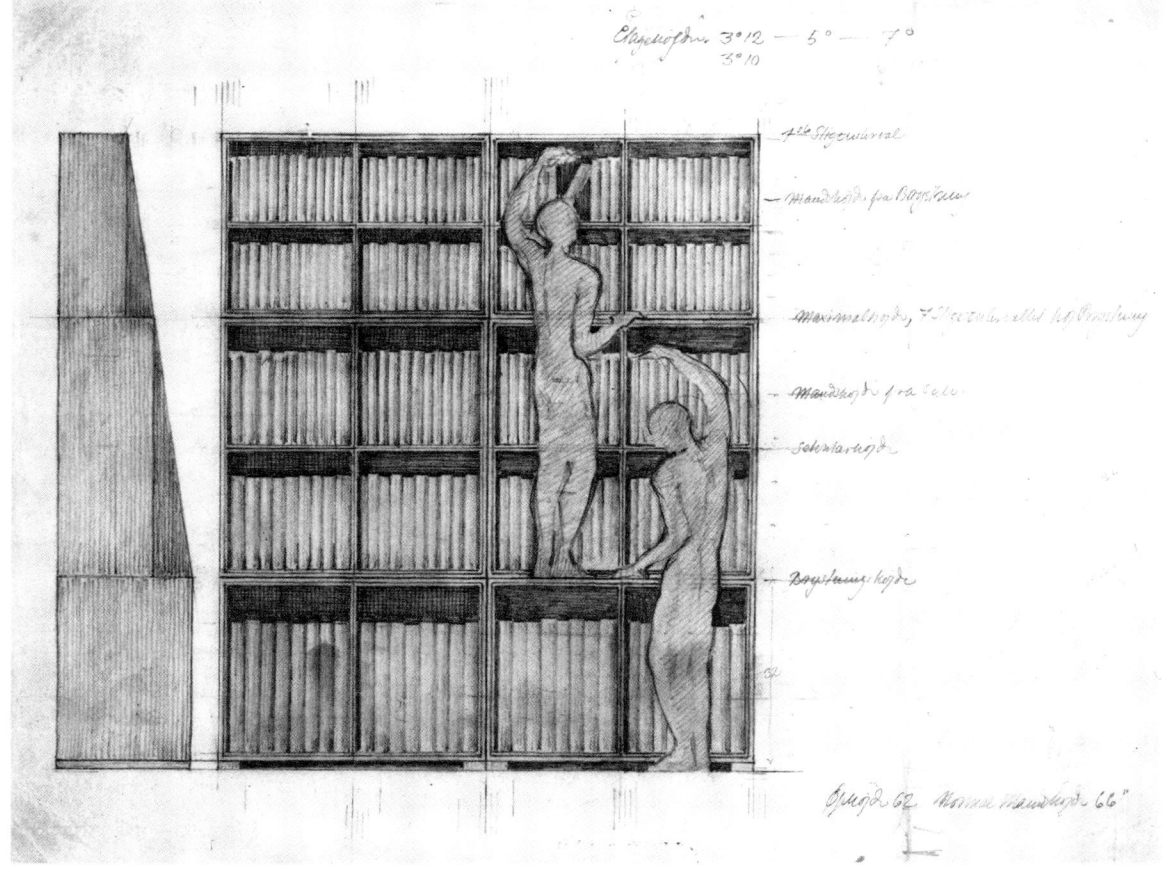

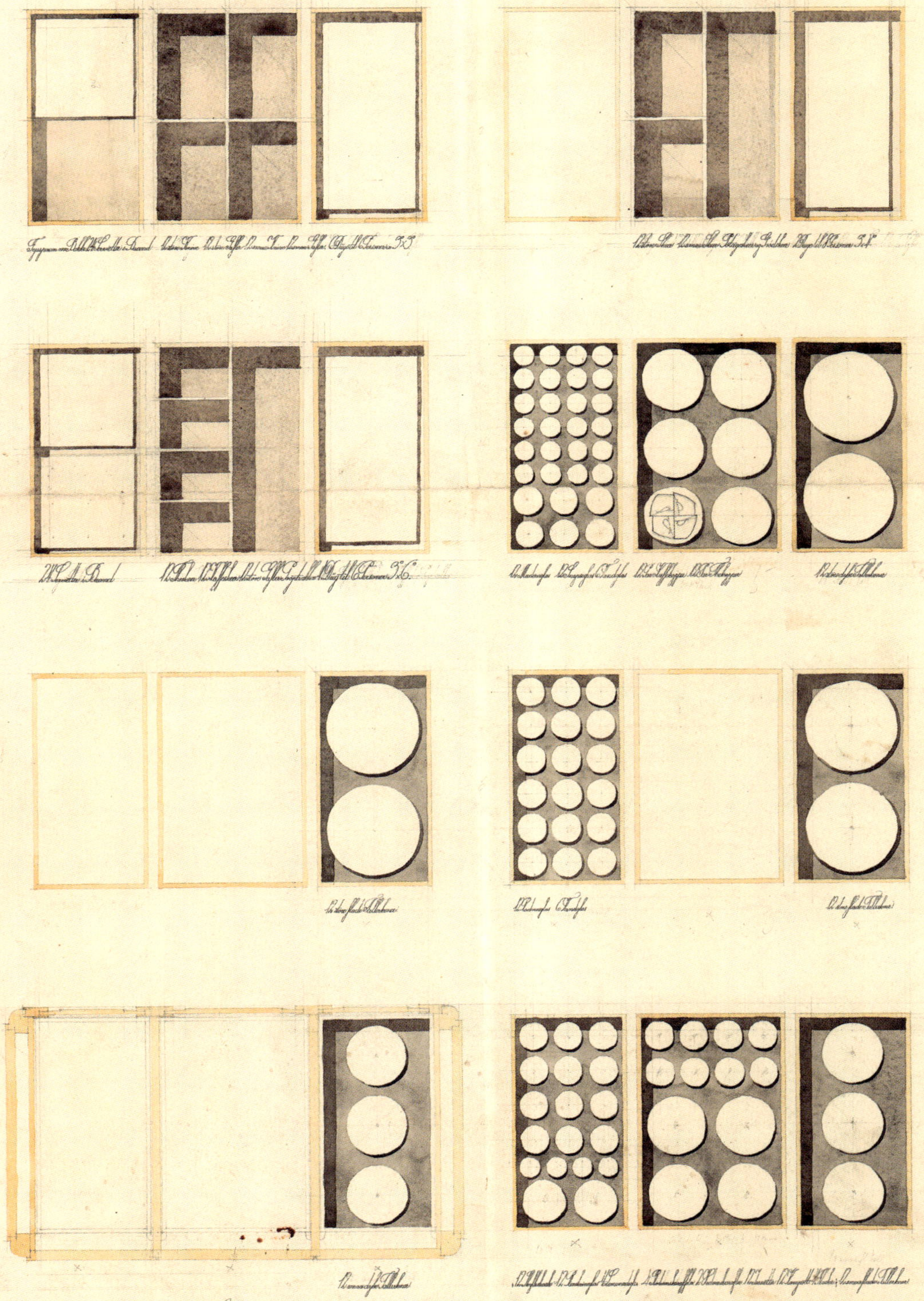

In 1927, Mogens Koch and his wife, Ea (Varming) Koch, moved into the modest rowhouse on the outskirts of Copenhagen that they would occupy for the rest of their lives. Faced with the problem of storing books, Koch imagined a modular box that could be combined to create the equivalent of built-in bookcases.[13] As the rooms in the house were rather small, the box should be small enough to allow flexible arrangements in different rooms. Moreover, the size of the box was limited by the fact that it should be easy for one person to move. Finally, Koch was confronted by the fact that books come in different formats with varied heights.

Koch was certainly familiar with Klint's 1917 project for modular office furniture, which was intended for mass production but never realized. And yet, Koch hoped to create a single piece of furniture that would accommodate books of different heights without the use of moving parts. His solution was a square box divided into six compartments that would hold books of two common heights, depending on the orientation. To maximize storage space, he reduced the thickness of the shelves and sides of the box to an absolute minimum dimension, which required the use of premium-quality wood. Aware that uneven floors might disrupt the alignment of the boxes, he created a narrow molding on the front edges of the box that creates shadow lines and obscures any minor gaps.

Shelving unit, 1930. These examples were produced in Douglas fir by Rud. Rasmussens Snedkerier. Rotating the square unit makes it possible to store books and other objects of different heights. → Mogens Koch. Study for stacking shelving unit. Ink on graph paper, 1928.

In 1928, Koch had a small set of square boxes made by a local carpenter. Two years later, Rud. Rasmussens Snedkerier, the old-line workshop that was already producing several of Klint's designs, initiated production of the MK bookcase in mahogany. As he prepared the working drawing, Koch increased the size of the box a few centimeters, to 76 x 76 cm, and also made the central bay slightly wider so that it appears the same width as the two outer bays. That refinement had the added advantage of providing a third height for books. In addition, Rud. Rasmussen instituted dovetail joints at the corners of the box, to provide equally strong joints no matter the orientation. Despite the high cost, Koch's handcrafted box has been in continuous production since 1930, in a variety of woods, and remains unsurpassed for ingenuity and flexibility.

In 1942, Koch and Klint's young assistant Børge Mogensen, who divided his time between the two architects' offices, was recruited to lead the new furniture design office at FDB, the joint association of consumer cooperatives in Denmark (now Coop Danmark). His task was to develop a collection of factory-made furniture that could be sold to FDB's members at low prices, within twenty-four months (p. 188). While he and his staff designed the most common items, he employed designs by friends and mentors for more specialized types. Hans J. Wegner supplied the design for a rocking chair, Kaare Klint designed an armchair that was never produced, and Mogens Koch contributed his 1935 design for a crib. Koch designed the crib with two nested elements that could be extended as the child grew. In the meantime, the removable railings could be used as a playpen.

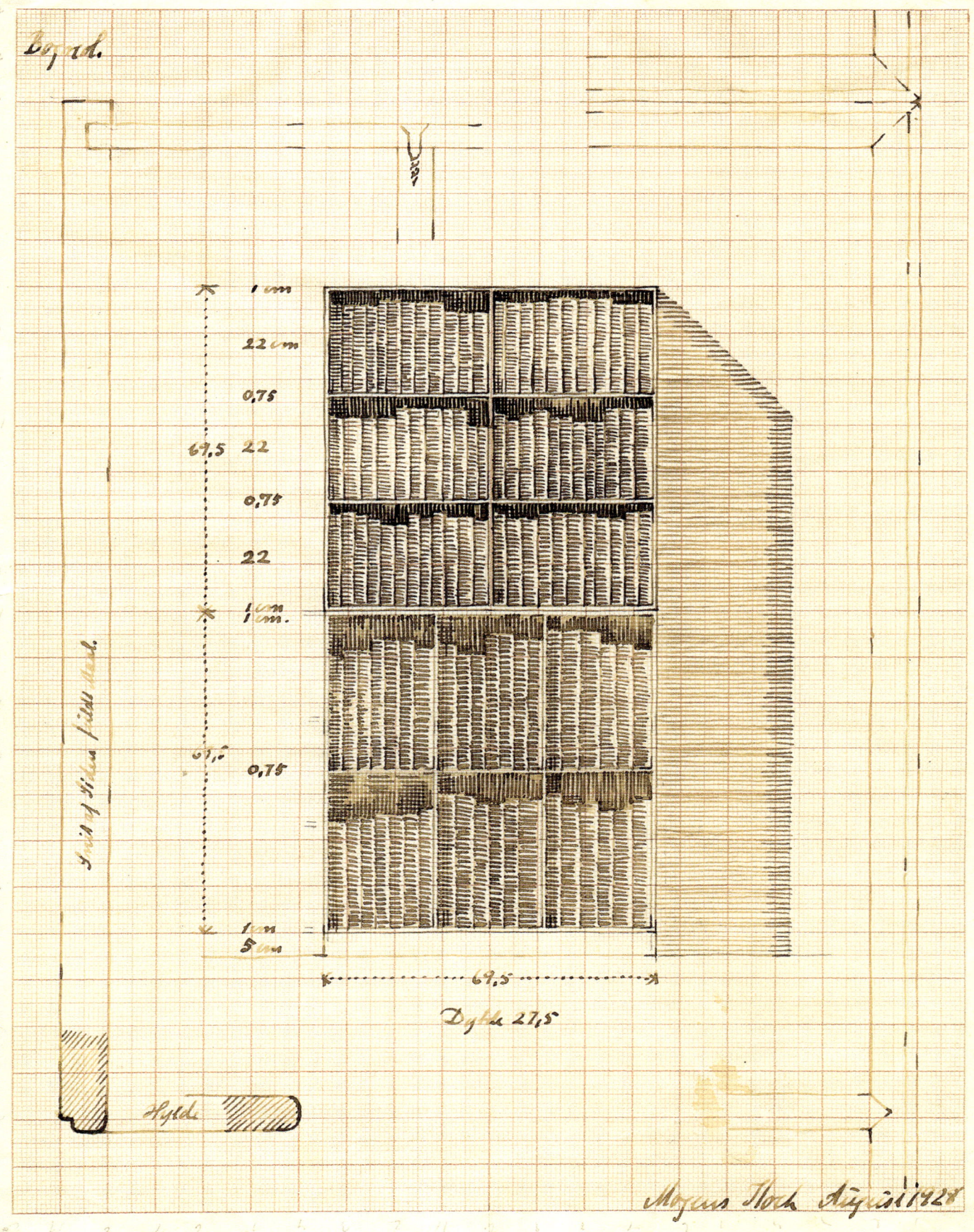

Koch's other contribution to the FDB furniture collection was a small rectangular box, 36 x 54 cm, with two compartments, made in pine in two depths.[14] Similarly to Koch's handcrafted bookcase, the small box could be rotated and stacked in different combinations. Those child-sized boxes for books and toys are clearly derived from Koch's square bookcase of 1928, which was indebted to Klint's modular furniture project of 1917. As such, we recognize the progression from an idea to a handcrafted object and, finally, an industrial product designed with the same care and concern as the original handmade item. FDB manufactured Koch's small pine box for about a decade and exited the furniture business in the early 1980s. Forty years later, Coop Danmark established a subsidiary — FDB Møbler — that has reissued several pieces designed by Børge Mogensen and his successors in the FDB furniture office as well as Koch's book box, which is now produced in oak and marketed for use by people of all ages.

Mogens Koch. Assembly of stacking storage units designed in 1940. Produced in pine for FDB furniture collection, circa 1943. / Stacking storage units, designed 1940 and produced in oak by FDB Møbler since 2022. / Child's bed and removable railings used as a playpen, 1935. Produced in beech for FDB furniture collection, circa 1943. ← Assembly of shelving units and cabinets designed in 1946. These examples were produced in pine by Rud. Rasmussens Snedkerier.

The twenty archetypal objects are arranged into four sections: Kitchen and Table, Table and Chair, Living Rooms and Terrace and Garden. That functional arrangement makes it possible to consider items that are naturally used together. Moreover, it becomes possible to move beyond the convention of ordering objects by chronology or material, which may obscure common threads between objects. Within each of the four sections, the objects are arranged chronologically, which is helpful when examining objects designed by the same person. Given the small cast of characters and their close connections, there are a number of references between chapters, which are supplied with a page number for easy location.

Each one of the twenty object or series of objects is examined in a chapter that provides a detailed description of the designer's intentions and locates the object in the context of their career. By necessity, those descriptions include biographical material that provides insight into the designer's character and, not infrequently, their struggle to see their design into production. The fundamental part of each chapter is the description of how the object is used or what is does, which is essential to appreciating both its archetypal status and its contemporary character. A number of the objects appear so simple that their true utility is often only discovered in use; this is especially true of the folding furniture.

Every one of the designers possessed a deep understanding of their working materials and the cultural background of the thing they were designing. Exploring the origins of their objects involves references to historical and technical factors that played key roles in the design process. Those factors ranged from solid geometry and the properties of different ceramic materials to the history of chairs and the basics of outdoor cooking. In addition to illuminating the objects, those brief excursions into other fields locate the designers' works in larger circles of history and reveal the complexity and depth of their methods.

The fundamental purpose of this book is to convey the extraordinary character of these archetypes as physical things. To that end, they are illustrated with new photos that were taken especially for this book. Where possible, the objects are presented at full scale in order to communicate their tactile quality. As a result, every one of the chapters opens with a full-scale image of the object, which presents the place at which the human hand meets the piece of industrial design and finds a comfortable point of contact. Those photographs are supplemented with archival material and with a series of line drawings that were made for this book, as the chapters were being written and the invisible aspects of the object became clear.

Those photos and drawings support an understanding of each object as the result of a process of design evolution, which is a defining feature of the archetype. As a matter of fact, not one of these objects suddenly appeared on a blank piece of paper as the result of a burst of inspiration. Instead, each one is the result of a long process of cultural development that was followed by the designer's attempt, sometimes lasting for years, to combine ideas and examples into a new and improved model. Presenting the sources of each object illuminates the designer's talent for transformation, while challenging the myth of individual artistic genius in applied art or (in Danish) *brugskunst*: useful art produced through the union of aesthetics and practical concerns.

Beyond the pleasure that follows an understanding of these archetypal objects, this book will hopefully serve as a resource for anyone seeking information about useful things. With that in mind, a number of the chapters include practical information that extends beyond the typical contents of a design history book. The people who designed these mass-produced archetypes did so in the hope of improving many people's daily lives. Each chapter concludes with a production history that describes the current status of the object or series of object. In several cases, there are remarks about second-hand options, which in some cases is the only viable source and in every case the environmentally sustainable option. And so, we can recognize these archetypes of Danish design as treasures from the past that will serve the present and provide the heirlooms of the future.

Børge Mogensen. Folding outdoor furniture, 1964–70.
Originally produced in beech by Søborg Møbelfabrik.
Now manufactured in teak by Carl Hansen & Søn.
During the 1970s, the pieces were sold in brown paper bags that recalled the packaging for charcoal.

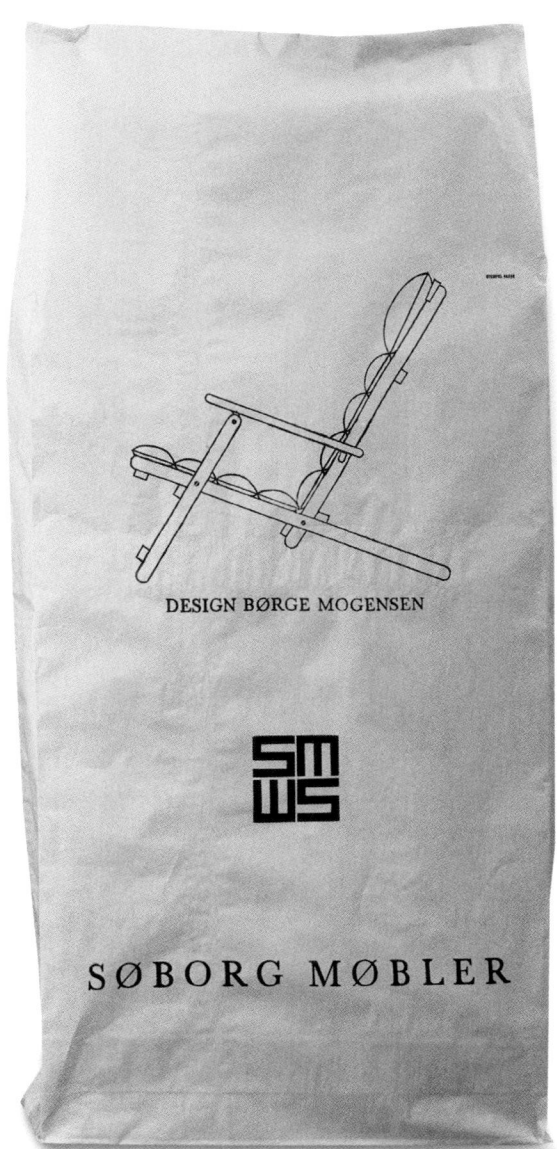
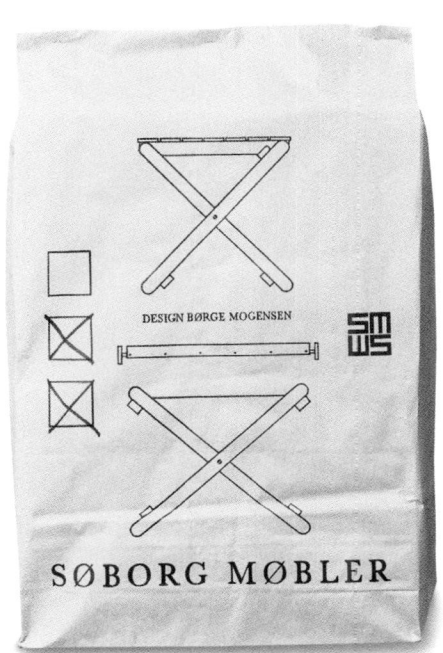
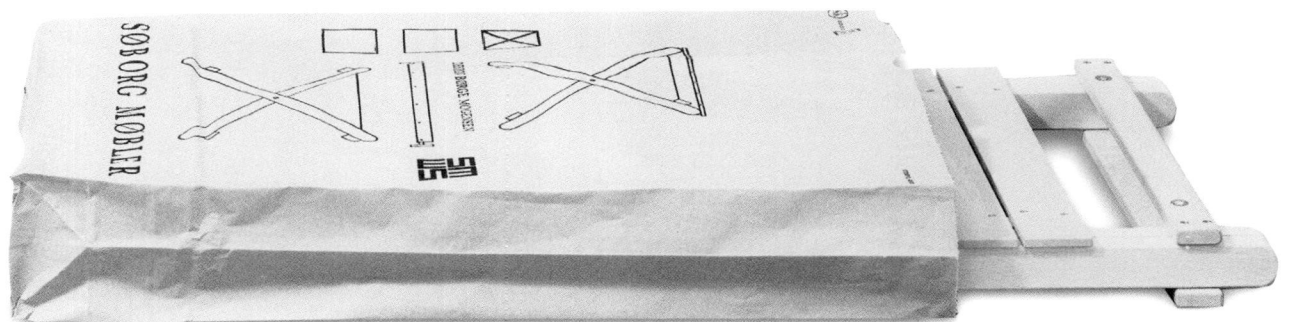

Kitchen

and Table

There is no more precise example of an archetypal Danish design — a mass-produced object with an anonymous and ideal form that resulted from a process of creative evolution and remains absolutely useful in our own time — than the stainless steel eating utensils designed by the silversmith Kay Bojesen. Most often remembered for the charming wooden toys that he created as a hobby, Bojesen is usually described as a genial fellow akin to Santa Claus: a round, jolly man with a workshop who created playthings for children.[1] The popular focus on Bojesen's toys and familiar stories about his playful persona have obscured his important work in several other fields, most notably the design of flatware, which he described as his primary interest.

Behind his cheerful demeanor, Bojesen was a "practical idealist"[2] who was entirely serious about his work and played many roles in Danish cultural life beyond the creation of toys: outstanding artisan, crusader for ethics in applied art, pioneering industrial designer and, finally, Denmark's leading designer of eating utensils during the twentieth century. He was also a visionary who recognized in the 1920s that the era of handicraft was ending, and that maintaining a genuine national culture would require a union of artisanal values and industrial methods. In 1953, Bojesen realized precisely that union with steel flatware that has not been bettered in seven decades and which encapsulates the arc of Danish design during 1925–75: from handmade luxuries for a few to factory-made articles for the many that were rooted in the values of the workshop.

Bojesen's first steps on his circuitous path to a leading position in Danish culture are oft-told tales: born to bon vivant publisher Ernst and artist Thyra (Rønsholdt) Bojesen; mediocre school grades; apprenticeship to a grocer, 1903–06; trainee for a wholesaler of oil and gasoline, 1906–07.[3] In 1910, Ernst Bojesen arranged an apprenticeship for his son with the silversmith Georg Jensen, who trained the young man in a new decorative style. In traditional silversmithing, thin sheets of silver are hammered into round vessels: hollowware, or flat pieces, such as jewelry and eating utensils: flatware. In both types of ware, the hammer marks on the exterior were usually removed during the finishing process. Jensen's artistic innovation was to preserve the hammer marks and incorporate them into his designs. The result was a new aesthetic for silver known as the "moonlight glow", which became an international commercial sensation.[4]

By 1913, Bojesen had completed his training and been admitted to the Copenhagen Goldsmith's Guild.[5] In 1919, he established his own workshop and became a father, with the birth of his son, Otto. Three years later, he designed his first wooden toy for Otto's amusement, as well as his own.[6] During the early 1920s, Bojesen worked in the decorative style developed by Georg Jensen, but that changed dramatically in the second half of the decade, as he rejected decoration and simplified his silverwares to emphasize the character of the material. A series of texts that Bojesen published during 1928–56 record his efforts to preserve the distinction between handicraft and industry, even as he worked to combine the best qualities of both fields.

Gunnar Biilmann-Petersen. Trademark for Kay Bojesen, 1933. Originally drawn by the artist Hans Tegner in 1913, Bojesen's trademark of a buoy floating on the waves was based on an old family emblem and well suited to his cheerful personality.
→ Grand Prix stainless steel flatware. 1:1 scale.

KAY BOJESEN 1938/1951–53
Grand Prix

The turning point in Kay Bojesen's working life occurred in 1928, as he adopted an ethical position on the use of machinery in applied art, established himself as the guardian of the workshops and created his first pieces of silver flatware. In July, he published a harsh critique of industrial silverwares that imitated artisanal products, entitled "Hammerblow."[7] The target of his outrage was the widespread practice of stamping factory-made silver with small depressions that mimicked the hammer marks popularized by Georg Jensen. Those stamped depressions created the illusion of handmade wares and promoted a higher sales price, while also concealing defects in the objects. Bojesen denounced the practice as a "commercial scam" and insisted on authenticity regardless of the production technique:

"No one is diminished by acknowledging the truth. This Machine Age is no less dependent on handicraft than any previous era. But both — handicraft and industry — must work according to their nature. It is truly reprehensible when industry, as shown here, applies false signs of craftsmanship to its products."[8]

Bojesen's revulsion with ersatz handicraft coincided with his turn away from the elaborate decorative style of his early work. As an alternative, he embraced smooth, voluptuous forms that emphasized the lustrous character of the material — what he later referred to as "the true nature of the silver" — and the skill required to create unembellished forms.[9] The earliest examples of Bojesen's new direction are the coffee sets he created during 1927–30, which display the robust curves, plain surfaces and fine details that would characterize his later work in a range of materials.

In the autumn of 1928, Bojesen exhibited two pieces of hand-forged silver flatware — a fork and a spoon — that signaled a new approach to handicraft based on the study of historical examples.[10] The same exhibition included a fork and spoon he had made to designs by architect Gunnar Biilmann-Petersen. It seems that the two friends had studied historic British flatware and designed their own versions of a favorite model. While Biilmann-Petersen looked to the Old English style of the late 1700s, creating threaded edges on teardrop-shaped handles, Bojesen found his lessons in an even earlier era.

In 1714, the coronation of George I, newly arrived from the Electorate of Hanover, ushered in a more restrained style of British silver.[11] Flatware in the Hanoverian style was functional and devoid of decoration, aside from a subtle ridge along the handle, which provides a resting place for the thumb. Surveying Georgian flatware, Bojesen recognized useful models for further development, including forks with tines long enough to spear food and spoons with bowls deep enough to hold a mouthful of liquid. Moreover, the handles have a gentle curvature that makes them easy to lift from the table and pleasant to manipulate. A decade later, the same curved handles would appear on Bojesen's next set of flatware, along with similar tines and bowls.

> Coffee set, 1927. Silver and teak.
> → Silver dinner fork and spoon, 1928.
> 1:1 scale. / Lunch fork. 1:1 scale.

Towards the end of 1928, Bojesen developed a plan for a permanent exhibition of Danish handicrafts for artisans who had no place to sell their work.[12] While Bojesen was well situated, not far from Christiansborg Palace, he knew that many of his colleagues suffered financially from their remote locations and would require support if a national handicraft culture was to survive. After Bojesen suggested a permanent exhibition at the Danish Museum of Applied Art (now Designmuseum Danmark), Christian Grauballe, the director of Holmegaard Glassworks, established an organization of artisans with a cooperative showroom not far from Tivoli Gardens, which operated for fifty years.[13] By the opening of that showroom — Den Permanente (The Permanent Exhibition) — in December 1931, Bojesen was no longer a working silversmith.

In 1930, as the worldwide economic depression decimated his trade, Bojesen closed his workshop and took a position with the Bing & Grøndahl Porcelain Factory, managing the flagship store on Amagertorv, in central Copenhagen.[14] Throwing himself into the work with his usual zeal, he created designs for porcelain, while also commissioning products from a range of leading architects and designers that included Kaare Klint.[15] Bojesen's ambitious plans and pursuit of practical forms with minimal decoration led to dire conflicts with the company directors. In April 1932, after fewer than eighteen months in the position, he resigned from Bing & Grøndahl. In the aftermath, he taught at the Technical Collage and worked as a freelance designer for other silversmiths, while searching for new premises.[16]

In 1932, Kay Bojesen published an article defending silver from avant-garde architects who questioned its relevance to a modern, egalitarian society. In doing so, he also laid out the principles that would guide his work with flatware for the next twenty years. As he observed,

"Another question is whether it might not be wise, as soon as possible, to consider silver from a functionalist point of view. That is to say, by looking at it naturally and treating it like all other metals, without old-fashioned reverence for the relatively expensive substance — a reverence that has led to silver being regarded as something elevated and thus mainly suited for 'artistic' purposes, so that strange ornaments have been added to peculiar forms that often have nothing to do with purely practical considerations. […] The way forward is elementary, if we just approach silver without snobbery, standardize it and pass it through the machines like any other metal. This would make silverware even more accessible to everyone."[17]

By the end of the year, Bojesen had rented a stand at Den Permanente that he would occupy for about two years, until he moved to a rented shop on Store Kongensgade, in central Copenhagen. In 1936, he rented the cellar at Bredgade 47, across the street from the Danish Museum of Applied Art, and established the small sales room and workshop that he would occupy for the rest of his life. Alongside his main business, Kay Bojesen Sølvsmedie, he created a separate company that would handle his toys and other woodenwares, Kay Bojesen Modeller (Designs), in the knowledge that he could not survive on sales of silver alone.

In 1938, the Danish Museum of Applied Art staged an exhibition of Bojesen's recent work in a variety of materials, which featured a vast assortment of toys that could attract visitors of all ages and generate sales at his shop across the street.[18] In hindsight, the most significant items in the exhibition were Bojesen's new pieces of silver flatware, which were rooted in his hand-forged fork and spoon from 1928. He had kept the gently curving handles of the forks and spoons, but straightened the edges, which made them easier to grasp, and shortened the handles for better balance. Moreover, the pieces could be stamped from a sheet of silver and then finished with hand tools. To provide a truly useful table knife, Bojesen created a curved blade that provides more contact with the plate. As he noted, "[…] the old-fashioned long, straight 'swords,' which only cut with the upper third, have been replaced by knives with shorter blades and a curved edge."[19]

Silver flatware, 1938. 1:1 scale. Left to right: cake fork, sauce scraper, dinner fork, dinner knife, lunch spoon, teaspoon. / Lunch fork. 1:1 scale.

Bojesen's 1938 silver flatware was recognizable as such, but it was unlike any previously seen in Denmark, which had been based on a decorative style and employed a common motif to unite the various parts into a pattern. Rejecting that approach, the silversmith followed his own advice of 1932 (cited above) and created flatware that was devoid of pretension or what he referred to as "snobbery."

The egg-shaped bowl on the spoons, four tines on the fork and gently curving handles with upturned ends on both utensils can be traced to eighteenth-century English examples. However, Bojesen had made a series of improvements on the historical examples by squaring the shoulders on the forks to hold more food, blunting the ends of the handles so that they rest easily in the palm, and thickening the necks at the transition to bowl or tines for greater strength. As such, we can recognize Bojesen's method of surveying past flatware and adopting features that were still useful, without mimicking the style. The result was a set of ideal tools for eating that were realized in silver but might also be rendered in other metals.

The Nazi occupation of Denmark (9 April 1940—5 May 1945) led to widespread shortages of materials, from basic goods, such as wood and wool, to every type of metal, including silver. During those years of sorrow and scarcity, Bojesen continued his artisanal research into practical articles for the table using whatever silver he could find. In the early years of the occupation, he extended his 1938 flatware with a variety of specialized utensils. Several of them look like toys for adults, but each one is a carefully designed tool for a specific type of food. While the curved tines on the serving forks prevent the food from escaping, the broad spatula on the honey spoon makes it easier to collect the thick liquid. The narrow rods that serve as handles on several of these utensils are easily rotated between fingertips and provide precise control over the implement. A decade later, a number of them would be produced in steel.

Bojesen's concerns for utility and convenience are also evident in one of the few pieces of hollowware that he created during the war years, which required melting older items for the silver.[20] His serving dish of 1942 included three loose dishes and a teak tray that provides an insulating layer between hot metal and tabletop. When serving smaller portions or several different types of food, the large dish can be subdivided with loose dishes and covered with the same lid. The accompanying teak tray includes a recess that prevents the large dish from sliding when carried. Bojesen's multi-use serving dish was typical of his mature work, in that he based the design on a concern for function while rejecting the dogma of Functionalism, which dictated the use of geometric forms that are alien to human anatomy. As Bojesen would observe, "After all, the mouth has the shape that a mouth should have —the hands as well."[21]

Silver serving dish and inserts with teak tray, 1942.
← Silver flatware, 1938–42. 1:1 scale. Left to right: oyster fork, honey spoon, marrow fork, serving trident, marmalade spoon, serving fork.

Kitchen knives, 1949. Stainless steel and Bakelite. Universal Steel Company. / Monkey, 1951. Teak and limba. → Double salad bowl and utensils, 1949. Teak. Diameter 26 cm. / Double-handled saucepan with matching spoon and tray, 1951. Silver and rosewood. Pan diameter 20 cm.

In 1938, Bojesen was asked his opinion on the future of Danish handicrafts. He answered in unequivocal terms, continuing the campaign for authenticity that he had begun ten years earlier, in the article "Hammerblow":

"First, I think we should liquidate the word 'handicraft', since so many of our products are created with the help of machines. [...] Let us therefore discard the word 'handicraft' as being misleading advertising and acknowledge to ourselves and our audience that we are *industrial artisans*, who are happy to enlist the help of machines to give as many people as possible the opportunity to buy *beautiful quality products at an affordable price*."[22]

The conclusion of the Second World War allowed Bojesen to put those words into practice. Over the following decade, he established himself as a leading industrial designer and worked with a wide range of materials, including various types of plastic, unconcerned with their low cost and social status. In 1946, he accepted a position as artistic director for the newly formed Universal Steel Company, a Danish concern geared to the export market.[23] His designs for USC included inexpensive steel flatware (Thule) and a vast range of cutlery, as well as carving sets and kitchen knives that display his concern for comfortable, secure handling. Other notable products include his melamine children's tableware for Dansk Bakelit Industri and a line of inexpensive cookware for Pan Aluminium A/S.

And yet, Bojesen never abandoned his workshop nor his practice of using precious materials to create new models of functional tableware; he famously declared, "I want to die a silversmith."[24] As a vast amount of teak flowed into Denmark from Southeast Asia, where the trees had been felled for road construction during the Second World War, Bojesen restarted his production of wooden articles and created an array of new bowls and trays. He also acted as an intermediary for architects Magnus L. Stephensen, Nils Koppel and Finn Juhl, shepherding their designs for woodenwares into production and presenting them in his shop.

In 1951, Kay Bojesen's work with silver entered a new phase that condensed two decades of creative research and produced a string of hollowwares that were the crowning glories of his career as a silversmith. The first of those late masterpieces was a double-handled saucepan with a flat lid that can be used as a serving dish, which would provide a prototype for industry. That same year, Bojesen created the teak monkey with movable limbs that became an immediate international success and remains his best-known toy. In the autumn, his silver flatware of 1938 was awarded *un Gran Premio* — the highest possible honor — at the IX Milan Triennal. He quickly christened that flatware **Grand Prix** and embarked on his most ambitious and consequential industrial design project.

Bojesen's definitive foray into industrial design was his collaboration with AB Motala Verkstad, an industrial conglomerate near Gothenburg, Sweden. In November 1953, Swedish newspapers reported on the new lines of cookware and flatware designed by a famous Danish silversmith and fabricated of fine Swedish stainless steel.[25] The first piece of cookware was an industrial version of Bojesen's double-handled silver saucepan. On the steel version, the hollow handles create a vacuum that provides insulation from the hot pan. The new Grand Prix flatware included thirty-four pieces, most of which can be traced to Bojesen's 1938 silver flatware and the accessories developed during the early 1940s. In Sweden, Grand Prix steel flatware was carried by two of the leading goldsmiths, both of them old friends of Bojesen, but was generally sold in hardware shops and department stores. While the parts could be purchased individually, the most common articles were offered in attractively packaged boxes of six pieces. Twenty-one years after Bojesen had first expressed the idea in print, he had realized his ambition of making the benefits of silverware available to all, by using a less expensive material. As he explained to a Swedish journalist,

"I probably wouldn't care if silver cost as little as steel, but as it is now, everyone can enjoy the steel. Everyone can have nice cutlery: lightweight and easy to clean and with a beautiful shine."[26]

Stainless steel pot and double-handled saucepan with copper bottom, 1951–53. AB Motala Verkstad. The two handles on the saucepan are hollow and contain a vacuum that provides insulation. → Grand Prix table knives. Kay Bojesen's devotion to well-balanced utensils resulted in knives that can be set on a table without the blades touching the surface. 1938 dinner knife with silver handle and stainless steel blade. 1953 dinner knife of stainless steel. / Packaging for Grand Prix stainless steel flatware, 1953.

Rather than replicate his silver flatware in steel, Bojesen adapted the forms to the properties of stainless steel and the requirements of industrial production. Working with the technical staff at Motala, he made a number of minute refinements to the original designs that reflected the immense hardness of the new material, blunting the points on the forks and grinding the edges on the bowls of the spoons. The steel utensils are slightly crisper than the silver versions, with squared ends on the handles and a subtle increase in the curvature of the necks on forks and spoons, as the handle flows towards the tines or into the bowl. Both refinements are actual improvements on the 1938 design. Because the forms are rooted in Bojesen's admiration for handmade silver flatware, his utensils are pleasant in the hand and mouth, no matter the material.

The transition between materials is most apparent in the knife. Because silver is a relatively soft material, it cannot hold an edge or cut any but the softest foods.[27] On the silver version of Grand Prix, Bojesen used a polished stainless steel blade with a bolster where the blade meets the handle. Developing the steel version of Grand Prix, he created a continuous form that is stamped from a single strip of steel. (To satisfy traditionalists, the steel version of Grand Prix originally included a knife with a hollow handle.) At the transition between handle and blade, two notches provide natural stops for the forefinger and thumb. To avoid any suggestion that his steel flatware was an imitation of silver, Bojesen specified a satin finish that has a gentle sheen and prevents bright reflections.

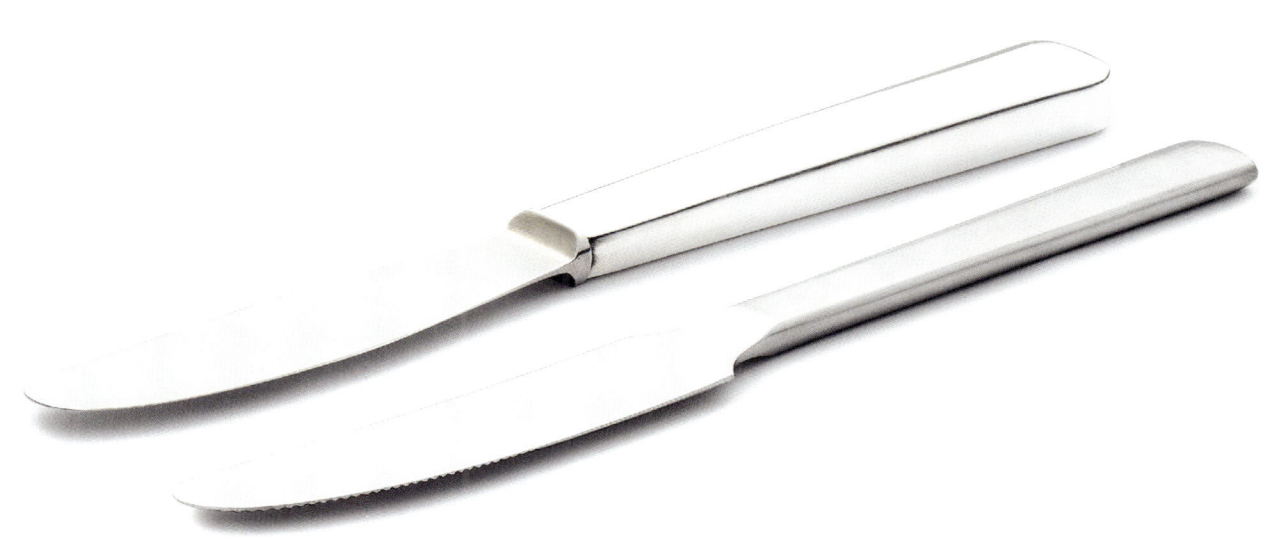

The basic parts of Grand Prix are the dinner fork, knife and spoon and the teaspoon, which are excellent for every meal. The strong and supple forms have the character of tools that perform so well they are hardly noticed, even as Bojesen's attention to detail significantly reduces the likelihood of dripping liquids or lost food. The gently curving handles on the fork and spoon can be traced to Bojesen's 1928 service — and then further back in time, to the practical and graceful forms of eighteenth-century British flatware, despite the different shapes.

The fork is Kay Bojesen's supreme accomplishment in flatware and the embodiment of a graceful instrument for spearing food and conveying it to the mouth. The entire piece of steel has a continuous curve that grows more pronounced as the handle flows into a wide, shallow scoop. The square shoulders allow food to be scooped without it falling off, such that even peas can be eaten with mashing them into a paste. Moreover, the four tines are thick enough and sufficiently strengthened by their curvature that they will not bend. While wide slots between the tines make it easier to spear and hold food, they also make the tines easier to clean, which is an often-neglected concern in flatware design.

Traditional table knives have long blades that can be traced to the serving knives used to disjoint and carve roast meat in the medieval era. Bojesen recognized that a long, straight knife is much less useful for seated diners consuming their own portions. In 1938, he had shortened the blade for greater rigidity and curved it so that more of the cutting edge comes into contact with the plate. In 1953, adapting the design to steel, he replaced the ground edge of the blade, which eventually loses its sharpness, with fine teeth that maximize cutting power and do not require sharpening.

Using a spoon with liquids is typically a balancing act. As such, the handle of Bojesen's spoon is slightly shorter than that of the fork, for greater control over the working end. The oval bowl is deep enough for broths and soups, and the spoon would appear generic except for the carefully calculated angle of the handle, the seemingly inevitable curvature of handle into bowl, and the ground edge on the bowl that limits dripping.

Grand Prix stainless steel flatware, 1953. Utensil details. 2:1 scale. On the fork, the two outer tines are slightly thicker and resist bending, while the depressions between the tines make it easier to hold solid food. With the knife, the small serrations are less damaging to a plate than a ground edge. The flat edge on the bowl of the spoon creates surface tension that holds the liquid. ← Grand Prix, 1953. 1:1 scale. Left to right: dinner fork, dinner knife, lunch spoon. Teaspoon above.

The fundamental challenge in flatware design is creating handles that will provide a cohesive set of tools, while also serving very different purposes. With Grand Prix, Kay Bojesen designed handles that fit naturally in the hand and reinforce the purpose of each utensil, whether cutting, spearing or scooping. → Grand Prix, 1953. Left to right: salt spoon, oyster fork, soup spoon, jam spoon, butter spreader. 1:1 scale.

Grand Prix embodies Kay Bojesen's belief that an eating utensil should feel like an extension of the hand. While the relatively short handles provide a secure grip, they have a rectangular cross-section that prevents the utensil from rotating in the hand. Moreover, the relatively wide ends of the handles, which fit comfortably into the palm, ensure the even distribution of weight that was one of Bojesen's primary concerns. As he noted,

"The people who work with the renewal of flatware are wise to study the types of the past, as the oldest are hand-forged and thus — in the best types — unsurpassed in balance. Machine processing has not yet achieved such a complete material distribution as in those well-proportioned and sensitive handcrafted eating utensils. [...] Cutlery with a solid weight does not have to feel heavy. If the right balance is present, the spoon or fork will not attract the user's attention in an irritating way."[28]

Confronted with a service of thirty-four parts that includes similar forks, knives and spoons for different meals and an array of special utensils, it is natural to wonder how many of those parts are actually necessary. The simple answer is that a handful of parts are absolutely necessary, while the value of the other parts varies according to individual taste.

Bojesen's multiple sizes of forks and knives are a reminder that foods vary in character enormously. While dense food might require heavy implements for cutting and spearing, the same utensils can destroy more delicate fare. Sweet and very rich foods are more enjoyable when consumed in small mouthfuls, which becomes simpler and more natural with small utensils.

Soup can certainly be enjoyed with the dinner spoon, but the wider bowl of the actual soup spoon more closely matches the shape of the mouth. Any one of the knives can be used to spread butter, but Bojesen's flat tool for that purpose will not tear the crumb of the bread. The smallest spoon is naturally more useful for salt than larger spoons, and the same utility is found in the specialized spoons for sauces, jams and other thick substances. An oyster aficionado will delight in the fork designed for extracting the bivalves, but many can live without it. All the same, the value of a utensil is not determined by its popularity but instead by its ability to satisfy the purpose for which it was designed. By that standard, every part of Grand Prix is necessary for someone.

Kay Bojesen completed Grand Prix with four utensils that help young children learn to feed themselves and gradually become accustomed to the habits of the table. Each one reflects Bojesen's sympathy for the frustration that children often feel as a result of their limited motor skills. Indeed, the two utensils for toddlers are not actually pieces of flatware, but chunky objects that are easy to grasp and manipulate. While the T-shaped pusher introduces the act of collecting food, the looped form of the baby spoon recalls a rattle. By designing children's utensils with the same care that he applied to adult flatware, Bojesen revealed his compassion for the people who would use his utensils, regardless of their age.

Following Kay Bojesen's death, in 1958, Erna (Drøge-Møller) Bojesen would operate the shop at Bredgade 47 and safeguard the quality of her husband's work until her death, in 1986. By 1962, after a decade of production, the dies used to produce the steel flatware were badly worn. After Motala declined to replace them, Erna Bojesen purchased the tooling and began searching for a new manufacturer.

Production resumed in 1970, under license to Raadvad Knivfabrik, which used several subcontractors over the following decades.[29] In 1990, the license was transferred to Rosendahl A/S, and production moved to Ohizumi Bussan, in Niigata, Japan. In 2008, Kay and Erna Bojesen's grandchildren assumed control of the flatware, while Rosendahl expanded the range of wooden toys. In 2011, production of Grand Prix resumed at Ohizumi Bussan, under the direction of Sus Bojesen Rosenkvist, who also revived production of the 1938 silver flatware in Denmark.

While Kay Bojesen was devoted to preserving the distinction between handicraft and industry, he happily translated his handmade silver utensils into mass-produced pieces of stainless steel. Within that apparent paradox lies the key to understanding Grand Prix steel flatware. As Bojesen explained, he based his forms on the shapes of the hand and mouth, which are independent of any particular metal or production method. By taking human anatomy as his starting point and incorporating practical details from historical examples, he created the most natural and graceful flatware that has yet to emerge from Denmark and quite possibly anywhere else. In the process, he made it possible for us to enjoy the virtues of handicraft — tactility, human scale, utility — while also providing us with the benefits of mass production. Similar acts of generosity are found in each of the other chapters of this book.

Serving set for jam and marmalade. Silver jars with gilded interiors and glass inserts, matching spoon and rosewood tray, 1955/56. / Kay Bojesen's shop in the cellar of Bredgade 47, Copenhagen, 1938–90. The offerings in the one-room shop ranged from silver hollowware and the silver and steel flatware in the display case to the wooden bowls on the shelves and the wooden toys that were an extension of his buoyant personality. ← Grand Prix, 1953. Left to right: child's fork-spoon, child's spoon, food pusher, baby spoon. 1:1 scale.

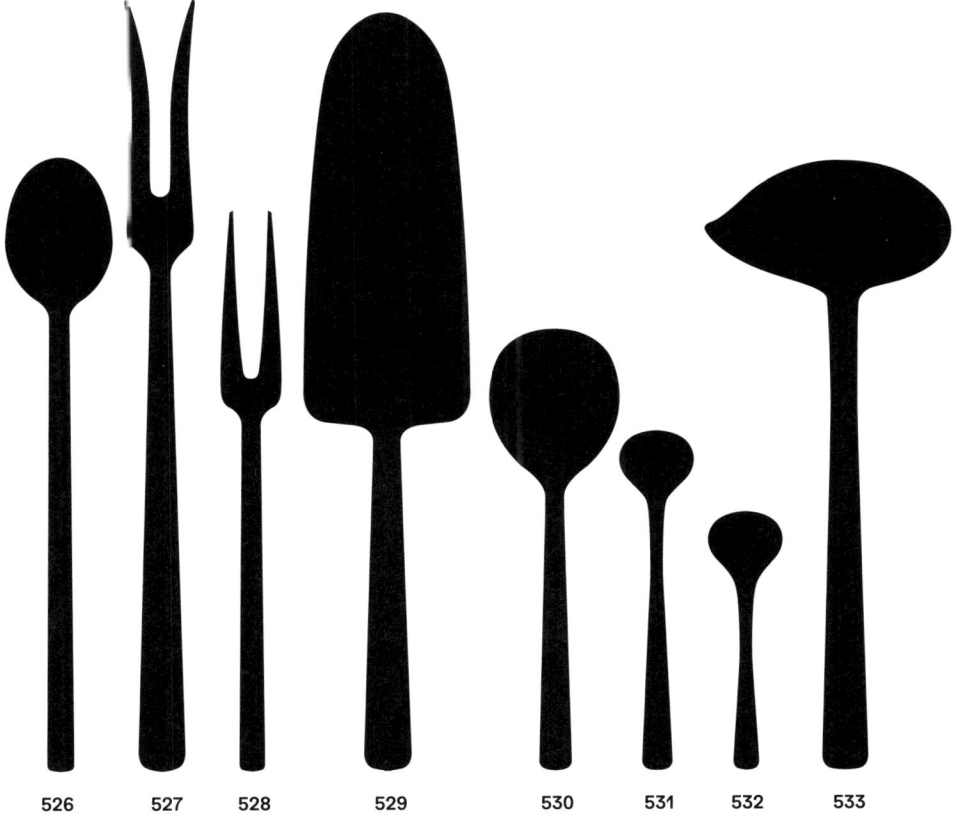

501	Dinner Spoon (194)
502	Dinner Fork (190)
503	Dinner Knife [hollow] (203)
504	Dinner Knife (202)
505	Lunch Spoon (169)
506	Lunch Fork (170)
507	Lunch Knife (196)
508	Dessert Fork (149)
509	Dessert Knife (172)
510	Butter Spreader (163)
511	Soup Spoon (153)
512	Fish Fork (169)
513	Fish Knife (189)
514	Oyster Fork (142)
515	Lobster Knife (142)
516	Large Teaspoon (157)
517	Teaspoon (140)
518	Coffee Spoon (127)
519	Demitasse Spoon (114)
520	Large Salad Spoon (238)
521	Large Salad Fork (238)
522	Small Salad Spoon (188)
523	Small Salad Fork (188)
524	Serving Spoon (238)
525	Fruit Spoon (188)
526	Iced Drink Spoon (182)
527	Meat Fork (229)
528	Serving Fork (165)
529	Cake Server (225)
530	Jam Spoon (132)
531	Mustard Spoon (110)
532	Salt Spoon (68)
533	Sauce Ladle (183)
551	Child's Spoon (157)
552	Child's Fork-spoon (159)
553	Food Pusher (94)
554	Baby Spoon (91)

Grand Prix steel flatware, 1953. Original model numbers and lengths in millimeters.

As they designed the **Stub** (Stump) series, Grethe Meyer and Ibi Trier Mørch combined the best features of tumblers and stemware, and created hand-friendly forms that are easy to use and difficult to overturn. While the range of sizes makes Stub suitable for every type of beverage, the eminently practical design allows the glasses to be stacked for compact storage. Introduced in 1960, the Stub series was a commercial sensation that remained in production for almost thirty years. Meyer and Trier Mørch's triumph is all the more remarkable because Stub originated in a glassware competition that saw their entry rejected, in the mistaken belief that it was a pastiche of familiar forms. Through a combination of good fortune and persistence, they arrived at a new paradigm for glassware that remains undiminished by the passage of time.

The two architects had first met as students at the Royal Danish Academy in Copenhagen, in 1941, and formed a friendship on their shared belief in a woman's right to her own identity, whether personal or professional.[1] Both were members of the student circle that formed around Professor Poul Kjærgaard and worked on his manual of building standards, *Byggebogen* (The Building Book); their colleagues included Bent Salicath, Børge Kjær and Erik Herløw.[2] During 1937–40, Trier Mørch had worked in Sweden on designs for standardized kitchens.[3] As such, she served as a conduit between research and practice by describing Swedish methods and technical advances to her friends. During 1947–48, she and Meyer worked on a kitchen survey that was managed by Bent Salicath and informed Danish kitchen research in the 1950s, as described in the following chapter.

Grethe Meyer and Ibi Trier Mørch.
Stub, 1957–59. Glassware dimensioned
for standard servings of liquor, beer
and wine. 1:1 scale.

GRETHE MEYER / IBI TRIER MØRCH 1957–59

Stub

After 1948, Meyer and Trier Mørch followed different career paths and pursued nearly opposite approaches to design, while remaining loyal friends. Ibi Trier Mørch abandoned the barren forms and industrial dogma she had adopted in Sweden during the 1930s, in favor of whimsy and decoration. As she explained in 1963, "I have struggled for decades to move beyond the rigid ideology of bare functionalism as the basis of my work."[4] To that end, she began designing silver hollowware for the court jeweler A. Michelsen that included sculptural saucepans and candleholders.[5] By 1952, she was teaching at the newly established Goldsmith's College in Copenhagen alongside Erik Herløw while also managing his design office. In 1956, he became the first professor of industrial design at the Royal Danish Academy's School of Architecture, and she joined his teaching staff.[6]

Meyer graduated in 1947 and took a full-time job with *Byggebogen*, while devoting evenings and weekends to her own projects. Following her survey work with Trier Mørch during 1947–48, Meyer became an expert in kitchen design. Her first public success occurred in 1950, when she and two friends won a competition for the design of a model row house for a large family, which was constructed for the exhibition *Kvinde og Hjem* (Woman and Home) in Copenhagen's Forum building; her main contribution was the ingenious kitchen/bathroom.[7] The following year, she won a competition for standard kitchens in high-rise buildings.[8] In 1955, Meyer joined the staff at the National Building Research Institute, where she continued the measurements of household objects that served as the basis of her design work, including the comprehensive storage system that she was developing with Børge Mogensen (p. 218).

In 1957, Grethe Meyer and Ibi Trier Mørch joined forces to enter a design competition that was sponsored by Kastrup Glassworks and organized by architect Jacob E. Bang, the company's artistic director. During 1928–41, Bang held the same position at Holmegaard Glassworks, Denmark's dominant producer of household glass, but ultimately resigned in frustration and left the glass industry.[9] In 1955, the new owner of Kastrup Glassworks hired Bang to renew the product lines and compete with Holmegaard. During his years at Holmegaard, Bang had worked in the shadow of the Swedish producers, notably Orrefors-Sandvik. By the time he arrived at Kastrup, the creative epicenter of the Nordic glass industry had shifted to Finland, where the glassworks at Iittala, Nuutajärvi and Riihimäki had all been revitalized during the late 1940s, with new owners and artistic directors.[10]

The leading figure in the rebirth of Finnish applied art was Kaj Franck, the artistic director of the Nuutajärvi Glassworks and the Arabia ceramics factory.[11] Like his modernist role models at the Bauhaus, Franck hoped to create industrial products that were free of historical decorations. To that end, he favored geometric forms, eliminated handles whenever possible and used color in lieu of decoration to add charm to his simple shapes. At both factories, Franck's assistants included Saara Hopea, whose colored tumblers established a new model for stacking glassware and were awarded a Silver Medal at the Xth Triennale in Milan, in 1954.[12] In contrast to the usual method of stacking tumblers, which exerts outward pressure on the rims, Hopea's molded cylinders placed the weight on the tumbler below and eliminated the risk of cracking.

Grethe Meyer and Ibi Trier Mørch. Competition drawing for Kastrup Glassworks with bowls, carafes, tumblers and two types of stemware, 1957. ← Saara Hopea. Stacking tumblers 1718 and pitcher 1618, 1954. Nuutajärvi Glassworks. / Kaj Franck. Cocktail mixer 1610, 1954, and 5027 tumblers, 1956. Nuutajärvi Glassworks.

In June 1957, Jacob E. Bang arranged an open competition for Nordic designers that was intended to discover uncelebrated talents and generate new designs for Kastrup.[13] The following February, he convened a jury to evaluate the 161 proposals. The jury included Kastrup's managing director, Erik Frandsen, architect Esbjørn Hiort, Professor Erik Herløw, glass engraver Åse Voss Schrader and none other than Kaj Franck. Both of the first prizes were awarded to Elisabeth Sass, for a set of stacking bowls and jars in colored glass and a set of stacking tumblers with a matching carafe. Second prizes were awarded to Tove and Edvard Kindt-Larsen, for their pitchers, drinking glasses and serving dishes, and Hans H. Henriksen, for his stacking beer glasses and stemware. Five other projects were awarded third prizes.[14]

Among the unsuccessful entries, no. 56712 — submitted by Grethe Meyer and Ibi Trier Mørch — included two series of drinking glasses, carafes that could be paired with both series and a variety of multi-purpose bowls and plates. All of the items displayed gently tapered forms, but the two types of stemware had such distinct proportions — tall and narrow vs. short and wide — that they might have been the work of the two different designers. Regardless of the proportions, the geometric shapes, smooth surfaces and absence of handles revealed a familiarity with recent Finnish glassware. Evidently, most members of the jury did not believe that Meyer and Trier Mørch's proposal contained any new ideas.[15] They probably regarded the tapered forms as imitations of Kaj Franck's work, including his carafe and glasses based on cones.

Following the competition, Jacob E. Bang convinced the management at Kastrup Glassworks to pay for prototypes of the first and second prize-winning designs as well as some of the entries that had not been awarded prizes. All of the prototypes would be exhibited at *Den Permanente* (The Permanent Exhibition), the showcase for handicraft and design in central Copenhagen that Bang had helped establish in 1931, along with Kay Bojesen (p. 24). Bang's selection of also-rans included Henning Koppel, Nanna and Jørgen Ditzel, Ib Kofod-Larsen, and Grethe Meyer and Ibi Trier Mørch. By working with the novice glass designers and shepherding their drawings into reality, Bang would be able to identify the technical challenges of each design and judge for himself if any of them might become viable products.

Grethe Meyer and Ibi Trier Mørch. Prototypes for Kastrup Glassworks, 1959. → Detail of pitcher with three spouts, 1959. The basic model can be traced back to the Etruscans.

The exhibition at Den Permanente opened in June 1959, with nearly 200 new objects by eighteen designers.[16] To Jacob E. Bang's certain delight, the exhibition received an extraordinary amount of favorable press coverage, which extended into Sweden and Norway. While the foreign journalists were amazed that Denmark could produce glassware of such quality, the local newspapers predicted bright years ahead for the Danish glass industry.[17] Frequent themes of the coverage included the simplicity of the forms, the abundance of multi-use parts and the profusion of stacking glassware, all of which signaled Kaj Franck's influence, although his name was rarely mentioned. As one reviewer noted, many of the designs had been radically altered during the transition from competition entry to prototype, and a few of the prize-winning designs proved to be technically impossible.[18]

To the certain dismay of the prizewinners in Bang's competition, a great deal of the press coverage was devoted to Meyer and Trier Mørch's prototypes, which included most parts of their original proposal in clear glass and a few green parts for serving white wine.[19] While various journalists admired the graceful bowl with a recessed foot and the carafe with three spouts, they were unanimous in their fascination with the two series of stacking stemware. As were their editors: Many of the headlines referred to the stacks and towers, and photos of the glasses appeared in nearly every article about the exhibition, occasionally as the only illustration.[20] Encouraged by the press coverage, Erik Frandsen decided to produce both of Meyer and Trier Mørch's glassware series.

Grethe Meyer and Ibi Trier Mørch with prototypes of serving bowl in clear glass and parts of Stub stemware in clear and green glass, which were produced for exhibition at Den Permanente in 1959. Background: elements of the Boligens Byggeskabe (Modular Cabinets) designed by Grethe Meyer and Børge Mogensen, as described in later chapter. → Grethe Meyer and Ibi Trier Mørch. Two types of stacking stemware with tapered bowls, 1957. / Three models of stacking glassware. Left to right: Saara Hopea, 1954; Hans H. Henriksen, 1957; Grethe Meyer and Ibi Trier Mørch, 1957–59.

Meyer and Trier Mørch's success was undoubtedly a shock to the competition jurors who had mistakenly dismissed their entry as lacking new ideas. Rather than mimicking Kaj Franck, the two architects had submitted innovative designs for stemware that were rooted in practical considerations and contained the seed of their later success. With or without a stem, most drinking vessels are wider at the opening than at the base, which makes them prone to overturning. Adding stems to the vessels greatly increases the risk of accidents. Meyer and Trier Mørch proposed a more stable type of stemware, in which the bottoms of the cups were slightly wider than the openings, to lower the center of gravity and reduce the risk of overturning. Those wide-bottomed cups would allow the duo to create a truly new type of stacking glassware by refining their original designs.

Despite Meyer and Trier Mørch's practical concerns, none of the glasses in their competition project could be stacked. In the interest of stability, the feet on the stemware had the same diameters as the openings. During the prototyping process, they made a minor revision to the feet that enabled their triumph at the Den Permanente exhibition. We can guess that Trier Mørch's colleague and friend Erik Herløw, who had served on the competition jury, explained the prize-winning entries to the disappointed duo following the jury meeting. Those entries included the stemware designed by Hans H. Henriksen that could be stacked for compact storage, because the feet were slightly smaller than the openings and could rest on bottom of the cup below. While the method of stacking was not entirely stable, it did protect the rims from chipping or cracking.

As Kastrup Glassworks created prototypes for the exhibition, Meyer reviewed several rounds of samples and responded with detailed notes to the glass-blowers. Those notes included frequent reminders that she had revised the drawings for the stemmed glasses and reduced the diameter of the feet by a few millimeters.[21] In doing so, she made it possible to stack the glasses, with each of the wide-bottomed cups resting on the rim of the cup below. While this protected the cups from cracking under outward pressure, the stems and feet were safely suspended in mid-air. By combining Hans H. Henriksen's idea of stackable stemware [B] with Saara Hopea's method of stacking tumblers [A], Meyer and Trier Mørch had invented a new model of stemware [C] that became the most successful result of Jacob E. Bang's competition.

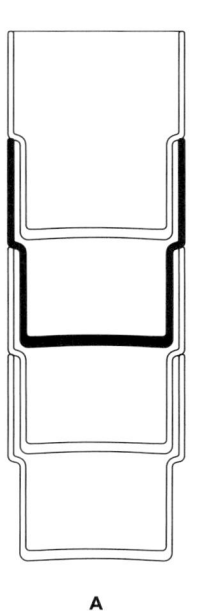

A

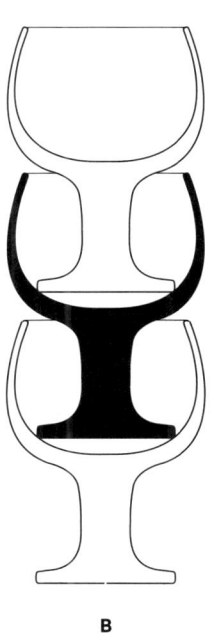

B

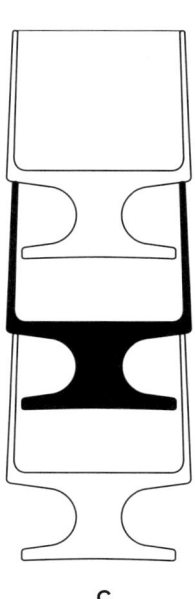

C

In January 1960, Kastrup Glassworks introduced two series of stemware with names that corresponded to their proportions, along with tumblers and carafes that were compatible with both series. While **Stamme** (Stem) has narrow and relatively tall cups on thin stems, **Stub** (Stump) has low and relatively wide cups on thick stems. Only one of those series could be stacked in any number, but that distinction only underscores all of the other differences between the two series. Stamme is easily overturned, due to the slender proportions, and fragile, due to the thin stems. Despite the undecorated surfaces, it is a simplified version of traditional stemware, with the elongated shapes taking the place of painted or engraved decoration. While the two series had a common root, Stamme would fade into history, even as Stub endures as an archetype.

Stamme stemware with tumblers, 1957–59.
→ Three carafes to be used with Stub and Stamme, 1957. / Stub stemware, 1957–59.

The nine parts of Stub are pleasant to use, easy to clean, and can be safely stacked in columns of three to six pieces, depending on the size. Moreover, Stub provides the benefits of conventional stemware without the fragility that discourages frequent use. While the raised bowls are easily lifted from the table and display the contents, the low heights and heavy bases resist overturning and prevent breakage. As such, we can recognize a hybrid of tumbler and stemware that was designed for use on a daily basis. That approach was undoubtedly rooted in Grethe Meyer's studies of household objects and her intense focus on practical concerns, which suggests that Stub was the basic design, and Stamme conceived as a whimsical alternative.[22] Whatever the sequence, Stub is the superior series in both practical and aesthetic terms, with graceful shapes that delight the eye and invite the hand.

Both series enjoyed strong sales during the early 1960s and were expanded with additional parts, beginning with the small glass for aquavit that was added to Stamme, in mid 1960. By 1962, sales of Stub had accelerated, and Meyer extended the series with two shallow glasses, one for cocktails and another for sparkling wine or dessert. In 1964, she created a cognac glass by extending the height of the port glass and increasing the taper to concentrate the aroma. That same year, she prepared new drawings for seven pieces of tableware that had been prototyped and exhibited at Den Permanente. By early 1965, Kastrup was producing the two serving bowls, three stacking bowls and both sizes of the three-spouted pitcher, all in clear glass. Those items would be discontinued after less than a year due to the merger with Holmegaard Glassworks.

Stub stemware in clear and smoke glass, 1965–95. Holmegaard Glassworks.

By the end of 1964, Kastrup's strategy of challenging Holmegaard in the Danish market for table glass had succeeded, largely due to sales of Stub and Stamme. In fact, that strategy was an important factor in the merger of the two companies that was completed in July 1965.[23] As the managers of the new Holmegaard-Kastrup Glassworks combined their catalogs and winnowed their product lines, they stopped production of the smallest tumblers and three carafes for Stub and Stamme as well as the bowls and pitchers that had been introduced earlier in the year. The remaining parts of Stub and Stamme continued to be produced in clear glass, while Stub was offered in Holmegaard's signature "smoke" glass, a gray-toned material developed in the 1950s based on Swedish examples. In 1968, Meyer designed a smaller version of the beer glass that is ideally sized for water, and Stub assumed its ultimate range of nine pieces.

Like any series of glassware, Stub has its limitations. Truly extraordinary wines and aromatic liquors are best enjoyed in glasses designed especially for those purposes. But But Stub is excellent for the beverages that most of us consume on a regular basis, from water and juice to soda and a variety of alcoholic beverages, because it was designed to fit the hand and serve the mouth. Those qualities make the series especially well suited to family life. Similarly to Kay Bojesen's Grand Prix flatware, Stub contains parts that are perfectly sized for young children. The range of sizes allows them to gradually become accustomed to the habits of the table, in comfort and with confidence, due to the low heights and heavy bases that make accidents less likely.

After 1965, production in two colors of glass introduced the question of choice, with conventional wisdom assuming that consumers would commit to one or the other color. Purists (or Puritans) might argue that a table should only be set with one color of glass, in the interest of harmony. And yet, harmony can be found in similar or identical forms of different colors, as seen in the clear and green prototypes exhibited at Den Permanente, in 1959. As such, the two colors of Stub provide the basis for mix-and-match services based entirely on individual habits and tastes, both visual and liquid. That relaxed approach is also a practical measure, due to the fact that Stub is not currently in production and only available from second-hand sources. As a result, some sizes can be difficult to locate in one or the other color.

Stub stemware, produced 1960–95. 1:2 scale.
→ Stub glassware with beverages. Left to right: white wine, red wine, beer and spirits.

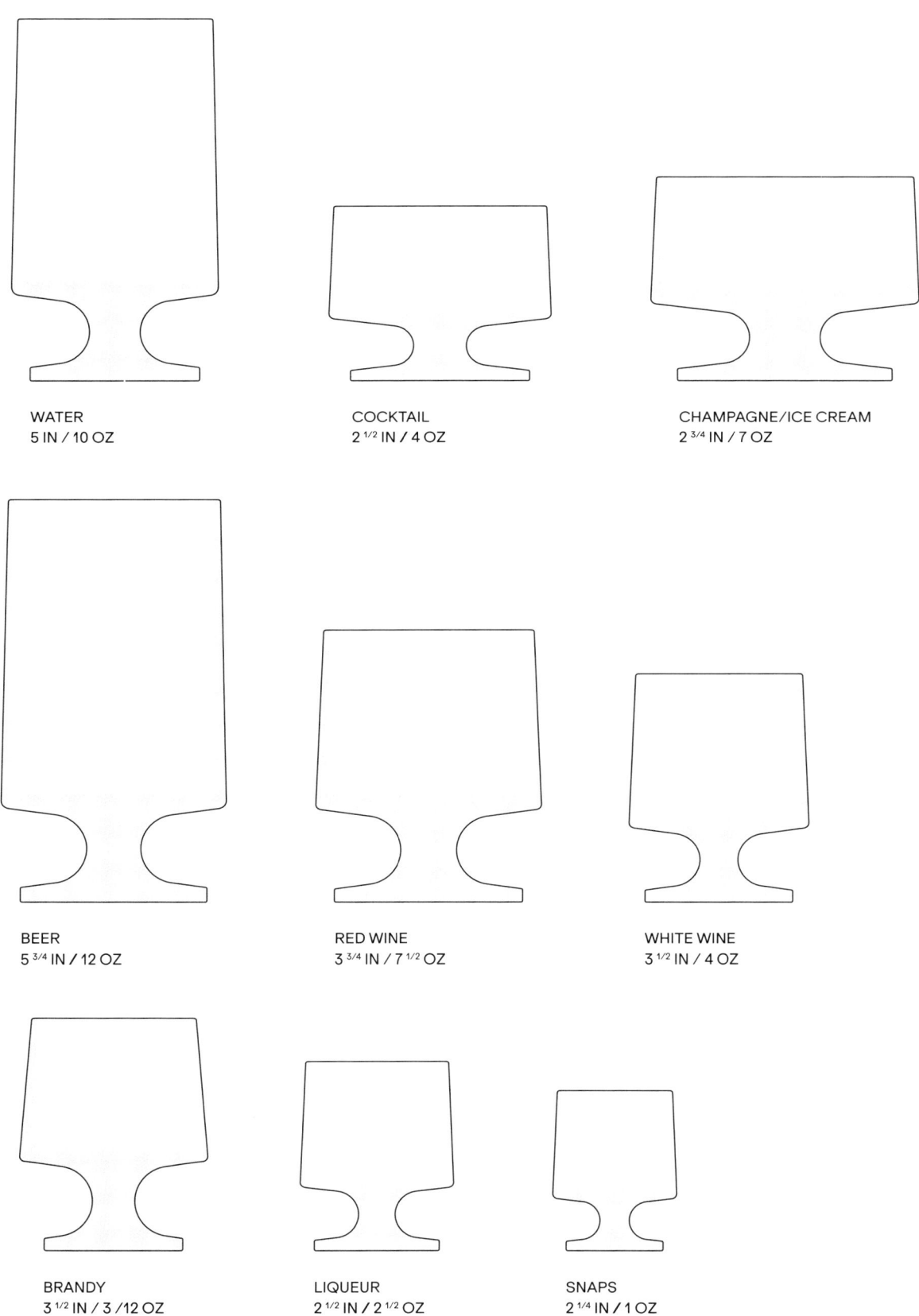

WATER
5 IN / 10 OZ

COCKTAIL
2 1/2 IN / 4 OZ

CHAMPAGNE/ICE CREAM
2 3/4 IN / 7 OZ

BEER
5 3/4 IN / 12 OZ

RED WINE
3 3/4 IN / 7 1/2 OZ

WHITE WINE
3 1/2 IN / 4 OZ

BRANDY
3 1/2 IN / 3 /12 OZ

LIQUEUR
2 1/2 IN / 2 1/2 OZ

SNAPS
2 1/4 IN / 1 OZ

In 1973, Stamme was discontinued due to low sales, but Stub would remain in production until 1995.[24] In 1977, the glassworks at Kastrup was closed, and the name of the company reverted to Holmegaard Glassworks. In 1985, Holmegaard was acquired by the Royal Copenhagen Porcelain Factory as part of a string of corporate schemes that eventually led to its demise.[25] In 2008, the Holmegaard brand was sold to Rosendahl Design Group A/S, the Danish company that also produces Kay Bojesen's wooden toys. Rosendahl revived the Stub glasses for beer and red wine, in 2019, but did not advertise their many virtues. Detached from the series and promoted solely on the basis of their forms, in a market filled with more eye-catching models, the two glasses proved difficult to sell. The revival of the dessert glass in 2020 failed to boost sales, and all three glasses were discontinued at the end of 2022.

As with all glassware, the best place to wash Stub is in the sink. However, some pieces can be placed in the dishwasher. As dishwashers became popular in the early 1970s, many glasses emerged with a cloudy coating etched into the surface: known in Danish as *glaspest*.[26] By 1975, Holmegaard had created a glass mixture that resisted etching, but it is almost impossible to date vintage glasses. The Rosendahl production is dishwasher-safe to 55° C (131 °F). As a matter of fact, Stub was designed with handwashing in mind, as home dishwashers were virtually unknown in Denmark during the late 1950s. The thick stems, sturdy rims and low cups that make Stub so durable also make it easy to clean, as seen in the vast number of vintage pieces that appear like new.

Given Stub's many benefits in the hand, on the table and in the cupboard, it will almost certainly return to production at some point. In the meantime, an ample supply of the most popular sizes can be located in vintage shops across Denmark and online. The beer glass is truly functional, in that it was designed to hold the standard serving of 33 cl and still provide room for foam. Among the late additions to the series, the low glasses sized for cocktails and dessert or sparkling wine were not produced in large numbers, and the 1968 water glass is rare. Regardless of size, each part of Stub has the character of a universal glass that has evolved through a succession of models and finally reached its essential form.

Following the introduction of Stub and Stamme, in 1960, the two designers remained loyal friends but returned to their separate paths. By that point, they had completed a second competition project, for a porcelain dinner service that would lead Grethe Meyer into a new career designing ceramic tableware and cookware, as described in two later chapters. The royalties from Stub and Stamme allowed Ibi Trier Mørch to step back from her teaching duties and pursue her own artistic and social interests.[27] During 1964–70, she designed exhibitions of applied art that were presented in Paris, Copenhagen and Moscow. After purchasing an old farmhouse on Tuse Næs, across the fjord from Holbæk, in 1968, she established a commune with her children and their friends and remained there until her death, in 1980.

The now-forgotten kitchen system designed by Hanne (Koch) Valeur — **K-60** — provided the model for several hundred thousand kitchens in Denmark, which were rooted in a blatant act of plagiarism that was generally ignored by her colleagues. The daughter of architect Mogens Koch and weaver Ea (Varming) Koch, she discovered her creative impulse during high school, but questioned the depth of her talent.[1] Rather than design her own furniture or textiles, she hoped to become an interior designer and arrange the works of others. Her father discouraged her from that path, worried that it was not a stable career and skeptical of the training she would receive from furniture designer Finn Juhl, who emphasized art over utility.[2] To satisfy her parents, she enrolled in a law program at the University of Copenhagen, but quit a few weeks later. After she confided her undiminished ambition to Børge Mogensen, a former assistant to her father, he convinced her parents to give their consent.

Hanne Valeur. K-60 kitchen system, 1962. Detail of cabinet door. 1:1 scale. Douglas fir veneer with brass pull. Valeur replaced the typical variety of handles and drawer pulls with a single pull that is easy to grasp from any angle or height. The uncoated brass conceals fingerprints and can simply be wiped clean.

In 1948, Hanne Koch began her studies at the School of Home Furnishing, where Finn Juhl greeted her on the first day and declared, "I never imagined a daughter of Mogens Koch would enter my school."[3] Three years later, Juhl found her final project for the interiors of a public building sufficiently impressive to award her a graduation prize. Soon after, she was rejected for a job with the non-profit housing society KAB, on the grounds that she had nothing to contribute to the work, which is ironic in hindsight. In early 1952, she found a job in noted architect Palle Suenson's studio, where her co-workers included the young architect Torben Valeur. They married in 1954. The following year, Torben Valeur and his colleague Henning Jensen established their own office. Hanne Valeur followed them and designed the interiors for their buildings.

In 1962, Børge Mogensen and architect Arne Karlsen (another former assistant to Mogens Koch) published a critique of recent trends in Danish crafts and design: "Applied Art Gone Astray."[4] The article was a response to the 1961 exhibition of the Copenhagen Cabinetmakers' Guild, but the subjects included tableware and factory-made furniture. Their central argument was that the practical and ethical approach to design established by Kaare Klint, circa 1930, had been eclipsed by the cynical pursuit of fashion, due to increased affluence at home and a booming export market. Moreover, the authors identified designers whose work they believed exemplified that trend, most notably Jens H. Quistgaard, Ib Kofod-Larsen and Finn Juhl. Several observers accused the duo of rejecting new ideas based on their own taste, while also admitting the substance of their argument.[5]

Mogensen and Karlsen's critique caused a minor scandal within the craft and design communities, which spread to the newspapers. As a result of the publicity, the chairman of the Cabinetmakers' Guild invited the two critics to support their position with some sort of installation at the Guild's 1962 exhibition.[6] They decided to create a model interior furnished with new designs that would demonstrate how established methods could be extended and developed. To realize that ambitious plan, they invited a cohort of architect-designers who worked on the basis of Klint's principles to collaborate with a group of like-minded cabinetmakers, under the motto "Tradition and Renewal". Occupied with his work on several parts of the model interior, Mogensen asked Hanne Valeur if she would be interested in designing the kitchen. She replied, "More than you could ever know."[7]

HANNE VALEUR 1962
K-60

As Hanne Valeur designed K-60, she abandoned the principle of specialized cabinets for different functions that had been doctrine in Denmark for decades. We can trace that principle to Sweden, but it originated in Weimar Germany. In 1926, Margarete Schütte-Lihotzky developed the Frankfurt Kitchen for a social housing program devoted to the smallest practical dwellings.[8] Inspired by the tiny kitchen in a railroad dining car, she created a narrow passage with specially designed cabinets that reflected the avant-garde ideal of the kitchen as a workplace or laboratory.[9] In Sweden, efforts to rationalize kitchen design began in 1921 and inspired a series of public exhibitions.[10] In 1928, architect Sven Markelius exhibited a kitchen based on the Frankfurt model of factory-like workstations and established the basis for kitchen studies in Sweden, and Denmark, for the next thirty years.

Danish efforts to rationalize kitchen design began in earnest in 1944 and spawned the kitchen survey that employed Bent Salicath, Grethe Meyer and Ibi Trier Mørch a few years later (p. 44).[11] After the Danish Ministry of Housing was established in 1947, vast resources were devoted to developing a standard kitchen that could be used in the compact space of social housing apartments.[12] The central figure in that research was Edvard Heiberg, a socially minded architect who regarded design as a rational process of solving problems using empirical data.[13] In 1947, he developed the first Danish version of a standard kitchen, which was based on the Swedish model.[14] As such, he treated the cabinets as functional elements of different widths and heights, each designed for a particular type of storage or activity, such as baking, peeling and chopping vegetables and grinding meat for meatballs and sausages.

In 1949, the Joint Organization of Non-profit Danish Housing Societies (hereafter the Joint Organization) formed a committee on kitchen research that included Edvard Heiberg, Bent Salicath and the housing architect Svenn Eske Kristensen.[15] Four years later, the Joint Organization established a research office and tasked Heiberg with developing a system of inexpensive cabinet that could be used in new social housing. The system would be known as the Danish Kitchen Set. By June 1955, he had designed seven specialized elements with six different widths that could be arranged in more than 130 configurations.[16] Heiberg's "element-kitchen" was sold to the public as the **Esto Kitchen**, through the Danish Consumers' Cooperative Society, also known as FDB (p. 188). In 1960, it was renamed the **Tectum Kitchen**.[17] Despite decades of research, the design barely differed from the Frankfurt Kitchen.

Hanne Valeur. Elevation drawing and cross section of K-60 with typical upper and lower cabinets and suspended cassettes for open storage, all based on a module of 60 cm. Drawers are 40 cm wide, while doors on upper cabinets are 30 cm wide. ← Model kitchen developed by Hemmens Forskningsinstitut (Swedish Home Research Institute) based on the Frankfurt Kitchen of 1926, complete with seating area, suspended bins for dry goods and specially designed cabinets of varied widths. / Installation view of *Bygge och bostad* (Building and Housing), Gothenburg, Sweden, 1948.

By early 1962, Hanne Valeur was well versed in Danish and Swedish kitchen theory through her training at the School of Home Furnishing and her experience designing kitchens for the social housing estates that were the basis of her husband's partnership with Henning Jensen. The kitchens at Slotsparken, near Kolding, which was designed in 1960–61, exhibit several features that would soon appear in K-60.[18] She certainly knew the system of elements promoted as the Danish Kitchen Set/Esto Kitchen and Tectum Kitchen, but rejected the mania for specialization that guided Edvard Heiberg's work, as well as his belief that aesthetic considerations interfere with an objective interpretation of facts. In her mind, aesthetics and practical concerns were inseparable and, ideally, integrated to the point that they were indistinguishable.

To that end, she designed the cabinets with a uniform width of 60 cm and a matching depth: a true module that followed the new Swedish standard and could accommodate the built-in appliances that were coming to the market.[19] The same module governed the heights of the cabinets and resulted in a series of cubes. In the process, she eliminated the varied counter heights that had originated in Germany during the 1920s and remained typical in Denmark for decades, based on the notion of ideal heights for different tasks. Working up from the floor, she established a recessed base of 20 cm, with a wooden plate that can be removed for access to plumbing and electrical wiring. Adding a 60-cm-high base cabinet and a 5-cm slab of wood, she arrived at a uniform counter height of 85 cm, which also corresponded to the Swedish standard.

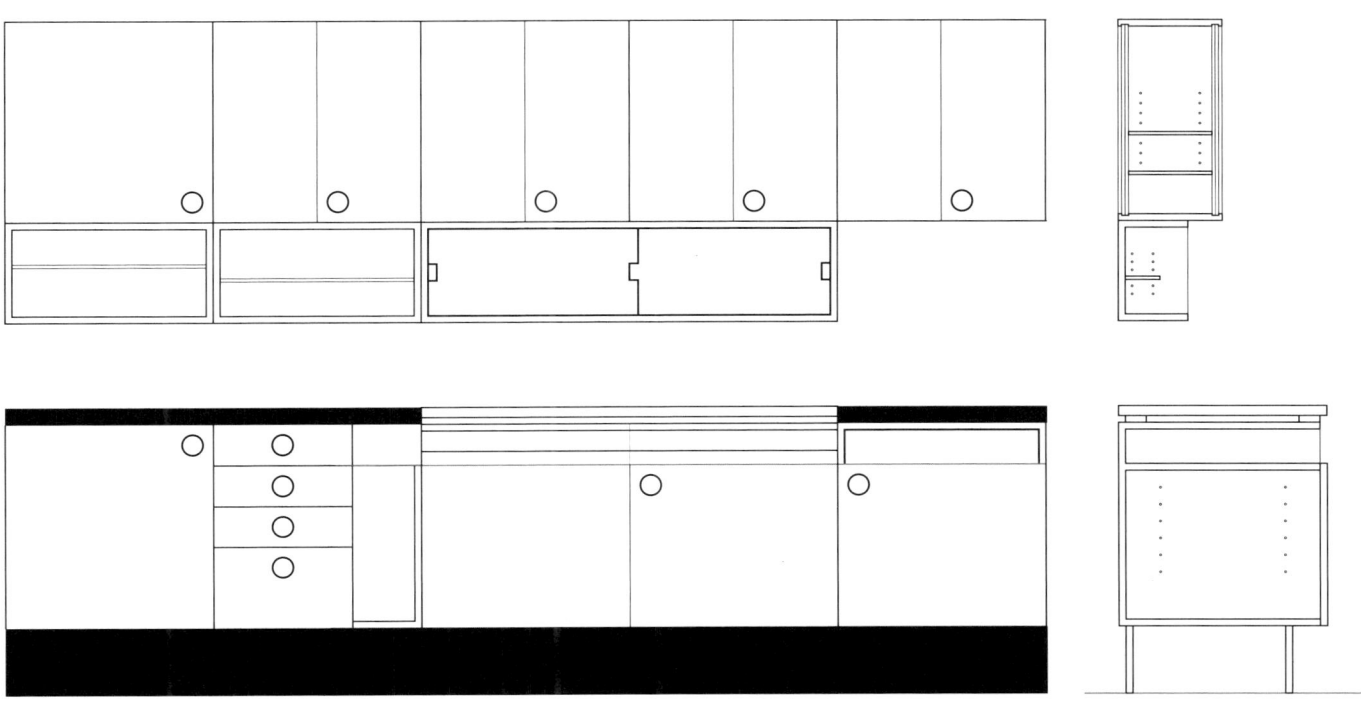

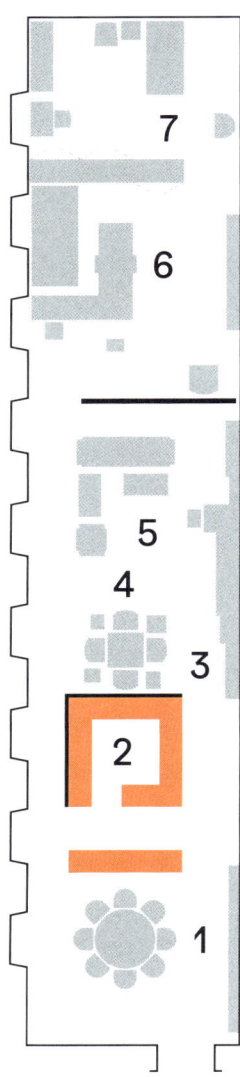

In early September 1962, the 36th annual exhibition of the Copenhagen Cabinetmakers' Guild opened at the Danish Museum of Applied Art (now Designmuseum Danmark), where the final gallery of the south wing was devoted to Børge Mogensen and Arne Karlsen's installation *Tradition og fornyelse* (Tradition and Renewal).[20] They arranged the furniture created by their team of architects and cabinetmakers in two sections, with the areas for dining, cooking and socializing near the entrance and two sleeping areas at the end of the gallery. Poul Henningsen designed the lighting scheme and also presented two new lamps. To promote the distinction between useful objects and fine art that was central to their critique "Applied Art Gone Astray," Mogensen and Karlsen juxtaposed examples of tableware and textiles with a variety of paintings, sculptures and prints. The sum of these efforts was a powerful statement that displayed Kaare Klint's enduring influence on Danish design culture.

Floor plan of *Tradition og fornyelse* (Tradition and Renewal), a special installation within the 1962 exhibition of the Copenhagen Cabinetmakers' Guild. 1:100 scale. 1: Dining set (Børge Mogensen/Virum Møbelsnedkeri). 2: K-60 kitchen (Hanne Valeur with Torben Valeur and Henning Jensen/Christensen & Larsen). 3: MK bookcase system (Mogens Koch/ Rud. Rasmussens Snedkerier). 4: Sitting group (Arne Karlsen/ Virum Møbelsnedkeri). 5: Sitting group (Vilhelm Wohlert and Jørgen Bo/Arne Poulsen). 6: Man's bedroom (Børge Mogensen/Erhard Rasmussen). 7: Woman's bedroom (Rigmor Andersen and Annelise Bjørner/Jørgen Christensen).

The centerpiece of *Tradition and Renewal* was the freestanding kitchen produced by cabinetmakers Christensen & Larsen, which was christened Køkken-60 (Kitchen-60) or simply K-60. In keeping with the Guild's practice of presenting architect-designed furniture, K-60 was credited to Torben Valeur and Henning Jensen with interior designer Hanne Valeur listed as a consultant. In fact, the opposite was true. While Hanne Valeur designed the kitchen, the two architects acted as hardware consultants.[21] Some months earlier, they had visited the Cologne Furniture Fair and discovered the special hinge that she would employ on the cabinets. As she searched for a recessed metal pull that would be flush with the surface of the doors, Henning Jensen designed the custom-made brass pull that was also used on the drawers.

Hanne Valeur's fundamental innovation was to treat kitchen cabinets with the same concern for aesthetics, materials and details applied to chairs and tables designed for the dining area and living room. In doing so, she advanced the idea of the kitchen as the central feature of the home, rather than a separate work area for the "housewife" that was distinct from family and social life. To that end, the sides and backs of her cabinets and doors were covered with the same veneer as the fronts, which allowed them to be used in an open floor plan. Freestanding rows of cabinets could be used as room dividers that were visible from all sides. As she explained,

"Each element appears as an independent piece of furniture, carefully finished outside and in. This allows for a free arrangement of the elements, which do not need to be stationary. The elements can be regrouped according to changing needs, and you can also build a kitchen little by little, element by element."[22]

She selected the materials for their beauty and durability and had them finished to ensure easy cleaning. The cabinets were veneered in Douglas fir, a dense wood with a straight grain and a warm, orange-brown color. All of the veneered surfaces were treated with a matt, acid-cured varnish that can be wiped clean of grease and food residue. The standard countertop was a slab of solid ash that was stained with the black, acid-proof solution typically used on laboratory worktops. Oiled teak countertops would be available by special order, along with square plates of Swedish Öland limestone for heat-resistant surfaces on either side of the cooktop. The wooden base plate was painted black to match the stained countertop, which also had the advantage of hiding scuffmarks.

Installation view of *Tradition and Renewal*, Danish Museum of Applied Art (now Designmuseum Danmark), September 1962. Interior of K-60 with Douglas fir cabinets and stainless steel countertop with integral sinks. The solid wood cassettes above the countertop are mounted on an exhibition partition.
← Installation view of K-60 in *Tradition and Renewal*. Left foreground: table and chairs designed by Børge Mogensen and illuminated by Poul Henningsen's new Contrast lamp. Henningsen designed the lighting for the installation and also introduced the small pendant that illuminated the path through the installation.

K-60 is a system of 60-cm cubes, multi-cubes and half-cubes that can be freely arranged within a three-dimensional grid. The base height of 20 cm and maximum height of 200 cm ensures that the shelves in the upper cabinets remain in reach for most adults. The cube provides two types of lower cabinets with adjustable shelves (with or without tray storage) and another type that includes vertical storage and either four or five drawers. The cube with an open front provides a frame for a wall oven, which Valeur located at standing height for comfort and convenience. A double cube provides a lower cabinet for a stainless steel countertop or a vitrine with sliding glass doors that can be suspended as a room divider. While a standing double cube provides the frame for a built-in refrigerator or freezer, the triple cube provides a storage cabinet that can also be equipped as a broom closet or ironing station. Upper cabinets take the form of a half-cube, 30 cm deep, with hinged doors and two adjustable shelves.

In her design of the lower cabinets, Valeur used vertical storage for trays to maintain her 60-cm module. While all of the shelves in K-60 are 60 cm wide, a drawer of the same width would require heavy-duty construction and metal slides to resist sagging and ensure smooth operation.

Instead, Valeur limited the drawer width to 40 cm and used vertical storage to fill the gap. Moreover, the 40-cm-wide drawers and 20-cm-wide storage unit could be installed as separate parts to fill any gaps along the wall and provide a harmonious effect.

Valeur supplemented the cabinets with solid wood boxes that are 20 cm deep and mounted on the underside of a vitrine or upper cabinet. While the single "cassette" provided open storage for anything at all, the double-wide cassette was equipped with sliding acrylic doors that would conceal dirty dishes.

Installation view of *Tradition and Renewal*. Interior of K-60 with black-stained ash countertop and solid Douglas fir cassettes for open storage. → Isometric drawings of cubic matrix and typical cubes, half-cubes and multiples. / Installation view of *Tradition and Renewal*. Interior of K-60 with open slots for tray storage. The vertical slot made it possible to reconcile 40-cm-wide drawers with the 60-cm module. The horizontal slots were dimensioned so that a loaded tray could be stored beneath the counter.

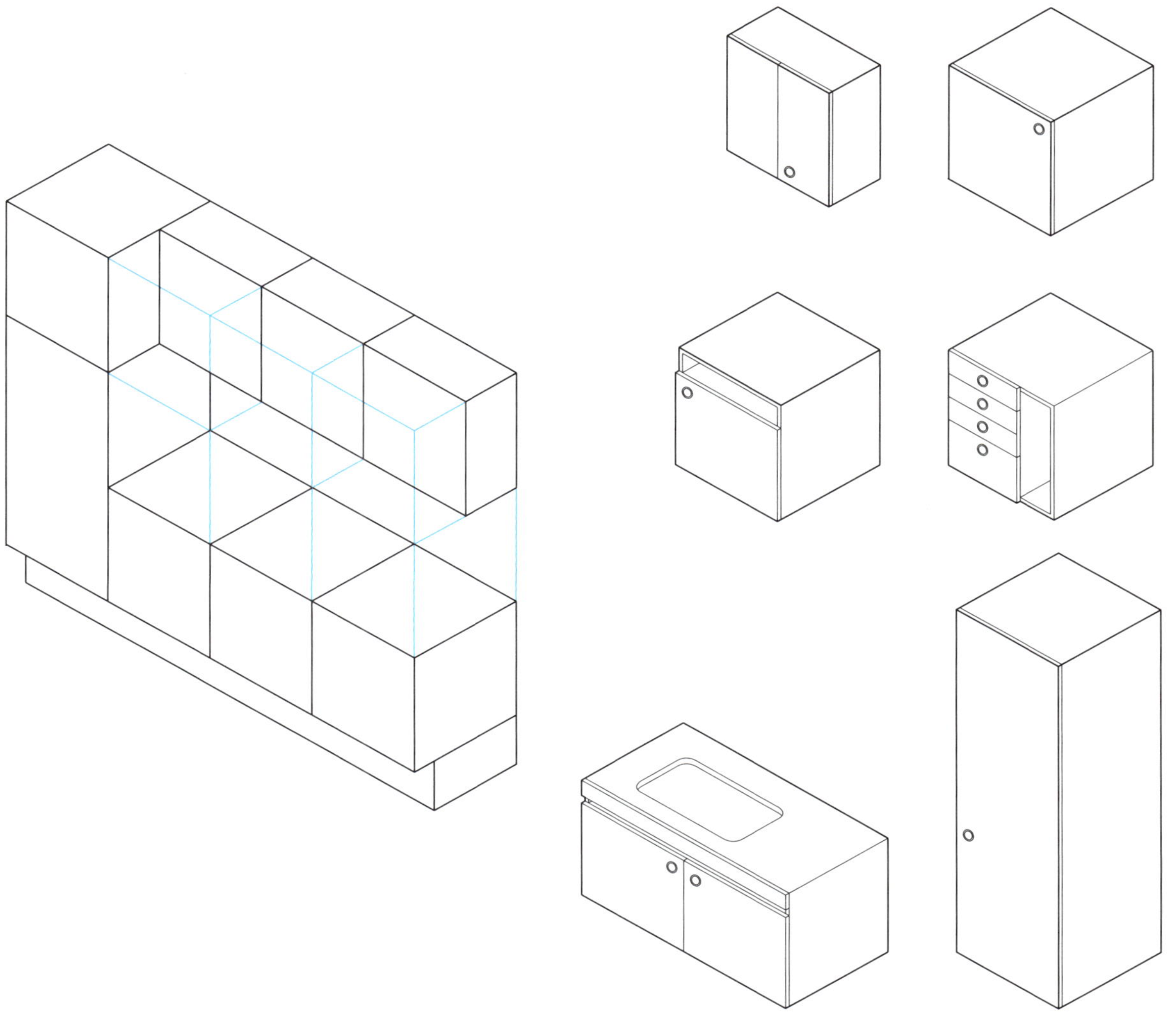

Hanne Valeur designed her cabinets so that it would be possible to access the entire width of the interior. While that simplified cleaning, it also allowed her to design removable trays and boxes that could be used for storage and simply placed on the counter. Towards those ends, she eliminated the narrow wooden frame that is typically applied to the front of a cabinet. That face frame, which is wider than the edges of the box, provides a place to attach hinges, braces the openings of large boxes and will conceal small imperfections in the construction. As K-60 was ultimately intended for factory production, Valeur was able to design with extraordinary precision and realize her ideal of an entirely useful cabinet.

She realized that ideal with the door that swings clear of the opening, even when it is only opened 90°. That door is slightly thinner than the wall of the cabinet and attached with the special hinge that Torben Valeur and Henning Jensen located in Germany. As the hinge is recessed into the interior surfaces of door and cabinet, an open door will clear the opening and align with the outside wall of the cabinet. That alignment allows the cabinets to be butted together, which is especially useful at a corner, because it eliminates wasted space and the resulting need for small pieces of trim to fill the gap. Within the cabinets, all of the shelves are supported on removable steel wires that are contained in the edge of the shelf and do not collect dirt.

K-60 was generally recognized as the outstanding component of *Tradition and Renewal* and received an overwhelmingly positive reception in the press. One of the headlines simply read "SUPER–KITCHEN."[23] Even Finn Juhl took a break from ridiculing Børge Mogensen and Arne Karlsen to exclaim,

"In this room, Henning Jensen and Torben Valeur and his wife, Hanne, have an unusually nice kitchen. Oregon pine, may not be the wisest choice, as it is very soft and quickly gets dirty. But this team manages to develop a holistic concept and see it through in every detail, such as hinges, grips, locks etc. What a pleasure to study it. [...] This is really a top-class team. My deepest respect."[24]

Christian Enevoldsen looked ahead to the time when K-60 would be mass-produced and predicted that the indelible character of the design would withstand changes in the type of wood veneer and even the use of paint:

"Naturally, these kitchen elements will not be very cheap. But there is also no reason to believe that they should become particularly expensive. With a rationally designed production, it should be possible to produce them at reasonable prices. [...] In the exhibition, the cabinets were shown in Oregon pine, which may be a slightly soft wood. But they can of course be made in other types of wood, or painted, which will have no significant impact on the appearance of the elements and none on the concept of this furniture."[25]

The most enthusiastic visitor to *Tradition and Renewal* was undoubtedly Ole Palsby, a young stockbroker and property developer who was more interested in art and design than accounting. Ole was the first son of Palle Palsby, the owner of Denmark's leading stock brokerage (L. Palsby, established 1917) and chairman of the Copenhagen stockbrokers' association. After finishing his studies at the Commercial College in 1957, Ole Palsby joined the firm founded by his grandfather and managed by his father. He might have settled down to the dull and comfortable life that was his birthright but for his budding cultural ambitions.

Detail of lower cabinet with the solid wood trays and storage bins that Hanne Valeur designed for K-60.
← The brass hinge discovered by Torben Valeur and Henning Jensen that became an integral feature of K-60. The recessed hinge makes it possible to open a door 90° and clear the opening to the cabinet. As a result, it becomes possible to access the full width of the interior. The recessed brass pull makes it possible to open doors against each other without damaging the wood veneer. As a result, it is possible to fit cabinets close together and make the most efficient use of available space.

In August 1958, the opening of the Louisiana Museum of Modern Art, 30 km north of Copenhagen, inspired Palsby to choose a new direction for his life. He would be a cultural entrepreneur. Within a few months, he had established a development company and commissioned Louisiana's architects, Jørgen Bo and Vilhelm Wohlert, to design a group of single-family houses for a plot in Rungsted as well as a house for his young family.[26] In 1962, Palsby's visit to *Tradition and Renewal* and encounter with K-60 catalyzed his desire to promote and sell beautiful objects of outstanding quality. He soon signed a contract with the Valeurs and Henning Jensen that made him the exclusive agent for K-60 and established a new company to market the system: K-60 Køkkenelementer ApS.[27]

 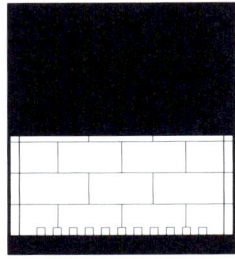 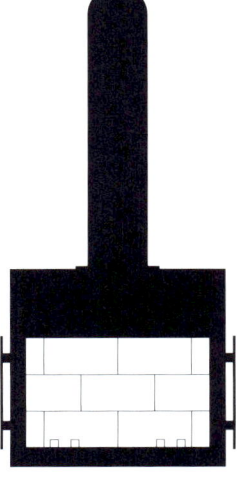 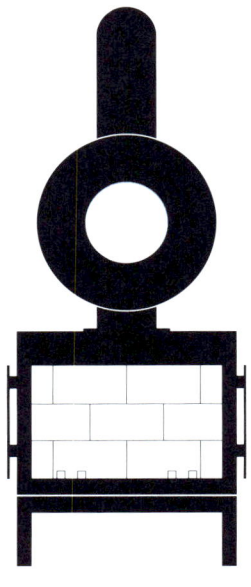

In 1965, Palsby left the world of finance and established a design showroom on the first floor of a historic building in central Copenhagen: Hovedvagtsgade 8. With an interior designed by Nils Fagerholt and a graphic identity by Bo Bonfils, Palsby's eponymous showroom presented a selection of exquisite objects anchored by K-60, Fagerholt's black steel fireplaces and furniture designed by Poul Kjærholm.[28] By 1966, the selection included Alvar Aalto's glassware, Dieter Rams's stereo equipment for Braun and chairs designed by Marcel Breuer in the 1920s. In addition to the commercial products, Palsby presented periodic exhibitions of contemporary Danish art. Indeed, the showroom was as much a gallery as a commercial venture and operated without any concern for turning a profit.

Jørgen Bo and Vilhelm Wohlert. Kirstineparken, Hørsholm, 1962–69. Interior of Kirstineparken 41 with dining area and K-60 kitchen. ← Bo Bonfils. Logo for K-60 Elementkøkken ApS, 1964. / Bo Bonfils. Logo for Ole Palsby, 1965. / Nils Fagerholt. Prefabricated steel fireplaces Pejs 1 (1959), Pejs 2 (1961) and Pejs 3 (1963). / Installation view of *Søren Georg Jensen*, Ole Palsby, Hovedvagtsgade 8, Copenhagen, 1967.

Palsby's final development project was Kirstineparken, which is located on a ridge in Hørsholm, 25 km north of Copenhagen. He purchased the property in 1962 and hired Bo and Wohlert to design fifty row houses that were based on a typical plan. By the early 1960s, residential construction in Denmark was dominated by "type houses": standard dwellings that were produced in large numbers by construction companies.[29] Typically, the builders did not hire architects but harvested ideas from publications and adapted them to their standard practices. Palsby's ambition was to construct type houses based on elevated standards of site planning, design and construction. Bo took the lead at Kirstineparken, which allowed him to exercise his rare gift for nesting buildings in the landscape.[30]

Bo based his work on a 1-1/2-story house of 137 meters, about 8 meters wide, which is framed by parallel brick walls and covered by a pitched roof of clay tiles. To provide the residents with private terraces, he arranged the houses in undulating bands that follow the topography and frame a common green space planted with oak trees. By February 1965, the model house was ready for visitors, who found that it was furnished with Hanne Valeur's K-60 elements and Nils Fagerholt's wall-mounted fireplace.[31] The same combination of kitchen and fireplace would eventually be installed in all fifty houses.

In April 1966, Ole Palsby participated in *Typehuset 1966* (Type House 1966), a public exhibition that catered to the thriving market for standardized single-family houses; his display included K-60 and Nils Fagerholt's prefabricated fireplaces. Making the rounds of the other stands, Palsby discovered a remarkably faithful copy of K-60.[32] Working for the Joint Organization, architect Børge Kjær and two assistants, Inger and Hans Zachariassen, had developed a less expensive version of Hanne Valeur's modular system.[33] While substituting some of the underlying materials and changing the surfaces inside the cabinets, they preserved the module of 60 cm, Douglas fir exterior and many of the signature details, including the round pulls, which were now made of plastic.

That plagiarized version of K-60 was presented as the Tectum Kitchen and displayed alongside another copy produced by Tectum that was painted gray and labeled the Atlas Kitchen. While FDB would sell the new version of the Tectum Kitchen to the public, the Atlas Kitchen would be used in housing estates constructed by the members of the Joint Organization. In the words of one visitor to *Tradition and Renewal,* previously cited on p. 67:

Kirstineparken 41. Detail of upper cabinet with open door and recessed brass hinge.
← K-60 cabinets with black-stained ash countertop and open cassettes of Douglas fir.

"But they [K-60 elements] can of course be made in other types of wood, or painted, which will have no significant impact on the appearance of the elements and none on the concept of this furniture."

The Joint Organization's decision to plagiarize the design of K-60 is not mysterious. Compared to the original Tectum Kitchen, Hanne Valeur's truly modular system offered lower production costs, more flexible installations and a clean break with the era of iceboxes and unheated kitchens. Above all, K-60 provided a more attractive design than the work of Edvard Heiberg and his fellow kitchen specialists, which is why the wooden copy created by Kjær and his associates was so faithful to Valeur's design. A few weeks after Palsby discovered the two plagiarized versions of K-60, he submitted a deposition to the Maritime and Commercial Court and filed a lawsuit against Tectum, alleging copyright infringement and violation of the Competition Act. The Court appointed two professional experts: master cabinetmaker Børge Jensen and architect Finn Juhl, and began the lengthy process of considering the case.[34]

Palsby's lawsuit had no effect on the marketing of Tectum's plagiarized design. In February 1967, an article in FDB's monthly magazine introduced the "New Tectum kitchen that has it all."[35] The kitchen was falsely described as a new version of the Danish Kitchen Set/Tectum Kitchen, which had been simplified and brought "up to date" to meet a higher standard of living. In March, the Joint Organization reinforced that fiction by publishing *Dansk Køkkensæt* (Danish Kitchen Set); a detailed description of the "new" Tectum and Atlas systems that provided a manual for architects and builders.[36]

In November 1967, *Køkkenet, Danmarks største arbejdsplads* (The Kitchen, Denmark's Largest Workplace) opened at Copenhagen's Forum exhibition building. The exhibitors included more than forty kitchen producers from Denmark, Sweden and West Germany, who participated in a juried competition for design excellence. The chairman of the jury was architect and kitchen specialist Esbjørn Hiort, who had reviewed K-60 in 1962 and was well aware of Ole Palsby's lawsuit against Tectum. Ultimately, Hiort's jury awarded a Gold Medal to the new version of the Tectum Kitchen, based on its "[...] extremely appealing overall character, elaborate details and many options for variation."[37]

The exhibition also included the first presentation of the Skarridsø Kitchen, which looked remarkably like the new Tectum Kitchen unveiled one year earlier. When a journalist asked the director of Tectum about the resemblance, he deferred to the director of the Joint Organization, who condemned this apparent case of plagiarism — with unintentional irony — while attempting to distance his painted copy of K-60 (Atlas Kitchen) from Tectum's facsimile in Douglas fir:

"I think the Skarridsø kitchen is a gross plagiarism of the Tectum kitchen. For now, we intend to present the case to our lawyer, Attorney Victor Hansen. I also think that the Skarridsø brochure is too close to the brochure for Tectum, which is not our kitchen; ours is called the Danish Kitchen Set and is sold to housing associations, while Tectum is only sold to private consumers."[38]

Ole Palsby's lawsuit against Tectum was never resolved, due to a personal catastrophe that rendered the matter moot. In the second week of February 1968, his father, Palle Palsby, was charged with raiding his clients' accounts to cover his losses on the stock market.[39] Ole Palsby was investigated and found blameless but nonetheless ruined: All of his business ventures — including the company that held the rights to K-60 — and his Bo and Wohlert-designed house had been financed years earlier by loans from his father.[40] After Palle Palsby's creditors called for the repayment of those loans, Ole Palsby was forced to declare bankruptcy. His showroom was shuttered, his companies were liquidated, and his home was sold to settle a fraction of his debts. As Kirstineparken was still under construction, the lender assumed control and completed the final cluster of houses in 1969.

Kirstineparken 41. Detail of vertical storage slot with pull-out drying rack for hand towels.
→ View from kitchen towards living room with lower cabinets, open storage cassettes and glass vitrines.

In the wake of Ole Palsby's bankruptcy, his lawsuit against Tectum was dismissed and the rights to K-60 reverted to Hanne and Torben Valeur and Henning Jensen. But there were no prospects for large-scale production of K-60 at a lower cost, because the market for factory-made kitchen elements was already glutted.[41] Tectum had many competitors, but it would remain the market leader, due to Hanne Valeur's design and FDB's large membership and sophisticated sales apparatus.

View from living room towards dining area and kitchen. Hanne Valeur. K-60 serving cart, 1962. Douglas fir and wicker basket. Nils Fagerholt. Pejs 1, 1959. Steel and refractory bricks. Over the decades, all but one of the fifty K-60 kitchens that were installed at Kirstineparken were painted white, disfigured or simply discarded. The only original example was the kitchen at Kirstineparken 41 shown on these pages. Prior to her death, in 2024, homeowner Kirsten Strømstad donated the kitchen to Designmuseum Danmark, ensuring that one example of this Danish cultural treasure will remain intact. → Detail of counter and cabinets at wall to living room. Alvar Aalto. Vase 3030, 1936.

As Valeur & Jensen's architectural practice prospered, Hanne Valeur withdrew from the office and pursued her own projects, which included perhaps a half-dozen kitchens with K-60 elements produced by Christensen & Larsen.[42] As for Palsby, he recovered from the scandal of his father's crime and played ever more important roles in Danish design culture (p. 132).

As the director of the National Association of Danish Arts and Crafts, Bent Salicath might have protested the plagiarism of K-60 in the pages of *Dansk Kunsthaandværk*, as he did in other cases of creative theft.[43] But his role in the design of the first Tectum Kitchen and close ties to the Joint Organization made that difficult. While the Joint Organization had commissioned the design and received some income from the Tectum Kitchen, Tectum and its parent company, FDB, earned enormous profits for decades. Reliable sales figures are difficult to locate, but a conservative estimate is that Tectum sold more than 400,000 kitchens during 1967–87.[44] Over time, the choice of veneers expanded, and the door fronts were updated by Børge Kjær and his associates to reflect shifts in taste.[45]

The extraordinary commercial success of the Tectum Kitchen is a tribute to Hanne Valeur's talent, her practical details and her ability to imagine the kitchen as an integral part of the home. With K-60, she advanced kitchen design beyond the poverty mentality of the 1920s and the rigid approach of the 1950s that was rooted in that mentality, and created a flexible system so practical and so attractive that it was not only copied but appropriated outright.

Another tribute to Valeur's abilities is the fact that many vintage Tectum Kitchens (made of better materials than is the norm today) are still in use and so highly valued that they are often renewed. Indeed, Valeur's design remains contemporary because it was rooted in a set of principles that can be continuously renewed.

In the end, the saga of K-60 confirms the underlying premise of Børge Mogensen and Arne Karlsen's controversial critique "Applied Art Gone Astray" and the resulting installation *Tradition and Renewal*. As Hanne Valeur developed kitchen cabinets with removable trays that were based on a single module, she extended the underlying principle of Kaare Klint's sideboard (p. 13) to an entire kitchen and demonstrated how his ideas and methods might be extended in new directions. In the process, she created another link in the chain of masterful storage solutions that have emerged from Klint's methods and values. They include the handmade bookcase and factory-made book box (p. 16) designed by Valeur's father, Mogens Koch, and the industrial system of cabinets (p. 218) designed by her supporter Børge Mogensen and his collaborator Grethe Meyer. The irony is that someone who doubted her talent so acutely in her youth would eventually create one of the most influential designs in the history of Danish furniture, which is now no longer forgotten and has been entered into the historical record.

Working as an architect, Arne Jacobsen created buildings that heighten our awareness of the natural world, by way of interior gardens, atmospheric surfaces and muted colors.[1] As an industrial designer, he created mass-produced items with pristine finishes and precise details that recall traditional handicraft. Most of Jacobsen's designs can be divided into two categories: organic forms that support the human body and geometric elements that serve a variety of purposes, from lamps to carpeting to plumbing taps. The common denominator in those categories was his delight in developing elegant solutions to practical concerns. Among the geometric designs, the most refined example of Jacobsen's functional artistry is the series of stainless steel hollowware that he named **Cylinda-line**.

Jacobsen's life and work have been so thoroughly examined, by this author and several others, that it is possible to leap forward to early 1964.[2] Attending a family dinner, Jacobsen found himself drawn into a gentle trap laid by his stepson, Peter Holmblad.[3] The young man had recently been hired at Stelton A/S, where he sold stainless steel tableware that he found too ugly to use in his own home. Holmblad hoped to convince his stepfather to design new products that would elevate the company's standard. At the dinner table, he pretended to struggle with the design of a serving dish and asked Jacobsen for advice, which was freely given and fairly harsh. Soon after, Holmblad raised the idea of making hollowware from ready-made tubes that were cut to useful lengths and fitted with bottoms and spouts. Jacobsen was intrigued and began sketching pitchers using the diameters of standard British tubes.

Arne Jacobsen. AJ stainless flatware, 1957. → Cylinda-line, 1964–67. Pitcher, teapot and detail of cocktail spoon. Stainless steel and thermoplastic. 1:1 scale.

Arne Jacobsen's designs for hollowware were not his first foray into stainless steel tableware. In 1957, he accepted an offer from A. Michelsen A/S, the venerable silversmithy and court jeweler, to design a set of steel flatware. Jacobsen abandoned the historical models of knife, fork and spoon in favor of continuous forms that he conceived as extensions of the fingers, which were stamped from sheets of stainless steel.[4] In the process, he allowed his ideal union of material, form and production technique to supersede the purpose of the utensils. While the flat handles are awkward in the hand, the implements are too narrow to hold a mouthful of food. Some of the spoons and serving pieces are useful, but the forks are best suited to eating dessert, when small bites are actually desirable.

Designing hollowware for Stelton, Jacobsen would once again pursue a union of material, form and production technique. But the use of a cylinder for all of the vessels freed him from the burden of inventing new forms and allowed him to focus on elegant details that support the purpose of each vessel. His penchant for geometric form was ideally suited to stainless steel, which is immensely hard and can only be shaped by machines. And yet, he would treat the industrial metal with the care and artistry previously reserved for silver. In doing so, he created a modern equivalent to traditional hollowware that could be sold at hardware stores for affordable prices.

ARNE JACOBSEN 1964–67
Cylinda-line

As Jacobsen sketched his cylindrical vessels, he gathered functional ideas from existing models, which were numerous. Cylindrical hollowware was a popular subject in Danish design circa 1960. Notable examples include a stainless steel service designed in 1963 by Søren Georg Jensen, a sculptor and son of the legendary silversmith Georg Jensen. While the sculptor's service may have spurred Jacobsen to design steel hollowware, his pots with semicircular spouts and handles are small works of art rather than useful models for further development. Nonetheless, Jacobsen found an important detail in Jensen's 1949 silver tea set: a pair of stacking cylinders with half-round folding handles.[5] Similar handles appear on Jacobsen's ice buckets, resting on bolts that prevent rattling (p. 85).

Søren Georg Jensen undoubtedly admired the set of black aluminum cylinders that Vilhelm Wohlert designed for the Louisiana Museum of Modern Art during 1958–59. Jensen lived nearby and his sculptures were included in the museum's collection. Both Jensen and Wohlert drew inspiration from designs of architect Magnus L. Stephensen, as did Jacobsen. During the late 1930s, Stephensen was a creative collaborator of Kay Bojesen, who tutored him in the design of silver hollowware and produced several of his vessels.[6] In 1950, Stephensen accepted an invitation to design silverwares for Georg Jensen A/S and he would also work in steel. His condiment set, three-armed tea strainer and insulated ice bucket provided useful models for Cylinda-line.

All four of these designers, architects and sculptor alike, were fundamentally inspired by the geometric hollowware designed during 1924–26 by Marianne (Liebe) Brandt, a student at Bauhaus Weimar and eventually a teacher at Bauhaus Dessau.[7] Determined to create revolutionary forms for everyday items, she reduced her vessels to sets of circles, hemispheres and cylinders that symbolized the arrival of a new industrial era, although her vessels were handmade. Jacobsen's improved version of Brandt's rotating ashtray includes handles of 4-mm steel rod that are easily manipulated with fingertips and recall Kay Bojesen's specialized utensils of the 1940s (p. 30).

Jacobsen found a fundamental source of inspiration in the black Bakelite handle that Erik Herløw designed for an aluminum pitcher in 1955, with a molded form that matched the voluptuous curve of the opening. Jacobsen dispensed with Herløw's sculptural approach but preserved the harmony of handle and vessel.

Søren Georg Jensen. Pieces of coffee and tea service, 1963. Stainless steel, rattan and enamel. Left to right: coffee pot, water pitcher and stacked pots for tea and hot water with creamer, sugar canister and ashtray in foreground.
→ Magnus L. Stephensen. Ice bucket with stand, 1959. Stainless steel and wooden lid (not shown). / Erik Herløw. Pitcher, 1955. Aluminum and Bakelite. / Marianne Brandt. Teapot, 1924. Nickel silver and ebony. / Marianne Brandt. Ashtray, 1924. Brass and nickel-plated steel. / Vilhelm Wohlert. Louisiana hollowware, 1958–59. Anodized aluminum and rattan. / Kay Bojesen. Serving fork, 1942. Sterling silver.

At its core, Cylinda-line is a set of cylindrical containers embellished with extremely practical details, which include the integral spout on the pitchers, the ice lip with welded tabs and the round lid with a raised disk that is easy to lift from any angle. The essential detail is the thermoplastic handle that makes it practical to pour the contents. The outer edges form a right angle so that the handle is aligned with the cylinder and provides precise control when pouring. On the underside, segments of circles provide a secure grip. The non-slip material was selected to withstand the dishwasher and initially produced in a dark shade of gray-green that signified Jacobsen's love of plants. To prevent heat transfer, the handles are attached to the vessels with two steel studs. The upper stud is slightly thicker than the lower, due to the greater stress on the connection.

Jacobsen's pots for coffee and tea are lighter and more durable than traditional models and so vastly improved in their function that they constitute reinventions of familiar types. The curved and tapered spouts on the pots contradict Jacobsen's system of simple geometric shapes for entirely practical reasons. The deep curve at the base of the spout creates a reservoir that ensures a steady flow of liquid, even as the tapered cross section makes it easier to control the flow.

At the end of each spout, a triangular opening with a tiny, beak-like projection cuts the flow of liquid and reduces dripping. Jacobsen placed the spouts near the bottom of the vessels, which makes it easier to empty them. No matter the pouring angle, the tiny steel sphere projecting from the rim of the pot will prevent the lid from falling.

Jacobsen's teapot embodies his underlying ambition for Cylinda-line, which was to create objects that are useful, beautiful and durable in equal measures. As every tea drinker can attest, the most vulnerable point on a ceramic teapot is the end of the spout. Typically, spouts are made as short as possible and pulled close to the vessel. Both of those precautions make it more difficult to control the flow of liquid. The brittle character of ceramics also makes it difficult to prevent dripping. On porcelain pots, the end of the spout might be ground to a thin edge that cuts the flow as sharply as possible, but only makes damage more likely. The enormous strength of stainless steel allowed Jacobsen to resolve the conflicts between performance and durability that are inherent to ceramic teapots and create a fundamentally new model.

Cylinda-line pitcher and pots, 1964–67.
Stainless steel and thermoplastic.
Detail of pitcher with ice-lip and handle attachment. → .75 L hot-water jug.
/ 1.5 L coffee pot. / 1.25 L teapot.

The smallest parts of Cylinda-line reveal the artistic root of the entire series. As a student during the 1920s, Jacobsen was enchanted by avant-garde architecture and design in Germany, where figures such as Marcel Breuer, László Moholy-Nagy and Marianne Brandt rejected traditional notions of beauty and worked to create a new visual language.[8] To that end, they created compositions of geometric elements — squares and cubes, circles and spheres, lines and bars — in which each element remained distinct. That artistic approach was rooted in abstract painting and generally known as Constructivism.[9] While many in the avant-garde viewed Constructivism as a source of spiritual enlightenment or a tool for social reform, Jacobsen regarded it as an artistic style that would allow him to design more beautiful buildings and objects.[10]

Cylinda-line offered Jacobsen an ideal vehicle for his constructivist tendencies, beginning with the basic form of the cylinder. The gaps between the plastic handles and cylinders limit the transmission of heat, but they also preserve the outline of the vessel. Designing the smaller vessels, he reinforced the separation of parts and employed loose elements whenever it suited the function. On the small pot for melted butter, the handle is separated from the cup by a single stud and appears to be an independent element. At the same time, the handle includes a finger notch for a secure grip and meets the cup at an angle that makes it easier to pour. Jacobsen's elementary approach is also reflected in his tea strainer and in the rotating ashtray that he based on Brandt's example. Both items include a 75 mm-cup of suitable height and a loose hemisphere fitted with 4-mm steel rods for handles.

While Jacobsen's details preserved the outline of his cylinders, they also improved the function of each object. His tea strainer can be understood as a microcosm of the entire series. While the Y-shaped pattern of drainage holes aligns with the three handles that are easily grasped from any angle, the number of holes increases at the bottom of the hemisphere, where the liquid pools. Rather than base his designs on specific functions, such as pouring water, brewing tea or deposing of cigarette butts, he incorporated those functions into his system of geometric elements. In doing so, he erased the distinction between form and function and created useful tools for daily life that are also abstract objects and radiate a rare, self-contained beauty.

Tea strainer in two parts. / Rotating ashtray in two parts. → Top views of tea strainer and rotating ashtray. 1:1 scale. / .3 L sauce server.

Three and a half years after Arne Jacobsen's fateful dinner with his wife and stepson, eighteen parts of Cylinda-line were introduced in October 1967. One of the factors in the delay was Peter Holmblad's decision not to present the line until he had enough pieces to demonstrate the beauty of uniform vessels.[11] Another factor was the need to invent a machine that could produce the cylinders. In 1964, Jørgen Knudsen, the owner of Dansk Rustfri A/S and eventual manufacturer of Cylinda-line, had suggested using ready-made British tubes. As it happened, the cost of those tubes would have made the finished goods astronomically expensive. After much trial and error, Knudsen's factory manager, Svend Sandgaard, invented a machine that could roll a flat piece of stainless steel into a cylinder and weld the seam.[12]

Holmblad's refusal to introduce Cylinda-line until he had an actual series of products proved to be a masterstroke. The introduction of the line, at a special exhibition at the Bella Center trade hall, generated a great deal of press, as did the annual ID Prize bestowed by the Danish Design Council. Nonetheless, a number of hardware dealers refused to carry Cylinda-line due to the strange appearance of the items. Several changed their mind after Holmblad dispatched his mother and sister to visit their shops anonymously and place orders for the elegant new hollowware they had seen in the newspapers.[13] By 1969, sales of Cylinda-line were sufficiently strong that Stelton introduced half a dozen new products, mainly pieces of barware that included two serving trays, which became best-selling items.

Outstanding parts of Cylinda-line. Left to right: 1.25 L teapot, 2 L pitcher (2004), 1.5 L coffee pot, tea strainer, 3.5 L insulated bucket, tong, 1.5 L insulated bucket. Stub glassware designed by Grethe Meyer and Ibi Trier Mørch. → Top view of insulated bucket.

Similarly to Kay Bojesen's steel flatware, Cylinda-line includes a number of specialty items, such as a toast rack and a cigar ashtray. But as with Grand Prix flatware, even the esoteric parts of the line are so excellent for their purposes that they will be necessary to someone. The most generally useful items are the pitchers that represent new forms of age-old vessels and the two insulated buckets with lids. As with the ice buckets introduced in 1967, the two buckets have a double-wall construction filled with mineral wool that provides excellent insulation. While the 3.5-liter bucket was promoted as a wine cooler and the 1.5-liter bucket as a serving dish for hot or cold food, both have nearly unlimited uses. No matter the temperature of the contents, the insulation prevents water from condensing and dripping on the exterior.

Arne Jacobsen's work on Cylinda-line included graphics, catalogs and packaging that communicated the geometric character and technical quality of the parts. He based the graphic identity on a circle and employed lowercase lettering derived from a standard industrial font to convey his ideal of neutral objects designed for mass production. The resemblance between Jacobsen's logo of offset circles and Marianne Brandt's 1924 teapot is not a coincidence. Despite the industrial character of Jacobsen's designs, he created boxes for the parts that recalled packaging for perfume or other luxury goods, which were made of cream-colored cardboard and printed with gray-green ink. Examples of Jacobsen's cylindrical boxes are now collectors' items.

Beyond the table, Cylinda-line provided the components for a set of plumbing taps, primarily designed by Jacobsen's assistant Teit Weylandt, that employ cylinders as handles and include narrow rods for adjusting water flow and temperature.[14] The first examples of the **Vola** series were installed in Jacobsen's new headquarters for the National Bank of Denmark, in the center of Copenhagen.[15] He lived to see the first stage of the building open in February 1971, a month before his death at the age of sixty-nine. In 1972, Weylandt shepherded several of Jacobsen's unrealized designs for Cylinda-line into production. Two years later, the introduction of his multi-set system of serving trays, bowls and cutting boards marked the completion of Cylinda-line.[16]

Arne Jacobsen, 1959. View of Jacobsen at home with the collection of cameo and antique medallions that he embedded in the wall above his fireplace. / Detail of cocktail mixer with spoon. / Lid for cocktail mixer. → Detail of multi-set tray with cutting board. Stainless steel and beech. / Arne Jacobsen. Packaging for tea strainer and marmalade jar, 1967

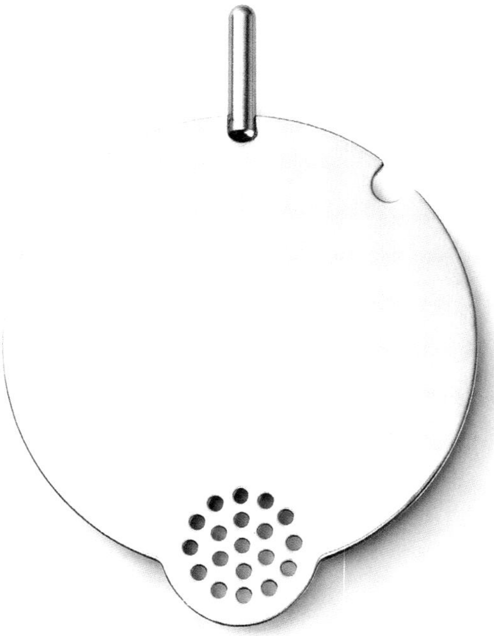

Six decades later, many parts of Cylinda-line remain in production, in China, with the original details mostly intact. While the handles are cast in black thermoplastic that resists fading, the precisely drawn grip has been preserved. Some parts of the line have been discontinued due to low sales, but most of them can be found in second-hand shops and through online sources. Other parts have been adapted to changes in popular appetites, such as the enlarged pitchers for drinking water and the insulated coffee press created by combining the 1.5-liter coffee pot with the strainer from the cocktail shaker. Those adaptations illustrate the durability of Peter Holmblad's original idea and the excellence of Jacobsen's forms, even as the purposes evolve.

With Cylinda-line, Arne Jacobsen created a series of nearly indestructible objects that provide decades of daily use and delight on a daily basis, even when sitting on the shelf. The beauty of the best parts of the series serve as a reminder of what is possible when artistic intelligence is applied to mass production. By focusing on the purpose of each object and using geometry to eliminate any trace of artistic signature, he created perfect examples of industrial design. That is to say that the best parts of Cylinda-line combine the precision of the factory and the accommodation of hand, eye and body that distinguish artisanal products. And so, beauty not only engenders delight but also gratitude and admiration.

Cylinda-line. Steel hollowware, 1964–67/1972/1974.

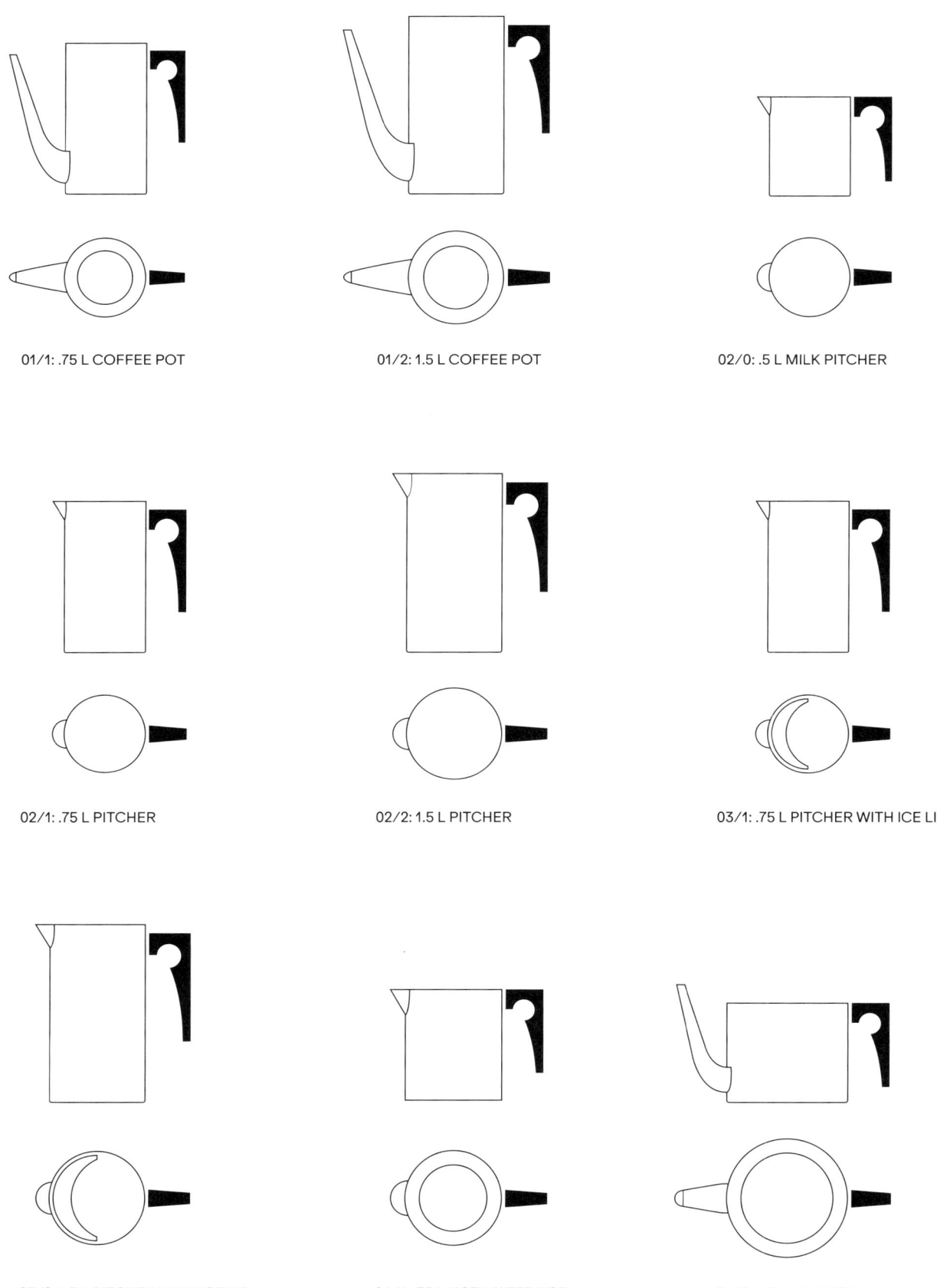

01/1: .75 L COFFEE POT
01/2: 1.5 L COFFEE POT
02/0: .5 L MILK PITCHER
02/1: .75 L PITCHER
02/2: 1.5 L PITCHER
03/1: .75 L PITCHER WITH ICE LIP
03/2: 1.5 L PITCHER WITH ICE LIP
04/1: .75 L HOT WATER POT
04/2: 1.25 L TEAPOT

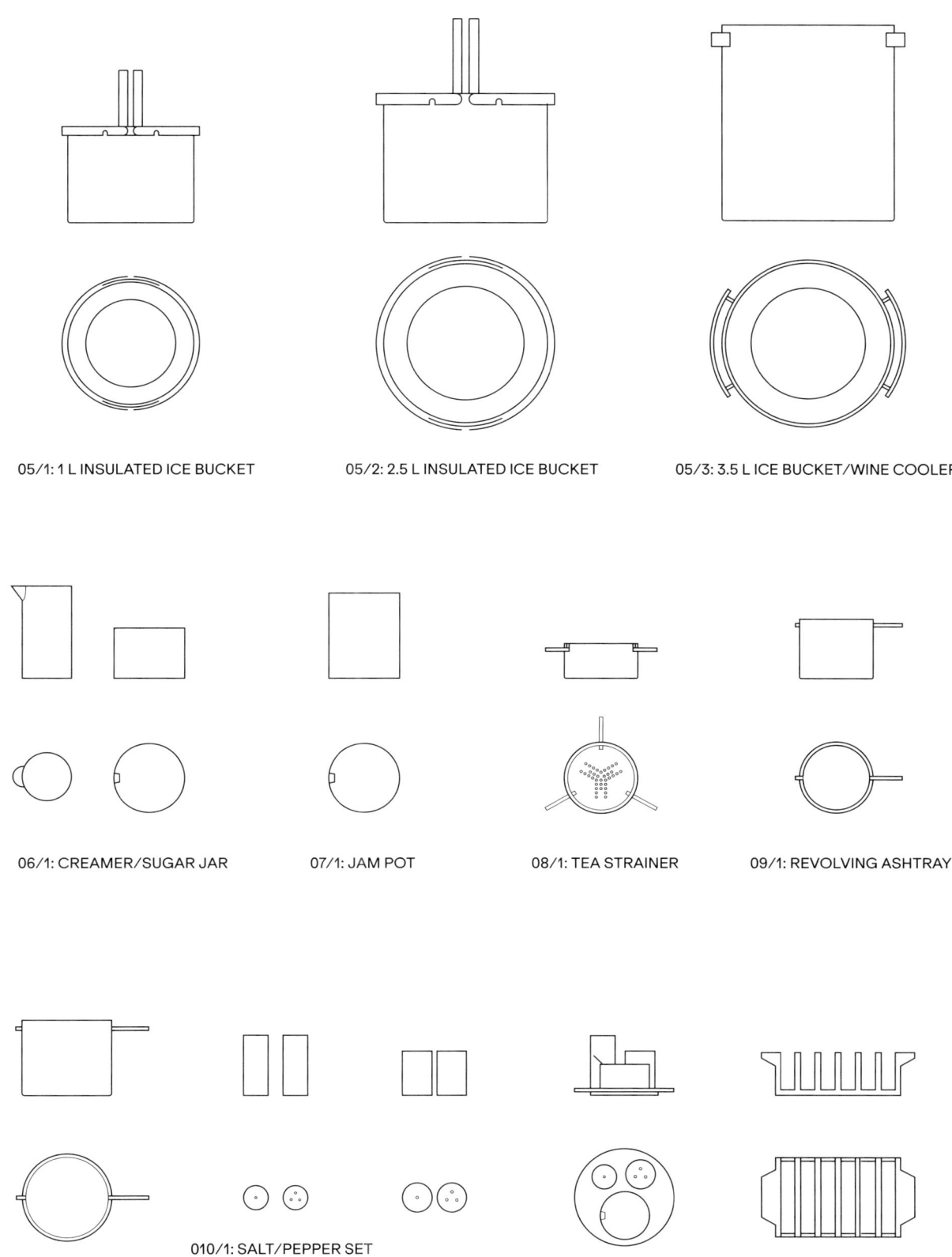

Cylinda-line. Steel hollowware, 1964–67/1972/1974.

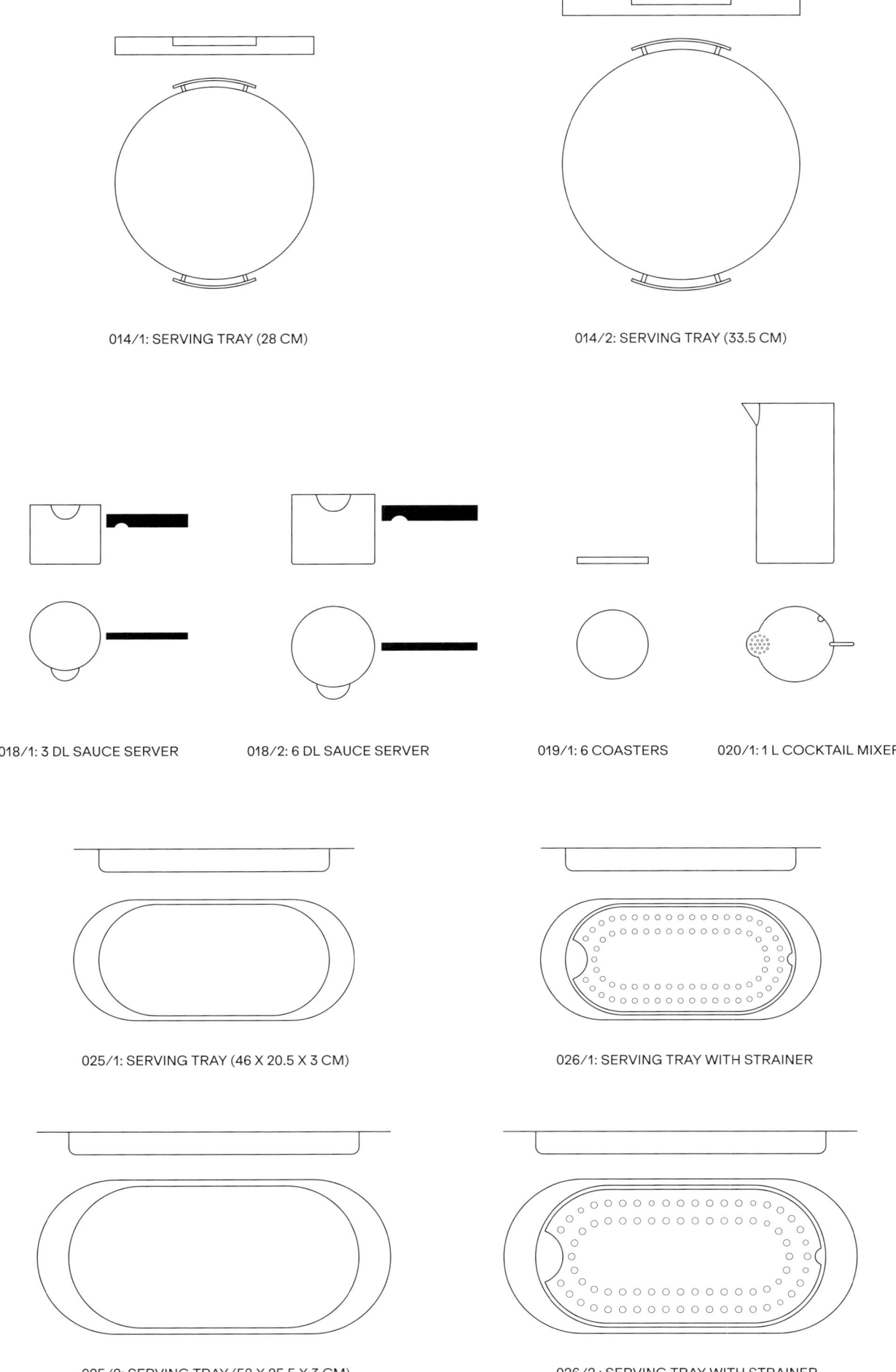

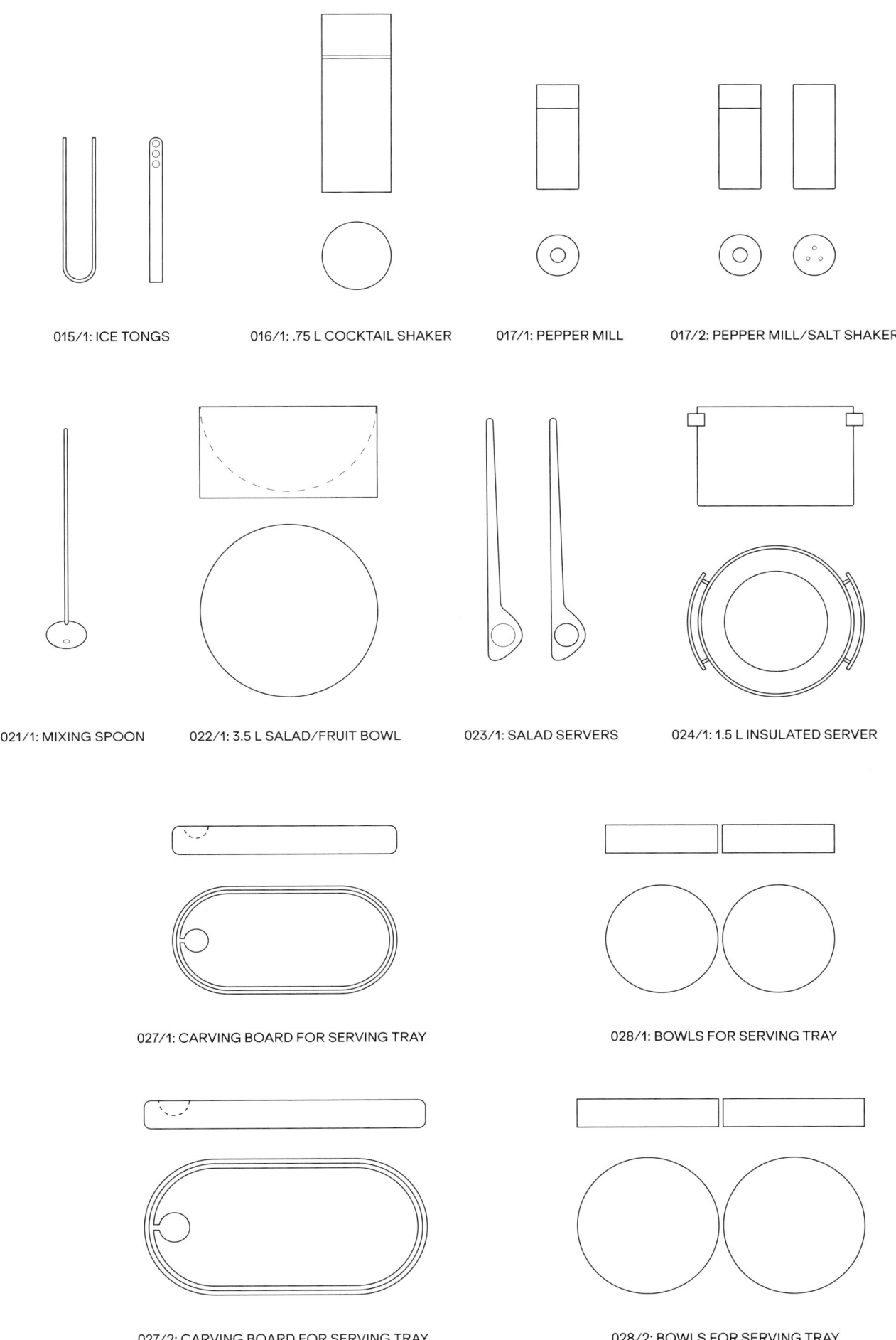

In June 1971, the Royal Copenhagen Porcelain Factory introduced **Hvidpot** (Whitepot), an economical service of undecorated parts that Grethe Meyer had designed to fit the hand, enhance the enjoyment of food and allow for compact storage. According to the press release, Meyer had worked on the service for five years, but we can trace the origins of Hvidpot to an unrealized service that she had designed with Ibi Trier Mørch, twelve years earlier. During the summer of 1959, as the public flocked to the Kastrup Glassworks exhibition and admired Meyer and Trier Mørch's stacking stemware (p. 44), they were designing plates and platters. In June, Porcelænsfabriken "Danmark" A/S (or Lyngby Porcelain) had announced a competition for a new service suited to industrial production.[1] As with their entry to the Kastrup competition, Meyer and Trier Mørch would be disappointed by the jury's response. But once again, their proposal would spawn an archetypal design for the table that condensed lessons from earlier models into a set of ideal forms.

Porcelain was a familiar material for Meyer.[2] After finishing her compulsory schooling in 1934, aged 16, she spent five years as a decorative painter at the Dahl-Jensen porcelain factory, outside of Copenhagen. During 1939–40, she worked as a secretary in an engineering office while attending evening classes and earning the diploma required to apply to the School of Architecture at the Royal Danish Academy. After graduating from the Academy in 1947, Meyer's research for *Byggebogen* and the National Building Research Institute focused on the dimensions of common household objects. By 1959, she had a solid grasp of porcelain production and extensive knowledge of tableware sizes, but Trier Mørch would contribute her own expertise to their competition entry. During the 1930s, her work on Swedish kitchen cabinets had naturally included a study of the contents and introduced her to the faience service that provided the model for her porcelain project with Meyer.

Grethe Meyer and Ibi Trier Mørch. Competition drawing for Porcelænsfabriken "Danmark" A/S, 1959. The competition project for a porcelain service was Meyer's first experience designing tableware and led to her new career as an industrial designer. → Grethe Meyer. Hvidpot, 1966–71. 1:1 scale.

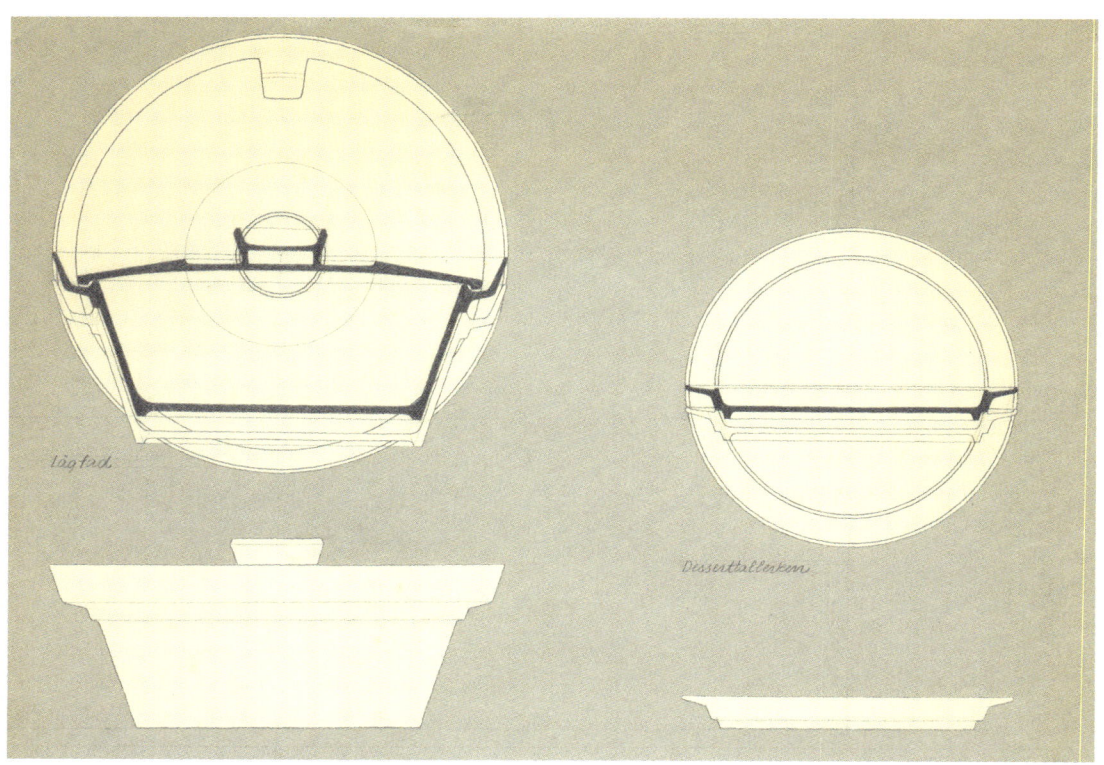

GRETHE MEYER 1966–71
Hvidpot

The 1959 porcelain competition that spawned Grethe Meyer's career as a ceramic designer was spurred by the same concerns that had inspired the Kastrup Glassworks competition, two years earlier. Confronted with shifts in popular habits, which included more casual approaches to table settings, the directors of Lyngby Porcelæn hoped to discover fashionable designs that would boost their sales. As with glassware, the most advanced Nordic designs for tableware were emanating from Finland, where Kaj Franck served as artistic director of the Arabia factory (p. 44). His goal was to "smash the services" and replace the traditional model of expensive, elaborately decorated parts with a handful of inexpensive items that could easily be combined with other types of tableware.[3]

In 1953, Arabia introduced **Kilta**: eight pieces of undecorated faience that were designed with simple geometric forms and accompanied by a set of covered jars. Most of the pieces had multiple uses, and many of them could be stacked for compact storage. Meyer and Trier Mørch were aware of Kilta as early as January 1953, when several pieces were exhibited in Copenhagen, at the Danish Museum of Applied Art (now Designmuseum Danmark).[4] Franck's influence on their 1959 competition entry is most pronounced in the covered dish they designed with a projecting collar and concave knob on the lid, which is illustrated on the preceding page. However, the essential model for Meyer and Trier Mørch's project was the Swedish service that served as the direct precursor to Kilta.

Kaj Franck. IS jars, 1949. Faience. / EE casserole, 1952–53. Faience. / Kilta/BA series with IS jars and EE casserole, 1951–52. Faience. Arabia. → Wilhelm Kåge. Praktika stacking bowls with "Weekend" decoration. / Drawings from 1933 catalog depicting interchangeable parts and compact storage. / Praktika, 1930–33. Faience. Gustavsbergs Porslinsfabrik. Assortment with "Kokvrå" decoration.

In 1933, following three years of study and testing, the Swedish ceramics manufacturer Gustavsbergs Porslinsfabrik introduced **Praktika**, a faience service designed by the company's artistic director, Wilhelm Kåge. Following the egalitarian ethos of the era, Kåge conceived the service for people of limited means who lived in small apartments. To that end, most of the parts could be used for more than one purpose and stacked for compact storage.[5] In a departure from the standard practice, which dictated the purchase of entire services for six or eight place settings, Praktika was sold as a series of individual parts, so that people could purchase only what they needed or could afford at the time. To promote public acceptance, the parts were offered with three types of painted decoration.

Despite Kåge's concern for consumers and painstaking attention to detail, his so-called Wonder Service was never embraced by the Swedish public.[6] But it was an enormous success with critics, architects and social reformers, who hailed Praktika as a new model for tableware based on social reality. Ibi Trier Mørch certainly encountered Kåge's masterpiece of functional tableware during her years in Sweden, 1937–40, while she was working on designs for standardized kitchens that included a careful study of storage needs. As part of her work, she may well have measured parts of Praktika and quite possibly saved a copy of the illustrated catalog that outlined the many benefits of Kåge's visionary design, including the stacking bowls and interchangeable lids for the pitchers.

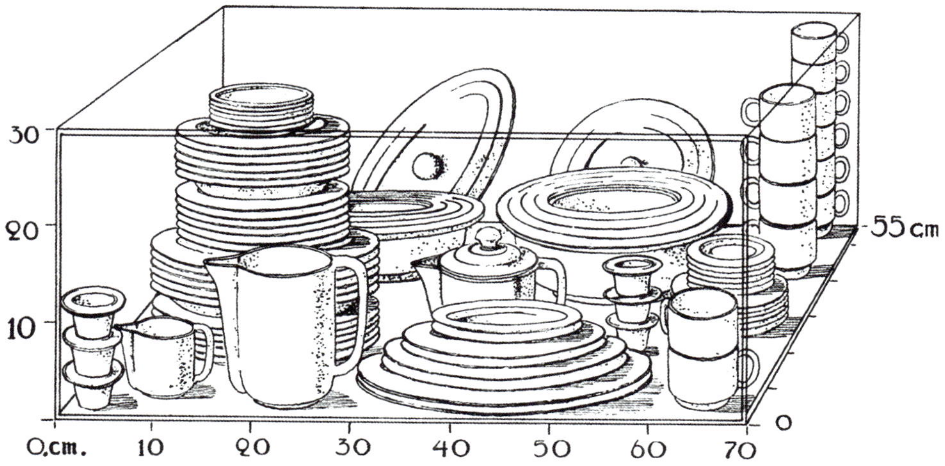

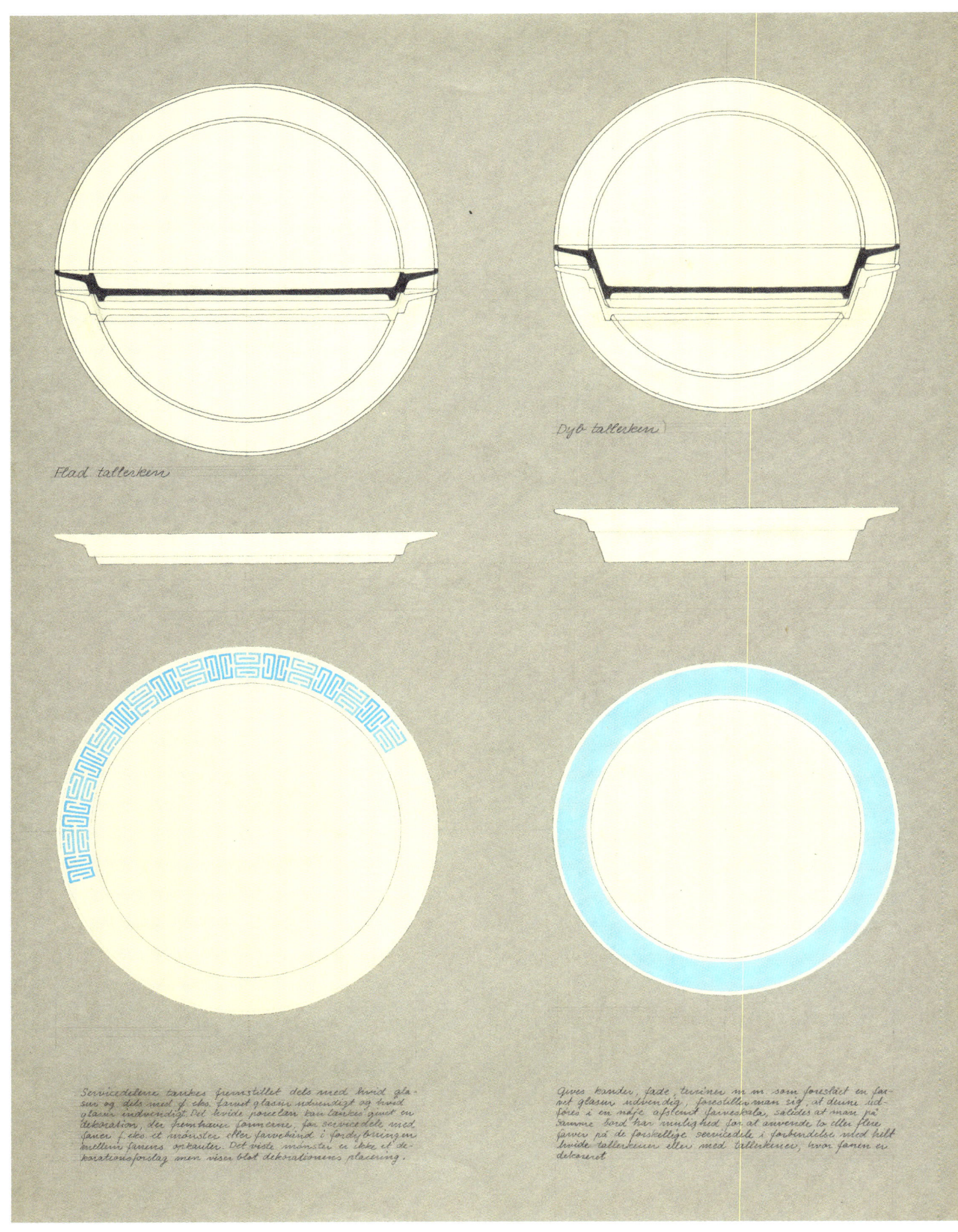

Grethe Meyer and Ibi Trier Mørch. Competition drawing for Porcelænsfabriken "Danmark" A/S, 1959. Proposal for plate and deep plate with options for painted decoration. → Proposal for teapot with two handles for ease of handling.

In November 1959, Lyngby Porcelæn convened an unusually large jury to review the ninety-one competition entries that included nearly 1000 drawings and models. The nine jurors included the two directors of the company and their artistic consultant, ceramicist Axel Brüel; a former Danish minister of commerce; the director of the National Hardware Dealers' Association; architects Arne Jacobsen, Esbjørn Hiort and Bent Salicath; and ceramicist Gertrud Vasegaard. The diverse viewpoints of the jurors made it impossible for them to reach a consensus, and they finally parceled out the prizes by nominating finalists and then eliminating them through successive rounds of voting.

Ultimately, the interior designer Alice Beckman was awarded first prize for a service that employed colored glazes to signify the contents of the parts and recalled Kaj Franck's Kilta series; a second prize went to Marianne Lyager and Knud Vodder for their sculptural designs of jugs and covered dishes. Third prizes were awarded to the architects Elizabeth and Søren Sass; V. Wismar Vestergaard; and Grethe Meyer and Ibi Trier Mørch. Three other entries received a fourth prize.[7]

Meyer and Trier Mørch's competition drawings reveal their intention to combine Wilhelm Kåge's model of stacking, multi-use parts with the precise forms and thin edges that porcelain allows, due to the high strength of the material. The common feature was a profiled rim on the plates and platters that would provide a secure grip, prevent damage when stacking and simplify washing.

Each rim featured two raised edges that would frame the area for handling the item and keep fingers out of the food; the flat surface between the edges could be decorated or could be left bare. Each of the parts would have a profiled base that would allow stacking with minimal contact, to protect the glazed surface from the unglazed foot. As a result, dirty plates could be stacked without coating the undersides with grease, which was a common concern in the era before automatic dishwashers.[8] The debt to the Praktika service was most apparent in the integrated spouts and ergonomic handles on the coffee- and teapots; both features would reappear in Meyer's next project for tableware.

The directors of Lyngby Porcelæn were unsettled by the lack of consensus among the competition jurors and quickly renounced the right to produce any of the prize-winning designs. Just as quickly, Meyer and Trier Mørch's friend Erik Herløw recommended their competition project to the Royal Copenhagen factory, where he served as the design consultant.[9] The factory had recently installed a new managing director, Erik Lindgren, who planned to introduce new and more fashionable designs. To that end, he invited Meyer and Trier Mørch to develop their porcelain project for Royal Copenhagen. For reasons that remain unclear, Trier Mørch declined the offer and left Meyer to continue the work on her own. By Christmas 1959, she had agreed to design a porcelain service with thirty-five parts and embarked on a new career path. Early in 1960, she resigned from the National Building Research Institute and established a design office in her small apartment on the outskirts of Copenhagen.

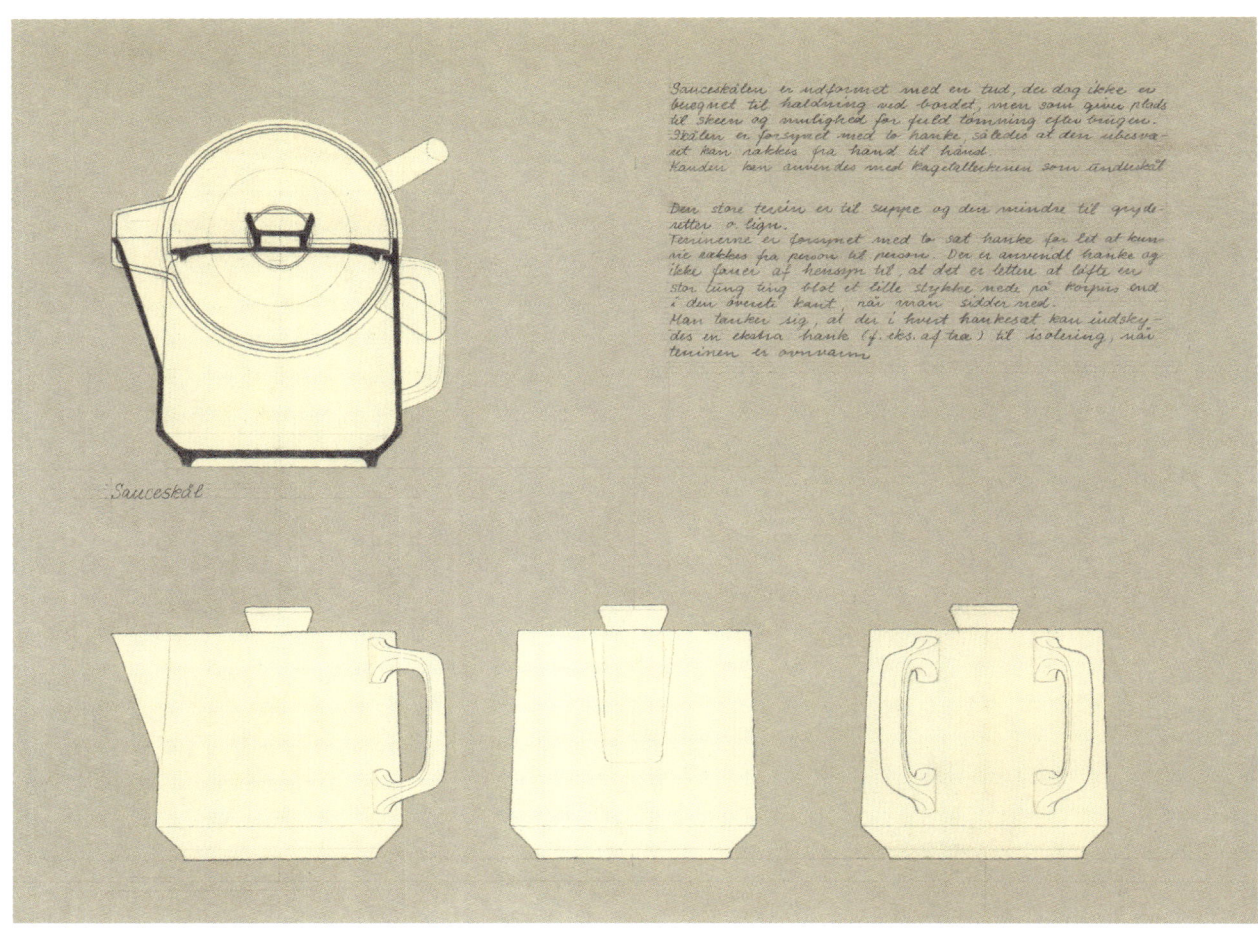

Gertrud Vasegaard. Two of eight parts from tea service, 1957. Porcelain. Bing & Grøndahl. The brown edges emphasize the varied shapes of the parts and were created by scraping off the glaze and applying an iron oxide solution. / Grethe Meyer. Decorated prototypes for faience service, 1964. After the management of the Royal Copenhagen Porcelain Factory insisted on some type of painted decoration, Meyer prepared a set of prototypes with an elaborate design that recalled her 1959 competition project with Ibi Trier Mørch. To her relief, management balked at the cost of painting the elaborate design and she was able to employ a single blue line. → Plate comparison. 1:1 scale. Meyer's concerns for ease of handling and compact storage first appeared in her 1959 porcelain project with Ibi Trier Mørch (top). The shift from porcelain to faience required Meyer to thicken her forms but the raised edge between rim and serving area remained intact.

As Meyer began her work at the factory, she found few friends among the technical staff, a tight-knit community of experts in ceramic chemistry and firing techniques who guarded their knowledge like members of a medieval guild. Moreover, that all-male circle of experts found it difficult to accept the self confident woman who entered their domain "like a hurricane" and expected them to follow her directions.[10] Meyer's difficulties were compounded by a change of material that nearly doomed her project. Towards the end of 1961, Director Erik Lindgren decided that Meyer's service would not be produced in porcelain but in faience, a cheaper material with lower density and less strength.[11]

The difference in strength between porcelain and faience is mirrored in the firing process. While pieces of porcelain pass through the kiln in a single line, faience items are fired in stacks that require less fuel and reduce the production cost. Those stacked pieces must support themselves until they gain the strength imparted during the initial firing; the rims of the plates must not sag, the cups must not buckle. Redesigning her porcelain service for production in faience would require knowledge that Meyer did not yet possess and would not learn from her uncooperative colleagues.

During 1962, as Meyer's failed firing samples accumulated, and frustration at the factory mounted, the directors of the factory began to question her ability to complete the service. The turning point occurred when Leif Lautrup-Larsen, a young engineer in the product development department, asked for permission to spend one day per week on the project, helping Meyer resolve the problems, which was granted.[12] Following his advice, Meyer straightened the walls of the cups and bowls to form a vertical collar around the openings that would keep them from collapsing in the kiln. Moreover, she altered the cross section of the plates and platters, and introduced a diagonal rib that would support the rim prior to firing. In doing so, she created the raised bead that characterizes the flat parts of the service, while recalling the raised edges of her 1959 project with Ibi Trier Mørch.

By the end of 1962, most of Meyer's technical problems had been resolved and she could turn her attention to aesthetic matters. Given a choice between the factory's two colors of faience clay: creamy yellow and bluish-gray, she chose the second option and specified a clear glaze that would reveal the warm tone of the material.[13] Within a few months, she had decided that her new service did not require any decoration, but that decision was vetoed by Royal Copenhagen's board of directors, who wanted to make certain that the factory's decorative painters were fully occupied.[14] Drawing on her teenage experience as a decorative painter at the Dahl-Jensen factory, she prepared two sets of samples. One set was decorated with intricate bands of blue lines that would undoubtedly keep the painting staff busy. The other set featured a single blue line that marked the raised bead on the plates and platters, and emphasized the openings of the bowls and cups.

The fact that Meyer's single blue line recalled the brown line on Gertrud Vasegaard's widely admired tea service for the Bing & Grøndahl porcelain factory was probably reassuring to the directors of Royal Copenhagen. Confronted with a vast difference in the cost of painting, they approved Meyer's preferred (and quite strategic) proposal for a single line.

As Meyer's project moved closer to production, she found herself at odds with the sales department over the price, which was slightly higher than normal for a faience service, as well as her name for the service: **Blåkant** (Blue Line), which recalled a faience service from the 1930s. Director Erik Lindgren supported her on both points, to the immense frustration of his sales director, who imagined that the new service would be a commercial disaster and predicted the company would only sell three complete sets — the traditional standard of success — to Grethe Meyer, Erik Herløw and Leif Lautrup-Larsen.[15]

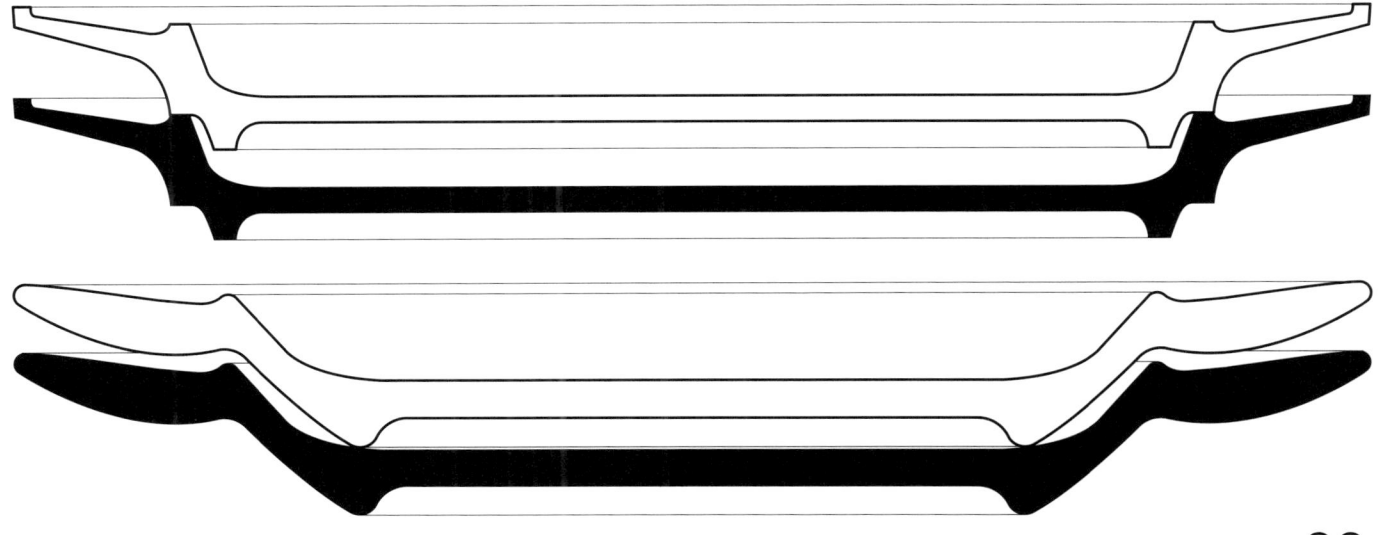

On 16 March 1965, Royal Copenhagen presented Blåkant in a special exhibition at the company's flagship store on Amagertorv, in central Copenhagen. Visitors to the exhibition encountered a table service that was devoid of historical symbols and devoted to the actual purpose of the parts. As Meyer explained, "When you set a table, it is not the service but the food that should be in focus, and plates and dishes should simply emphasize this. It is also important that the individual parts can be used for different purposes and in combination with other items that are used on the table, for example in wood or oven-proof materials. I did not attempt to find new shapes but to improve on traditional ones."[16]

True to her word, Meyer pursued an evolutionary approach by combining age-old models, such as the "deep plate" that also serves as a bowl, with lessons from Kaj Franck's Kilta series and Wilhelm Kåge's Praktika service. And yet, her forms were simpler and more precise than Kåge's examples, even as she avoided the strict geometry and extreme simplification that undermined some parts of Kilta.[17] She based the design of Blåkant on three principles that can be traced back to her 1959 porcelain project with Ibi Trier Mørch:

Firstly, Meyer reduced the number of different forms to simplify production and limit the cost to consumers. As with Kilta, a simple vessel provided the basis for a range of parts that could be covered with a single lid.

The same principle is found in the jugs for coffee and tea and the jugs without handles, all derived from Kåge's Praktika. Secondly, Meyer designed the plates and bowls so they could be combined to keep food warm or be stored in the refrigerator. As with Praktika, overturned plates can serve as lids for large bowls, and vice versa, with the two parts held in place by the raised edge on the top of the plate. Meyer's third principle was the necessity of compact storage that had guided the design of Praktika.

The exhibition of Blåkant generated an enormous amount of positive press; one journalist even predicted that the design would still appeal to the public in the year 2000.[18] Within twelve months, sales of the service exceeded all expectations, and it would remain in production for more than forty years. While Blåkant may be the ideal service in faience, the material has limitations. The coarser ingredients and lower firing temperature that make faience less expensive than porcelain also make faience slightly porous, such that it can absorb water molecules through the glaze.[19] As a result, vintage cups and bowls often have crackled glazing, due to expansion of the underlying material. Of course, placing faience in the dishwasher only heightens the likelihood of water absorption and crackled glazing. Meyer's next service would address those shortcomings, as she finally realized her goal of an undecorated porcelain service composed of multi-use parts.

Grethe Meyer. Blåkant, 1960–65. Faience. Royal Copenhagen. Typical parts with characteristic painted blue line around rims and openings. Three principles of Blåkant: The service should employ as few forms as possible; the parts should have multiple uses; and all of the parts should be easy to stack for compact storage.

In 1966, as sales of Blåkant took off, Royal Copenhagen enlisted Grethe Meyer to design a new porcelain service for hotels, colleges and other institutions that serve large numbers of people.[20] During the 1950s, many of the porcelain factories in then-West Germany, the historical center of European production, had been rebuilt and modernized with automated equipment that lowered costs and increased volumes. The resulting torrent of inexpensive wares crippled Royal Copenhagen's sales of hotel porcelain and rendered its existing service obsolete. Aware that the company could never compete with the German factories on price, Director Erik Lindgren asked Meyer to design a service that could also appeal to better-quality restaurants and might even interest home cooks. Her first step was a careful study of the turning machines that Royal Copenhagen had purchased to produce cups and plates for the new hotel service, as she pursued a union of form and technique that would ensure a moderate sales price.

Seven years after her initial studies for a porcelain service, created with Ibi Trier Mørch, Meyer would continue the principles of multi-use parts based on a handful of forms that could be stacked for compact storage. And yet, five years of development for Blåkant had sharpened her knowledge of useful serving sizes and volumes and provided her with a set of dimensions that could be developed in other materials. While Blåkant can be seen as a prototype for Hvidpot, Meyer would create a new set of forms that reflected the change in material and the primary market of hotels and restaurants. Porcelain designed for hotels and institutional use is typically 15–20% heavier than household wares, because the items are used several times each day and handled with much less care than in a home. With that in mind, Meyer would pursue a balance between durable forms and comfortable weights, designing forms that are at once strong and slender.

Meyer began her work with the plate, which is the most common part of any service, and focused her attention on the rim. Determined to provide a secure grip when plates or platters are laden with food, she created a shallow curve on top of the rim that provides a natural depression for the thumb. Within the rim, a more pronounced curve around the serving area keeps food where it belongs, while also making it easier to scoop, spear and cut. As with Blåkant, Meyer's porcelain plates have a deep base that provides a generous well for food and elevates the rim above the table, for ease of handling. That base also separates the underside from the serving area when plates are stacked, which is especially welcome when the plates are dirty. Meyer was so enchanted by the play of light on the contrasting curves of rim and well that she considered naming the design "shadow play" (*skyggespil*).[21] Ultimately, she settled on Hvidpot to emphasize the absence of decoration and the universal character of the service.

Grethe Meyer. Hvidpot, 1966–71. Porcelain. Royal Copenhagen. As Meyer applied the three principles of Blåkant to porcelain, she used the increased strength of the new material to create forms that are softer and easier to handle. The deep base on the plates makes it easy to separate them when stacked.

Plate comparison. 1:1 scale. / Cup comparison. Blåkant 3042. Hvidpot 6231. → Hvidpot. Grethe Meyer was so enchanted with the play of light on the rims of the plates that she considered naming the service "Shadowplay." Top to bottom: deep plate 6290, flat plate 6294, platter 6326.

The shift from faience to porcelain affected every aspect of Grethe Meyer's new service, from the rim of the plates and the shape of the spouts to the overall aesthetic character. On Blåkant, the warm tone of the clay creates a subtle contrast with the geometric forms and decoration, softening the appearance of the parts. With Hvidpot, Meyer recognized that a machine-made service of white geometric objects could easily appear mechanical and bereft of charm. Working with the precision that is possible with porcelain, she avoided completely flat surfaces in favor of gentle curves that seem to swell and capture light. Due to the difference in firing methods, she could extend the curved wall on the cups and bowls to the edge of the opening, making them slightly easier to empty. As a result of the more relaxed forms, some parts of Hvidpot are less eye-catching than the equivalent parts of Blåkant, but they are also less obviously the work of an industrial designer and more compatible with older things.

As Meyer designed Hvidpot, she reduced the number of parts whenever possible and created smooth, uninterrupted surfaces. In doing so, she addressed the two primary concerns for buyers of hotel porcelain: economy and ease of cleaning. Beyond the prices of the individual parts, the most economical service is the one that reduces the total cost by allowing more types of food to be served with fewer parts. Hygienic concerns are paramount in public establishments: a dirty plate might cause a patron to never return and tell their friends to avoid the place.

With Hvidpot, the same curved rim on the plates and platters that provides secure handling also simplifies washing, due to the absence of any raised edge that might trap food residue. Considering the primary market, Meyer designed her new service with automatic dishwashers in mind and devoted special attention to the rinsing and drainage cycles.

Ultimately, Meyer's careful planning realized Royal Copenhagen's goal of an economical service. In the 1970s, most parts of Hvidpot were comparable in price to the same parts of Blåkant, and occasionally less expensive, despite the more costly raw materials and firing technique.[22] As with Blåkant, Meyer struggled with the factory's board of directors over the question of decoration for the retail market. Once again, she preferred an undecorated service, while they (once again) insisted on some motif that would keep the decorative painters busy. After negotiations with Director Erik Lindgren that Meyer compared to a sailing on a stormy sea, they agreed on two options for retail customers that would be available by special order.[23] The first option was a painted circle that recalled Blåkant but in several different colors; the second was an abstract version of Royal Copenhagen's historic logo, three wave-like blue lines that symbolize the Danish straits. As neither option proved popular, both were discontinued in 1981.

Butter plate 6321 can be used as a lid for the serving bowl 6224. → Bowl 6281 provided the basis for the bouillon cup 6234, teacup 6232 and coffee cup 6231. The two sets of stacking bowls are based on the same form as the cups. The lid on the covered serving dishes 6300 and 6245 also fits two of the stacking bowls 6260 and 6225.

Hvidpot includes two covered serving dishes that are high and low versions of the same vessel and display Grethe Meyer's devotion to practical details. On Blåkant, she designed the covered dishes with a projecting collar in place of attached handles, which was based on Kaj Franck's Kilta casserole. The corresponding parts of Hvidpot have a flared rim that is also rooted in Kilta and provides an integral, nearly unbreakable handle. Moreover, the two dishes have the same diameter, so that the lid with a solid knob (which will not trap water or residue in the dishwasher) can be used on both of them. The flat form of the knob allows the lid to placed upside down on the tabletop, where it will not wobble or drip condensate, while the low height allows dishes to be stacked with the lids in place. The same lid can be used on two of the large bowls that provide further examples of Meyer's drive for a reduced number of parts.

Hvidpot bowls are so plain that Meyer's work is only evident in the surprisingly large capacities. As with Blåkant, she used overlapping spheres to provide a large volume in a compact shell but employed more generous curves that make it easier to wash the bowls.

In contrast to Blåkant, which includes nine variations on the same bowl, Hvidpot provides two sets of four bowls with different heights and sizes that suit a wider range of uses. The set of four large bowls includes pairs of low and high vessels with coordinated diameters that allow both types to be stacked. Four smaller bowls with unique diameters have countless uses, and the three smallest bowls can be stacked in the fourth, which is the same size as the large teacup.

As Meyer transformed the four small bowls into cups for coffee and other hot drinks, her customary concern for a comfortable grip reappeared in the handles. Exploiting porcelain's capacity for thin edges and precise details, she created an ear-shaped loop that makes it easy to lift and control a cup filled with hot liquid. While the large opening tapers to accommodate the forefinger, the flat top provides a resting place for the thumb. For all of her attention to the hand, Meyer was also attuned to mechanical functions: the cups and saucers are supported on a low foot that promotes complete drainage in the dishwasher.

Hvidpot includes a set of jugs that are easily stacked, with or without lids, and useful for every sort of liquid. Most of them have a short spout that is integrated into the body, to reduce the likelihood of chipping, but the jugs for coffee and tea have longer spouts that provide more control when pouring. The high strength of porcelain allows a thinner edge than faience or stoneware, which is better at cutting the flow of liquid and preventing drips but also more vulnerable to damage. Meyer's novel solution was a robust spout with a Teflon-insert that prevents drips through surface tension with the liquid. However ingenious, the drip-free spout is completely dependent on a loose piece that is easily lost. Moreover, the jugs are rather heavy, even when empty, such that we can recognize them as the weakest parts of Hvidpot. Better options include Arne Jacobsen's stainless steel jugs for coffee and tea (p. 81).

Meyer completed Hvidpot with seven jars of varied sizes that can be used for serving sugar and other condiments, but are so versatile they could easily be an independent series Each of the jars can be covered with a flat lid that also fits one of the cups, bowls or small jugs; a slight curvature on top of each lid prevents stacked jars from sliding sideways. Meyer was clearly inspired by the jars that Kaj Franck designed to complement his Kilta series.

While Franck's jars have one diameter and three heights, Meyer designed jars with a variety of diameters and integrated them into a larger system of parts. By coordinating those diameters with other containers and creating interchangeable lids, she extended the utility of Hvidpot from table to kitchen and into the refrigerator. In doing so, Meyer created a porcelain service that exceeds the limits of a traditional model and encompasses the entire cycle of preparing, serving and storing food.

Meyer's concern for economy makes it possible to enjoy the benefits of Hvidpot with only a handful of parts, some of which are still in production. Discontinued and vintage items can be found online and in second-hand shops. Among the five flat plates, the 24-cm model (6295) is an ideal size for breakfast, lunch and dinner and can be paired with one of the two deep plates (6290/6291) to serve nearly every type of food. Beyond those two basics, a small plate (6292 or 6293) for starters, sides and desserts, the 14-cm bowl for individual portions (6224) and one of the oval platters (6205 or 6206) will create a harmonious arrangement that emphasizes the food. The 20-cl cup for coffee and tea (6232) is still in production and can be stacked with the saucer as an intermediate layer. Among the second-hand parts, the small jugs, covered serving dishes and large bowls are all especially useful. Unfortunately, the jars and lids are rare.

Jars on teak tray from Ildpot. Left to right: 6240, 6241, 6256, 6285. ← Cream pitcher 6250 with stacked coffee pots 6220 and 6221. / Sauce pitcher 6265 with stacked creamers 6211, mustard jar 6270 and coffee pot 6305. / Assortment of jars. Left to right: 6286, 6275 (3), 6240 (2), 6285. Jar 6240 is sized for salt and spices but also serves as an eggcup.

Grethe Meyer believed that the traditional model of a table service — a set of decorative pieces united by a common motif that would be collected over a lifetime, but used only on special occasions — was an obstacle to enjoying everyday meals. Her intention was not to "smash the services", as Kaj Franck had proposed in 1949, but to promote a relaxed and convivial approach to setting the table.[24] To that end, she suggested combining parts of Hvidpot with parts of other services. As she explained,

"Like other items for daily use, a table service should be designed so that you like it more and more — it should grow on you. So Hvidpot is neither way-out nor trendy, but neutral and based on a tradition which has been carefully developed to meet the needs of today. It can be used as a complete set, but individual items may well be used on their own without looking like parts of a set, or they may be combined with other items for the table or serve as bowls and vases."[25] Meyer's reference to "other items for the table" certainly included family heirlooms, parts of traditional services and unique pieces of handicraft, but the most natural supplement to Hvidpot is actually Blåkant. Despite their differences in color and form, both services embody Meyer's respect for the people who would use her things and for the food they would serve. Moreover, the two services are complementary because each provides what the other lacks.

Blåkant was designed for household use and includes an array of specialized parts that can accommodate a universe of habits and menus: two butter dishes, fourteen different bowls, serving dishes of every shape, size and volume and so forth. While Royal Copenhagen hoped that Hvidpot would appeal to home cooks, Meyer designed the service for restaurants, where food is typically served in individual portions using a minimum number of items. The parts of the service are standardized to simplify serving and storage, and serving leftover food is taboo. As a result, a commercial service only requires two sizes of platters; butter dishes that can be stored in the refrigerator are unnecessary, because a server brings each guest their own portion.

While Hvidpot provides items for daily use that can withstand the dishwasher, Blåkant provides special parts that receive less frequent use, many of which are better washed by hand — including the square and rectangular serving dishes that can be tightly packed to conserve table space, the raised platform that ennobles every kind of cake, pie or tart, and the enchanting set of nine stacking bowls that provides a vessel for any occasion. Together, Hvidpot and Blåkant provide the tools for a nearly infinite variety of table arrangements, even as their neutral character provides a framework for other items. The result is a culinary kit-of-parts that transcends the limits of any single service and applies Meyer's special talent for useful elegance to nearly every type of tableware. Fortunately, most parts of both services are widely available.

Selected parts of Blåkant. Nine stacking bowls, diameters 7–30.5 cm. → Layer cake platter 3075, diameter 28.5 cm. / Low serving dishes 3078 and 3096. / Bowl 3084, diameter 43 cm.

During 1965–2010, Royal Copenhagen produced Blåkant at the Aluminia faience factory in Frederiksberg, a municipality within Copenhagen. Over time, the blue-gray color became slightly darker due to adjustments in the clay mixture, which ensured greater consistency during the firing process. During the 1980s and '90s, Royal Copenhagen produced several variations on the service in a variety of color schemes; none equaled the success of the original.[26] As a result of Blåkant's longevity, a vast number of parts are available in Denmark through open-air markets, second-hand shops and online merchants. During 2019–24, the Bodum kitchenware company produced ten parts of Blåkant in porcelain, matching the original color, form and decoration, under the name **Blue**. The limited number of parts made it difficult to create complete table settings, and production was discontinued due to low sales.

Over the decades, Hvidpot has been produced at five different factories, in varied levels of quality. The initial production occurred at the Royal Copenhagen porcelain factory in Frederiksberg, during 1971–87. During the mid 1970s, the company subcontracted production to Vista Alegre, a Portuguese factory, but the quality of those parts (stamped VA) was relatively poor, and the effort was abandoned within two years, with production returning to Frederiksberg.[27] Following the 1987 merger between Royal Copenhagen and its primary competitor Bing & Grøndahl, Hvidpot was produced at the B&G factory in the Valby district of Copenhagen, until the service was discontinued in 1990.

In 2001, Royal Copenhagen revived Hvidpot in a reduced service of twenty-three parts that was produced in Portugal, by Bonvida Porcelana, and labeled with the three-digit system that Royal Copenhagen had instituted in 1990. While those items are certainly useful, the manufacturer struggled to provide eliminate iron spots and to match the precise forms of Meyer's original design.[28] Consequently, it can be difficult to stack plates from 1971–90 (excluding the abysmal Vista Alegre production) with plates from the early 2000s. The Bonvida production was discontinued in 2009, primarily due to misguided marketing and correspondingly low sales.

In 2014, under the supervision of Grethe Meyer Design, which administers Meyer's estate, the retail giant Coop Danmark (formerly FDB) revived Hvidpot with a number of the basic parts. Those parts that are once again manufactured in Portugal, now by Porcelanas da Costa Verde, and sold for surprisingly low prices online and in supermarkets. Despite the low cost, the level of quality is comparable to the Frederiksberg/Valby production of the 1970s and '80s.[29] Moreover, the parts are sufficiently faithful to Meyer's drawings that new and vintage plates can be stacked together. Due to advances in filtering the raw materials, the Costa Verde porcelain is a shade brighter than the original production.

One of the extraordinary aspects of Grethe Meyer's work with ceramics was her ability to balance multiple and apparently contradictory priorities, including utility and cost. Her goal was not the lowest purchase price, but instead the best solution that would be generally affordable and provide the true economy that results from decades of use.

In 1973, on the occasion of Meyer receiving the Nordic Crafts and Design prize, the Danish Society of Applied Art and Industrial Design presented a retrospective of her designs that included Blåkant and Hvidpot.[30] In his review of the exhibition, design critic Axel Thygesen described the character of Grethe Meyer's work in terms that have only become more relevant with the passage of a half-century:

"Grethe Meyer has created things that will stand forth as external examples. It is conceivable that fashion may knock them temporarily out of production now and then […] but they will always emerge as sources of inspiration. Like our old trusted, well-tried implements and tools, they display severe logic and a deep understanding of humanity; they are willing workers, warm and friendly without being impertinent and ingratiating. In the true sense, they represent culture. They should have ecological awards showered on them; they should be held forward as shining examples for design schools the world over. If we concentrated more on working in the spirit of Grethe Meyer, we would avoid much of the material waste and pollution that plague us. And our lives would be happier, richer."[31]

Three years later, in 1976, Meyer completed a system of ceramic cookware that was based on the same union of logic and humanism that produced Blåkant and Hvidpot, and constituted her final masterwork in ceramics, as detailed in the following chapter.

Together, Blåkant and Hvidpot provide a comprehensive range of tableware that can be combined to serve any type of food or occasion. The subtle difference in the color of the wares and the appearance of Grethe Meyer's blue line provide variety, even as the items are united by her thoughtful and intensely practical approach to their forms.

Hvidpot. Porcelain table service, 1966–71.

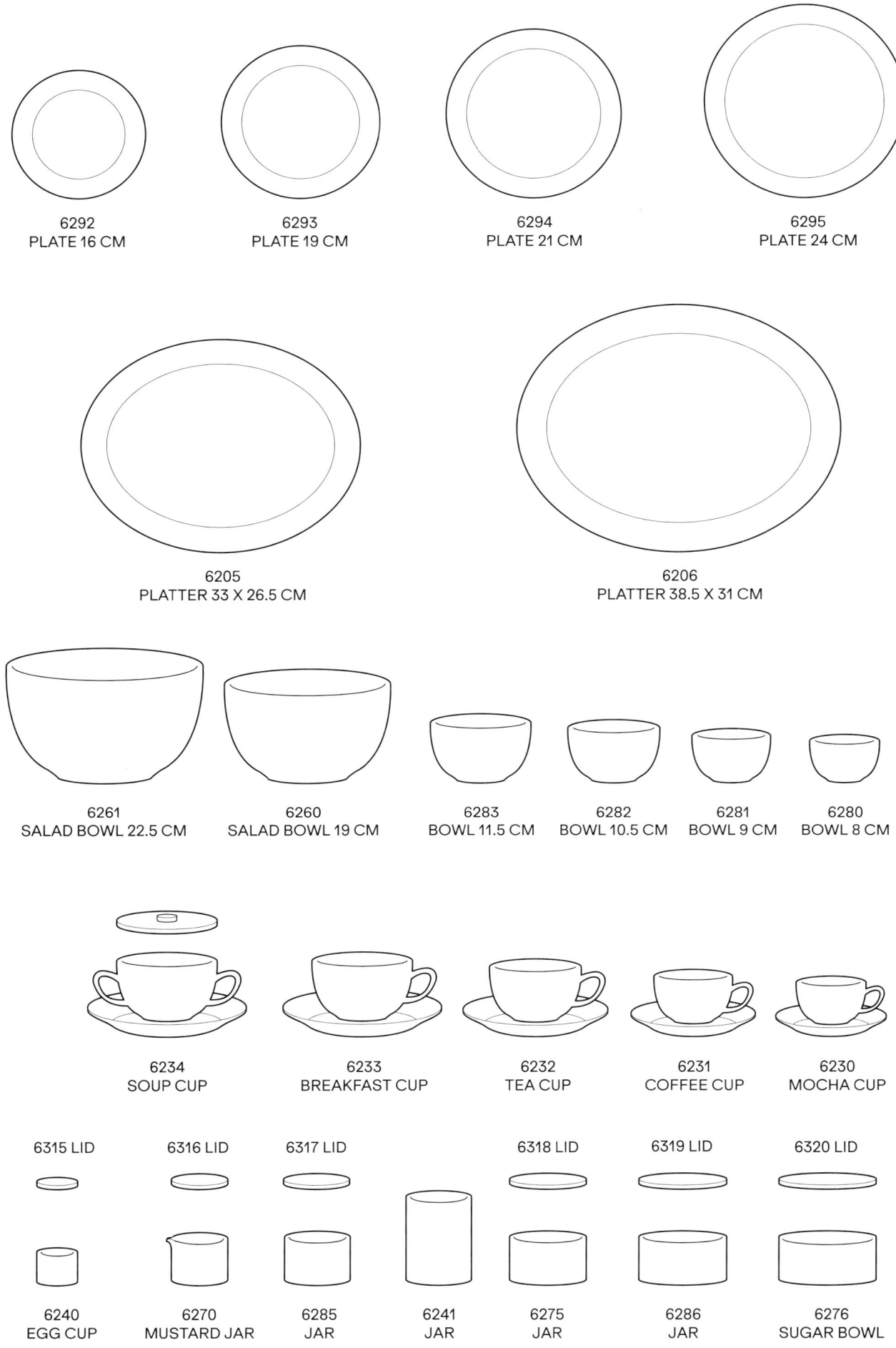

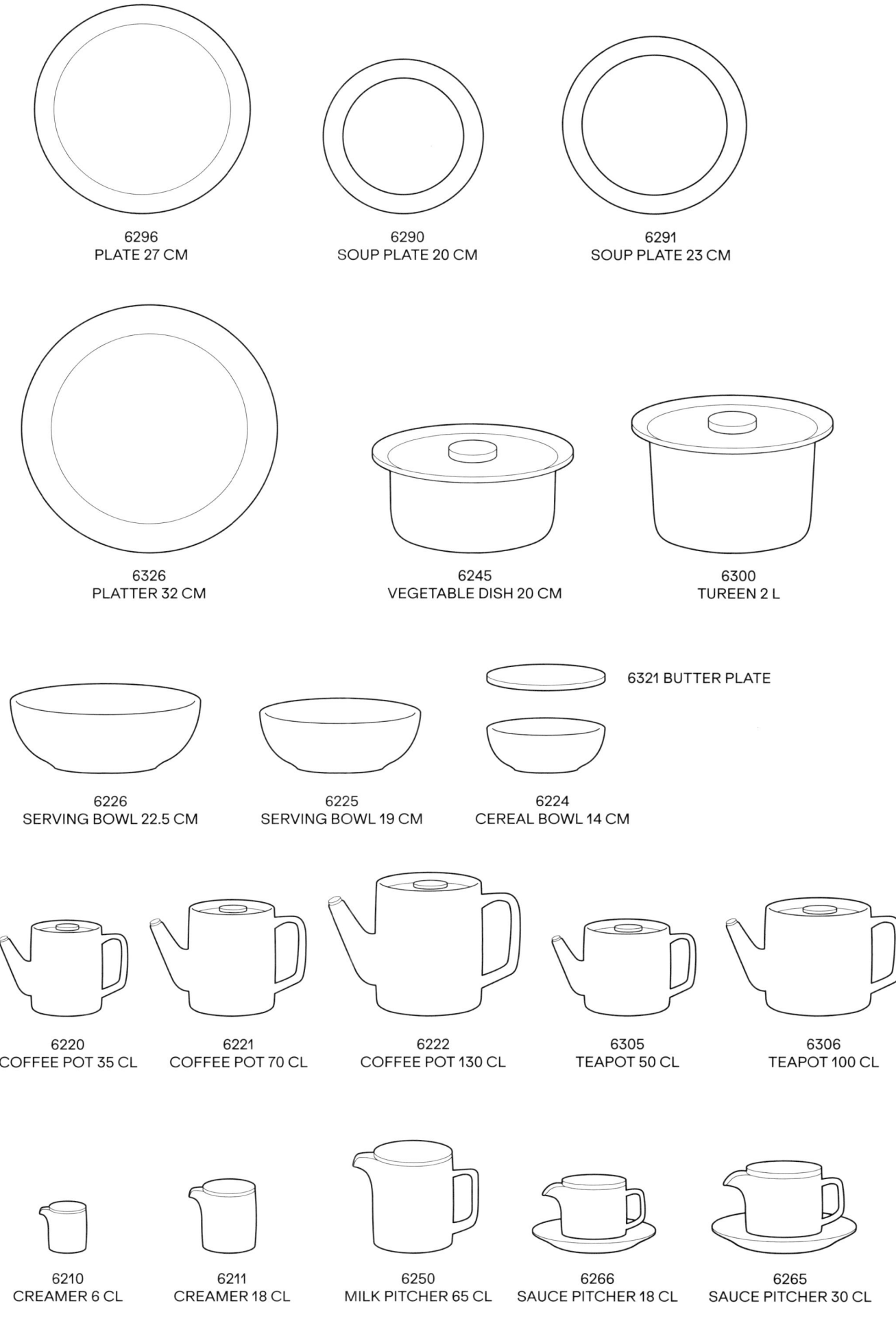

Working with a new type of clay, Grethe Meyer applied her mastery of ceramics to the design of cookware, creating versatile pots and dishes that are suitable for almost any type of cooking and become more beautiful with use. Her crowning achievement for the Royal Copenhagen Porcelain Factory was rooted in an increasing number of requests from consumers for dishes that could go directly from freezer to oven at the end of a long day.[1] In 1970, Meyer surveyed the most popular cooking appliances in Denmark, Sweden and Germany, searching for the typical sizes of burners and ovens. Her underlying goal was cookware that could be used with gas and electric appliances in all three countries. After completing Hvidpot (p. 92), she spent five years designing the series of stoneware vessels that she named **Ildpot** (Firepot), which was introduced with a special exhibition at the Royal Copenhagen flagship store, in March 1976.

We can trace the origin of Ildpot to a decades-long effort in the Nordic region to erase the distinction between dishes for preparing and serving food, which was rooted in ancient custom.[2] Before the advent of enclosed cooking fires and packaged ingredients, cooking was generally hard, grubby work that involved breaking down raw foodstuffs and preparing them in vessels valued more for durability than appearance. In wealthy households, servants would transfer prepared food to serving dishes that were placed on the table, distancing cooking from consumption and servers from masters. That practice also allowed royals and the upper echelons of society to display their status and taste through the use of elaborately decorated tableware, often made of precious metals or porcelain.
In doing so, they established habits that were adopted by people of lesser means and proved to be remarkably persistent.

Around 1900, social reformers and home economists in Sweden began to campaign for well-designed objects that would benefit ordinary households. The leading voices included educator and writer Ellen Key, who promoted the idea of "beauty in the home", and her follower Gregor Paulsson, who advocated the production of "better things for everyday life" that would appeal to families with limited incomes.[3] One result of their efforts was the **Pyro** line of cookware, which was designed by Wilhelm Kåge for the ceramic factory Gustavsbergs Porslinsfabrik and introduced at the 1930 *Stockholm Exhibition*.[4] Hoping to eliminate separate serving dishes, Kåge created ovenproof vessels with a painted flower motif that would appeal to popular taste. To encourage the use of Pyro on the table, Kåge designed a matching service in faience that eventually grew to more than 200 parts. The rapid success of Pyro allowed Kåge to develop the **Praktika** service, which provided the basic model for all of Grethe Meyer's ceramic systems (p. 95).

Grethe Meyer. Study for vessel sizes within an average-sized oven, 1970–73. Meyer began her work by studying oven sizes and dimensioned the parts of Ildpot so that several dishes could be prepared at the same time.
→ Grethe Meyer. Ildpot, 1970–76. Stoneware. Large roasting pan 22524 with loose cooking ribs. 1:1 scale.

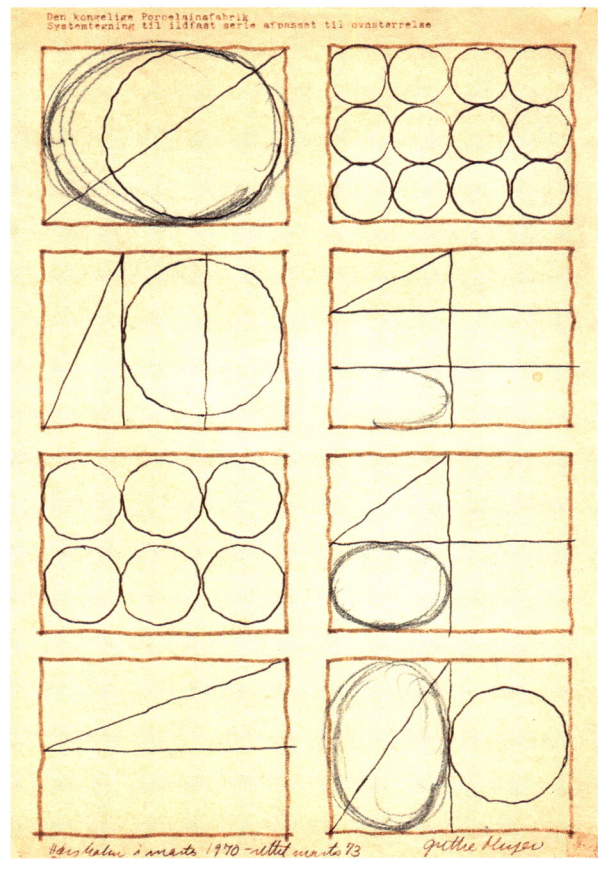

GRETHE MEYER 1970–76
Ildpot

In 1955, the Swedish Society of Crafts and Design arranged a housing exhibition in Helsingborg that was generally known as *H 55* and celebrated a quarter of a century of progress since the *Stockholm Exhibition*.[5] As in 1930, Gustavsbergs used the exhibition to introduce a variety of new product lines, now designed by Kåge's successor as artistic director, Stig Lindberg. The main attraction was **Terma**, a line of flameproof pots and pans suitable for both stovetop and oven, molded from a new type of clay that Gustavsbergs had developed for rocket engines.[6] The factory also introduced **Spisa**, an undecorated table service that was produced in a variety of colored glazes. For the sake of economy, the parts were fabricated of stoneware, bone porcelain or faience, according to their purpose.[7] Regardless of the material, all of the parts had an angled rim inspired by Kaj Franck's **Kilta** series (p. 94). By coordinating the diameters of the plates and round serving dishes, Lindberg was able to use plates as lids and reduce the cost of the service.

The solid-colored versions of Spisa introduced at *H 55* were only produced for five years, due to consumers' discomfort with the absence of decoration. Moreover, the use of plates as lids on the serving dishes was considered bizarre. But **Spisa Ribb**, the decorated version of the pattern, which soon included conventional lids with knobs, became immensely popular and would remain in production until 1974. Meanwhile, Lindberg's model of plate-lids, which can be traced back to Wilhelm Kåge's Praktika service, would endure as a defining feature of Ildpot.

In the aftermath of *H 55*, the major Danish tableware producers introduced new lines of ovenproof cookware, in porcelain, "flint porcelain" and stoneware.[8] All three materials are fired at much higher temperatures than those used for cooking, but each has its limitations. Faience is porous, which makes it susceptible to cracking, and even the addition of pulverized flint (to make "flint porcelain") does not extend the safe temperature beyond 150° C (375° F). Stoneware should not be placed under a broiler for browning foods at 288° C (550° F) or exposed to a direct heat source. Some types of porcelain can withstand temperatures up to 300° C (572° F), but it is generally a poor conductor of heat and less than ideal for baking dishes. Finally, all three materials are vulnerable to cracking from thermal shock. As a result, none of them can safely be placed in a hot oven, let alone survive a direct transfer from the freezer, as the temperature rises from -20° to 200° C (-4 to 392° F) in a matter of minutes.

Stig Lindberg. Terma refractory wares (top) and Spisa Ribb (bottom), 1955. Gustavsbergs Porslinsfabrik. / Original version of Spisa tableware with ovenproof serving dishes at top. → Grethe Meyer. Ildpot cocotte with teak tray. Meyer valued unglazed stoneware for its warm color and subtle character.

In 1969, as Royal Copenhagen's customers clamored for cookware made of some miracle material, the company hired civil engineer Ebba (Grue) Jespersen to develop a new type of stoneware that would be impervious to thermal shock.[9] In contrast to porcelain, which is based on highly refined kaolin clay, stoneware is based on common "ball clay" and fired at a lower temperature, typically 1,300° C (2,372° F). During the firing process, the quartz particles in the ceramic mixture are melted to form a glass-like (vitreous) mass with a non-porous surface that does not require glazing. By experimenting with various blends of ball clay, aluminum oxide (which allows an unusually high firing temperature) and talcum (which promotes the fusion of ingredients), Jespersen finally arrived at a stoneware mix that could be fired at 1,450° C (2,642° F) — the same firing temperature as porcelain. After firing, her improved version of stoneware had a thermal expansion rate near zero, allowing it to withstand extreme and rapid changes in temperature.

As a matter of fact, stoneware is almost ideal for most types of cooking and unparalleled for oven use.[10] Firstly, the non-porous surface does not absorb flavors or affect the taste of food, as is the case with unglazed faience (also known as earthenware). Furthermore, the density of stoneware causes it to slowly absorb heat and then radiate it into the food, eliminating hot spots and providing even cooking temperatures. Among its other virtues, stoneware is perfect for most types of baking, because it provides a crisp crust while preserving a moist filling. The utility of stoneware is increased by omitting the customary glazing that makes it possible to maintain a pristine appearance, but also reflects heat and lowers the cooking temperature by a few degrees.[11] Beyond these typical properties, Royal Copenhagen's engineered stoneware could go directly from freezer to hot oven, be placed under the broiler and used with gas and electric burners as well as the new microwave ovens that were becoming increasingly popular. Indeed, Ildpot can be used with any heat source except open fires and induction cooktops.

Stoneware was a new material for Grethe Meyer, but she was no longer a ceramic novice struggling to understand the difference between porcelain and faience. In contrast to porcelain, which allows for thin edges and tight curves, stoneware requires rounded edges and gentle curves that will prevent cracks during drying and firing, as the ceramic body shrinks.[12] To that end, Meyer employed relaxed forms that eliminated sharp corners and ensured gradual transitions between surfaces at right angles. Working with a compass and triangles, she simplified the details to a handful of radii that would allow interchangeable parts and ensure consistency at the factory, at least in terms of form. During the firing process, minute variations in the batches of raw materials and atmosphere of the kiln produced minor variations in color, which imbued Meyer's industrial ceramics with a slightly rustic character.

Comparison of plates from Hvidpot (top) and Ildpot (bottom). 1:1 scale. → Ildpot pots 22508 and 22509 with plate-lid 22515. Meyer's designs for cookware display the same concern for handling found in her tableware.

Ten years of intense work with faience and porcelain had endowed Meyer with a set of principles that could also be applied to stoneware. As with Blåkant (Blue Line) and Hvidpot, Meyer based her design on a profiled rim that provides a comfortable grip, which is a matter of safety when pulling hot dishes from the oven. The essential detail on Ildpot is the flared rim that is easily grasped between thumb and forefinger, and provides an integral handle for all of the parts. On each part, the width of the rim is proportional to the size, so that the largest and heaviest parts allow the most secure grip.

Drawing inspiration from Spisa, Meyer created lids that can be used as plates for cooking and serving, and provide intermediate layers for stacking. Similarly to Hvidpot, most of the plate-lids can be used on several vessels, reducing the cost to the consumer and preserving space in the cabinet. On the rim of each vessel, a narrow groove provides a resting place for the foot of the plate-lid and prevents it from sliding off. When covered dishes are removed from the oven, the combination of rim and lid increases the thickness of the integrated handle and provides more surface area for the thumbs.

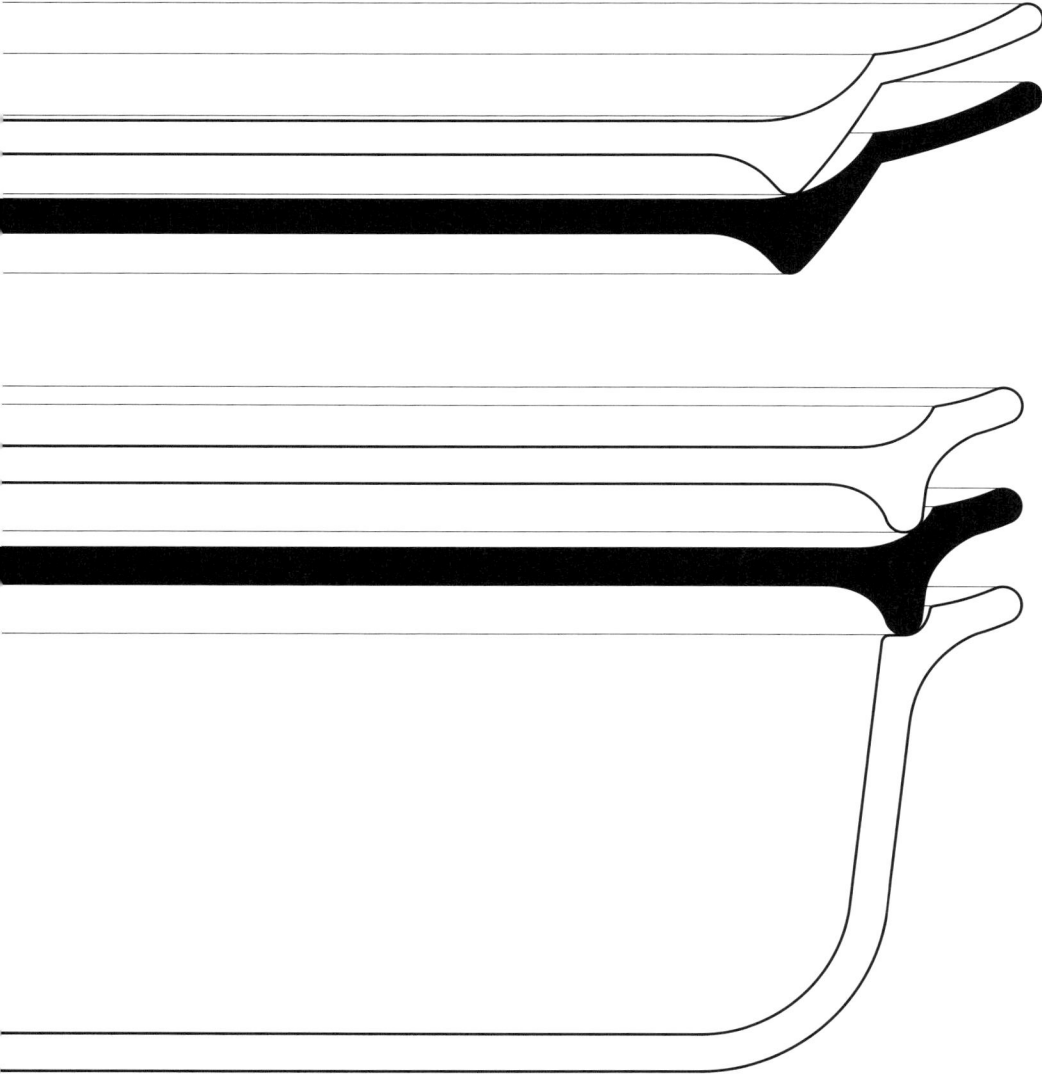

From the outset, Grethe Meyer imagined a system of cookware that could be used for almost any type of food. To make that possible, she created three types of vessels: round pots, rectangular dishes and narrow forms with rounded ends. As with her tableware, Meyer standardized the dimensions as much as possible, using common diameters and rectangles that could be molded at different heights to provide smaller or larger vessels. She referred to the smallest pots as *cocottes*, using the French term for a baking dish that provides an individual serving; classic preparations include baked eggs, and onion soup with a cheese gratin. Meyer designed her cocottes for a variety of recipes and courses, with two smaller vessels that are especially well suited for desserts, and a slightly larger model that is excellent for stews and single portions of main dishes.

The most versatile parts of Ildpot are the round pots with capacities of 1–3.5 liters, which are equally useful on the stovetop and in the oven. As such, they are ideal for cooking that begins with braising or sautéing on the stovetop and continues with baking or broiling in the oven. The only type of cooking with Ildpot that should be avoided is deep-frying. Meyer supplemented her pots with a low dish dimensioned for quiches, tarts and pies. As stoneware retains and then radiates heat, the dish will not scorch the crust if the dough is partly baked, filled and returned to the oven.

Pot 22509. With regular use, the unglazed stoneware acquires a patina that personalizes each vessel or baking dish. → Vessels with lids: Pots 22508 and 22510. Low cocotte 22512. / Baking dishes. Roasting dish 22524. Baking dish 22530 and plate-lid 22522. Tart dish 22599. Oblong dish 22532.

Abandoning the traditional oval form, which is rooted in handicraft, Meyer designed rectangular dishes that allow for close packing in the oven. Aside from the largest dish, which was dimensioned for a large leg of lamb, the rectangular dishes can be covered with one of the plate-lids. The narrow forms are especially useful for baking bread, cakes and pâtés, due to the rounded ends that ease removal, but equally well suited for preparing fish, because the proportions concentrate the cooking liquid. Regardless of shape, the gentle curves that prevent cracks during firing also promote convection in the cooking liquid. As with the cocottes and round pots, all of the dishes can be placed directly under the broiler for browning and finishing.

Through regular use, Meyer's unglazed stoneware develops a patina, as airborne fats within the oven are deposited on the surface. The change in color can be accelerated by rubbing the vessels with a small amount of oil before using them. As the stoneware darkens, the slightly rough exterior becomes increasingly smooth and the interior develops an organic, non-stick surface, as on a seasoned iron skillet. The mutable character of the cookware reflects Meyer's belief that household goods should become more familiar with use (p. 110). Just as Hvidpot "grows" on the user, Ildpot parts become increasingly specific to the owners. As the traces of cooking habits accumulate on the surface, the varied shades of the pots and dishes provide a visual record of the cook's favorite foods.

Drawing on her own experiences in the kitchen, which included testing all the parts of Ildpot at home, Meyer created accessories that are as thoughtfully designed as the vessels. Mindful that many types of food, such as fish and vegetables, benefit from not being submerged in cooking liquid, she designed stoneware ribs that can be placed in the bottom of the pots and dishes. While the triangular ribs are easily arranged with fingertips, the two lengths allow for varied arrangements in all of the vessels, except the cocottes. For cooking that requires food to be raised more than 2 cm from the bottom of the vessel, the ribs can be stacked at right angles in two or three layers. Rather than an afterthought, Meyer's ribs are an integral feature of Ildpot and equally useful with other types of cookware.

Meyer completed Ildpot with a series of teak trays that protect the tabletop from heat and also prevent scratching. Introduced in 1977, the round and rectangular trays follow the standardized dimensions of the pots and dishes; most of them can be used with two or three different vessels. The larger trays can accommodate a number of cocottes and pots, and each of them has myriad uses in the kitchen. With her customary concern for handling, Meyer designed three types of rims that become wider and thicker as the size of the tray increases, to ensure a secure grip. She believed the trays would grow more beautiful as the teak aged to a warm gray tone and suggested they be left untreated, but an occasional dab of oil will prevent cracks and stains.[13]

Production techniques for Ildpot varied according to the shape of the vessels. While the cocottes and pots were turned on the same automated wheels used for Hvidpot, the rectangular and oblong dishes were formed by slip-casting. In that laborious process, liquid clay (slip) was poured into a plaster mold that absorbed water and formed a layer of the necessary thickness, which would eventually dry and be placed in the kiln. On taller vessels, particles in the liquid clay would sometimes settle during the drying process, producing horizontal lines that reinforce the rustic character of the wares.[14] Due to the time and labor required, the slip-cast parts of Ildpot were relatively expensive in comparison with the pots, which resulted in lower sales. By 1986, as production of Ildpot drew to an end, only two rectangular dishes and a single oblong dish were still in production. While vintage pots are plentiful, the rectangular dishes and the narrow forms are difficult to find, and the lids for those parts are rare.

Roasting dish 22527 with teak tray. In 1977, Meyer designed a series of teak trays that can be placed on the table and used instead of a trivet. ← The cooking ribs could be placed in the bottom of a vessel to raise food above the cooking liquid. The two lengths of 12 (22588) and 20 cm (22589) allow them to be combined in every part of Ildpot except the cocottes. Due to their triangular form, the ribs could be used with any orientation, while the curved sides made them easy to grasp with fingertips.

An assortment of vessels and trays displays Grethe Meyer's devotion to natural materials that were treated as simply as possible. Her stoneware vessels have a slightly rustic character that recalls traditional wares and blurs the distinction between industrial design and handicraft. And yet, the precise forms and close fit of the plate-lids would not have been possible without the use of machinery. While the vintage items display a range of shades, the recent production of Ildpot (foreground right) employs a refined version of the original stoneware mix and has a consistent color.

Introduced in 1976, Ildpot was an immediate commercial success, but sales slowed during the 1980s, as consumers experimented with new types of cooking equipment.[15] Following the merger with Bing & Grøndahl A/S, in 1987, the porcelain kiln at Royal Copenhagen was modified to increase production of the annual Christmas plates that provided both companies with a steady income. That modification also made it impossible to produce Ildpot, which was discontinued by the end of the year.[16] In 2019, following the successful 2014 revival of Hvidpot, Coop Danmark relaunched Ildpot through its subsidiary FDB Møbler. Working with Grethe Meyer Design and a retired engineer from Royal Copenhagen, FDB Møbler located a German factory capable of producing Ildpot in the original material. While refinements to the recipe and ingredients ensure a uniform shade of brown, the rectangular parts are cast in pressurized molds that provide unblemished surfaces.[17] Meyer would almost certainly be pleased with the consistent appearance of the new parts, especially as they still develop a patina with use.

Ildpot was the final stage in the series of ceramic designs that Grethe Meyer began in 1959, as she developed a competition project for porcelain with Ibi Trier Mørch (p. 92). Having traced the root of that project, we can recognize Ildpot as the final stage in a sequence of Nordic tableware that began with Wilhelm Kåge's Praktika service, continued with Kaj Franck's Kilta and Stig Lindberg's Spisa, and included Meyer's Blåkant and Hvidpot. It is unlikely that any manufacturer today would support a five-year-long process of design and development for a ceramic service, as Royal Copenhagen did — three times over — during 1960–76. As a result of that support, Meyer was able to pursue her ideal "compromise between practical demands, possibilities of production and aesthetic design" in a variety of materials.[18] Basing her designs on the natural color and character of faience, porcelain and stoneware, she created three sets of ceramic tools that remain unsurpassed in their union of comfort, utility and grace.

During the late 1970s, Grethe Meyer expanded her range of materials and subjects to include a series of table linens and prototypes for cast-iron cookware. In the 1980s and '90s, Meyer worked with Royal Copenhagen on several variations of Blåkant and created a string of new designs in glass, metal and porcelain, but few progressed beyond prototypes or a very limited production. In 1991, she found renewed success with **Copenhagen**, a graceful set of stainless steel flatware for Georg Jensen A/S that remains in production. Following her eightieth birthday, in 1998, Meyer retired to the small courtyard house at Ved Stampedammen in North Zealand that she had purchased in 1963, when the salvation of the Blåkant service for Royal Copenhagen assured her a future income. She spent her final decade at home surrounded by the treasures she had created over the course of her prolific career, including the pioneering storage system that she and Børge Mogensen designed during the 1950s: Boligens Byggeskabe, as described in a later chapter.

Bowl 22668. The smallest part of Ildpot is the miniature version of a cocotte that Meyer dimensioned for butter and salt. 6.5 cm. 1:1 scale. → Interior of Grethe Meyer's home in Hørsholm, 2002. Meyer stored her ceramic wares in customized examples of Boligens Byggeskabe, the system of shelving and cabinets that she designed with Børge Mogensen during 1952–57. Circa 2000, she and the industrial designer David Lewis, who happened to be a neighbor, developed a special shade of brown paint that would complement the warm colors of Ildpot and provide a rustic background for her designs in porcelain and faience.

Ildpot. Stoneware and teak trays, 1970–76/1977.

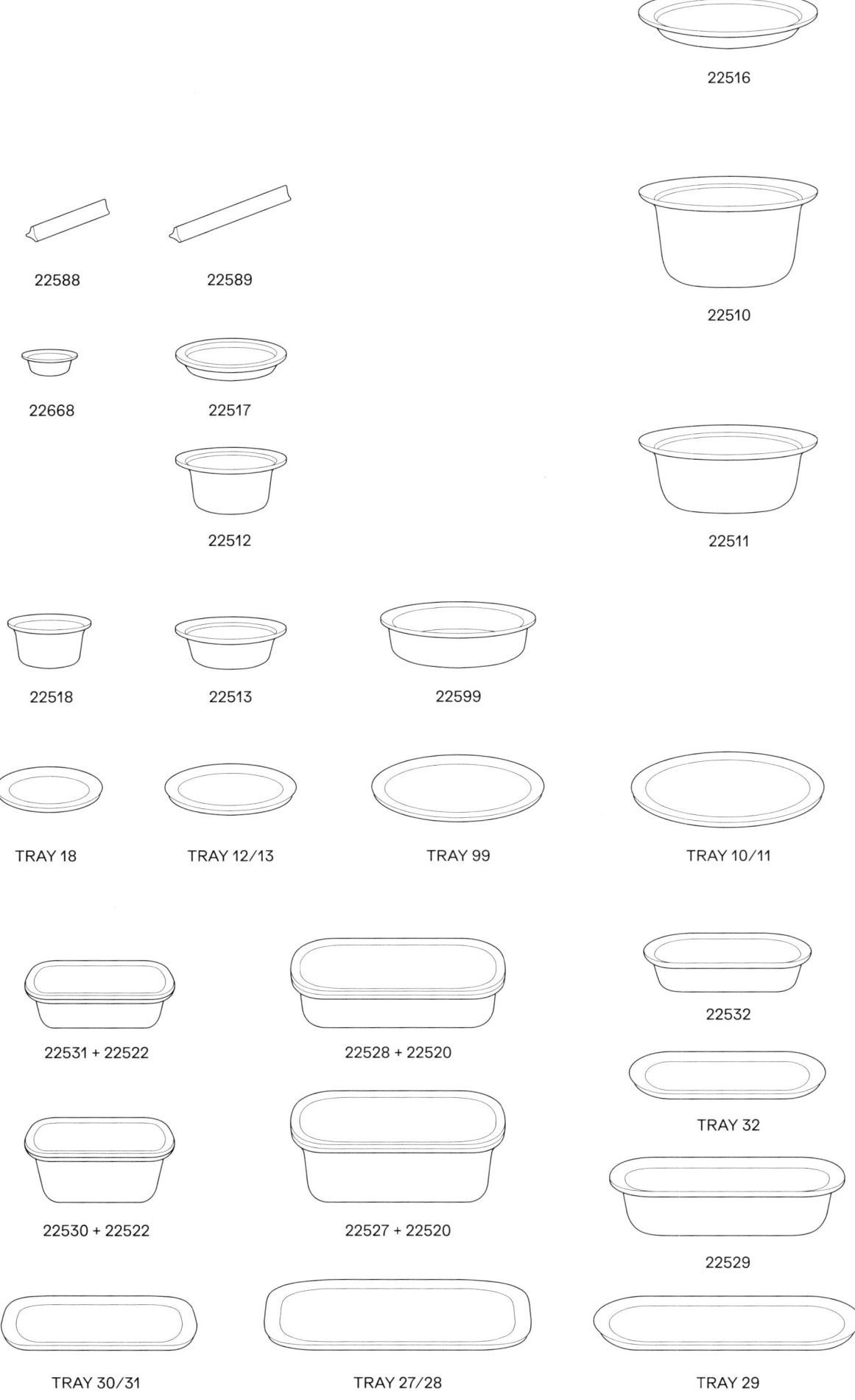

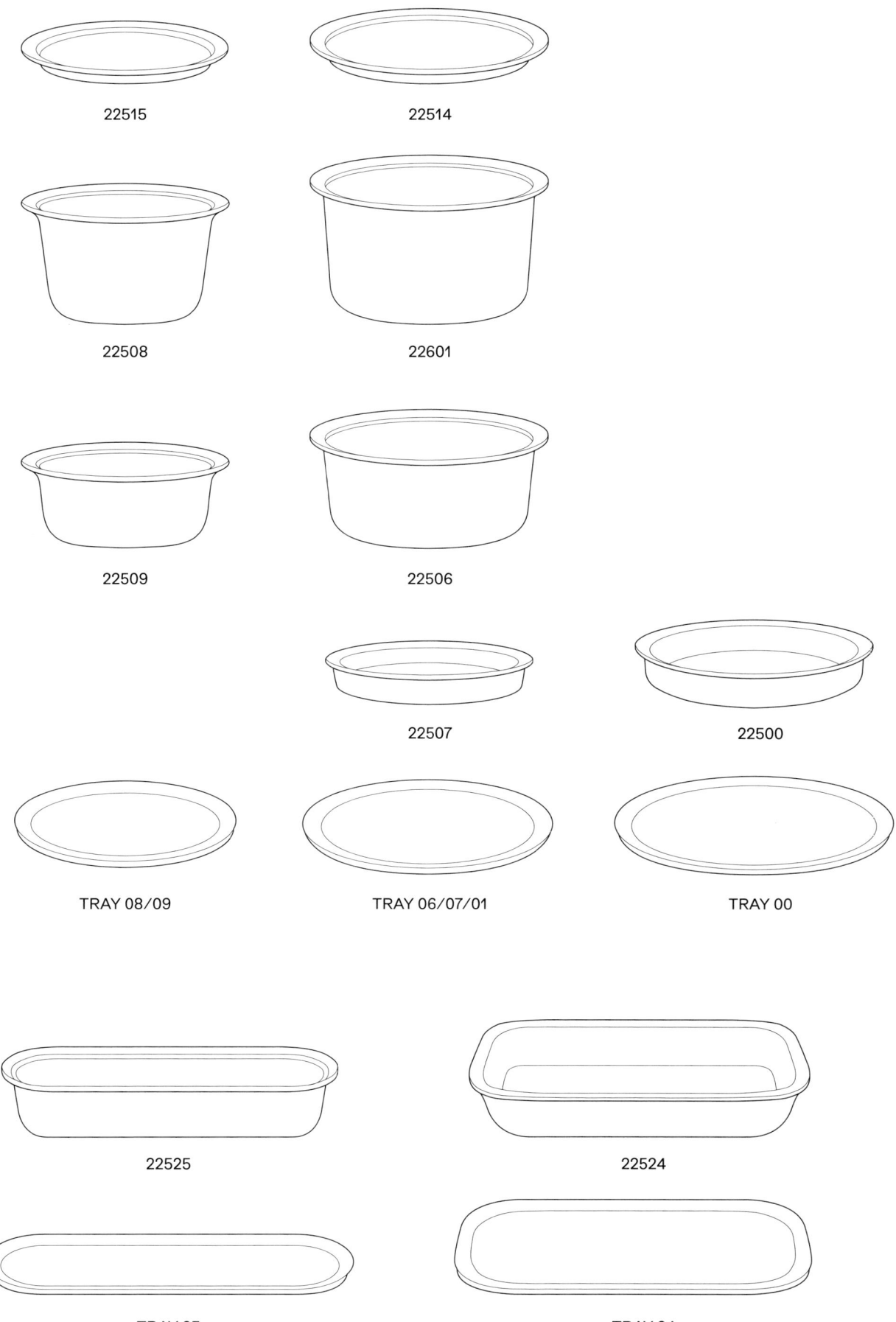

Among Danish designs for the home, few can rival Ole Palsby's groundbreaking system of cookware for widespread appeal and enduring impact. Examples of those rare specimens include Hanne Valeur's K-60 kitchen system and the laminated wood chairs designed by Arne Jacobsen, which are described in two other chapters. In Denmark, Palsby's pots and pans have been so much a part of daily life, in so many homes and for so many decades, that their origins have been forgotten and so too, the magnitude of his achievement. Revisiting the genesis of Palsby's cookware system reveals his fortitude in the face of commercial failure, his ethical regard for consumers and his persistent efforts to offer them excellent goods that would increase their pleasure in cooking and eating.

In the autumn of 1968, Ole Palsby began to emerge from the shadow of his father's financial crimes, which had bankrupted the son and caused him to lose his home, design showroom and credit rating (p. 72). Despite those losses, he still had close friends who believed in him. By pooling small sums of money from a number of them, including Torben Valeur, Henning Jensen and Keld Helmer-Petersen, Palsby was able to open a small shop devoted to imported cookware and tableware; what the French refer to as *materiel de cuisine*.[1] While he sourced most of his stock from the shops around Les Halles, the historic market district in the center of Paris, he found his business model in central London, at the cookery shop Elizabeth David Limited named after the eponymous English food writer.

Ole Palsby. Interchangeable lids for Eva Trio cookware, 1976–77. Stainless steel plate with 4 mm rod. Diameters 16, 20, 26 and 28 cm. 1:1 scale.

Beginning in the late 1940s, Elizabeth David established herself as the leading promoter of foreign food in Britain, with magazine columns and cookery books that extolled the virtues of traditional Mediterranean cuisine.[2] While much of her early work was greeted with incomprehension or disdain, her book *Italian Food* (1954) established her place in popular culture. An ardent proponent of simple food based on high-quality ingredients, David hoped to liberate people from a national diet that was heavy on canned foods and light on fresh vegetables. Following the publication of *French Provincial Cooking* (1960), she and a group of affluent friends established a shop in Pimlico offering cookware and accessories that met her exacting standards, including the French series of enameled cast iron, Le Creuset, and the British series of cast aluminum known as Gateware.[3]

On 1 October 1968, fewer than eight months after declaring bankruptcy, Palsby opened his kitchenware shop at Læderstræde 7, in the historic center of Copenhagen, between the pedestrian street known as Strøget and Gammel Strand. As with Palsby's design showroom on Hovedvagtsgade, the interior of the shop was designed by Nils Fagerholt, and Bo Bonfils created the graphic identity. Inspired by Elizabeth David's example, Palsby worked to renew food culture in his native land by importing cookware that had been previously unavailable in Denmark, along with cutlery and glassware. Similarly to David, Palsby offered a variety of French products that included Sabatier knives, copper saucepans and Le Creuset cast iron, as well as the aluminum Gateware that she championed.

Ole Palsby regarded his kitchenware shop as a commercial venture, but it was also a cultural project akin to the design showroom he had operated during 1965–68. Rather than install art exhibitions, he produced new types of cooking equipment and tableware that met his high standards of quality and utility. In 1971, he introduced a series of grills designed by Karsten Ravn and Lars Lundquist (p. 316). As Palsby later explained,

"What was characteristic of the enterprise [...] was that we didn't just find good professional cookware that already existed but couldn't be bought anywhere in Denmark. The business was, at least as much, a place where we developed up-to-date products, the ideas of which were probably known but had not been developed. This applies, for example, to our entire grill series, where the idea was since the garden grill was here to stay, it should not just be a cheap toy that was left to rust but a durable consumer product on a par with stoves and refrigerators. Of course, all good kitchenware is a durable consumer product, so for us it was really just continuing a tradition."[4]

OLE PALSBY 1976–77

Eva Trio

By the early 1970s, Palsby had established himself as Denmark's leading source of specialized cookware, advertising in popular magazines and printing seasonal catalogs designed by Bo Bonfils.[5] In July 1974, Palsby opened a second shop devoted to culinary culture, along Strøget.[6] But he would only occupy the space for a year. The success of Palsby's first shop had inspired a number of other businesses to create new kitchenware departments. Due to economies of scale, his larger competitors could offer many of the same products at lower prices. As importantly, sales of Ravn and Lundquist's grills were being undermined by a spate of inexpensive copies and near-copies.[7] Meanwhile, the global oil crisis of 1973–74 precipitated an economic downturn across Europe that would persist through the late 1970s.

In August 1975, Palsby's business collapsed, and he would declare bankruptcy in November. By the end of January 1976, he had liquidated most of the stock at Læderstræde 7. He remained in the shop through 7 February, attempting to sell the display fixtures and last unwanted items. That morning, George Kringelbach, the food writer at the newspaper Politiken, used his column to announce the demise of Palsby's shop in the afternoon. The article included a brief interview that allowed Palsby to reflect on the failure of his business.

Ole Palsby in his cookware shop at Læderstræde 7, Copenhagen, circa 1973. Foreground from left: Karsten Ravn and Lars Lundquist. Garden table and concrete elements. Both described on pp. 327. → Promotional poster for Ole Palsby's cookware shop. The sampling of cookware and kitchen tools illustrates the range of Palsby's wares and includes several items that would inform his work on Eva Trio, including French copperware (rows 1 and 5) and cast aluminum Gateware (rows 1, 4 and 5) as well as the hand grill designed by Ravn and Lundquist (row 4). The hanging displays in Palsby's shop would be fundamental to his conception of Eva Trio.

After describing the loss of revenue from sales of the grills series, he explained his belief in an ethical approach to commerce and his hope for the future,

"There is always someone who can produce things a little more poorly and a little cheaper. I don't know if consumers are not sufficiently quality-conscious, but the majority are probably too ill-informed, because few retailers are able to give their customers the guidance that would enable them to make a sensible choice. What the consumer buys is often an illusion that he will be able to cook good food if he buys a copper pan. You are told that copper is good because it retains heat so well. Well, my God, it's exactly the opposite property you need — a good heat conductor, which copper is. [...] The truth is that if you buy the right tools for your kitchen, you can get by with far less equipment than if you don't make an effort to understand how things work and your family's needs. [...] I think it is strange that the people who have the capital and the sales apparatus but who are not exactly awash in good ideas — rather than stealing other people's ideas — do not say: How about we cooperate and come up with something great together? [...] I am still naive enough to believe that originality and quality can pay off in the long run, even if I now have to close my small business."[8]

Kringelbach's readers on 7 February 1976 included Erik Mangor, the owner of Denmark's leading producer of kitchen tools: Eva A/S. In the afternoon, he walked into Palsby's almost empty shop and asked the proprietor if he could design cookware that would equal the imported wares. Palsby answered, "Yes I can, as long as I have a free hand."[9] On 1 April 1976, Palsby signed a contract to develop a new line of cookware that would employ all of the knowledge that he had accumulated during his years as a merchant and his ten preceding years as a patron of architecture and industrial design.

Since the introduction of **Eva Trio**, Ole Palsby has often been described as a self-taught designer. However, he received an informal design education from the architects and designers who worked on his various business ventures during 1959–75. That virtual apprenticeship began when he commissioned Jørgen Bo and Vilhelm Wohlert to design his own home and continued as he established the design showroom on Hovedvagtsgade, where his associates included Nils Fagerholt, Bo Bonfils and Poul Kjærholm (p. 69). Palsby's training concluded at his kitchenware shops, where he continued working with Fagerholt and Bonfils and found new associates in Karsten Ravn and Lars Lundquist. Through the years, Palsby absorbed a practical approach to design that employs geometric elements to create systems of related objects.

Beyond those general principles, Palsby spent seven years importing cookware for his shops. As a result, he was an expert in the properties of various metals, useful sizes of pots and pans, and a wide range of cooking techniques. He also found useful lessons in a number of Danish specimens that include the enameled steel pots that Jørgen Ditzel designed for Rafa A/S with removable wire handles of stainless steel, which is a poor conductor of heat. Palsby was certainly impressed by Taverna, a line of copper cookware produced by Georg Jensen A/S with stainless steel handles designed by Henning Koppel.

While the vessels were modeled on traditional French wares, they were lined with silver, which provides a more durable surface than tin and is nearly ideal for many types of cooking.[10] The handle on the smallest part of Ravn and Lundquist's grill series, which Palsby produced and sold in his shops, inspired the signature feature of his new cookware.

Palsby was also able to draw on his experience designing porcelain cookware. In 1972, he and Nils Fagerholt entered a competition sponsored by the Royal Copenhagen Porcelain Factory. Their project included casseroles with three different diameters that matched the burners on a typical electric stove and removable stainless steel handles that recalled Jørgen Ditzel's pots.[11] Five years later, working for Eva A/S, Palsby imagined a system of pots and pans with four diameters that were based on the burners of a typical electric stove, but slightly larger. By adding 2 cm to the typical burner sizes, he created a rounded transition at the bottom of the vessels to ease stirring and cleaning and arrived at diameters of 15, 20, 24 and 28 cm. While the limited number of diameters allowed the use of interchangeable lids, all the parts could be stored on hooks, as in his kitchenware shops. By November 1976, Palsby had distilled his cookware project to a handful of principles and a set of dimensions that he could present to Erik Mangor.

> Essential influences on Eva Trio: Jørgen Ditzel. 24 cm casserole for Rafa A/S, 1956. Enameled steel, stainless steel. / Henning Koppel. 20 cm sauté pan (8042) for Georg Jensen, 1971. Copper, silver, stainless steel. / Karsten Ravn and Lars Lundquist. Hand grill for Ole Palsby A/S, 1971. Cold-rolled steel. → Ole Palsby. Eva Trio drawings, 1976–77. Sketch for modular system with standard diameters and universal lids. / Sketch for combination of three metals, 1977. / Presentation sketch, 1 November 1976

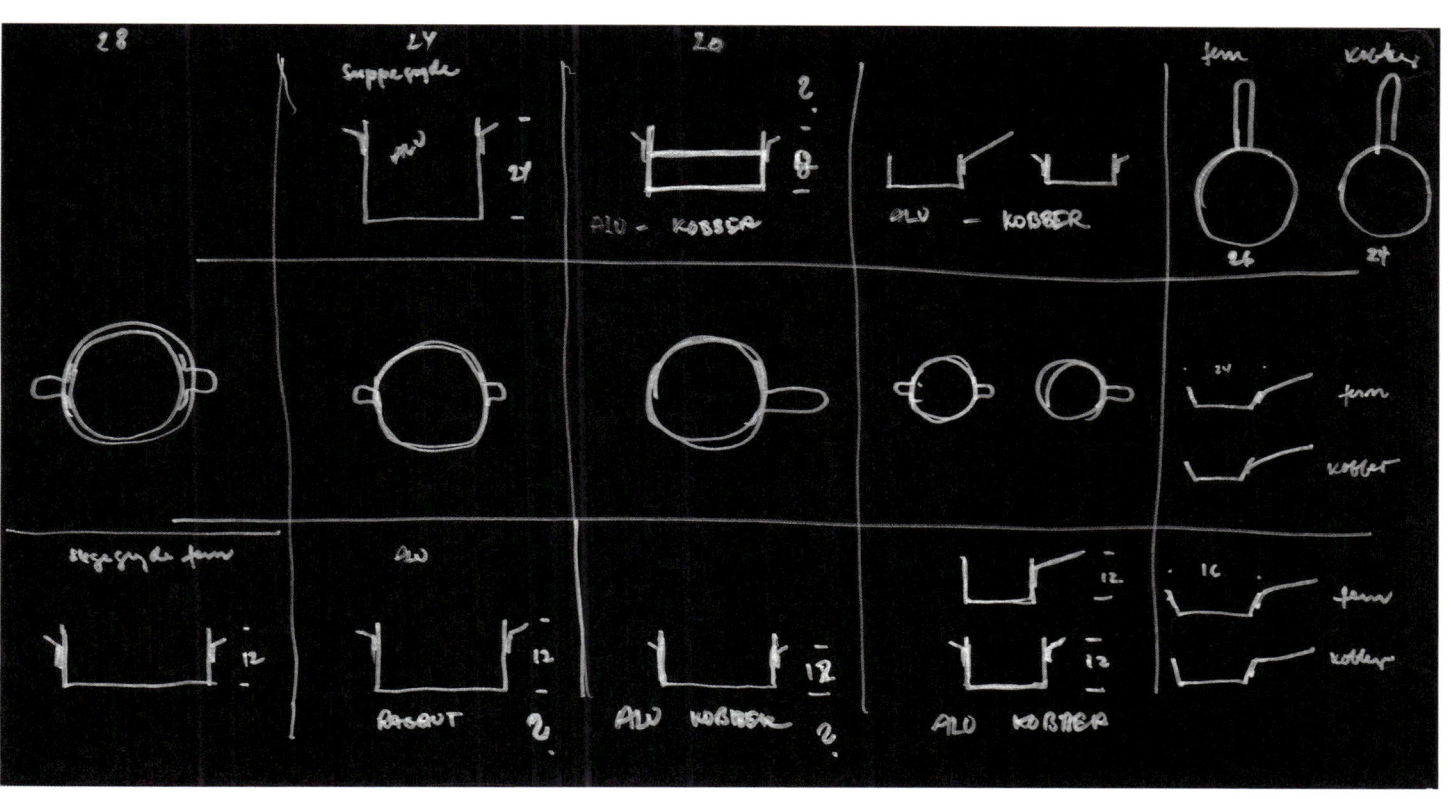

1-11-76

At the onset of the project, Ole Palsby and Erik Mangor agreed that the new cookware would encompass a range of techniques, from the everyday to the elaborate. It would be a *gourmet series* for people who might like to broaden their culinary horizons and explore the type of cooking promoted by Elizabeth David and many others. Palsby's project was rooted in his knowledge of traditional cookware, but he pursued a radically new approach to the design of pots, pans and lids. Historically, producers of metal cookware have employed one type of metal that was locally available and shaped by a process rooted in handicraft, such as hammering copper, forging steel or casting iron. As a result of that historical pattern, traditional cookware lines such as Le Creuset and Mauviel have distinctive forms that are specific to the metal, which makes it difficult to combine pieces from different lines, particularly the lids.

Palsby's quantum leap in cookware design was to reject the traditional union of metal and form, and instead create generic pots and pans that could be fabricated of different metals. The result was a true industrial design that could be mass-produced without a loss of quality and sold at affordable prices. This radical rethinking of cookware was rooted in Palsby's commitment to the people who would use his pots and pans. He understood that excellent cooking requires a variety of metals, because they conduct heat at different rates. Dense metals (such as cast iron) absorb and release heat slowly, which makes them superb for foods that benefit from prolonged cooking. Highly conductive metals (such as copper and aluminum) absorb and release heat quickly, which makes them superb for rapid cooking of thin or delicate foods. Determined to create an ideal line of cookware that was suited to almost any cooking technique, Palsby selected three types of metal and named his gourmet series Eva Trio.

The first edition of Eva Trio included eighteen pieces.[12] Half of the series was made of raw aluminum, which is lightweight, inexpensive and conducts heat quickly. Drawing on his experience selling Gateware, Palsby designed nine saucepans, frying pans and stockpots. His second metal of choice was high-carbon steel, which has many of the same properties as cast iron but absorbs heat more quickly and weighs much less. The four frying pans can be seasoned like iron skillets, to provide a natural, non-stick surface that is ideal for meat, fish and eggs. He completed the series with a small pot and four pans made of copper, which requires a lining to prevent poisoning. Inspired by Georg Jensen's Taverna line, Palsby lined his vessels with silver and created a union of metals with an unparalleled sensitivity to heat.

Drawing a further lesson from Taverna, Ole Palsby designed stainless steel handles that will not conduct heat from an electric stove. During the design process, he paid several visits to the blacksmith who had prototyped Ravn and Lundquist's grill series, carrying boxes of French copper cookware that were stripped of handles and used to test new solutions.[13] Palsby's objective was to determine the optimum angle for the handles on his frying pans and saucepans, which proved to be 25°. All of the handles would be made of 8-mm rod and riveted to the vessel for maximum strength. He modeled the flat lids for the series on a classic French type but imagined them as stainless steel disks equipped with handles of 4-mm rod. After Palsby presented his drawings and prototypes to Erik Mangor, the sales manager at Eva announced that it would be impossible to sell the new cookware, because it resembled "boy scout equipment."[14]

Three pieces of Eva Trio, 1977. Left to right: 24 cm carbon steel sauté pan, 4.7 L raw aluminum stock pan, 1.2 L copper sauce pan. → Interchangeable lids. Stainless steel plate with 4 mm rod. / Profile of standard lid. / Detail of handle for 1.6 L sauce pan.

Despite the skepticism among his staff, Mangor's commitment to Palsby's cookware never wavered. In September 1977, Eva Trio was introduced at a trade show for hardware dealers in the Bella Center, in Copenhagen, where it attracted a great deal of interest and some skepticism about the unusual handles.[15] Later in the autumn, Ole Palsby and chef Poul Lannik embarked on a marketing tour with press conferences and public events in Denmark's six largest cities. In each city, evenings were devoted to a demonstration and dinner for twenty hardware dealers and their staff, so they could provide customers with the informed guidance that Palsby regarded as an ethical obligation. The general public learned about the cookware in December, a week before Christmas, when George Kringelbach, who had mourned the demise of Palsby's kitchenware shop, celebrated the arrival of Eva Trio in his column "a la carte":

"When you consider how much junk and foolishness is presented in the trade under the name 'gastronomic kitchenware,' it almost brings tears to your eyes to finally meet the real thing: a new series of kitchenware based on the highest quality — and on the highest practical sense. This sensible approach is not only evident in the choice of materials and design but, in fact, also in the price. It is neither the cheapest nor the most expensive option in this tired and widely abused genre."[16]

.3 L butter warmer, 1978. Copper, silver and stainless steel. Diameter 8 cm. 1:1 scale. → A trio of specialized pans, 1978. Copper, silver and stainless steel handles. Top to bottom: 2.8 L sauce pan (20 cm). 2.5 L multi-purpose *fait-tout* (24 cm). 28 cm frying pan.

Kringelbach advised his readers that he had tested the new pots and pans in his own kitchen — and planned to replace his traditional cookware as soon as he could lay his hands on the corresponding pieces of Eva Trio. In the wake of that endorsement, sales of Palsby's gourmet series soared and reached one million Danish kroner within six months.[17] The best-selling pieces were the copper frying pans and saucepans lined with silver.

Commercial success allowed Palsby to extend the concept of a gourmet series with specialized copper vessels, several of them based on French models. While metal pots differ in height and diameter, their functions are essentially identical. Pans not only vary in height and diameter but also in purpose, with certain shapes better suited to specific cooking techniques. As Palsby extended the series, he devoted special attention to the low pans, creating different heights and profiles that would provide ideal conditions for frying, sautéing and braising. The original 26-cm frying pan in copper was replaced with three different models and supplemented with several new saucepans; larger vessels were equipped with a second handle for comfort and safety.

Palsby also created his own version of the French model known as *fait-tout* — "does everything" — a hybrid of sauté pan and frying pan that is equally suited to making omelets and meatballs. The sloping sides make it easier to monitor the cooking and turn the food, while also increasing the surface area and promoting evaporation of liquids. At the opposite end of the spectrum, in both size and specialization, Palsby created a miniature pot for melting butter that remains the single most charming part of Eva Trio. The narrow rod that serves as the handle is easily rotated between fingertips and provides precise control over the contents, as with various items designed by Kay Bojesen and Arne Jacobsen (p. 24, 76).

By 1980, Palsby had expanded Eva Trio to include twenty-two pieces of silver-lined copperware and a spirit warmer (*réchaud*) that can be paired with a standard copper pot for cooking or warming food on the table. Palsby's excursion into tabletop cooking was surely inspired by the popular interest in fondue during the 1970s, but the *réchaud* and other spirit warmers he created for Eva Trio are useful for a wide range of foods from every part of the world. Working with a traditional model, Palsby created three sizes of baking pan in copper or aluminum. Pairs of pans can be nested to create a *bain-marie*, a French precursor to the double boiler that allows slow cooking in hot water and is especially useful for making sauces and custards or working with chocolate.

Roasting pan with steaming grid, 1978. Copper, silver, stainless steel. 24 x 32 x 7 cm. → *Réchaud* with 2.2 L pot and spirit burner, 1978. Copper, silver, stainless steel. Diameter 21 cm.

Palsby's fascination with French cooking techniques recalls the origins of our own culinary era, which began in the early 1970s through the intersection of two disparate cultural forces.[18] On the one hand, the counterculture of the 1960s had rejected the industrial food chain and advocated sustainable farming and eating habits, notably vegetarianism. On the other hand, food writers such as Elizabeth David, George Kringelbach and Julia Child had convinced a great many people that they could prepare and enjoy fine food at home, with an emphasis on French techniques. Through the combined influence of hippies and gastronomes, cooking practices and eating habits in much of Europe and the Americas underwent a profound shift. The now-familiar results include the farm-to-table movement, widespread embrace of organic food and popular fascination with foreign cuisines. Palsby's gourmet series, which was designed to make sophisticated techniques accessible to home cooks, can be seen as both a product and an instrument of that culinary evolution.

The Silver Age of Eva Trio lasted for five years. During the late 1970s, the price of silver skyrocketed, driven by speculation that originated in Texas, where three brothers hoped to control the global supply.[19] They eventually went broke but not quickly enough. In 1982, the silver linings on Eva Trio were replaced with a white-bronze alloy — "Silver-look" — that is nearly as conductive as copper and has a higher melting point than silver.[20] Production with Silver-look continued until the end of 1984, when new regulations made it impractical to apply the material. During 1985–94, the copper parts of Eva Trio were produced with a lining of stainless steel and an aluminum core that provided fast thermal response. Between 1996 and 1998, the copper parts were simply lined with a thin layer of stainless steel. While none of these combinations matched the performance of silver, the resulting expertise in bonding different metals led to the Multi-line (now Multi) version of Eva Trio, which was introduced in 1999 and remains in production.

Bottom of 24 cm sauté pan. Copper, aluminum inner layer, stainless steel.
→ Multi-line: 1.8 L sauce pan (16 cm) and 3.6 L pot (20 cm). Stainless steel, aluminum inner layer.

Since 1977, Eva Trio has been produced in a variety of metals that followed changes in cooking habits and technology.[21] The three metals of the original series were gradually retired, with carbon steel replaced by stainless steel in 1985, and raw aluminum replaced by anodized aluminum in 1990. In 2000, solid copper vessels were discontinued, and the use of copper reduced to a thin layer on stainless steel. Despite the use of different metals, Ole Palsby's designs for the vessels and lids are essentially unchanged from 1977. In 1986, he extended the series with flat glass lids that make it possible to keep an eye on the food without disturbing the cooking. In 1997, the addition of magnetic steel bases to the stainless steel vessels made them compatible with induction cooktops; the same bases were soon applied to the other parts of Eva Trio.

Over the decades, the substitutions of metals have transformed Eva Trio from a gourmet series of specialized parts into a system of general-purpose cookware produced in several combinations of metals and coatings. The Multi-line that grew out of the 1980s experiments in bonding different metals can now be regarded as the most successful extension of Palsby's original design, due to its superior cooking properties. The two outer layers of stainless steel are fused to an aluminum core that extends to the rim of each vessel, which ensures a uniform distribution of heat and also provides a forgiving surface. As the aluminum cools faster than the two layers of steel, it becomes easier to remove any food that has stuck to the interior. Due to the three layers of metal, the parts have especially thick walls that promote durability and ensure decades of service.

The persistent appeal of Palsby's vessels, lids and handles, which have resisted the passage of time and appear as new, is a tribute to his inspired union of beauty and utility. A near parallel is found in Kay Bojesen's steel flatware, in that both men used their knowledge of traditional wares to create ideal designs for factory production (p. 24). Much like Bojesen, Palsby was a "practical idealist" who refused to abandon his commitments to excellence and to the people who would use his wares. As he explained in 1976 (p. 134), "I am still naive enough to believe that originality and quality can pay off in the long run." Two years later, that belief was validated by the commercial success of Eva Trio, which separated cookware from its artisanal origins and made excellent cooking equipment more widely available to the public.

After nearly fifty years, so many pieces of Eva Trio have been produced in such a wide variety of metals that it is possible to assemble a personal *batterie de cuisine* tailored to almost any combination of tastes and techniques. In addition to the new products, many vintage items can be found at second-hand sources, including copper vessels with 2 mm-thick walls and the occasional *réchaud*. Because the diameters remain unchanged, new lids are compatible with old vessels. The benefits of using silver-lined copperware for certain recipes are so pronounced that ambitious cooks with an induction cooktop will find it worthwhile to purchase an induction plate that allows their use. By mixing old and new pieces, according to occasion and appetite, it becomes possible to enjoy the unlimited cooking experience that inspired Ole Palsby to create his visionary system of culinary tools.

Contemporary *batterie de cuisine* composed of articles in aluminum, carbon steel, copper and stainless steel, with stainless steel and glass lids, 1977–2023. By combining articles of different metals and vintages, it becomes possible to create an individual cooking experience that realizes Ole Palsby's original vision for Eva Trio.

Table

and Chair

Arne Jacobsen was obsessed with technology that would allow him to construct more elegant and enchanting structures, from buildings to lamps to chairs.[1] In 1929, years before it was legally possible to construct a Danish house of reinforced concrete, Jacobsen employed plastered brickwork to mimic the houses erected at Bauhaus Dessau, in Germany.[2] Beginning in the early 1950s, as the materials and methods available to Jacobsen caught up to his artistic ambitions, he was able to design buildings and furniture that remain entirely contemporary. The furniture includes the stacking armchair of plywood and steel tubing that responds to subtle movements by the person sitting in the chair — **FH 3207** — and remains Jacobsen's supreme work as an industrial designer.

Jacobsen designed his first plywood chair in 1935, for the Bellevue Theater building that he had designed in Klampenborg, along the coastal road that connects Copenhagen and Helsingør. His first piece of plywood furniture engendered his first collaboration with the Fritz Hansen furniture factory. While the company was founded as a workshop in the 1870s, the eponymous cabinetmaker soon shifted to mass production. After the First World War, Fritz Hansen's son, Christian E. Hansen, initiated a research project to discover the process of steam-bending wood: a trade secret of the global enterprise Thonet-Mundus.[3] One of the byproducts of that research was expertise in producing plywood seats and backs for the new bentwood chairs.

In 1933, the cabinetmaker's grandsons Poul and Søren Hansen became co-directors of the company and turned their attention to making furniture from bent steel tubing, followed a recent trend emanating from Germany. Jacobsen's furniture for the Bellevue building employed plywood, bentwood and steel tubing for individual models, and several of them anticipated his masterful forms of the 1950s and '60s. But twenty years would pass before he combined plywood and steel in a single structure. During the 1930s, he was experimenting with curved elements and becoming accustomed to working with industrial materials.[4] The most successful of those experiments was the theater seat of molded beech that he designed under the influence of architect Alvar Aalto, the Finnish pioneer of plywood furniture.

> Arne Jacobsen. Bellevue Theater, Klampenborg, Denmark, 1935–37. Detail of auditorium with seating. Stained beech plywood. → FH 3207, 1955. Birch plywood with Douglas fir veneer, steel tubing. 1:1 scale.

ARNE JACOBSEN 1954–55
FH 3207

Marcel Breuer. B33 side chair, 1927. Steel tubing, canvas seat and backrest. / Alvar Aalto. Armchair, 1932. Painted steel tubing, birch plywood. / Eero Saarinen and Charles Eames. Armchair, 1940. Plywood and solid wood, foam rubber covered with wool. / Charles and Ray Eames. DCM (dining chair metal), 1946. Birch plywood, steel rods, rubber shock mounts. / Peter Hvidt and Orla Mølgaard-Nielsen. Ax chair, 1948. Solid and molded birch with mahogany cores, birch plywood with teak veneer. → Arne Jacobsen. FH 3100 (Ant), 1952. Birch plywood, steel tubing, rubber bumpers. Recent examples veneered with beech and Douglas fir. / Low table and lounge chair with arms for the American-Scandinavian Foundation. Birch plywood with rosewood veneer, steel tubing, foam rubber covered with wool. Exhibited at the Danish Museum of Applied Art (now Designmuseum Danmark), Copenhagen, 1952.

Aalto's inventive use of plywood was rooted in his dismay with furniture made of chrome-plated steel tubing. During the 1920s, avant-garde architects in Germany —most notably Marcel Breuer — used the material to pursue the dream of mass-produced industrial furniture.[5] Aalto was enthusiastic about the structural possibilities of steel tubing but found the hard shiny surface to be cold to the touch and unforgiving to the eye. In his words, the German models were "not satisfactory from the human point of view."[6] As an alternative, he combined a base of painted steel tubing with a curved layer of plywood that supports the body. Very quickly, he and his architect-wife, Aino (Mandelin) Aalto, developed models made entirely of molded wood that would have an enormous influence around the world.[7]

The primary agent of that influence was Finnish-American architect Eero Saarinen, whose family had immigrated to the United States, in 1923.[8] After finishing his studies in 1935, Eero Saarinen spent time in Helsinki, visited the Aaltos and returned home filled with enthusiasm for molded wood furniture.[9] In 1941, he and his colleague Charles Eames won a first prize in an international furniture competition for their chairs with molded plywood shells.[10] Those shells had defects, but Eames and his wife, Ray (Kaiser) Eames, spent the next five years developing a machine that could mold plywood in two directions at once.[11] In 1946, they unveiled a dining chair with a pair of plywood elements that are joined and supported by bent steel tubes.

The combined efforts of the Aaltos and the Eameses inspired Danish architects Orla Mølgaard-Nielsen and Peter Hvidt to design the AX chair, which was produced by Fritz Hansen and provided the company with even greater expertise in molding plywood.[12] That expertise proved invaluable after Arne Jacobsen appeared with a cardboard and wire model of a lightweight stacking chair that would employ a one-piece plywood shell for seat and back. The greatest challenge in developing that chair was the curling of the veneers where the backrest curves in two directions. Over the course of ten prototypes, the technical staff discovered that cutting away material reduced the problem, which prompted Jacobsen to draw the elegant profile that defines the chair.[13]

The first batch of chairs was produced in black-painted beech and labeled FH 3100. But a Swedish journalist provided the more common name when he observed, "[...] designed in black, it is a little reminiscent of an ant and probably just as useful."[14]

Introduced in 1952, the Ant is generally recognized as the first chair with a one-piece plywood shell that curves in two directions. By that point, Jacobsen was already wrestling with the challenge of providing armrests, as seen in the experimental lounge chair that he exhibited the same year. While the separate elements for seat and backrest recall the work of the Eameses, the sculptural wooden armrests anticipated Jacobsen's definitive union of plywood and steel tubing.

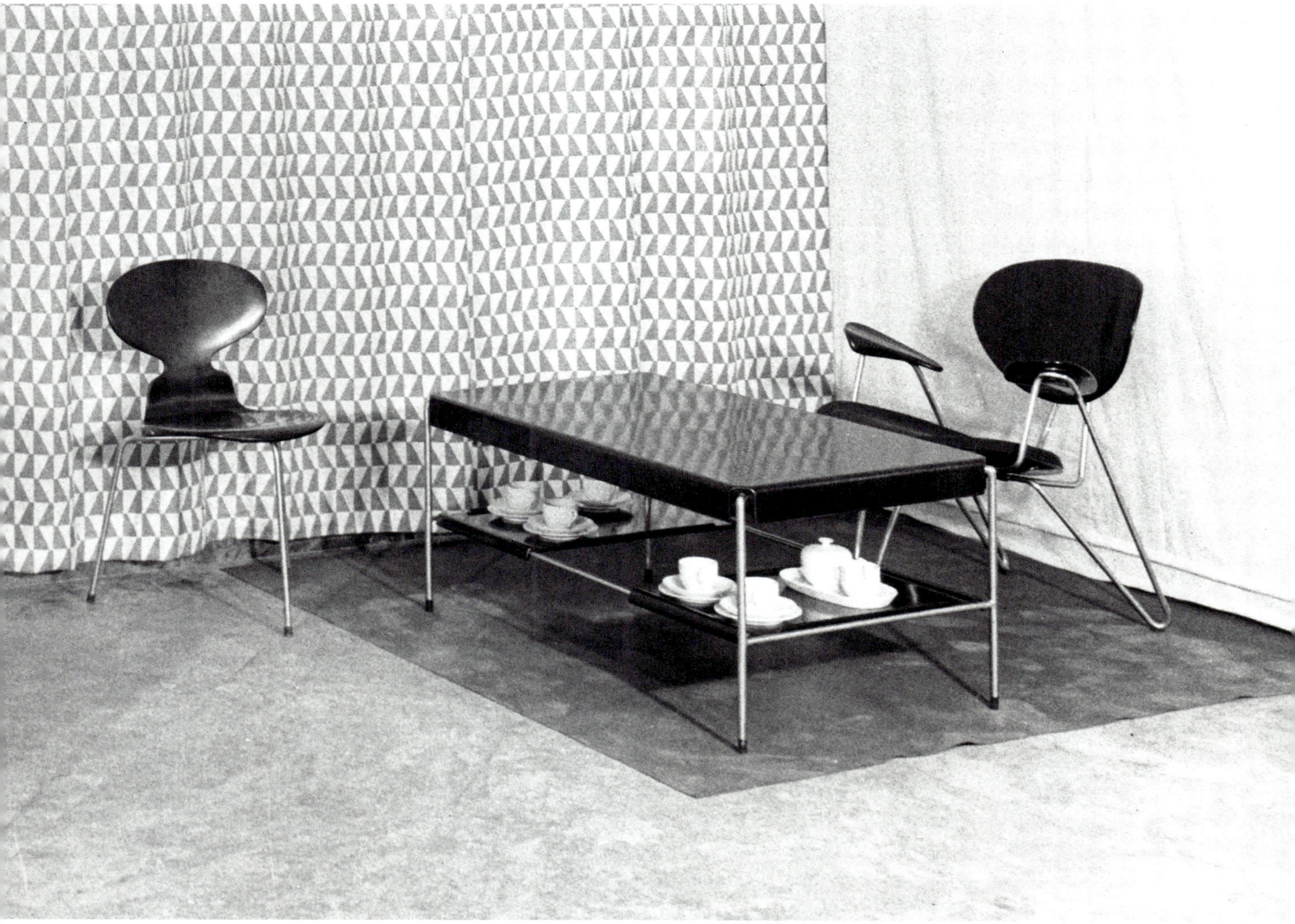

The design of an armchair required Jacobsen to make a fresh start. He would employ the same materials used for the Ant, but there was never any question of adding arms to his three-legged masterpiece. By its very nature, an armchair requires a symmetrical structure with four legs to ensure stability. In a deft stroke of formal economy, he extended the back legs of his four-legged structure to a point just above the seat and bent them forward to create arms. Those bent steel arms determined the profile of the plywood shell that Jacobsen designed as an extension of the human body. While the Ant was composed of two separate parts that corresponded to the materials, the new armchair would integrate plywood and steel tubing and create an organic and interactive structure.

By 1955, technical advances at the Fritz Hansen factory had eliminated the problem of curling veneer that inspired the narrow waist on the Ant. As a result, Jacobsen was able to design his ideal plywood shell, which incorporated lessons from his mentor and role model, the Swedish architect Erik Gunnar Asplund. In 1937, Asplund completed the new courthouse for the Gothenburg District Court, which is an addition to the eighteenth-century city hall.[15] His work on the building included all of the furniture and lighting and provided Jacobsen with a model for the city halls in Aarhus and Søllerød, Denmark, that he completed in 1942.[16] Designing chairs for the judges in Gothenburg, Asplund created backrests that mimicked the human torso and conveyed the compassionate character of the Swedish legal system.

As Jacobsen adapted Asplund's example to his plywood shell, he arrived at a flaring backrest that supports the spine but preserves freedom of movement for the upper body. In comparison with the Ant, the seat is wider and deeper, and the front edge has a more pronounced curve that ensures comfort behind the knees. Jacobsen also increased the slope of the seat and backrest by a few degrees, which make it easier to recline. He completed the armchair with narrow plywood armrests that make it possible to enjoy a variety of seating positions, for prolonged comfort. As the steel tubes extend out on either side of the seat, the armrests rotate inward to provide resting points for the forearms and slope backwards to support the elbows at a natural angle.

Erik Gunnar Asplund. Armchair for Gothenburg Courthouse, 1935–37. American hickory and goatskin upholstery. / Contrasting shells of FH 3100 and FH 3207. 1:10 scale. → Arne Jacobsen. FH 3207, 1955. Douglas fir.

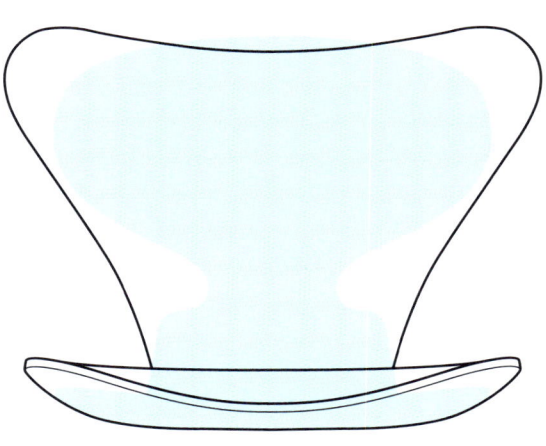

Rubber bumper. 1:1 scale. / Top view with locations of rubber bumpers. / FH 3207 with veneers of Douglas fir and cherry.

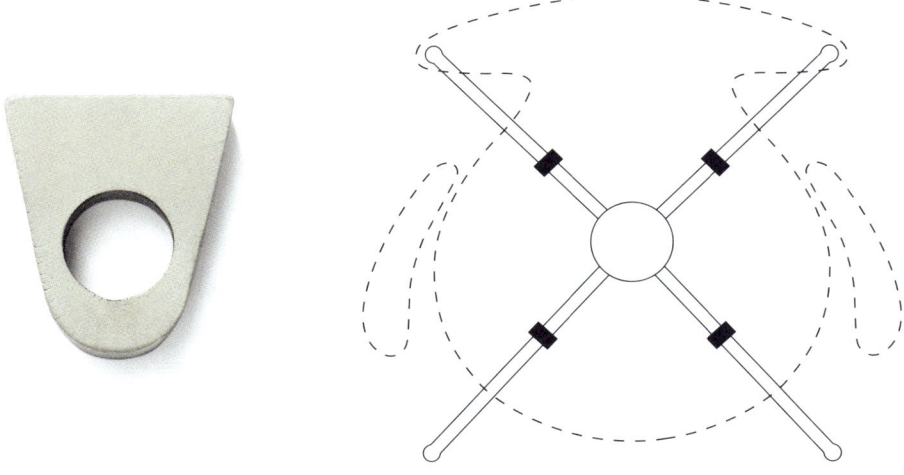

In the summer of 1955, the Swedish Society of Arts and Crafts staged the *Helsingborg Exhibition 1955* (*H55*) in the coastal town of the same name, across the Øresund strait from Helsingør, Denmark, which included recent examples of architecture and design from ten nations.[17] As Jacobsen had designed the Danish display of handicrafts and industrial design, it was a natural setting to introduce his new armchair, which was labeled FH 3207. Elsewhere in the exhibition, a model apartment designed by Finn Juhl included a version of Jacobsen's new chair without arms, which was labeled FH 3107 and attracted little notice.[18]

Visitors to the Danish section encountered one of those rare phenomena in furniture history: a new version of a familiar type made possible by the innovative use of materials. The essential feature of FH 3207 is the slightly springy structure that flexes as a person sitting in the chair adjusts their position within the shell or leans on the armrests. While the rigid structure of a conventional chair will resist those movements and promote muscle fatigue, Jacobsen's interactive assembly of three resilient materials (plywood, steel tubing and rubber) registers the changing distribution of weight and actively promotes relaxation.

As with the Ant, the plywood shell of FH 3207 consists of nine layers of veneer and two inner layers of canvas. Once again, Jacobsen insisted on the thinnest possible steel tubing, to ensure resilience. The plywood shell and base of steel tubing are only connected at a central point beneath the seat, but a rubber bumper threaded over each of the four legs provides additional support to the shell and acts as a shock absorber. As the rubber bumpers eliminate the need for additional connections between plywood and steel tubing, they also preserve the resilience of both materials such that the shell and legs can respond to movement. Indeed, those bumpers are essential parts of the interactive structure.

While the rubber bumpers preserve the flexibility of shell and tubing, Jacobsen's carefully wrought arms preserve the visual separation of the two materials. Rather than curve the steel tubing as it rises above the seat, to mimic the plywood shell, he simply bent the tubes at two points. In doing so, Jacobsen made certain that the arms are perceived as extensions of the legs and reinforced the distinction between steel and plywood that is fundamental to the comfort of the chair. The steel tubing does not curve until it passes under the narrow plywood armrest that was formed to fit the hand.

The plywood armrest is cantilevered from the steel tubing and restates the underlying principle of the chair in miniature. Cherry veneer. → Light breaking on the back of the shell reveals the compound curves that correspond to human anatomy. Oak veneer.

Jacobsen lavished as much care on the design of the armrest as on the shell that provides the seat and back. While the rounded upper surface fills the palm, the concave underside provides a recess for fingertips. Jacobsen's attention to touch reveals the essential nature of his work on FH 3207. By shaping steel tubing and plywood to accommodate the body, he humanized technology. The result is a mass-produced chair with the tactile character most often found in handcrafted items. While the torso-shaped shell displays Jacobsen's concern for the human form, the depth of his concern only becomes apparent in use. Leaning, stretching and turning, we experience Jacobsen's armchair as an extension of our body and enjoy a sense of well-being that is at once physical and psychological.

As Jacobsen adapted industrial materials to human factors, he built on the efforts of Alvar Aalto, Eero Saarinen and the Eameses and created a more comfortable chair than any of his predecessors, by virtue of his artistic modesty.

Rather than invent new forms on the drawing board, he preferred to work with a model and pursue a more perfect union of purpose, material and form that was suited to the problem at hand. With Cylinda-line, the use of geometric shapes allowed him to concentrate on proportions and practical details (p. 76). With FH 3207, his reliance on Asplund's model in Gothenburg allowed him to focus on the design of the arms, the contours of the shell and the resilient structure.

The plywood shell that Jacobsen designed to accommodate the arms on FH 3207 provided the basic element for a range of chairs that are suited to many different purposes. With or without arms, the shell can be combined with a range of upholstery options and a variety of bases to provide chairs for offices and town halls, schools, lecture halls, and almost any other setting that requires upright seating. As every one of the model numbers ended in 7, the range eventually became known as the Seven Series or Series 7. The stacking chair without arms — FH 3107 — that appeared in the Helsingborg exhibition, and was generally ignored, would become what is almost certainly the best-selling chair of the twentieth century and remains a pillar of Fritz Hansen's production.

FH 3207 has been in continuous production since 1955. The only significant alteration to the design has been an increase in the seat height, from 44 to 46 cm, due to the general increase in stature since 1945. Initially, 3207 and the variants were available in black-painted beech and a choice of teak, rosewood or oak veneers. The shell is still produced in a range of natural wood veneers that includes Jacobsen's favorite: Douglas fir. In the late 1960s, he selected a palette of colors for the painted beech version that is periodically updated. The shell is also produced in stained ash, with a range of colors. As natural wood is more forgiving of wear than paint or stain and more resistant to fashion, it provides the most durable option. Vintage examples in every finish can be found internationally.

Jacobsen published few statements and was tight-lipped with the press, refusing to adopt a philosophical position or describe his work in intellectual terms. But late in life, he delivered a speech that revealed his fundamental convictions:

Two offshoots of the armchair: FH 3177 (1970) and FH 3107 (1955). Douglas fir veneer. ← Four armchairs can be stacked for ease of storage. Veneers, bottom to top: dark oak, cherry, Douglas fir, oak.

"We are living in times greatly influenced by technology, in which, unfortunately, aesthetics have not been recognized as having a function. People feel at ease, are happier in their work, and feel more cheerful, within aesthetically resolved conditions rather than those that are purely technically perfect. [...] The greater part of my observations is small nudges, reflecting my worries about the devaluation of the coming generation of architects. A devaluation that I believe we can avoid when we add an absolutely necessary touch of humanity to the inhumane nature of industrialization and raise building to an art form called architecture."[19]

Jacobsen was summarizing his approach to designing buildings, but he might just as well have been describing his work as an industrial designer. Despite the vast differences between a city hall and a coffee pot, all of Jacobsen's work after 1950 embodies his obsession with technology. Reading the passage above, it becomes clear that he regarded beauty as a necessity alongside daylight and fresh air. And that he believed the raw products of industry could be softened and made beautiful through artistry. And so, it also becomes clear that Jacobsen's aesthetic obsession with technology was rooted in his desire to delight and comfort people. The most direct expression of that desire is the interactive plywood armchair that Jacobsen designed as an extension of the human body, which remains unique in the history of modern furniture.

The simple wooden chair that Vilhelm Wohlert designed to furnish the Louisiana Museum of Modern Art, in Humlebæk 30 km north of Copenhagen, is an overlooked treasure of modern Danish furniture that has been hidden in plain sight for more than six decades. That chair was the finishing touch to a building that is indivisible from its setting, because the design was based on the features of the landscape: the terrain, trees and views of a small lake and the sea.[1] As a result, a visit to the building provides a picturesque stroll in which the natural attractions of the place are experienced in tandem with the works of art. To avoid competing with nature or art, Wohlert and his co-architect, Jørgen Bo, distilled their work to a series of geometric elements and constructed a building with an anonymous character; Wohlert's chair extended that project to the furniture.

In 1954, the art collector Knud W. Jensen purchased a derelict estate named *Louisiana*, which had been established a century earlier by forester and beekeeper Alexander Brun. During 1856–75, Brun planted the grounds with rare trees, constructed a modest two-story villa and named the estate after his third wife, Louise (Wolff) Brun.[2] The lush setting was ideally suited to Jensen's vision of exhibiting art in the landscape and also provided him with a name for his new museum.[3] In 1956, Jensen commissioned Bo and Wohlert to design an exhibition building for his collection of modern Danish art. While the building was under construction, he decided the museum would host concerts in one of the large galleries. Suddenly, Louisiana required several hundred lightweight chairs that could be stacked for compact storage.

The exhibition building that opened in 1958 was the joint work of Bo and Wohlert, but Wohlert designed the custom-made lamps and furnishings on his own. He had spent the better part of twelve years studying and working with Kaare Klint, absorbing the principles that shaped most of his later work.[4] One of those principles was the use of geometry as a design tool. Following Klint's lessons, Wohlert understood geometry as a fundamental language of forms and proportions that are independent of any particular style. As such, they provide the basis for buildings and objects that are devoid of artistic flourishes and possess an essential character. The plain black hollowware that Wohlert designed for the new building (p. 79), using the form of a cylinder, was rooted in that principle and anticipated the **Louisiana Chair**.

Another of Wohlert's guiding principles was the idea of the furniture-type: a basic model defined by purpose and structure that has existed for centuries or even millennia. Common examples include the table with a useful height for eating; the low table for small objects; and chairs for upright seating, with or without arms. Very rarely, a new type will appear as the result of a new function or material, such as the cantilevered chair of steel tubing (p. 150). From this perspective, furniture design is a gradual and communal process, as artisans and designers adapt existing models to their own work. One example of that modest approach is the chair that Wohlert designed for Louisiana by combining parts of several models, including one of his own designs and another that would have surprised Kaare Klint.

Jørgen Bo and Vilhelm Wohlert. Louisiana Museum of Modern Art, Humlebæk, Denmark, 1956–91. Terrace of 1958 exhibition building with Louisiana Chairs in black-stained beech. → Vilhelm Wohlert. Louisiana Chair, 1957–58. Solid and laminated teak with leather seat, 1959. P. Jeppesens Møbelfabrik. Detail of backrest. 1:1 scale.

VILHELM WOHLERT 1957–58
Louisiana Chair

Finn Juhl. Chair 108, 1946. Teak with leather seat. Niels Vodder. / Hans J. Wegner. Model 30, 1952. Oak, leather seat. Carl Hansen & Søn. / Vilhelm Wohlert. Model 402, 1956. Teak, leather seat. Søborg Møbelfabrik. → Vilhelm Wohlert. Model 401, 1957. Teak, leather seat. Søborg Møbelfabrik.

Wohlert's design for the Louisiana Chair fused ideas and forms from two opposing sources into a new and singular model. One of those sources was the sculptural approach pioneered in Denmark by Finn Juhl, who regarded furniture design as a vehicle for artistic expression.[5] As a result, Juhl chafed at many of the principles promoted by Kaare Klint, including the idea that materials should be treated according to their natural properties, in the belief that they limited his creative freedom. While wood has a linear structure, Juhl treated it like clay and relied on master cabinetmaker Niels Vodder to realize his complex structures of curved forms. After 1945, Juhl reinforced the sculptural character of his chairs by treating the seats and backrests as independent elements that were distinct from the wooden structure.

Juhl's sculptural approach had a liberating effect on his contemporary Hans J. Wegner, a trained cabinetmaker whose designs were rooted in his mastery of wood construction. Wegner also possessed an innate artistic talent that first appeared in the wooden figures that he carved as a youth.[6] While he sympathized with many of Klint's principles, he was committed to a more personal approach that allowed him to explore the sculptural potential of wood. In 1950, Wegner began his long partnership with the Carl Hansen & Søn factory by designing dining chairs that adapted Juhl's strategy of detached seat and backrest to the reality of wood construction, as seen in CH 30. The detached elements were ideal for the factory, because they could be upholstered and attached to the finished structure at the end of the production process.

After Klint's death in 1954, Wohlert experimented with different approaches to form, as he worked to establish his own professional identity.[7] In 1956, he designed a teak dining chair for Søborg Møbelfabrik with a petal-shaped backrest and a dish-shaped seat supported on inverted wooden pyramids: SM 402. Considering his training with Klint, it becomes clear that Wohlert regarded Wegner's CH 30 as a new structural type that was ripe for further development. Indeed, Wohlert developed his own details for SM 402, while the back legs have a double curve that recalls the ancient klismos-type. Nonetheless, CH 30 is so much a product of Wegner's personal approach to form that it is difficult to recognize Wohlert's own contributions to SM 402 or to regard the chair as something other than an awkward experiment in Wegner-style.

Wohlert's second chair for Søborg Møbelfabrik, designed in 1957, marked a return to his first principles, as he used geometry to create a new version of an older furniture type. SM 401 (the Circle Chair) was based on the corner armchair that was developed during the early 1700s for use with writing tables.[8] While the rotated frame allows the chair to be pulled very close to the table, the front leg provides maximum support for someone leaning forward. The backrest on SM 401 is woefully inadequate, and the vertical legs undermine stability. And yet, the design includes the round seat supported on a square frame of straight rails that would appear on the Louisiana Chair. Wohlert's next chair would provide both comfort and stability by incorporating the flared legs and shaped backrest that he had employed on SM 402.

Vilhelm Wohlert, Louisiana Chair, 1957–58. 2017 edition in black-painted ash with leather seat. Stellar Works. / Louisiana Chairs, 1958. Stained beech with vinyl seat. P. Jeppesens Møbelfabrik. Wohlert's geometric structure makes it possible to stack more chairs than is typical in a spiral column that is extremely stable. → Louisiana Museum of Modern Art, Humlebæk. Seating area for cafeteria, circa 1964. The immediate and unexpected popularity of the museum resulted in a crush of visitors that far exceed even the most optimistic projections. As a result, the chair that Wohlert designed as temporary seating for concerts was permanently installed as a dining chair in what had been designed as a tranquil reading area. To accompany the chair, Wohlert designed a simple trestle table that was made of beech and remained in place for decades.

The color and character of the Louisiana Chair were determined by the architectural setting. Bo and Wohlert constructed the building of organic materials, which have an impersonal character in the sense that the colors and textures were determined by natural processes, rather than artistic choices. The only instances of applied color in the building were monochromatic hues that would not compete with the setting or the art — the whitewashed brick walls and fireplace, black posts between the windows and gray wall in the double-height gallery overlooking the small lake. As the architects explained,

"The buildings had to be white, inside the house because of the works of art, and outside in order to contrast with the green park, and to link the old and new together. The natural effects of the material in the brickwork and the woodwork are neutral, and yet they increase the effects of the works of art."[9]

The chair that Wohlert designed for that singular building represents a union of human factors, aesthetic concerns and technical requirements. Indeed, the Louisiana Chair marked the transition in his work with furniture, from collaborator with cabinetmakers to industrial designer. His designs for Søborg Møbelfabrik had been tentative steps in that direction, but they were products of the handcrafted approach he had absorbed in Klint's office. Louisiana's requirement of several hundred chairs compelled Wohlert to design for mass production.

To that end, Wohlert turned to Poul Jeppesen, the owner of P. Jeppesens Møbelfabrik in Store Heddinge, southern Zealand. Jeppesen's small factory was already producing furniture designed by Grete Jalk and Professor Ole Wanscher, Kaare Klint's successor as head of the Department of Furniture Design at the Royal Danish Academy. Wanscher's work with the factory served as a stamp of approval and assured Wohlert of quality production. The three hundred chairs that Jeppesen delivered to Louisiana in the summer of 1958 had beech frames, which were treated with the hardwearing black stain used on laboratory worktops and finished with round seats covered in blue-gray vinyl. While the vinyl was easily wiped clean, the color harmonized with the gray-green marble parapet around the lower level of the cafeteria.

Wohlert's combination of a simple frame, circular seat and black finish imbued the chair with an elemental character that harmonized with the whitewashed brick walls and geometric patterns of wood, paving tile and stone. It was also an ingenious answer to Knud W. Jensen's requirement for compact storage. The truly innovative aspect of the chair is only apparent when the chair is being stacked. Rather than sitting directly on top of one another, in the conventional manner, Wohlert's chairs are stacked by rotating them and inserting one of the back legs between the legs of the chair below. As the chairs are stacked, they form a spiral of interlocking units that allows more chairs to be stacked in a single column and reduces the area needed for storage.

In 1959, Poul Jeppesen decided to test the market for the Louisiana Chair and produced a number of chairs in teak along with additional examples in black-stained beech.[10] Both versions were advertised in furniture journals and displayed in shops. While the black version of the chair has the character of an abstract element, in which the species of wood is irrelevant, the lighter color and exposed grain of the teak chair make it easier to appreciate the simplicity of Wohlert's industrial design. He had reduced the chair to a minimum number of elements: four legs cut from the same tapered length of wood, four identical rails that support the circular seat and a curved plywood backrest that is attached to the rear legs with wooden pegs. The only detail is the graceful cut at the top of the back legs, which provide a flat surface for attaching the backrest.

Wohlert designed the Louisiana Chair by combining parts of his two chairs for Søborg Møbelfabrik. While Model 401 supplied the round legs and circular seat supported on a square frame, Model 402 provided the curved backrest and splayed legs. He created that hybrid structure by renouncing any sculptural ambitions for the design — eliminating hand-drawn curves and straightening the elements — while also abandoning the rigid geometry of his Circle Chair.

Rather than create another formal experiment, he followed his training and used geometry as a design tool, guided by Poul Jeppesen's requirement for simple forms suited to factory production. As a result, the parts of the chair coalesce into a whirl of curved edges and surfaces and imbue the structure with a unified character. Indeed, the entire design is governed by a system of proportions that unite comfort, strength and stability.

The basis of Wohlert's design is a 45-cm cube that corresponds to the height of the seat at the front edge. Because a cube is equally stable in width and depth, a structure with the same proportions will resist overturning in both directions. With that in mind, Wohlert arranged the legs at 45° to the center of the cube, which coincides with the center of the circular seat. As they rise from the floor, the legs slope towards the center of the cube and brace the square frame supporting the seat, which reduces stress on the joints and makes the chair more durable. Having arrived at the basic structure, Wohlert sloped the seat by 3°, to counteract our natural tendency to slide forward when leaning back, and inclined the backrest at an angle of 105°, which promotes relaxation without lulling a person to sleep.

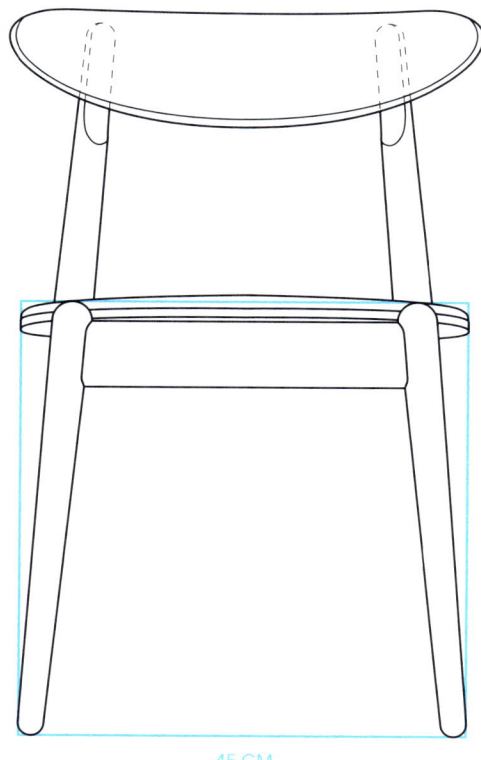

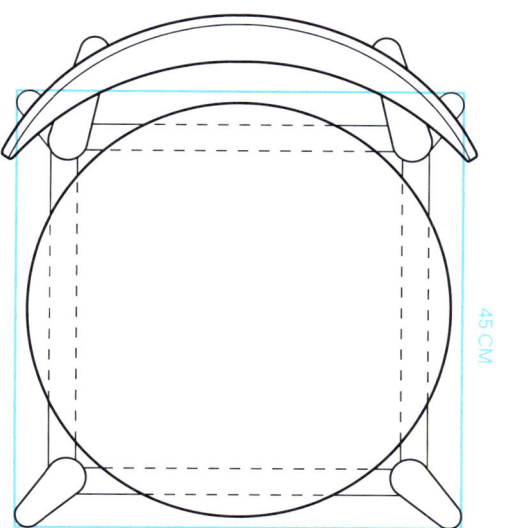

Front view and plan illustrating Wohlert's use of a cube to design the base of the chair. The uniform placement of the legs makes it possible to stack the chairs in a spiral, so that they hold each other in place.
→ Louisiana Chair. Teak, leather seat.

The essential part of the Louisiana Chair is the back leg, which was turned on a lathe from a straight piece of wood, softened with steam and bent back on itself. At one and the same time, the back legs brace the seat, support the backrest at a natural angle and allow the chairs to be stacked. Wohlert accomplished that remarkable feat of formal economy by extending the back legs above the seat and bending the top of each leg towards the centerline of the seat. In doing so, he made it possible to support the backrest at the ideal height, while limiting the width of the chair and ensuring close spacing for concerts.

What Wohlert could not have known as he designed the Louisiana Chair for concert seating is that he was also creating a dining chair. In 1957, Knud W. Jensen had imagined that Louisiana might only attract 40,000 visitors per year, due to the remote location and the fact that he was exhibiting *modern* art.[11] On the opening weekend in August 1958, 4,000 people showed up. One year later, Louisiana had received 225,000 visitors; the number would only increase over time. By 1963, the reading room facing the sea had been converted into a seating area for the cafeteria, which was furnished with Wohlert's black chairs. Even if he had anticipated the second purpose of the chair, it is unlikely that he would have altered the design. The seating angle of 3° that allows people to lean back during concerts also allows them to lean forward and enjoy their meal with minimal effort.

Wohlert's multi-purpose chair for Louisiana realized the impulse that had spurred him to design his experimental models for Søborg Møbelfabrik and confirmed Kaare Klint's theory of furniture design as a gradual process of evolution. Just as Hans J. Wegner found useful ideas in Finn Juhl's work and adapted them to his own ends, Wohlert used lessons for Wegner's work to create a new and improved model of the furniture type. The Louisiana Chair might be regarded as a generic design — which is certainly what Wohlert intended — except for the fact that it is so excellent in so many ways. By restricting himself to human factors and functional concerns, above all the necessity of stacking, Wohlert created a model that transcends its original purpose and setting: a universal object of uncommon grace and unsurpassed utility for its type.

Detail of double-curved back leg with notch for attachment of backrest. The back leg is formed from a single length of wood that was first turned on a lathe and then steamed, so that it could bent in two directions at once. As a result, it supports the curved backrest at the required angle but also slopes inward to allow stacking. → 1959 edition. The curved backrest is based on the same circle that provides the seat but angled to provide comfortable support for the spine. The curved parts of the chair are united by the shape of the seat, creating a unified, organic structure that recalls handcrafted chairs. / Cross section of upright and reclining seating positions. Wohlert angled the backrest following the standard for relaxation (105°) but limited the angle of the seat to 3°, to prevent people from falling asleep. The 3° angle proved ideal after the chair was converted to cafeteria seating.

After 1958, the Louisiana Chair was lost to history and remained out of production for more than fifty years. Despite its many excellent qualities, the chair does not appear in many or any of the numerous books on Danish furniture.[12] We can attribute that lack of recognition to the anonymous appearance that is one of the chair's chief virtues. Poul Jeppesen's attempt to sell the Louisiana Chair to the public appears to have been unsuccessful, despite the extraordinary popularity of the museum and resulting exposure to Wohlert's masterful design. After 1960, Jeppesen ran few advertisements, if any, which suggests that the chairs that he manufactured in 1959, in teak and black-stained ash, were the only examples that he ever produced for the public.

During 1958–2002, most of Louisiana's three hundred black chairs remained in use, in the cafeteria where they were periodically repaired and repainted. The fact that so many survived for more than forty years, in a setting that received several hundred thousand visitors each year, is a tribute to their durable design and construction. By 2002, the number of serviceable chairs had dwindled to the point that they were sold to museum employees, and the cafeteria was furnished with Arne Jacobsen's side chair FH 3107, the offshoot of his armchair FH 3207 (p. 150).

In 2012, the Japanese design brand Stellar Works revived the Louisiana Chair along with a number of Vilhelm Wohlert's other chairs. The new examples of his multi-purpose masterpiece were produced in natural walnut, with the option of a soap treatment, or in natural ash, with several options for a stained finish, including black. In 2021, Stellar Works substituted oak for ash, but the options for stained finishes still include black, and Wohlert's original design for the Louisiana Chair remains intact, even as the version in walnut recalls the teak production of 1959.

In 2018, to celebrate Louisiana's sixtieth anniversary, the cafeteria was refurnished with new examples of the copper lamps that Wohlert designed for the 1958 building and the Stellar Works edition of the Louisiana Chair, in black-stained ash with seats covered in gray-green leather. As a result, visitors to the museum can enjoy the benefits of Wohlert's chair in the building for which it was designed, which is now vastly expanded.

In early 1959, fewer than six months after Louisiana opened, Jørgen Bo and Vilhelm Wohlert began work on the first project to extend their 1958 exhibition building. During 1966–91, they expanded the museum in four phases, which include an exquisite concert hall with handcrafted chairs designed by Poul Kjærholm and three wings of galleries that are collectively suited to every type of artwork.[13] Each one of those extensions was designed in harmony with the terrain and based on the movement of the visitors as they progress through the landscape, above and below ground. Amid the multiple extensions, Bo and Wohlert were able to maintain and expand the low pavilion that contains the cafeteria, preserving a union of architecture, landscape and furniture that remains a cultural archetype in itself.

> Louisiana's architects, Vilhelm Wohlert and Jørgen Bo, August 1958. Similarly to the Louisiana Chair, Bo and Wohlert's 1958 exhibition building represents a union of handicraft ideals and abstract aesthetics, which was rooted in the beauty of the natural setting. The wall of projecting brickwork behind the architects (also visible on p. 162) is simply the result of two intersecting grids, as the pavilion that contains Wohlert's Louisiana Chair rotates to face the sea. → The domesticated version of the Louisiana Chair produced in 1959 represents a union of traditional sensibilities and industry production, such that it bridges the gap between eras and has an ageless character. In fact, it is an ideal example of a wooden multi-purpose chair, no matter the species and finish.

Architect Poul Henningsen (also known as PH) was a modernist Renaissance man who played an extraordinary variety of roles in Danish cultural life from the 1920s until his death, in 1967, and whose persona has assumed almost mythical status. An incomplete list of his accomplishments includes his work as a critic and driving force behind the journals *Klingen* (The Blade) and *Kritisk Revy* (Critical Review); political activist and public intellectual devoted to the maintenance of a decent society; building architect and designer of furniture, kites and a piano; songwriter and composer of musical reviews; and historian of erotic art. Since his death, Poul Henningsen has been the subject of several full-length biographies and his writings has been collected and dissected in numerous volumes.[1]

Given the astounding range of Henningsen's activities, it can be easy to forget that he was the most innovative lamp designer of the twentieth century, who invented a new method of controlling electric light.[2] He made that invention in the 1920s but achieved his greatest success thirty years later with the pendant that he designed to illuminate a dining table: **PH 5**. A number of basic facts have been published repeatedly: PH 5 was designed to conceal the light bulb following Henningsen's "conversion." The name is derived from the 50-cm diameter of the largest shade. The curved shades are based on a logarithmic spiral that ensures even reflections. And yet, those familiar facts do not illuminate the union of science and sensibility that produced Poul Henningsen's most personal lamp.

As a matter of fact, Henningsen designed his earliest lamps for dining rooms, during 1916–20. In most cases, he used glass bowls and dangling glass prisms to shield the incandescent bulbs that he despised for their cold light, extreme brightness and correspondingly deep shadows. While those fixtures appear entirely decorative, they were based on segments of a circle and marked Poul Henningsen's first attempts at using geometry to control glare.[3] In 1924, he began the collaboration with lamp producer Louis Poulsen A/S that would continue for more than forty years. The first result of that partnership was the copper pendant that Poul Henningsen designed to illuminate the Danish porcelain display within the Grand Palais, at the 1925 World Exposition in Paris..[4] The interior surfaces of the copper shades were coated in nickel silver that provided a dull luster and reflected light.

Henningsen was awarded a Gold Medal for the Paris Lamp, but he was appalled by reflected glare from the underside of the shades. As a result, he abandoned metallic finishes in favor of white paint, while also pursuing a mathematical solution that would allow him to control the distribution of light. During the winter of 1925–26, he found that solution in the logarithmic spiral that occurs in some natural structures and has been known to mathematicians since the 1600s. In early 1926, Henningsen developed a pendant based on a logarithmic curve that would illuminate Copenhagen's new Forum exhibition building.[5] That fixture, made of three copper shades with white interiors was the first example of the PH Lamp, which immediately became a sensation.

In 1928, Poul Henningsen published a lengthy article entitled "Lighting the Home." Rather than simply promote the PH Lamp, he described his ideal for domestic lighting in terms that precisely anticipate the design of PH 5, nearly thirty years later. He began by recalling the pre-electrical era:

"After millennia of using an ordinary flame as a light source, which has been appropriate in terms of clarity (intensity of the luminous parts) and which has an exceedingly fortunate spectral composition, the entire traditional culture, which rested so confidently and well on the good properties of the flame, was blown up with the use of gas and electricity for lighting. [...] There is, in and of itself, no more reason to applaud the past for the lighting culture we know from candles and kerosene lamps as there is reason to applaud it because it did not know how to misuse a telephone; however, it is fortunate that there was a fine lighting culture which we can learn from in theoretical, if not in practical, terms.

Poul Henningsen. PH 5, 1955–58.
Aluminum, steel. Diameter 50 cm.
1:1 scale.

POUL HENNINGSEN 1955–58
PH 5

The question of lighting culture is identical to the question of coziness (*hygge*), and although cozy is often confused with decorative, you will always find that it is the culture of lighting that creates coziness, and not the decorative quality of the lighting fixture. [...] In the home, light is widely used as an artistic way to marking the spaces that are suitable for work or for relaxing. [...] The low-hanging lighting that is, of course always required above a table, a workplace, a reading area, must hang so low that it provides just enough diffusion for the table, but no more."[6]

Having described the location and height of a pendant, he described the importance of color to the atmospheric character of light:

"In the home, to obliterate the difference between day and night by some imitation [of daylight] would be an impoverishment of human existence. [...] A very important issue for domestic lighting is the spectral composition of the light, often expressed in popular terms: the light should be warm and cozy. [...]

The degree of coldness of the light depends on the temperature of the glowing body, so that the higher the temperature of a glowing body, the colder we call the light. When the temperature is increased, the position of the spectrum shifts, as there are fewer red rays in the spectrum, and more yellow, green, blue and violet. [...]

It follows from this that the candle should provide better illumination for assessing material characteristics than the electric light bulb, and this is in fact the case. [...] There is probably also a reasonable explanation why the light should contain a certain absolute minimum share of red rays, and it is precisely this level that makes the lighting festive, because these red rays make the silverware, glasses, tablecloth, flowers and dishes stand out with their strong and beautiful material character."[7]

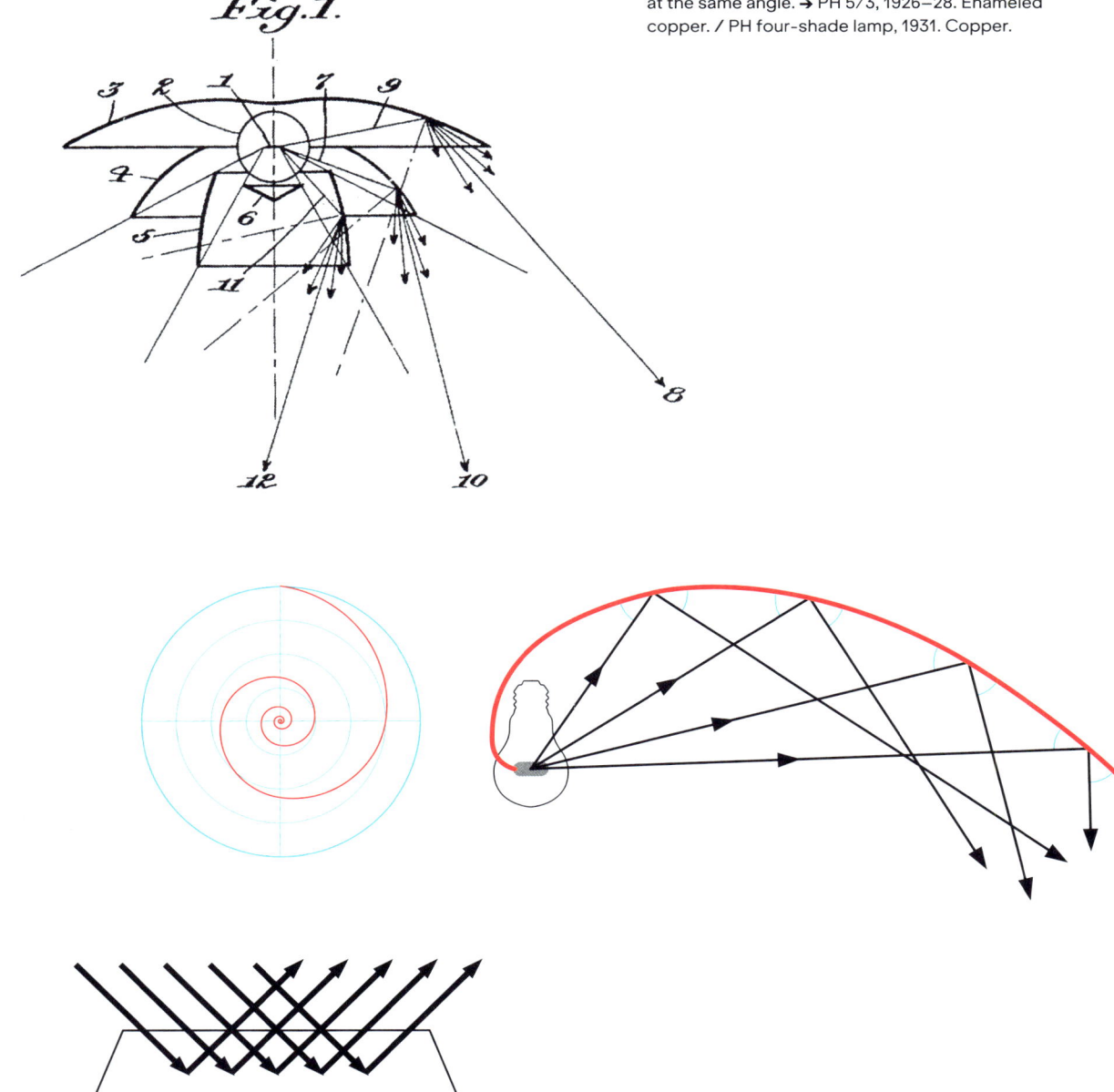

Poul Henningsen. 1927 patent drawing with arrows indicating reflections at a uniform angle. / A logarithmic spiral extends out from the center at a constant angle of rotation. As a result, a surface that follows that spiral will reflect light at a uniform angle. / Light striking a smooth surface is reflected at the same angle. → PH 5/3, 1926–28. Enameled copper. / PH four-shade lamp, 1931. Copper.

The starting point for Poul Henningsen's lamps — from the first to the final — was the fact that light striking a smooth surface is reflected at the same angle. During 1916–24, he designed curved shades that were based on a parabola and reflected light in parallel rays. His breakthrough, in December 1925, was to abandon parabolic curves as the basis of his work and design shades using a logarithmic spiral, in which a line or surface grows at a constant angle. As a result, the angle at which light strikes the spiraling surface also remains constant — and so, too, the angle of reflection. That single angle of reflection made it possible for Henningsen to predict how light would be distributed and to control its direction by rotating the curved shades.[8]

His next challenge was to eliminate direct glare, which occurs when the eye is exposed to a source of light, such as the sun or an incandescent bulb. He realized that goal by stacking three curved shades in such a way that that they block the view of the filament in the light bulb. He referred to the lines between the filament and the shades as *vizier lines*, based on the visors used on medieval armor.[9] While the middle and lower shades are nested, the top of the middle shade is aligned with the bottom of the upper shade. As all three shades are derived from the same curve, the distribution of light along the outer surfaces is consistent, and the shades form a harmonious body. That simple arrangement provided the basis for every PH Lamp, including PH 5.

By the end of 1926, Henningsen and the technical staff at Louis Poulsen had developed an entire family of PH pendant and table lamps for offices, homes and shops.[10] Floor lamps and chandeliers would soon follow. The material for the shades varied from painted copper to translucent glass that would diffuse part of the light and provide a pleasant glow. Colored glass shades were introduced the following year. No matter the material, the lamps were numbered based on the sizes of the shades, with the first numeral corresponding to one-tenth of the diameter of the upper shade and the second number referring to the sizes of the middle and lower shades. For example, PH 3/3 includes an upper shade with a diameter of 30 cm that reflects 50% of the light and two lower shades that are proportioned to the remaining 50% of the light.[11]

During 1929–31, Henningsen developed a four-shade lamp that could be mounted close to the ceiling and illuminate an entire room.[12] To that end, he added an inverted "trumpet" shade that received light from below and directed it towards the walls. The four-shade series was introduced in 1931, in metal or colored glass, but was discontinued in the early 1940s. By that point, the Second World War had broken out and Nazi Germany was occupying Denmark. In autumn 1943, Henningsen and his wife fled to neutral Sweden to escape the planned round-up of Danish Jews and anti-Nazi agitators, such as Poul Henningsen.[13] Arriving in Sweden, he set up a factory to produce pleated paper versions of the PH Lamp. After returning home in 1945, he devoted much of his time and energy to political causes.

During the mid 1950s, Poul Henningsen experienced a creative resurgence and designed a string of fixtures that gave new forms to familiar obsessions. In 1957, he was commissioned to create lamps for the new Langelinie Pavilion, designed by Eva and Nils Koppel and located on the Copenhagen waterfront, near the statue *The Little Mermaid*.[14] Within a few months, he had developed the monumental pendant known as the Pinecone or the Artichoke lamp, which is made of copper leaves with a pink coating on the inside that emits a rosy glow. The other lamp for the pavilion is the Plate, an assembly of copper rings that obscure the bulb and provide reflected light to the table.

The design of the Pinecone was rooted in the Louvre, a smaller fixture of concentric rings that Henningsen had recently designed for the chapel at Skodsborg Sanitorium, north of Copenhagen.[15] The Louvre also provided the starting point for the small fixture known as the Snowball, which was constructed of polished aluminum shades with matt white interiors. Even prior to this burst of activity, he was developing a new pendant for the home that could be suspended at a low height over the table, as he had described in 1928. He named the pendant PH 5.

In April 1958, Henningsen unveiled the Louvre, Snowball and PH 5 in the exhibition *Glas, Lys og Farver* (Glass, Light and Colors), at the Danish Museum of Applied Art (now Designmuseum Danmark).[16] The exhibition was a three-man survey that presented works by Poul Henningsen and two old friends: Jacob E. Bang, artistic director of Kastrup Glassworks, and the painter and scenographer Svend Johansen.

The design of PH 5 was rooted in Henningsen's frustration with what he regarded as the miserable quality of incandescent light bulbs, which he still found lacking in every way, as he had in the 1910s and '20s. In a famous declaration, the designer announced his "conversion" to the reality of incandescent bulb design:

"After 33 years of fairly Christian conduct, I have, as will appear from this booklet, gone over to Islam — in my relationship with incandescent lamp manufacturing. For a lifetime, I believed that consideration for consumers and common sense would prevail, but now, I have become a fatalist. I bow to fate and, with the permission of LP [Louis Poulsen], I have constructed a PH lamp, where you can use anything — a glowworm, Christmas lights and 100 watt metal-filament lamps. However, a fluorescent tube in its current form would be too long.

I hereby abandon all dreams that any incandescent lamp technician would take an interest in quality and produce light with reasonable regard for the characteristics of the human eye. This may also be expressed with a well-established moral tenet: It is no use making demands on others; you must make them on yourself. Or, in lighting terms: The luminaire designer cannot expect the slightest support from the incandescent lamp manufacturers. [...] I have come to this realization during my deep spiritual crises: The luminaire designer must proceed with the incandescent lamp available at any time."[17]

Eva and Nils Koppel. Langelinie Pavilion, Copenhagen, 1954–58. Interior of main dining room with Poul Henningsen's Pinecone and Plate lamps. → PH 5. / Installation view of *Glas, Lys og Farver* (Glass, Light and Colors), Danish Museum of Applied Art (now Designmuseum Danmark), April 1958. Poul Henningsen's three new fixtures were suspended in rows, with the Snowball along the inner wall, the Louvre above the central aisle and PH 5 tucked between partitions along the outer wall and suspended at an extraordinary height.

Comparison of PH 5/3, 1926, and PH 5, 1958.
→ PH 5. / Viggo Johansen, *Aftenpassiar*
(Evening Talk), 1886. Oil on canvas, 142 × 105 cm.
SMK — National Gallery of Denmark.

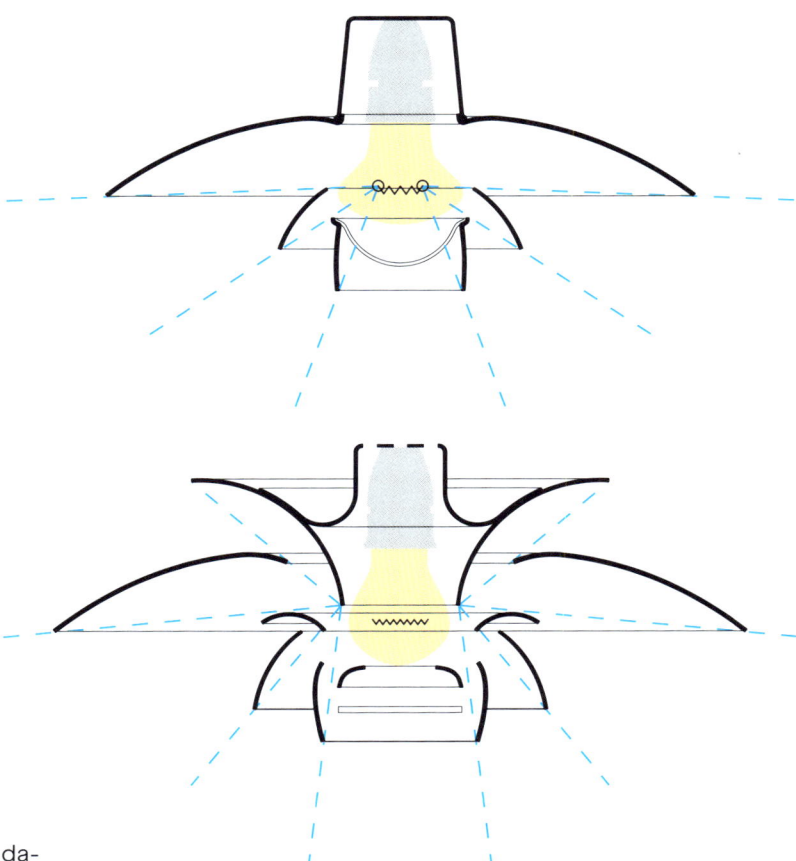

As he designed PH 5, Henningsen solved two fundamental concerns that had preoccupied him since he began working with electric light, circa 1916: direct glare and the perception of color. He realized that solution by combining the three shades of the classic PH lamp with the trumpet shade developed in the 1930s. The precise arrangement of the four shades concealed the bulb without blocking the flow of light:

"When the lamp shade is closed, the fitting can be set in all directions without any risk of producing glare. I hope that the new PH-lamp will delight other people as it delights me when I see its reflection in my coffee cup — ah, well, why should daily life by ugly and prickly and not beautiful and harmonious? Minor issues may grow into major vexations if one does not try to resolve them."[18]

Because the bulb is completely shielded, the fixture could be suspended just above eye level to provide gentle light on the tabletop. The trumpet shade that Henningsen had originally designed to reflect light onto walls would now illuminate the people seated around the table. Moreover, it would play a role in the color of the lighting.

His second concern, beyond the appearance of the bulb, was the character of the light that it emitted and the resulting effect on the perception of color. For all of his mathematical insight, Henningsen had a fundamentally artistic conception of lighting that was rooted in his childhood. As architect and cultural critic Allan de Waal noted, Henningsen was raised by the light of kerosene lamps until the age of thirteen, when he and his mother moved from Roskilde to Frederiksberg, in the center of Copenhagen.[19] De Waal employed Viggo Johansen's painting *Evening Talk* to illustrate the evening atmosphere that Henningsen knew as a boy and explained:

"This warm, subdued kerosene lighting presented the starting point for Poul Henningsen's work with electric light."[20]

And yet, as Henningsen explained in 1928, his goal was not a return to a late nineteenth-century way of life. Instead, he hoped to recreate the cozy evening atmosphere that he had experienced as a child in Roskilde, using warm light with a reddish undertone:

"Over the years, there have been several experiments with colored shades for the PH lamp, which I would prefer to forget all about. [...] The street lighting of the St. Mark's Square in Venice has slightly lilac glass globes. [...] Everything suggests that yellow shades also ought to be banished from people's homes — if they want to be able to see colors in the evening. [...] There is a reason why the daylight is most blue in the middle of the day, when its intensity is at its peak, and most red in the morning and the evening, when it is faint. It is the task of man to bridge the gap between evening and morning with artificial light, and this can hardly be done correctly by imitating the bluish light of noon — it must hold the many reddish rays of the evening and the morning. [...] However, the decisive factor is that the filter we use should accentuate the blue and, in particular, the red ends [of the spectrum] and should never accentuate the yellowish-green middle that is favored by lamp manufacturers."[21]

Henningsen designed PH 5 with the knowledge that the human eye is most sensitive to yellow and green light (an evolutionary trait that made it possible to distinguish between the colors of edible and toxic plants). Designing the first PH lamps in the 1920s, he employed matt white surfaces that would reflect white light containing all of the visible wavelengths: from red to violet. However, a colored surface will reflect light of the same color and absorb wavelengths of other colors. Complementary colors such as red and green or yellow and blue absorb each other.

To boost the perception of red and blue wavelengths and attain his ideal evening light, Henningsen employed colored surfaces within PH 5 that are barely visible from the outside but exert a subtle effect on the light, as it is reflected between the shades. The red ring shade and interior of the trumpet shade suppress green wavelengths by absorbing them and so imbue light with the long wavelengths that Henningsen found comforting and restful. At the same time, the blue surface on the underside of the anti-glare shade absorbs yellow wavelengths and improves our color perception, which is generally desirable when looking at food.

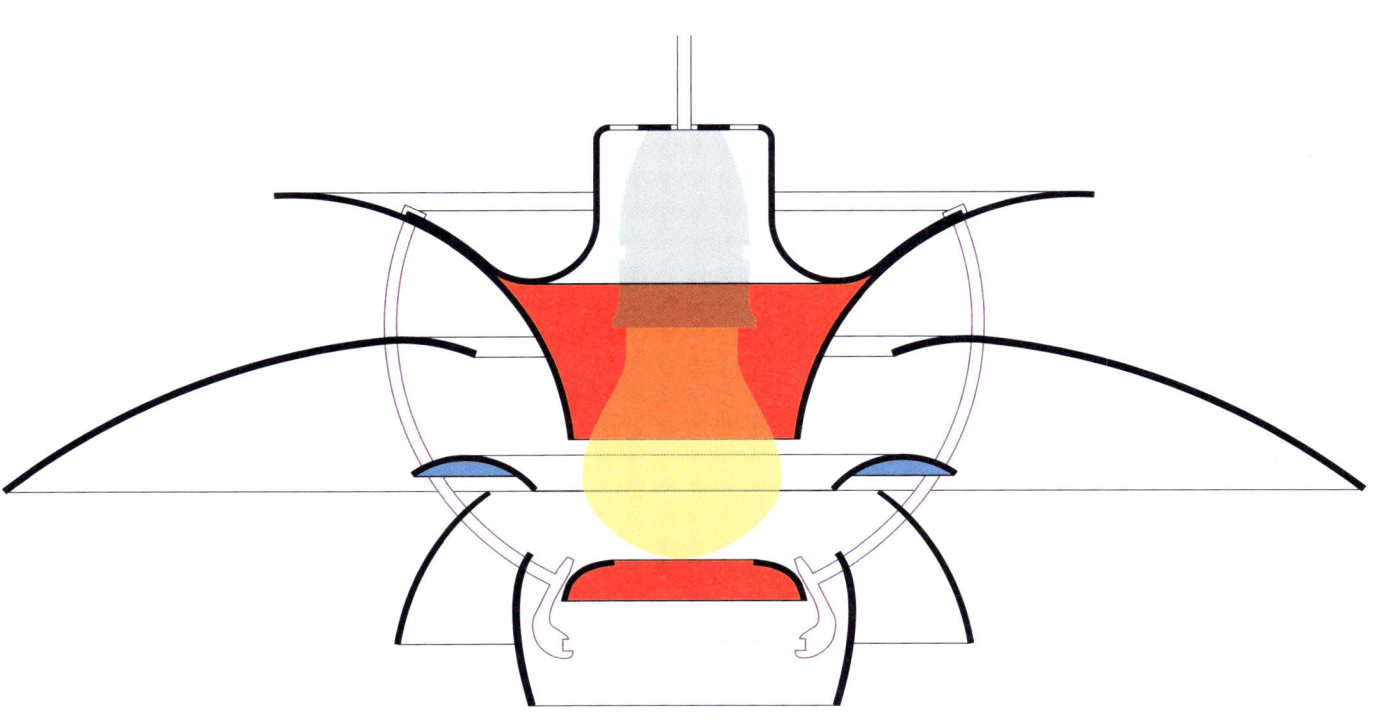

Cross section through PH 5 with colored shades and red interior of the trumpet shade. Poul Henningsen used red and blue surfaces to absorb yellow and green wavelengths of light and shift the tone towards the shades he found most pleasant and relaxing. / Visible light contains a full spectrum of wavelengths, but a colored surface will only reflect light with the same wavelength. → A disassembled lamp reveals the concealed interior shades with colored surfaces. Below: trumpet shade with red interior.

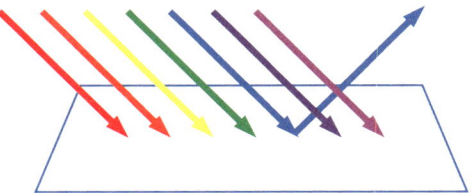

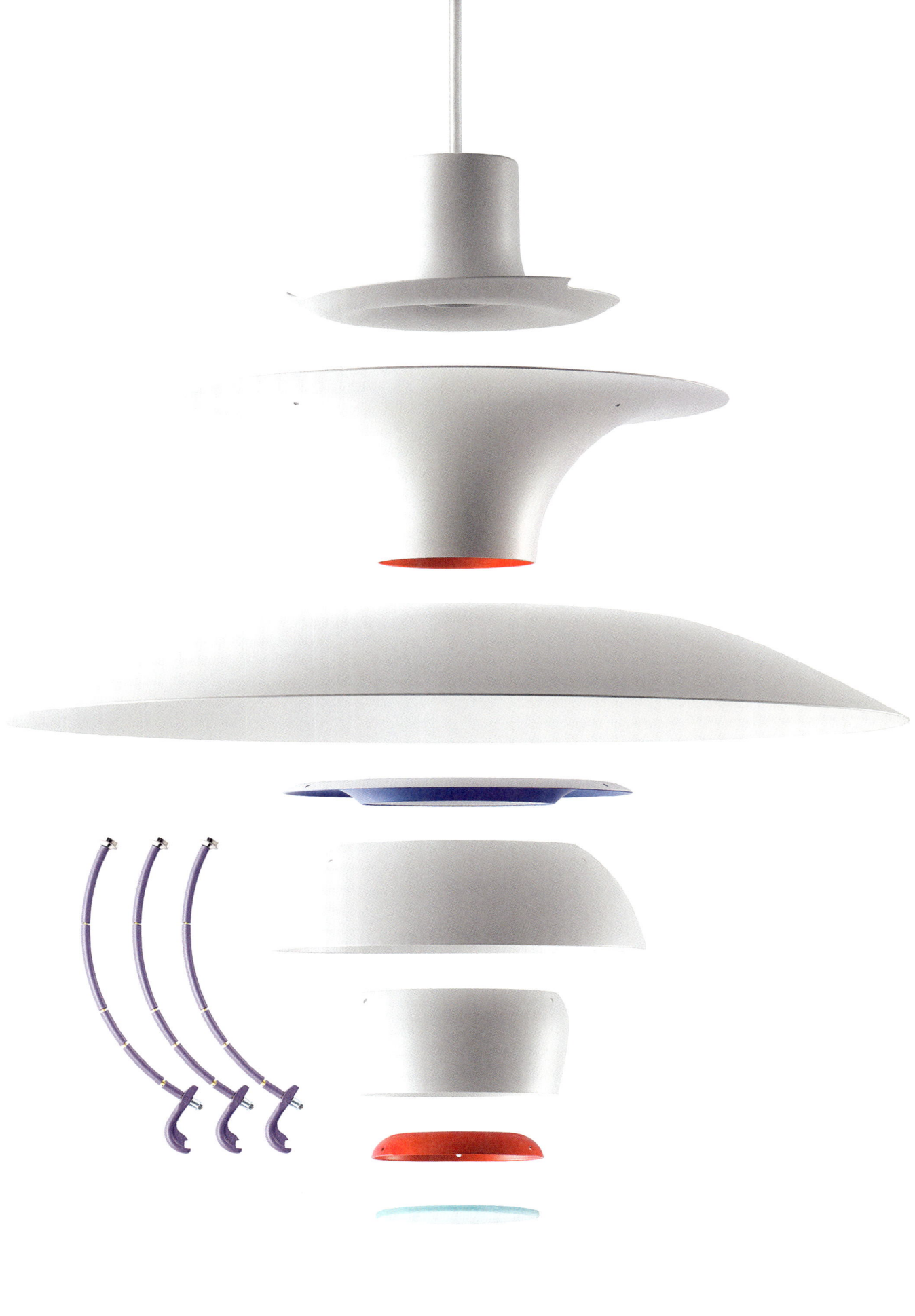

Vintage examples of PH 5 display Poul Henningsen's preferred palette of colors, which correspond to his preferred wavelengths of light. → View of PH 5 with removable top of trumpet shade for changing the bulb. Interior of trumpet shade with red surface for absorbing green and yellow wavelengths.

Beyond the masterful manipulation of light, PH 5 is a small marvel of structural engineering that certainly involved the technicians at Louis Poulsen. The six shades are assembled with three curved brass wires, which are threaded through holes in each shade. Each wire is encased in segments of purple metal tubing that act as spacers and ensure a correct distance between the shades. Moreover, the spacers stiffen the brass wires and create a rigid structure that will not fall to pieces if the lamp falls. After the shades, wires and spacer have been threaded together, the nuts on the top of the trumpet shade are tightened to created a rigid assembly. Changing the light bulb is easily accomplished by rotating the removable cap of the trumpet shade.

With PH 5, Poul Henningsen created his ultimate lamp for the home: an inexpensive industrial fixture that could be used with any type of bulb and which provided gentle evening illumination. It was at once efficient, beautiful and unbreakable. The only problem is that it was somewhat stingy with the dispersion of light.

In his zeal to conceal the light source and prevent glare, Henningsen installed a blue metal cap in the opening of the lower shade that matched the color of the anti-glare shade. As a result, a tabletop only received indirect light from the middle and upper shades and PH 5 gained a reputation as a beautiful lamp that provided limited illumination. In 1999, Louis Poulsen replaced the blue cap with a frosted glass lens that is held in place by extensions to the three curved struts. While the light bulb is still concealed, the glass lens provides diffused light to the tabletop and more fully realizes Poul Henningsen's original intentions for the lamp.

Over the decades, some modifications have been made to the design and construction of PH 5. Due to the complex form, the trumpet shade was originally made of two parts. In 1980, as the light socket was revised to reflect the recently standardized sizes of 60, 75 and 100-watt bulbs, the fabrication of the shade was altered to create a single piece of metal.[22]

PH 5 was initially produced in white, blue, red and lilac versions that corresponded to Poul Henningsen's preferred wavelengths for evening lighting. In the 1970s, lilac was softened to purple, and several colors were added to the palette. More recently, the lamp has been produced in combinations of muted colors and exposed metals, with each shade in a different color or metal. On many of those versions, the red and blue interior surfaces that Henningsen devised to absorb yellow and green wavelengths have been replaced with colors that match the outer shades. As a result, the lamp no longer functions as Henningsen intended, and the character of the design has been lost. Due to its extraordinary popularity, vintage examples in the original colors are numerous and easily found.

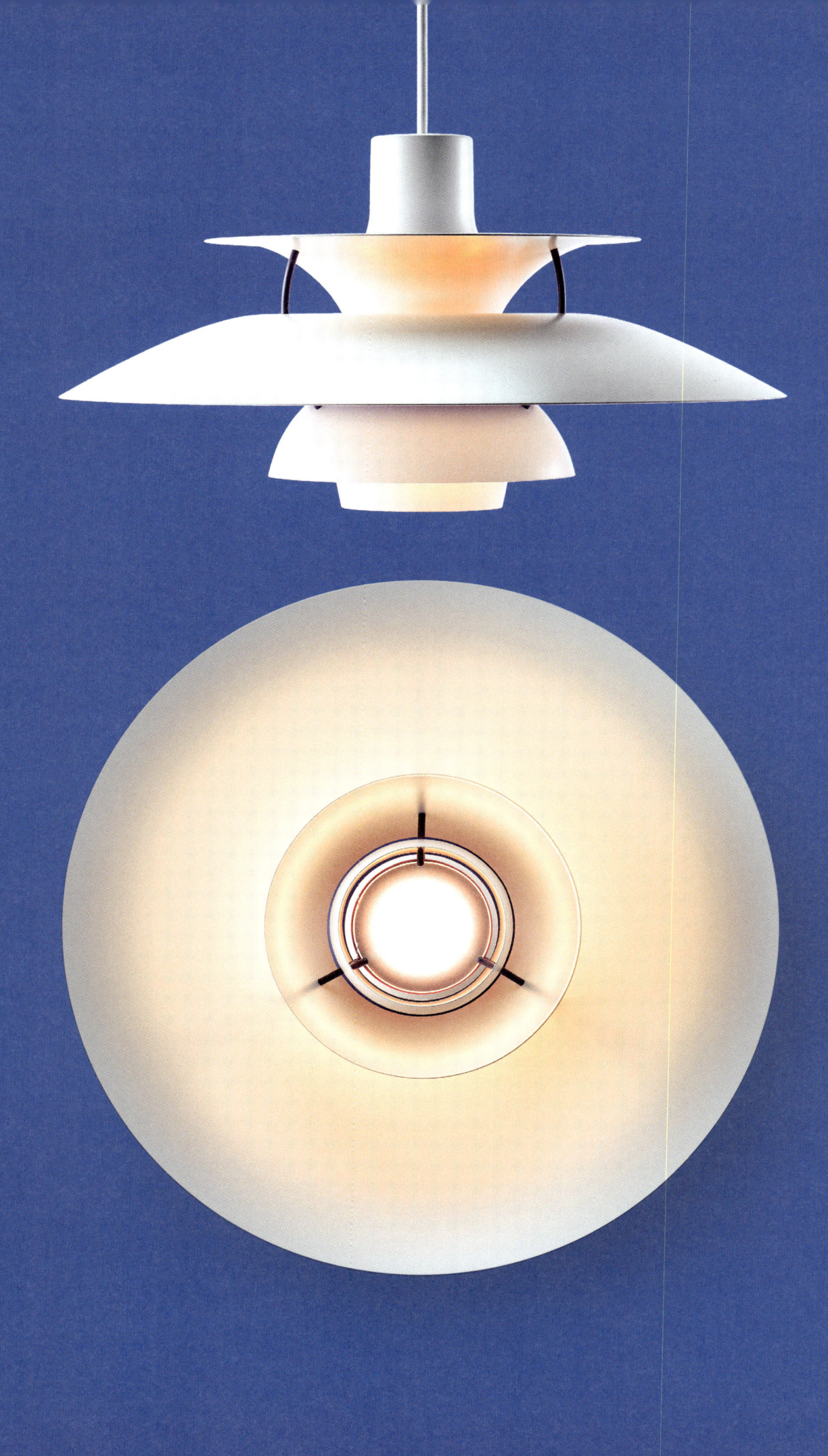

Poul Henningsen continued to develop new lamps based on long-held principles through the early 1960s. Those efforts included PH Contrast, an intricate structure that made is possible to raise and lower the bulb and adjust the color tone of the light. In 1966, as Poul Henningsen was struggling with his final illness, Louis Poulsen introduced PH 4/3, a simplified version of PH 5 that omitted the trumpet shade and internal reflectors in the interests of economy, which became immensely and justifiably popular.

Taking into account Poul Henningsen's formative years in a home illuminated by candles and kerosene and his resulting attempts to domesticate the incandescent bulb, it becomes clear that PH 5 was his most personal lamp. It can also be regarded as his most useful lamp for the home, due to his "conversion" and his decision to conceal the light source. In recent decades, tremendous resources have been devoted to producing LED bulbs that mimic the light of incandescent bulbs. Those new bulbs would have drawn Henningsen's ire for their color tone, particularly the frosted glass bulbs that reduce the output. While clear glass bulbs provide more light (lumens) per watt, they also expose the diodes. But as Henningsen designed his autobiographical masterpiece to even accept a Christmas tree bulb, it will create a cozy atmosphere no matter the light source.

Poul Henningsen, circa 1962, as he contemplates the lamp that embodied his lifelong fascination with cozy evening illumination and can be regarded as a form of autobiography.
← Two views of PH 5.

The essential fact about furniture architect Børge Mogensen is that he was trained as a cabinetmaker in his youth, during 1931–34, in his hometown of Aalborg, the industrial center of northern Jutland.[1] Designing factory-made furniture as an adult, he employed his deep knowledge of wood construction to create improved versions of common types, often refining his designs over the course of several decades. His most practical and versatile dining table — **Fredericia 6286** — was the result of twenty-three years of development that began in the 1940s with his legendary furnishing program for FDB, the joint association of Danish cooperative consumer societies.[2] While the design can be traced to the nineteenth-century religious sect known as the Shakers, Mogensen created an industrial equivalent to handicraft that embodies his unique approach.

Following his apprenticeship in Aalborg, the young journeyman moved to Copenhagen and enrolled in the furniture program at the School of Arts and Crafts, which provided higher education to qualified artisans. His teacher was Orla Mølgaard-Nielsen, who had been Kaare Klint's student at the Department of Furniture Design at the Royal Danish Academy (p. 6). In 1938, Mogensen finished his studies at the School and began attending Klint's lectures at the Academy, although he was not registered as a student. Evidently, Mølgaard-Nielsen recommended Mogensen to his former teacher, because the young man soon found himself enrolled in Klint's department and employed in his design office. He would continue his studies with Klint until 1941 and serve as his teaching assistant during 1945–47, which led to Mogensen's first encounter with future collaborator Grethe Meyer (p. 218).

During 1938–42, Mogensen worked for both Kaare Klint and Mogens Koch, applying his artisanal expertise to their furniture designs and preparing the full-scale working drawings. Along the way, he contributed to Klint's furnishings for Grundtvig Church and Koch's furnishing program for the state hospital in Sønderborg as well as their designs for the annual exhibitions of the Copenhagen Cabinetmakers' Guild.[3] Beginning in 1939, Mogensen participated in the exhibitions more years than not, designing showpieces and interiors for one or more of the master artisans. At the 1940 exhibition, he demonstrated his range in three installations fabricated by different workshops. Beyond his own dining suite of Cuban mahogany, he and Aage Windeleff designed a simpler dining set of the same material and a set of larch furniture for a maid's room: Hanne's Attic.[4]

Børge Mogensen. Fredericia 6286, 1964–66. Oak. 195 x 97.5 x 73 cm. 1:1 scale. The defining feature of Børge Mogensen's simplest and most durable trestle table is the 33-mm-thick top made of solid oak selected for its hardness and stability. The design of the table was based on his twenty years of work with the type and drew on models from the nineteenth-century Shaker sect, whose craftsmen provided Mogensen with enduring standards of beauty and utility.

BØRGE MOGENSEN 1964–66
Fredericia 6286

In 1937, Frederik Nielsen — who had been part of the cooperative movement since the age of sixteen — became managing director of FDB.[5] The association used its purchasing power to reduce the cost of food and other goods sold in its nationwide network of shops. Nielsen was convinced that those goods should include inexpensive, practical furniture that was scaled to ordinary homes and would provide his members with long-term value.[6] Beyond his concerns for economy and utility, Nielsen also had a cultural agenda, in that he hoped to promote a natural and unpretentious approach to furnishing that recalled rural traditions. As Børge Mogensen observed,

"Throughout his life, Frederik Nielsen has carried a sense of utility and the value of traditional qualities that he probably acquired in the farmhouses of his childhood. The servant's hall with the long whitewashed table and sand on the floor, somewhere up there in North Jutland, which he often described so beautifully, might be seen as a symbol of the lost territory that would now be reclaimed through the efforts of FDB."[7]

In pursuit of this ambitious goal, Nielsen enlisted Steen Eiler Rasmussen, professor of architecture at the Royal Danish Academy, to outline a program under which FDB would design, produce and sell its own collection of furniture.[8] According to that program, FDB would establish an independent design office and subcontract production to a network of factories. In place of the typical matching sets for bedroom, living room and dining room, the pieces would be sold individually to allow people to buy only what they needed or could afford. Moreover, the pieces would be devoid of traditional decoration or stylistic associations, so that new purchases were easily combined with earlier purchases or other types of furniture. Following Rasmussen's advice and Klint's assent, Nielsen recruited Børge Mogensen to lead the design office.

Børge Mogensen and FDB Furniture Office, 1944. Two FDB chairs developed on the basis of traditional models. J 52 Windsor armchair and J 12 armchair based on English Sussex type. → FDB model interiors, 1944. Bedroom furnishings and display of Shaker trestle tables with two types of spindleback chair.

Mogensen assumed his new position in October 1942 and quickly developed a program that was rooted in Klint's principles and methods:

"The social task of drawing furniture for regular people suited me, and I had a good legacy to manage in my learning from Kaare Klint. Without it, I would have been at a loss. From the outset, it was clear to me that Kaare Klint's specific requirement that the furniture should, above all, be a utilitarian tool, was indispensable in this case, if I were to realize Frederik Nielsen's idea of giving the regular man his natural environment back."[9]

Mogensen and his small team of assistants divided their furniture program into two categories that corresponded to the type of construction.[10] On the basis of Klint's studies for sideboards and shelving, Mogensen developed a modular system of pine cabinets that could be stacked to provide various types of storage throughout the home. For more technically complex items, such as chairs and tables, Mogensen and his team adopted vernacular models from several countries, including the Windsor chair from Britain and the Swedish spindle-back chair. Rather than design new models, they revised the existing designs to improve their function and align with the demands of factory production. The result was a collection of inexpensive furniture that was vastly superior to any other factory-made furniture available in Denmark.

The first batch of FDB furniture was introduced in 1944 and included a variety of dining tables, most of which had four legs.[11] Mogensen's preferred model was the trestle table that had been developed by members of the United Society of Believers in Christ's Second Appearing — popularly known as the Shakers due to their ecstatic gyrations during worship services — which flourished in the eastern United States circa 1800–60.[12] According to Shaker doctrine, which prohibited private property and required withdrawal into self-sufficient communities, there is no distinction between spiritual pursuits and physical efforts. As such, the construction of a table, broom or any other necessary object was an act of devotion that required perfect handicraft.

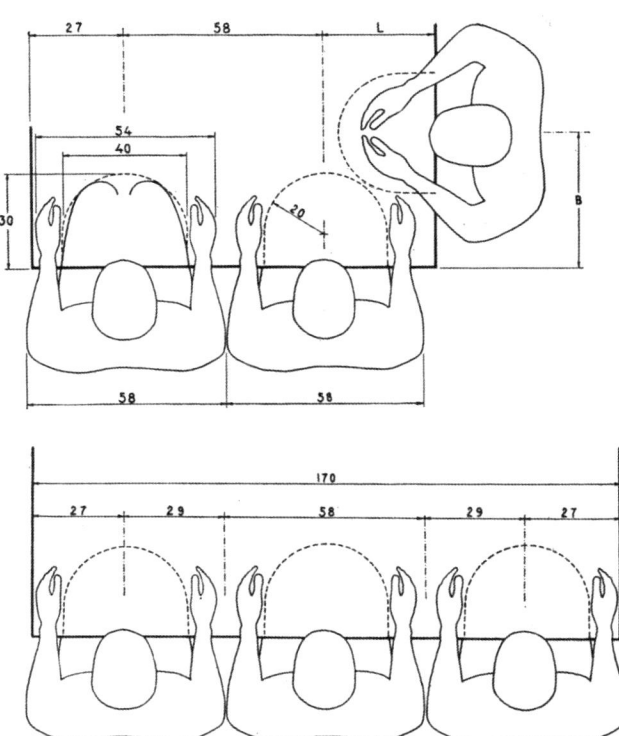

Børge Mogensen. Logo for Fredericia Furniture, 1961. / Erik Berglund. Diagram with spacing of place settings, 1957. Mogensen was so impressed with Berglund's presentation methods that he adopted the graphic style for his own planning diagrams. ← Communal dining room, Hancock Shaker Village, Massachusetts, USA, circa 1830. The Shakers' preoccupation with utility led them to install wooden pegboards on the walls of every room for hanging every sort of item, including chairs, and make it easier to wash the floor. / Børge Mogensen and FDB Furniture Office, C 18 table and J 39 chair, 1947.

Converts to Shakerism often donated simple pieces of furniture, such as trestle tables and ladder-back chairs. Those donations provided prototypes for the sect's craftsmen, who refined them according to the Shaker tenets of utility, modesty and formal purity.[13] The Shakers quickly developed a thriving trade with the "outside world" based on furniture and vegetable seeds. After 1860, a dearth of converts to a faith that required celibacy led to a decline in numbers, such that the sect was generally forgotten by the 1920s. The Shakers were saved from obscurity by the publication of *Shaker Furniture: The Craftsmanship of an American Communal Sect*, in 1937.[14] Four years later, a copy of the book was purchased for the library of the Danish Museum of Applied Art (now Designmuseum Danmark), most likely at the request of Kaare Klint, and found a devoted reader in Børge Mogensen.[15]

In 1947, Mogensen extended the FDB collection with a refined version of his 1944 Shaker table that was designated C 18.[16] He increased the stability of the table by dividing the uprights into two posts with chamfered corners, which protect the knees of those seated at the ends of the table. At the same time, he added a second plank beneath the tabletop that strengthens the entire structure. Produced in solid oak, C 18 became a mainstay of the FDB collection and remained in the catalog for decades, although the top was changed to veneer during the 1950s. To accompany C 18, Mogensen designed a beech chair — J 39 — that was also based on a Shaker model and became the most widely known piece of FDB furniture.

In 1950, Mogensen resigned his position at FDB and established his own design office. Two weeks later, the owners of Søborg Møbelfabrik asked him for a system of storage furniture in the same vein as his work for FDB. By 1955, he had established relationships with a handful of furniture factories and was providing them with a stream of designs that matched their equipment and expertise.[17] The twin pillars of his production were Karl Andersson & Söner, in Huskvarna, Sweden, where he adapted his designs to local woods, and Fredericia Stole- og Polstermøbelfabrik (hereafter Fredericia), located in the eponymous town in Jutland. In Fredericia, Mogensen found his ideal manufacturer in Andreas Graversen, an interior designer who turned to furniture production and purchased a factory in 1955 with the ideal of producing Mogensen's designs.[18]

In the early 1960s, Mogensen returned to the design of dining tables with renewed zeal, using measurements compiled by Erik Berglund, the head of furniture research for the Swedish Society of Arts and Crafts. Berglund's 1957 handbook for designers and manufacturers, *Tables for Meals and Work in the Home*, continued the studies that Kaare Klint had pioneered in the 1920s, with particular attention to the spacing of legs and place settings.[19] Fortified by Berglund's data, Mogensen designed a quartet of tables for Karl Andersson & Söner with solid oak legs and veneered tops that include several of his best works with the type.[20] He reserved his new version of a trestle table for Fredericia, where Andreas Graversen would not only provide him with an ideal sparring partner but also with the finest grade of oak.

The Shakers' development of rural furniture types anticipated Mogensen's work for FDB and provided him with an aesthetic standard. At the same time, his decision to include trestle tables in the FDB furniture program was mostly a matter of utility. He recognized, as the Shakers had before him, that a trestle table with central posts offers several advantages over a conventional table with four legs. Firstly, the absence of legs at the corners makes it possible to use the entire edge of the tabletop and seat more people. Secondly, the absence of a narrow frame beneath the edge of the tabletop (an apron) provides more clearance and makes it possible to push armchairs under the table. Moreover, the structure is at once simpler and stronger than a table with corner legs, which increases durability and saves money at the same time.

Børge Mogensen. Fredericia 6286, 1964–66. Oak. 195 x 97.5 x 73 cm. → Diagram of Fredericia 6286 with comfortable place settings for eight. Posts shown in solid blue.

In 1964, Mogensen channeled two decades of experience designing trestle tables into an immaculately simple oak structure that can be used for many generations. He retained the paired posts and dual planks of his C 18 table from 1947 but employed Erik Berglund's research to refine the dimensions of the tabletop. Mogensen increased the width of the top by 7.5 cm, which might seem a slight difference, but provides extra space for place settings when people are seated at the ends of the table. He also increased the height of the table by 2 cm and designed the top in three lengths: 130 cm (model 6287), 150 cm (6289) and 195 cm (6286).[21] The longest model will comfortably seat eight people. On each model, the 34-cm overhang at either end of the table ensures that persons seated there will not bump their knees on the trestles.

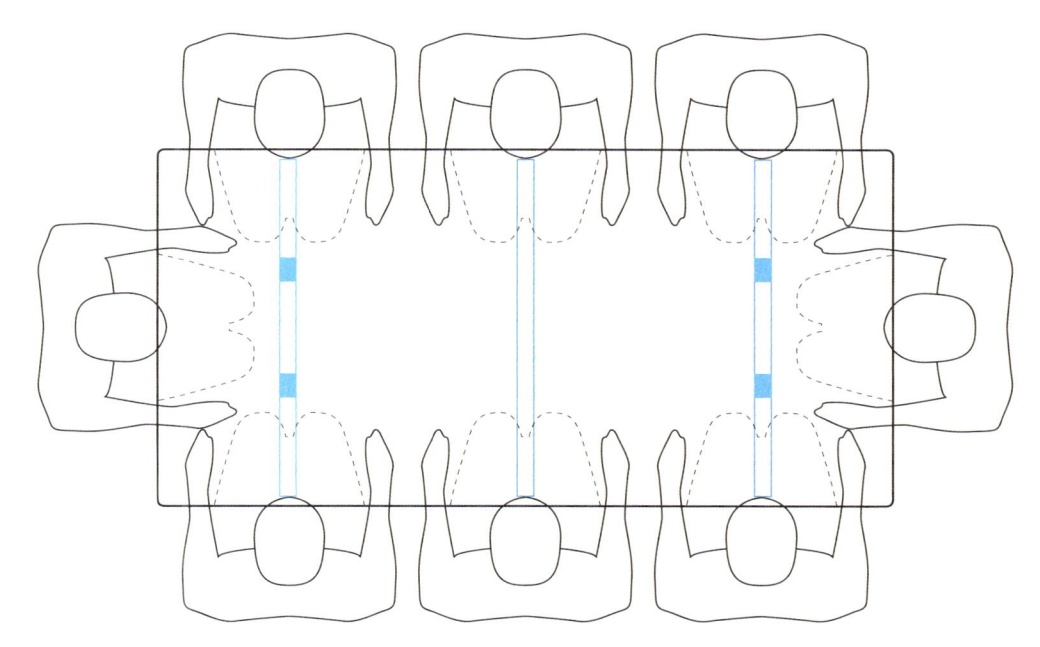

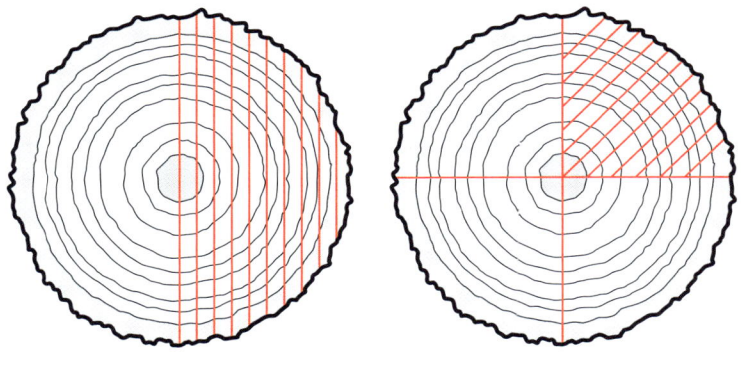

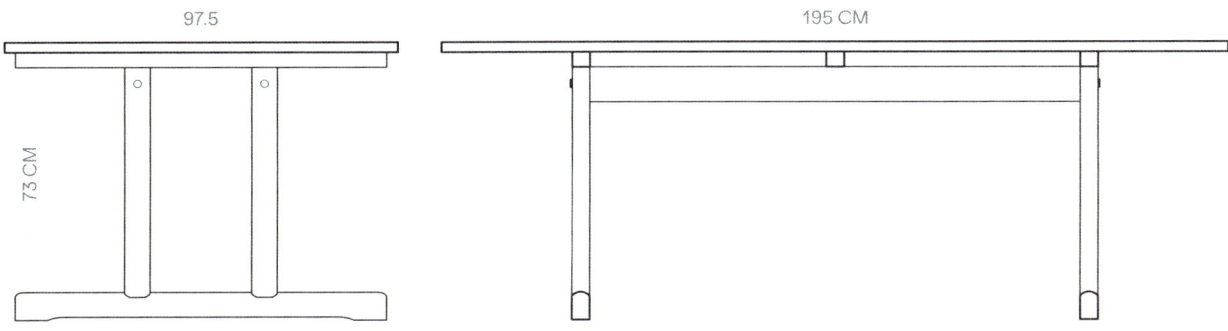

As with his earlier variations on the Shaker model, Mogensen's final trestle table features a top of solid oak. Veneered tabletops are less costly than solid wood but vulnerable to damage from liquids and zealous scouring. Barring a disaster, a solid wood tabletop that appears worn can be sanded and refreshed for additional decades of service.

With that in mind, Mogensen specified the use of quartersawn oak, which requires more labor at the sawmill but produces an especially stable grade of lumber. The most common method of sawing a log is plainslicing it into parallel boards. Because the angle of the wood grain varies considerably, plainsliced boards are vulnerable to changes in humidity and may warp or cup, as sometimes seen on wood floors. When a log is quartered and the quarters turned during sawing, the boards have a fairly consistent grain that is nearly perpendicular to the surface. The parallel grain imparts great strength and the right angle prevents the boards from warping or cupping.

Diagrams of plainsawing and quartersawing techniques for converting logs into lumber. / Side views of Fredericia 6286. 1:10 scale. → Underside of Fredericia 6286. The unusually thick top made it possible to reduce the depth of the crossbars, which reduces obstructions for people seated around the table.

As Mogensen developed his oak structure, he simplified the joints and eliminated any details apart from the shaping of the wooden elements. The ends of the horizontal elements and the outer faces of the posts are gently rounded, to eliminate sharp edges and protect the wood from wear. At the bottom of the trestles, the horizontal elements have projecting feet that ensure stability and make it easier to move the table. While the parts that make up the trestles are joined by mortise and tenon for lasting strength, the trestles are connected to the stretchers and tabletop with wood screws. The result is an immensely durable union of material and form that has the simplicity of traditional handicraft, but was based on practical research and designed specifically for factory production.

With the design of Fredericia 6286, Mogensen arrived at a contemporary equivalent to the Shaker model that he had admired for over twenty years. Comparing the two models, we can recognize the same unity of thought and action, in which the furniture embodies a set of beliefs. While the Shaker cabinetmakers pursued perfect handicraft in the service of their faith, Mogensen pursued an ideal factory-made table in the service of his craft and resulting concern for the people who would live with his furniture. In doing so, he displayed the ethics of the artisan: You are defined by what you make and personally responsible for the quality of your work. In both instances, we find the same concerns for durability, utility and an apparently artless beauty rooted in the construction.

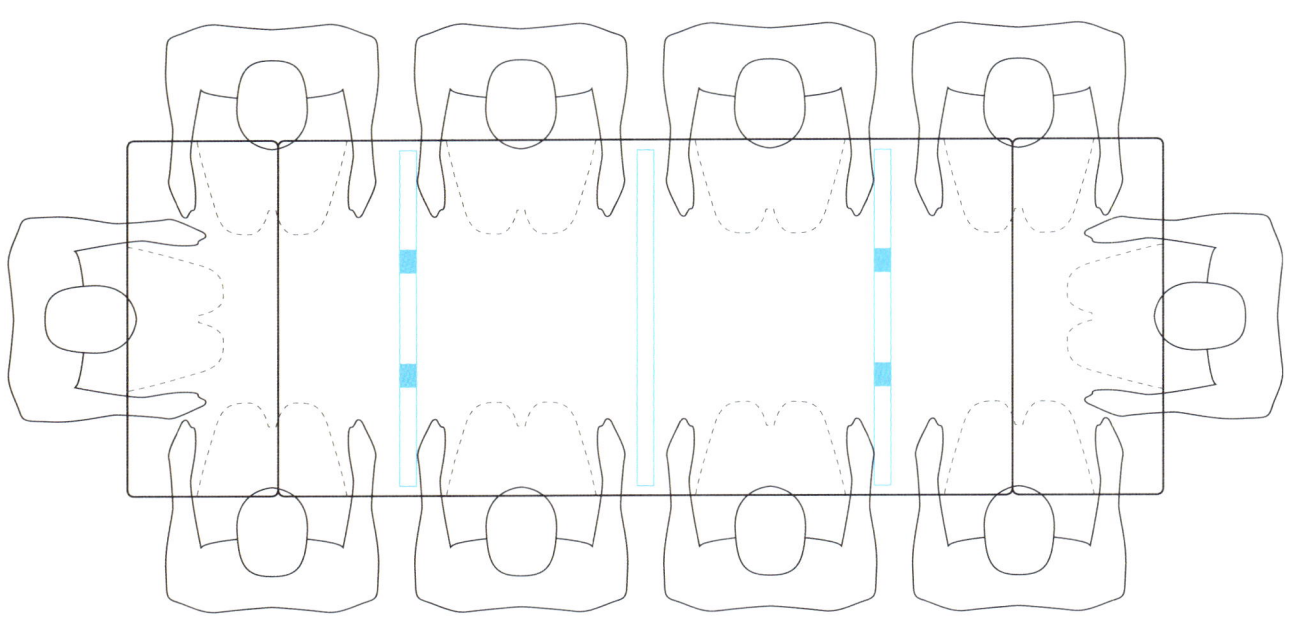

Mogensen's drawings reveal his conviction that a truly useful dining table can be extended for guests and for the nearly infinite variety of household tasks. To that end, most of his tables with four legs have a split top that can be pulled apart and extended with loose leaves. The simple structure of a trestle table precludes a split and sliding tabletop, because the top is attached to the horizontal plank that connects the trestles. Moreover, there is no apron to conceal the sliding mechanism The solution, which Mogensen had previously employed on his C 18 table, in 1947, was a loose plate with battens that fit into metal loops at both ends of the tabletop. The method is inexpensive, due to the absence of moving parts, and also prevents wear and tear on the table.

Seventeen years later, Mogensen replicated that method using better-quality materials. On Fredericia 6286 and its related models, the extension leaves were made of MDF and coated in a durable enamel paint, initially in a deep shade of red.[22] More recently, the leaves have been produced in neutral shades. No matter the color, the leaves are large enough to provide extra place settings and can also be used as a serving station. Through his attention to practical concerns, Mogensen created a table that transcends any single use and can serve as the central piece of furniture in the home. By virtue of its size, 6286 can accommodate a variety of activities at the same time. Moreover, the extension leaves also provide easily cleaned surfaces for children's art projects, food preparation and various household chores.

Diagram of Fredericia 6286 with two extension leaves and comfortable place settings for ten. Posts shown in solid blue. → Underside of tabletop with metal loop and extension leaf with beech stave.

Production of Fredericia 6286 and the smaller versions were discontinued in the early 1980s, due to low sales. Nonetheless, a number of Mogensen's designs for Fredericia remain in production after more than sixty years. Moreover, the company has acquired the rights to a number of his designs that originated with other producers, notably the C 18 table and the J 39 chair. In 2021, Fredericia revived the 6286 table and introduced a new version with a length of 220 cm that will comfortably seat twelve people: 6386. Vintage examples of 6286 and the related tables with solid wood tops can be found on the second-hand market and refurbished, which is also true of Mogensen's Shaker tables from the 1940s.

In 1984, FDB sold the production rights for its designs and exited the furniture business.[23] In 2013, in the wake of successful revivals of Mogensen's FDB designs — by Fredericia Furniture[24] and the design brand Hay — Coop Danmark (formerly FDB) established FDB Møbler. The new company revived Mogensen's J 52 chair (p. 190) along with designs by his successors at the head of FDB's furniture studio: the cabinetmakers Poul M. Volther, Ejvind A. Johansson and Jørgen Bækmark. The success of FDB Møbler spawned a chain of shops and an expanded product range that includes the new version of Grethe Meyer's Ildpot cookware (p. 116).

Børge Mogensen's work for FDB laid the foundation for most of his later furniture by fusing two opposite approaches. On the one hand, he was transformed into an industrial designer whose designs were enriched by his knowledge of handicraft. On the other hand, his association with Frederik Nielsen renewed Mogensen's connection to the rural culture that he left behind when he moved to Copenhagen and enrolled in the School of Arts and Crafts. Mogensen was not a religious man, but his description of working with Nielsen recalls the union of belief and action that guided the Shaker craftsmen:

"Through Frederik Nielsen's conscious sense of tradition and my own sense, which at that time was more unconscious, we developed a spiritual connection that shaped the furniture resulting from our collaboration. I too come from a farming background in North Jutland, and despite my youth, I suppose this legacy was reflected in the designs. Later, as the urban environment enhanced my expertise, I have often looked back to the FDB furniture, and despite their, perhaps, somewhat more naive aspect, I do see something genuine in them that I find difficult to maintain in my current work."[25]

During 1950–72, Børge Mogensen pursued an industrial equivalent of vernacular furniture that would have the same utility and simplicity as the historical models that he so admired. The most direct expression of that pursuit is the trestle table that he based on the Shakers' model and distilled to its essence — Fredericia 6286. Other examples include the pioneering storage system that Mogensen designed with Grethe Meyer (p. 218), which was rooted in his work for FDB; the adjustable lounge chair that he specifically designed for industrial production (p. 234); and the folding deck chair that constituted his final masterpiece (p. 304).

> Børge Mogensen at his drawing table, 1964.
> ← MDF extension leaf with parts of Eva Trio and Ildpot. The exposed corners are rounded to prevent injury, and the rounding is mirrored on the other corners for a balanced appearance.

Living

Rooms

Inspired by homemade Christmas ornaments, Mogens Koch created a pleated paper lantern that radiates warm diffused light and displays the mastery of geometry that characterized his work as an architect and as a designer. In high school, Koch studied mathematics with more enthusiasm than aptitude.[1] But he discovered his special gift under the tutelage of his architect-uncle Hans Koch: a mathematical genius devoted to intricate patterns and three-dimensional forms, who is now best remembered for his partnership with Carl Petersen, the architect of the Faaborg Museum, on the island of Funen.[2]

In 1918, Carl Petersen was appointed to a professorship at the School of Architecture within the Royal Danish Academy and moved into his official apartment in Charlottenborg Palace, where he set up his architectural practice with Hans Koch. Mogens Koch had entered the school the previous year and was soon recruited as their assistant. He was already aware of his uncle's enchanting paper ornaments from family gatherings, but would now learn the arcane technique of creating them. As his cousin Peter (Hans Koch's son) recalled,

"In their spare time, Hans Koch and Carl Petersen competed to invent, draw and fold regular and semi-regular polyhedra, by their own account completely surpassing Archimedes. In private, H. Koch struggled with the triangulation of the angle; MK was one of the few who were initiated into this secret knowledge."[3]

Neither Hans Koch nor Carl Petersen reached the age of fifty, and both were gone by 1923. In their absence, Mogens Koch fell into the orbit of their former associates Ivar Bentsen and Kaare Klint; Klint had designed furniture for the Faaborg Museum.[4] Upon completing his studies, in 1925, Koch joined Klint's office, where he would spend five years working on interiors for the Danish Museum of Applied Art (now Designmuseum Danmark) and Copenhagen City Hall, a vast amount of furniture and a series of small items for churches.[5] In the process, Koch collaborated with a variety of artisans — weavers, cabinetmakers, upholsterers, silversmiths, bookbinders — and gained insight into their materials and techniques. In 1927, he married Edel "Ea" Varming, a weaver who would enrich his understanding of textiles and produce his most notable works in the field. Koch left Klint's office to gain experience on large building projects, but his accumulated knowledge of handicrafts would sustain him during the early years of his own practice and shape all of his later work.

Hans H. Koch. Christmas decorations, circa 1918.
→ Mogens Koch. Le Klint 105, 1942. Paper. Height 39 cm, diameter 32 cm. 1:1 scale.

In 1932, after two years with Povl Baumann and Ole Falkentorp, Mogens Koch established his own architectural practice.[6] Over the following decade, he cobbled together an income by teaching technical drawing and surveying, drafting for Kaare Klint, designing a few small houses, restoring a historic home in Hamburg and working with various forms of handicraft. In 1933, Koch won prizes for textile designs in a competition for church furnishings and made his first appearance at the annual exhibitions of the Copenhagen Cabinetmakers' Guild, with the carpets that Ea Koch had woven to his designs.[7] In 1935, he presented his first pieces of furniture at the Guild exhibitions, where he later displayed prototypes of a chair and a table (pp. 292, 256). In 1937, he took a part-time job with the Society for Ecclesiastical Art and was soon assisting the Association for the Promotion of Needlework.[8] And so it was that by 1942, Mogens Koch was impeccably qualified to assemble the exhibition of Danish handicrafts that led him to design a pleated paper lantern with an ideal geometric form.

MOGENS KOCH 1942

Le Klint 105

In October 1942, *Danskt Konsthantverk* (Danish Handicrafts) opened at the National Museum in Stockholm. The exhibition was initiated by the Swedish government, as a sign of solidarity with its beleaguered neighbor, which had been occupied by Nazi Germany since April 1940.[9] At the invitation of the National Museum and the Swedish Society for Crafts and Design, Vilhelm Slomann (director of the Danish Museum of Applied Art) assembled an advisory committee that included architects Kay Fisker, Kaare Klint and Steen Eiler Rasmussen.[10] That committee chose Mogens Koch to curate and install a selection of recent Danish handicrafts and designs that would form a cohesive cultural statement. Working with a schedule of five months and an equally tight budget, Koch gathered objects from a wide range of workshops and factories and expanded the program to include graphic arts and factory-made furniture.

In Stockholm, *Danish Handicrafts* was at once a popular and a critical success, with a great many visitors and a series of admiring reviews that lavished special praise on the furniture.[11] In Copenhagen, the exhibition infuriated the leading manufacturers of porcelain, glass and silver, who bitterly resented Koch's authority to select items based on his cultural criteria, rather than their marketing strategies; despite the fact that all of them were represented in the exhibition. Angry letters appeared in the press, accusing Koch of being a "dictator" — an outrageous slur in a country under Nazi occupation — who represented a "clique" (presumably the circle around Kaare Klint) and selected the items based on his own taste.[12] But, as Koch explained, personal taste is an unreliable basis for assembling an exhibition, because it changes over time. His standard of selection had been a natural relationship between purpose, material and form.[13]

Beyond the quality of the objects, several Swedish critics praised the lighting and exhibition design. Koch had obscured the museum's ornate neo-Renaissance interior with hectares of draped canvas, creating tent-like rooms that provided neutral backdrops for items of varied sizes and materials. While most of the rooms were illuminated with glass pendants designed by Arne Jacobsen, Vilhelm Lauritzen or Poul Henningsen, Koch designed a pleated paper lantern for the silver gallery that provided diffused light and enhanced the luster of the polished metal. In an apparent favor to Kaare Klint, Koch credited the lantern solely to the manufacturer, which resulted in some confusion among the reviewers as to who had designed the lantern:

"Finally, mention should be made of the excellent luminaire, which had been arranged in a spiritual way in all the exhibition halls. Poul Henningsen's PH lamps — deeply appreciated in Sweden — appeared here in a new, successful design, and Tage Klint's pleated paper lanterns in the silver gallery were the best of their kind that I have ever seen. They created an absolute sensation at the show."[14]

Mogens Koch drawing the pleated paper lantern that would become known as Le Klint 105, August 1942. → Installation view of *Danskt Konsthantverk* at the National Museum in Stockholm, October 1942. Silver gallery with Mogens Koch's lantern and trestle tables designed by Gunnar Biilmann-Petersen.

Mogens Koch's lanterns were even more prominent in the second showing of the exhibition, now titled *Dansk Kunsthaandværk*, which opened at the Danish Museum of Applied Art in January 1943.[15] Koch not only re-created the silver gallery from the Stockholm installation but also used a string of lanterns to guide visitors through the furniture section. The room devoted to Kaare Klint's work included a mahogany table lamp with a pleated paper shade produced by his older brother, Tage Klint, which had also appeared in Stockholm.

Towards the end of 1943, Kaare Klint wrote a brief text that traced the origin of his brother's enterprise to a petroleum lamp created by their father, the architect and engineer P.V. Jensen-Klint.[16] Working from a traditional example, circa 1901, Jensen-Klint devised a pleated paper shade that would diffuse the harsh light from the flame but struggled to develop a stiff collar that would hold the shade in place. In time, it was found that diagonal folds between the pleats made it possible to bend the paper at a right angle and create a collar that was secured with string. Over the next several decades, even as petroleum was replaced by electricity, members of the Klint family would fold paper lampshades for their own use and as gifts for friends.

Installation view of *Dansk Kunsthaandværk* at the Danish Museum of Applied Art (now Designmuseum Danmark), Copenhagen, January 1943. The room devoted to Kaare Klint's work included the wooden table lamp with a paper shade produced by his brother, Tage Klint. → Mogens Koch, Le Klint 105. Recent production. / Kaare Klint. Table lamp (later Le Klint 1), 1942. Mahogany with later shade. / Kaare Klint. Bethlehem Church, Copenhagen, 1930–38. View of nave with the pleated paper lanterns that Klint designed based on a traditional Japanese model.

Kaare Klint was the first to imagine a wider audience for the family lampshade. In 1927, he tested large versions in the lecture hall at the Danish Museum of Applied Art but finally hired Poul Henningsen to design fixtures using his new three-shade system (p. 147).[17] In 1937, Klint hoped to illuminate the interior of his new Bethlehem Church in Nørrebro, Copenhagen, with Japanese temple lanterns made of mulberry paper that were nearly two meters high. After the building committee rejected that idea, he designed pleated paper columns modeled on the Japanese specimens, with rounded ends that employed Hans Koch's cross-pleating technique.[18] Klint had learned the arcane technique twenty years earlier, while assisting Carl Petersen on an art gallery and participating in meetings of Koch and Petersen's "Polyhedra Club."[19]

By 1937, Tage Klint imagined a commercial production of pleated paper lampshades and cajoled his teenage daughter Lise "Le" and several of her friends into doing the laborious handwork.[20] The next year, he invented a machine that could emboss the intricate pattern of folding lines on a sheet of paper, which made it possible to mass-produce the shades. By 1942, he had improved the shade with a cross-pleated collar and edge, for added stiffness, and patented an ingenious wire frame that connected the shade to the lamp socket. Koch's exhibition in Stockholm offered Tage Klint a golden opportunity to promote his budding enterprise, and Kaare Klint promptly designed a table lamp for his brother's shade, so that it could be included in the furniture section. Moreover, Tage Klint could produce Koch's lanterns for the silver gallery.

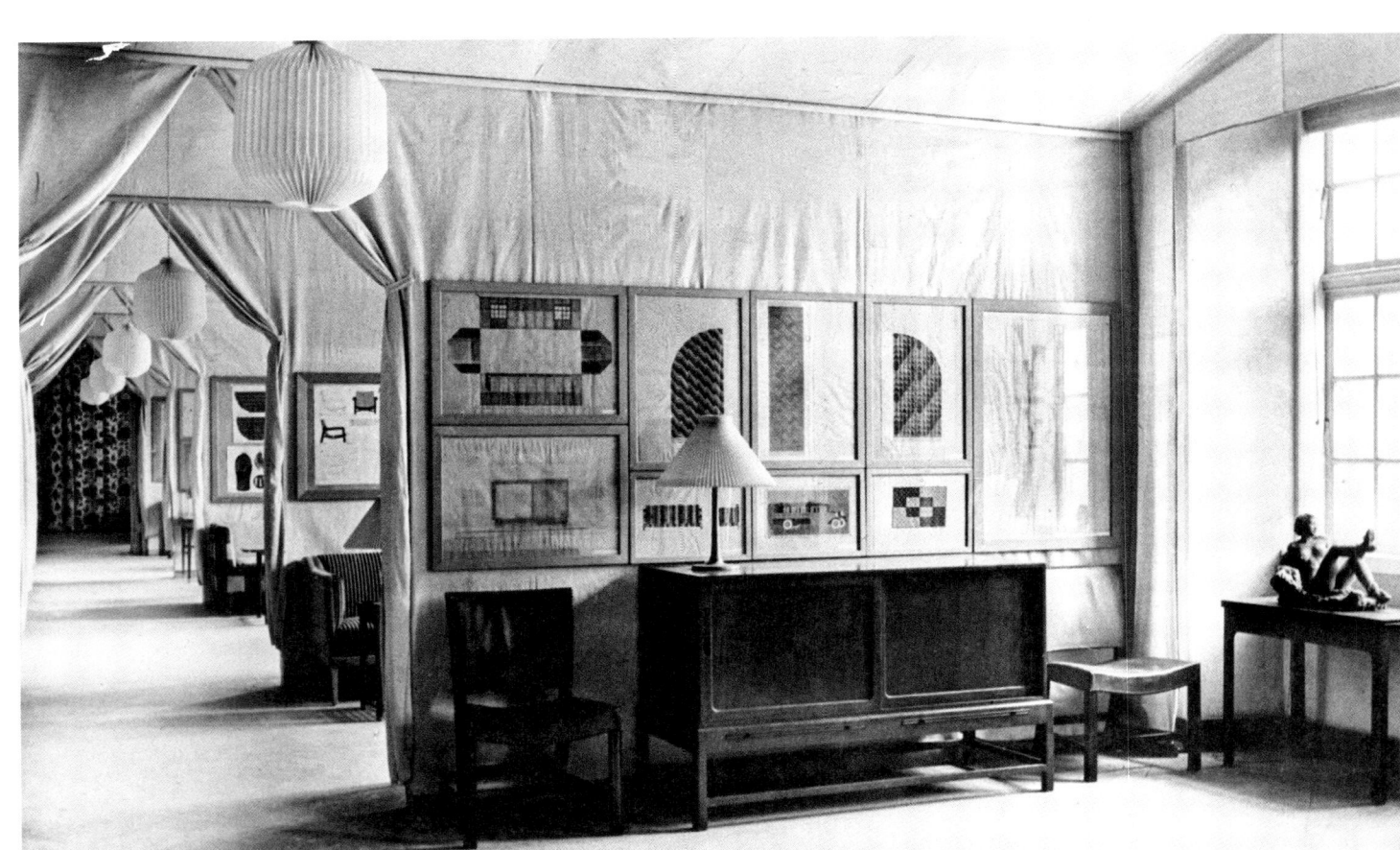

The lantern that Mogens Koch created for *Danish Handicrafts* was typical of his designs of useful objects, in that he used a geometric formula to determine the form, proportions and details. Geometry allowed Koch to create patterns and structures that are based on an inner logic and devoid of an artistic signature. As a result, many of his designs appear inevitable, as if they were simply discovered in the process of studying the task and material at hand, which is essentially how he worked.

One of Koch's primary sources was the visual manual written and illustrated by the Renaissance artist Albrecht Dürer and published in 1525, with a title that can be roughly translated as *Instruction in Measurement with Compass and Ruler in Lines, Planes and Solid Bodies*.[21] In the final part of Dürer's manual he describes the five geometric bodies (polyhedra) with identical faces that are known as the Platonic solids; one of them provided the basis for Koch's lantern. He surely knew the manual from his time with Hans Koch and Carl Petersen — Dürer had been the first to "unfold" polyhedra into two-dimensional patterns that can be cut from a sheet of paper and folded into three-dimensional forms.

As Mogens Koch learned from Hans Koch, the secret to folding paper into a complex three-dimensional shape is the use of diagonal folds between the parallel pleats — cross-pleating. Those diagonal folds allow the parallel pleats to bend and change direction to ultimately form a closed body. However, the folding angles must be consistent and are subject to the rule of the triangle: the sum of the three angles is 180°.

Koch based the design of his lantern on the icosahedron, a twenty-sided shape made of equilateral triangles. Among the five Platonic solids, the icosahedron most closely approximates its internal sphere, which makes it excellent for diffusing light from a central point. Rather than use the twenty-sided shape as a model, Koch adapted it to the cross-pleating technique and created his own faceted polyhedron, which is based entirely on 30° and 60° angles.

Koch began with a rectangular sheet of paper (200 x 58 cm) and divided it into seventy-two strips of equal width. By folding those strips at an angle of 60°, he arrived at a cylinder of thirty-six vertical pleats with a diameter of 32 cm, which determined the width of his lantern. He reserved the central portion of those pleats (50%) for a horizontal band that provides stiffness to the lantern and diffuses most of the light sideways. Above and below the band, diagonal folds — cross-pleats — allow the vertical pleats to bend by 30° at two points and taper toward the vertical axis, to complete a form with a height of 40 cm.

Folding the extra material at the top and bottom of the form produced rigid collars that were initially tied with string and later fixed with a wire ring. After the folding was completed, the two ends of the paper sheet were sewn together to create a rigid structure. Through his mastery of mathematics, Koch created a rigid, three-dimensional pattern of folded surfaces that provides maximum diffusion of light with a minimum weight and use of material. That faceted body delights the eyes as well as the mind.

The five Platonic solids include the icosahedron (second from bottom) that provided the basis for Mogens Koch's lantern. / Koch's transformation of icosahedron with the original solids at left: side views and top views. → Half-model of Le Klint 105. The cross-section through the lantern reveals the diagonal pleats above and below the central band that comprises 50% of the lantern and ensures excellent diffusion of light.

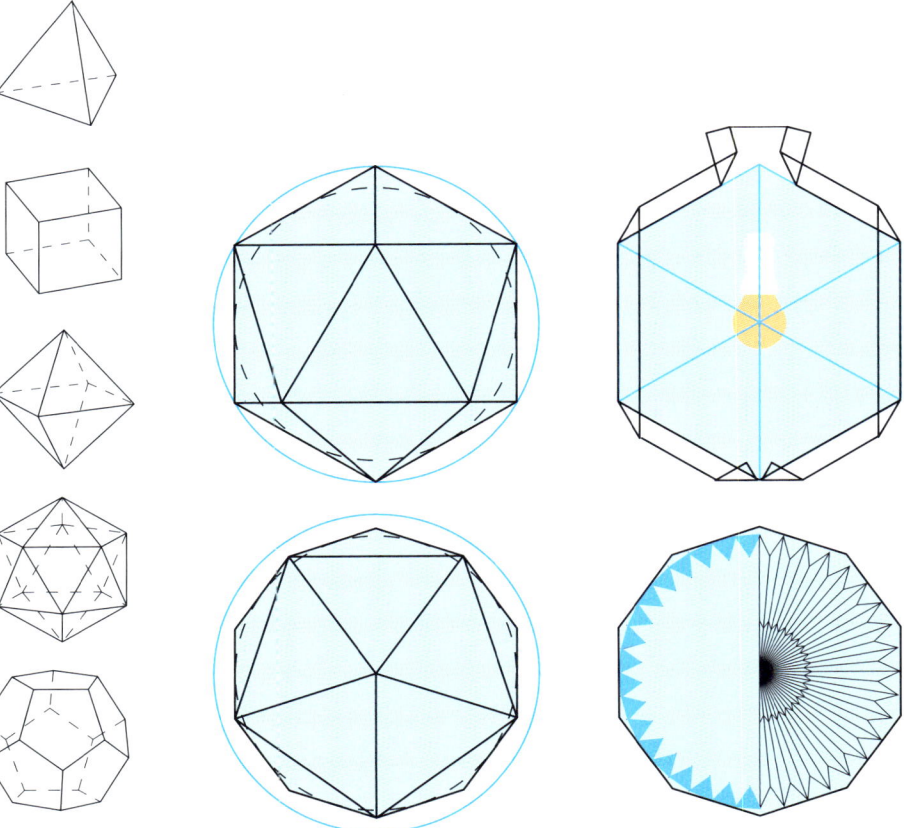

Koch's lantern has a mutable character that varies with the brightness of the room and level of illumination, shifting back and forth between opaque shell and translucent screen. When the lamp is off, the lantern is a decorative object that captures every nuance of ambient light and reveals the wonders of solid geometry. When it is switched on, the pleated surface appears to dissolve into a three-dimensional mesh of folded edges. As the edges nearer the lamp become brighter and less distinct, the projecting edges appear as a web of darker lines that give tangible form to immaterial light, so that it becomes part of the space. The effect can be tailored to the hour and atmosphere using a dimming switch to adjust the brightness.

The glare-free lighting that radiates from the translucent shell is indivisible from the faceted surface. The most common sources of diffused lighting are translucent globes of glass or plastic. While a thinner material transmits more light, it also produces a hot spot; a thicker material will prevent the hot spot but also reduce the transmission of light. Koch's equilateral pleats scatter the light within the lantern at so many angles that it creates an even level of illumination. On the exterior, the multitude of pleats breaks up the bright surface and prevents the sharp contrast with the surroundings that results in glare. As such, we can recognize the same unity of purpose, material and form that guided Koch's selection of objects for *Danish Handicrafts*.

The neutral character of Koch's lantern is illustrated by a comparison with Kaare Klint's lantern for his Bethlehem Church. In 1938, Klint created a site-specific design with a slim proportion that would harmonize with the narrow vaults of the sanctuary. In 1942, Koch created a placeless, abstract form akin to his tent-like exhibition rooms within the Swedish National Museum. To that end, he based the design on the size of a paper sheet and the laws of solid geometry. The form that resulted from those two factors has an objective beauty that recalls natural structures, such as crystals, pinecones and spiral shells, each of which is also governed by a simple mathematical formula. As a result of that neutral character, which is devoid of stylistic references, Koch's lantern is compatible with any setting.

In October 1945, Koch created a slightly smaller version of the lantern for rooms with lower ceilings than the National Museum, as are found in most homes. By reducing the width of the pleats by 19%, he preserved the original proportions and arrived at a lantern with a diameter of 26 cm and height of 31 cm. In time, the smaller model would become known as **105a**, while the larger was designated **105b**. Already, Koch's original lantern had bolstered Tage Klint's commercial ambitions and become a source of fascination for Kaare Klint, whose brother pressured him to create new designs for paper lanterns.[22]

Two states of Mogens Koch's lantern. When the lantern is switched off, it provides an abstract decoration that appears to shift in density and visual weight according to the position of the observer. When it is illuminated, Koch's ideal geometric object gives tangible form to immaterial light and provides gentle, even illumination that is indivisible from the room, due to the pleats that project and recede at the same time.

Lise "Le" Charlotte Klint with Mogens Koch's apparently magic lantern. Probably taken in Stockholm during 1944.
/ Mogens Koch. Le Klint 105. Recent production.
→ Installation view of *Le Klint Lampeskærme*, Svenskt Tenn, Strandvägen 5, Stockholm, May 1944. While Mogens Koch provided a drawing for the cascade of his lanterns, Estrid Ericson provided the blue shantung silk that formed the backdrop. The exhibition designer was architect Jørn Utzon, who emphasized the handcrafted origin of the shades by decorating the room with straw mats from Bali and woven baskets from Mexico. The centerpiece of his design was a display of Kaare Klint's Fruit Lamp under a small canopy, which included several of the early, colored examples that were printed by hand.

The lavish praise that greeted Koch's lantern in Stockholm and the publicity generated by the exhibition in Copenhagen catalyzed Tage Klint's ambition to establish a lampshade company. He named that company after his daughter Lise, using her nickname: Le Klint Lampeskærme. In October 1943, he opened a small shop on Store Kirkestræde, in central Copenhagen, which was designed and furnished by his brother Kaare and a young Vilhelm Wohlert; Koch arranged the display of shades and lanterns.[23] The shop remains in place, absent the original interior.

In 1944, Tage Klint dispatched his daughter Le and some lampshades on a promotional visit to Stockholm. After a chance encounter, she and Danish refugees Jørn and Lis Utzon spent some days and nights folding additional shades and lanterns for an exhibition at Svenskt Tenn, the city's premier shop for home furnishings.[24] When the exhibition opened in May, visitors encountered an array of Koch's lanterns and the first examples of the **Fruit Lamp** that Kaare Klint had designed a few months earlier.[25] Klint had also worked with a Platonic solid, but generated a vastly more complex shape that reflected his delight in solving the most difficult problems he could create for himself. A comparison of the pleated masterpieces underscores Koch's pursuit of the simplest possible form that would suit the purpose and display the character of the material.

Le Klint's promotional visit to Stockholm was a direct challenge to Poul Henningsen, who had been there since October 1943, after fleeing Denmark on account of his anti-Nazi activism. He quickly set up a small factory to produce pleated paper versions of his three-shade lamps and applied for a Swedish patent on the underlying technique, which was granted.[26] By early 1945, he had designed a ten-sided, pleated paper globe that was difficult to distinguish from the Fruit Lamp exhibited at Svenskt Tenn. In 1946, Louis Poulsen A/S began production of the **PH Globe** in four sizes and several colors. But in fact, Tage Klint had already filed a lawsuit against the company, alleging plagiarism.[27]

During the trial, both parties acknowledged that the actual inventor of cross-pleated spheres was Hans Koch, who had failed to patent his technique before his death.[28] As such, Louis Poulsen could continue producing the PH Globe, but it was discontinued by 1950. Henningsen returned to his work with metal shades, eventually designing the **PH 5** pendant (p. 174). Wary of further trials, Tage Klint copyrighted his products and received a patent for a durable plastic material that can be pleated like paper but is easier to clean and also flameproof.[29] While Le Klint would continue to produce paper shades and lanterns, the plastic film eventually became the more popular material.

Assembly hall of the Royal Danish Academy of Fine Arts, Charlottenborg Palace, Copenhagen, 1956. Pleated paper and bamboo. Constructed by Mogens Koch. / Mogens Koch. Sketch for three-lantern fixture, November 1948. / Top view of fixtures with three or six lanterns. 1:20 scale. → Le Klint 105 seen from below.

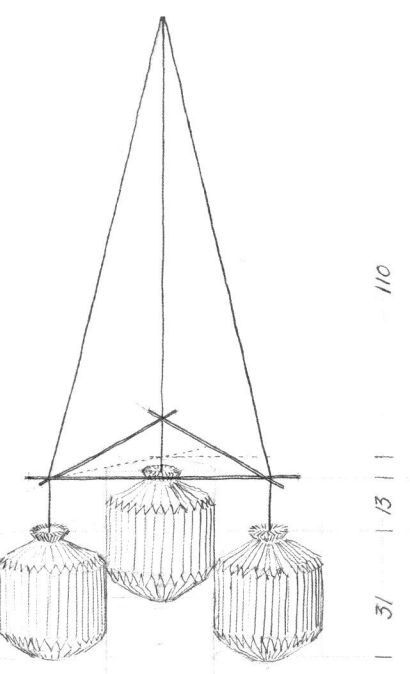
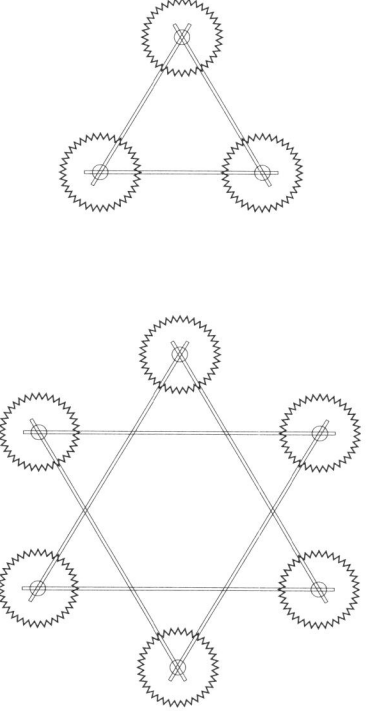

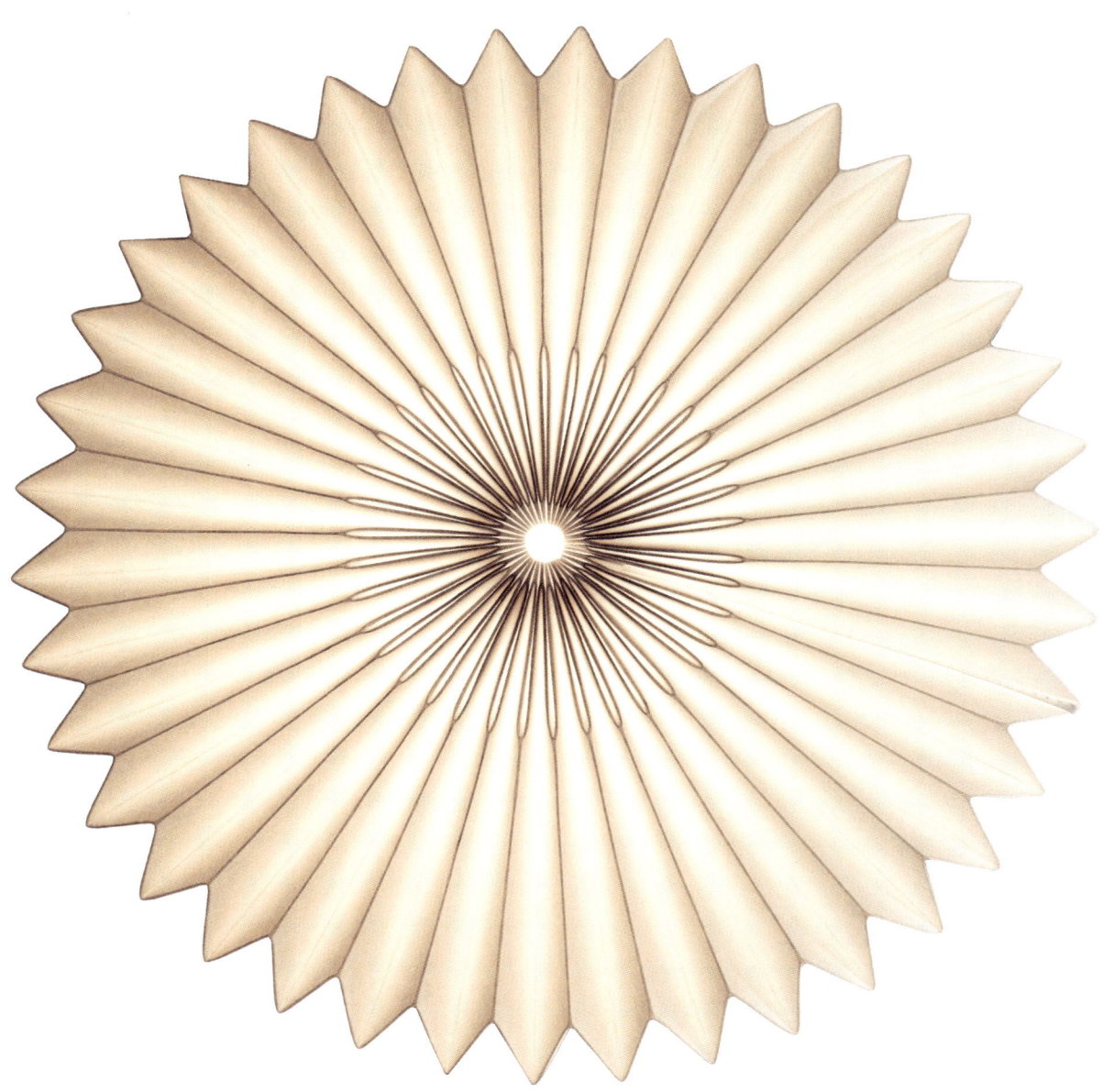

Like so many of Mogens Koch's furnishings, including bookcases and folding tables, his pleated paper lantern can be assembled in multiples to suit the size and purpose of a room. Koch designed his first multi-lantern fixture in 1948, for the official residence of the roads inspector in Frederiksborg County. As he planned the interiors, he found that the cost of the furniture left only a pittance for lighting. His economical solution was a three-lantern fixture made of bamboo rods and sailing line, which would hang over the dining room table. While the design recalls a chandelier, Koch's fixture was an improvement on the historical model, because the diffused light would illuminate a larger area. A few months later, he designed a six-lantern fixture for the inspector's home, although the proposed location is unknown.

There is no evidence that either of Koch's multi-lantern fixtures ever illuminated the county inspector's home, but the six-lantern fixture saw the light of day in spectacular fashion. In 1954, Koch fabricated at least six of them for the lecture hall of the Royal Danish Academy, where he had been appointed as a professor in 1950.

Suspended amid the neoclassical decor, Koch's abstract constellations revealed the degree to which his lanterns are at home in almost any setting, by virtue of their simplicity. On each fixture, the bamboo framework revealed the geometric root of the lantern, in the central hexagon and equilateral triangles. As such, lantern and fixture have an organic relationship, like the acorn that contains the seed for an oak tree.

After realizing his ideal structure in pleated paper, Mogens Koch never worked with that material/technique again. Eight decades later, his geometric marvel remains in production at the Le Klint factory in Odense, Denmark, where the female artisans, who refer to themselves as "folding girls", transform embossed sheets of plastic or paper into **Le Klint 105**, now made in four sizes. Traditionalists who desire a gentle patina will choose paper, while those who dislike dusting will choose plastic. Regardless of the material, the lantern works well with any light source and maximizes the output, due to the extensive surface area. Indeed, Koch's lantern is ideal for LED bulbs and embodies his project of using ancient knowledge to enhance the present.

Some years before either architect created their most enduring individual works, Grethe Meyer and Børge Mogensen merged their talents and created a joint work that remains a highpoint of both their careers. Conceived in a burst of extraordinary optimism and corresponding ambition, **Boligens Byggeskabe** (Modular Cabinets) is an adjustable system of built-in cabinets that can be tailored to any room and contain a universe of objects. By absorbing those objects into the walls of the home, the system increases the apparent size of the room, even as the architects' careful calculations ensure that none of the storage space is wasted. As the cabinets make it possible to enjoy one's possessions without being overwhelmed by them, the benefits of the system extend beyond beauty and utility to include serenity.

Meyer and Mogensen met for the first time in 1946–47, in the Department of Furniture Design at the Royal Danish Academy, where he was Kaare Klint's teaching assistant and she was attending Klint's lectures during her final year of architectural studies.[1] Those lectures were a formative experience for Meyer, as she absorbed Klint's practice of measuring household goods and using their dimensions as the basis for the design of storage furniture. That practice provided the foundation for her career as a researcher during 1948–60, which culminated in her work on Boligens Byggeskabe. Moreover, those lectures instilled the obsession with compact storage that informed Meyer's archetypal designs for glassware, tableware and cookware (pp. 44, 92, 116).

Five years after their first meeting, Mogensen was an independent furniture designer, and Meyer was a full-time researcher for *Byggebogen* (The Building Book), the manual of design and construction standards initiated by Professor Poul Kjærgaard (p. 44). As Meyer developed a new section of the manual that focused on storage and furniture arrangements, she enlisted Mogensen as a consultant.[2] In the course of that project, they employed the research practices that both had learned from Kaare Klint and amassed a trove of new dimensional data. By 1953, Meyer and Mogensen had joined forces to design a system of modular cabinets that could accommodate the needs of individual households, rather than impose a one-size-fits-all solution on the infinite variety of human needs and habits.

As the two architects formulated their ambitious project, they had a specific application in mind. While *Byggebogen* was intended for general use, Kjærgaard and his staff were especially concerned with the construction and furnishing of social housing.[3] Meyer and Mogensen conceived their modular cabinet system as a parallel project, in the hope of providing social housing residents with built-in cabinets that could make the most of the available space and ease their daily routines. Describing that ambition, Meyer compared their project to earlier efforts to standardize kitchen cabinets in social housing, which included her work on the kitchen survey of 1948–49 and her prize-winning kitchen designs of 1950–51. As she explained,

"The effort to improve kitchen design has resulted in the kitchen types and furnishings prepared by a kitchen committee (consisting of the architects Edvard Heiberg, Eske Kristensen and Bent Salicath) set up by the Joint Organization of Non-Profit Danish Housing Associations. [...] In this area, we are thus following in the footsteps of our Swedish colleagues, whose pioneering work in the kitchen area has provided a basis for our work. Unfortunately, the picture looks rather more disappointing when we compare the built-in cabinets in our modern homes with those of the Swedes. [...] The need for cabinet space is no less in this country among the residents of small, modern and often overcrowded apartments."[4]

Grethe Meyer and Børge Mogensen. Key for Boligens Byggeskabe cabinets and detail of recessed door pull. The key is easy to grasp with fingertips and serves as a handle for all of the doors. As the key is completely recessed in the door pull, it will not catch clothing or damage walls and other doors when opened. 1:1 scale.

GRETHE MEYER / BØRGE MOGENSEN 1952–57
Boligens Byggeskabe

Meyer and Mogensen created their storage system through a union of theory and practice that was rooted in their earlier individual experiences. Mogensen's furniture program for FDB (p. 188) included storage for a wide range of common household items. Beyond the sideboards and bedroom cabinets, he created an entire system of modular units — "byggemøbler" — that could be aligned or stacked in many combinations. And yet, the built-in cabinets that he envisioned with Meyer presented a new challenge. While his units for FDB included fixed partitions, the new cabinets would be simple containers with flexible dividers. Moreover, there were gaps in Mogensen's expertise. He had expert knowledge of book formats and tableware, but his provisions for clothing were based on averages and somewhat imprecise.

Meyer's experience with the storage of household objects was theoretical, but it was also much more detailed than Mogensen's experience for FDB. Similarly to his work, her research was based on the detailed measurement of things, but it was also devoted to analysis and focused on the most efficient use of space. Her meticulous approach led her to measure folded pairs of socks (and pajamas and sweaters and every other type of garment) and made it possible to calculate how much space was required to hold a week's supply of clothing for a typical man or woman. As a result, Meyer and Mogensen could design cabinets that utilized the entire height of the wall, saving both space and materials. However, she had limited knowledge of furniture materials and no experience designing for factory production.

As they developed their storage project, Meyer and Mogensen were guided by a handful of principles.[5] Their fundamental principle was that it should be possible to see and easily reach every item without standing on a footstool. To that end, the cabinets were scaled to the human body, and the subdivisions were based on eye height and arm's length. The second principle was that the shelves and drawers should be sized for specific things, using the data that the two architects had amassed and would continue to gather. The third principle was that the cabinets should fit into every room in the home, by aligning with standard ceiling and door heights, and by presenting more or less neutral surfaces that would be compatible with all sorts of furniture.

By early 1954, the analyst and the artisan had advanced their studies to the point that they were ready to construct a full-scale mock-up. In the spring, they won first prize in the annual competition that was sponsored by the Copenhagen Cabinetmakers' Guild (the following spread) with the goal of finding new designs for the guild's annual exhibition in the autumn. Each of the competition winners received abundant publicity, and their projects were constructed and presented to the public. Meyer and Mogensen's prize-winning entry was a one-room, 35-square-meter apartment with all of the storage and most of the furniture built into the walls.[6] It was clearly intended as a model for new residential construction and might be regarded as such today, due to the charming and practical design.

The two architects brought complementary experiences and bodies of knowledge to their collaboration. Grethe Meyer was a seasoned analyst with special expertise in the storage of clothing and housewares. Børge Mogensen had already designed cabinets for most types of household items and was unmatched in the design of factory-made furniture.
→ Børge Mogensen. Selection of furniture for FDB, 1942–50. Mogensen's work for FDB endowed him with vast experience with the design of cabinets for industrial production.

Starting with a ceiling height of 250 cm, the two architects subtracted a 10-cm gap at the floor and subdivided the remaining wall surface into four horizontal bands of 60 cm.[7] The height of the bands provided a vertical module and yielded a table height of 70 cm, shelving increments of 30 cm and an upper shelf height of 190 cm: the practical limit for a typical adult. The horizontal module of 104 cm corresponded to half the length of a standard bed. Both modules were visible in the wall that included the folding bed — which doubled as a sofa — alongside two shelving units with folding work surfaces. The hinged, wall-mounted tables and sliding doors around the dining area were veneered in water-resistant teak, while the other woodwork was veneered in pine.

In September 1954, Meyer and Mogensen's model apartment was constructed by Søborg Møbelfabrik and installed in Copenhagen's Forum building as a central attraction of Bo Godt (Live Well) — a special edition of the cabinetmakers' exhibition that celebrated the guild's 400th anniversary. As the two architects later explained,

"The exhibition of the cabinets in Forum was a good opportunity for us to carry out a necessary first trial in our study of the objectives and the technical and aesthetic design. [...] The great interest shown by the public at the exhibition and the numerous subsequent inquiries to the manufacturer and architects indicate that people largely accept this new approach to furnishing, even when it affects the living room, which does not normally contain built-in furniture.

However, the prerequisite for an extension of the fixed cabinets of the home and for raising their quality is that this can be done on a reasonable economic basis, which in turn requires mass production of the cabinet elements. One can therefore hope that the housing associations, the responsible authorities and the architects creating the designs will show sufficient interest in the matter to help enable a rational and financially sound production approach."[8]

Grethe Meyer and Børge Mogensen. Model apartment with built-in cabinets. Installed at Bo Godt (Live Well), 400th anniversary exhibition of the Copenhagen Cabinetmakers' Guild, Forum exhibition building, Copenhagen. September 1954. To make the most of the limited space — 35 square meters — Meyer and Mogensen incorporated most of the furniture into the walls of cabinets, including the bed that can be used as a sofa and two wall-mounted tables that can be combined in either location.

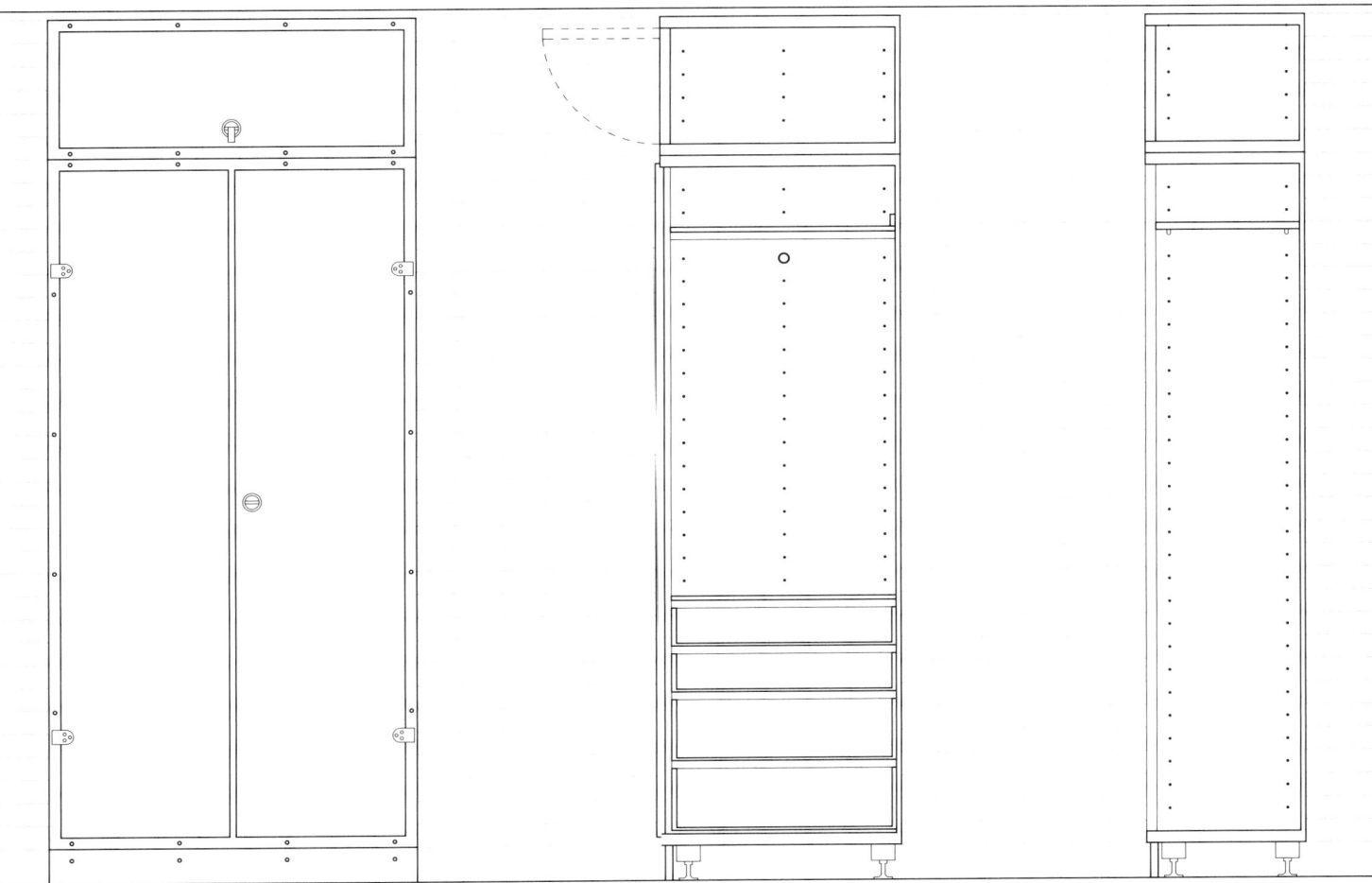

There is no indication that Meyer and Mogensen were ever contacted by any organization involved in the construction of social housing regarding their space-saving storage system. Nonetheless, they forged ahead with the project, using the measurements of clothing and other items gathered since 1952. To maximize the efficient use of space, they revised their modular system and employed a much smaller unit that would exploit every cubic centimeter of the cabinet interior. Moreover, the small module would promote the use of standardized parts that could be mass-produced at an affordable price. The result would be an ideal storage system that could be reconfigured, as household needs changed, and dismantled for transport and reassembly when changing dwellings.

Mogensen established the underlying module following Kaare Klint's penchant for using 12 as the basis of dimensional systems, because that number can be evenly divided by 2, 3, 4 and 6 to provide a variety of modules.[9] As in 1954, Mogensen and Meyer began with a ceiling height of 250 cm. After subtracting the height of a baseboard and a piece of trim at the ceiling, they arrived at a working height of 237.6 cm.[10] Dividing that number into 36 equal segments yielded a module of 6.6 cm, which established the heights of the cabinets and drawers and the spacing of adjustable shelves. While a base cabinet is 30 units high (198 cm), the gap at the ceiling can be filled with an upper cabinet that is 6 units high (39.6 cm) and, depending on width, fitted with a top-hung door or two sliding doors.

The cabinets were designed with two depths that correspond to shelving (30 cm) and clothing storage (60 cm).[11] The six standard widths of the cabinets were determined by the minimum useful width of a shelf for folded clothing (34.6 cm) and the maximum practical width of a drawer (69.2 cm). Combining the two dimensions produced a cabinet that would hold a week's supply of clothing for an average person, which could be subdivided with drawers and shelves of various widths depending on their wardrobe. The widest of the standard cabinets (135.3 cm) could accommodate two equal stacks of drawers or used entirely for hanging space. Two additional cabinet widths (52.8 and 87.4 cm) made it possible to fill almost any wall surface.

As the two architects developed their modular system of drawers and shelves, they prepared for mass production by revising the materials and drawing a distinction between outer and inner surfaces.[12] While the edges of the cabinets were covered in solid wood (Douglas fir), the sides of the cabinets and the interior partitions, shelves and drawers were all fabricated of fiberboard over wooden frames. The fiberboard was sprayed with an especially durable paint (Durolit) in a warm shade of gray that provides a neutral background for every sort of object. The solid wood edges of the cabinets, which were attached with brass screws, made it possible to attach hinged or sliding doors, which were constructed of furniture-grade plywood and veneered with Douglas fir or teak.

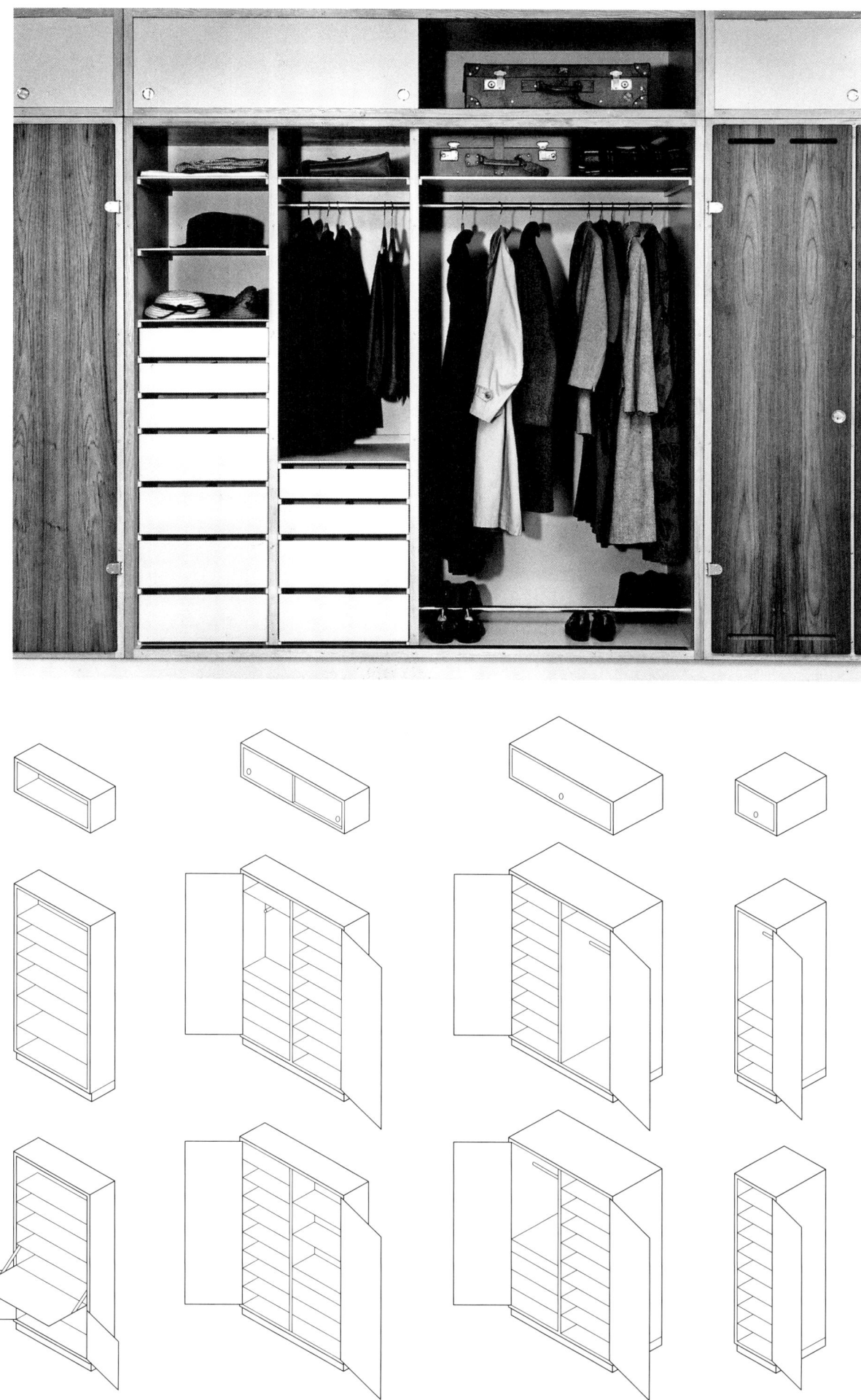

Closet with men's clothing, 1957. The typical cabinet for clothing has a width of 102 cm that corresponds to the length of the hanging rod and is easily subdivided. The doors on the upper cabinets have sliding doors. / Isometric drawing of typical cabinets and overhead units. ← Master dimensions for cabinets in two depths with a vertical module of 6.6 cm that determines the possible arrangements of adjustable shelves and drawers. 1:20 scale.

The brass hardware that Mogensen designed for the cabinets is integral to their use.[13] All of the doors include a round pull that is recessed into the plywood (p. 219). As a result, it is possible to install a cabinet next to a wall and still open a hinged door. The key that serves as a handle for hinged and sliding doors alike is contained by the round pull, which prevents damage to walls and other doors. As the key is fully recessed, it will not snag a person's clothing. Mindful that many cabinets would be installed in small rooms, Mogensen created a hinge that ensures a door need only be opened 90° to pull out a drawer. The upper boxes with top-hung doors include a flexible leather strap that makes it easy to lift the door whether standing on the floor or a footstool.

In the interest of economy, the cabinets were designed so that they could be shipped in pieces and assembled by a carpenter. Knock-down furniture had existed for centuries, as seen in medieval trestle tables and Ming Dynasty armchairs. Moreover, the Swedish retailer Ikea had been selling flat-pack chairs and tables by mail order since 1948, undoubtedly inspired by the designs of architect Elias Svedberg. Indeed, Svedberg's Triva-Bygg collection, introduced in 1944, established a new model for the Nordic furniture industry.[14] Meyer and Mogensen's signal innovation was to devise a panelized system of cabinets that reduced the cost of transport and simplified installation. They named that system Boligens Byggeskabe and presented it at the exhibition *Tidens Møbler* (Furniture of Our Time), which was staged at Tivoli Gardens in October 1957.

Following the exhibition at Tivoli, architect Ole Dybbroe (Meyer's colleague at the National Building Research Institute) published a detailed assessment of Meyer and Mogensen's storage system. In doing so, he identified the conflict between utility and cost that had already doomed their original ambition for the cabinets:

"Boligens Byggeskabe stands out with a quality in terms of both interior layout and technical execution that far surpasses, one can safely say, what is normally achieved with ordinary built-in cabinets. [...] However, that is also the biggest obstacle for the sales of the cabinets in a time when everyone, with the Ministry of Housing as the most vocal among them, is calling for 'lower costs at any price' — and where, unfortunately, the price often *is* exactly the quality. [...] Although the built-in cabinets can probably compete in price with loose cabinets and the existing cabinets made on-site *of similar quality*, with the stated prices, it will be difficult to compete with ordinary cabinets made on-site without interior fittings of any notable kind – that is, like most 'fixed cabinets' in residential architecture."[15]

As Dybbroe noted, the cost of Meyer and Mogensen's cabinets was a reflection of their quality, rather than the materials. Painted fiberboard and veneered plywood are both inexpensive, and the cost of the veneer, whether beech or teak, is minor when compared to the labor. Moreover, the amount of solid wood required for the edges of the cabinets makes that expense negligible. Mogensen's brass hardware would have been less costly in stamped steel but also less durable. The actual cost of Boligens Byggeskabe lies in the details that make it possible to assemble and disassemble the components again and again, and in the inserts — partitions, adjustable shelves, drawer glides and dividers — that make it possible to customize the interiors of the cabinets.

Typical shelving, 1957. The 30-cm-deep cabinets provide adjustable shelving with or without folding writing surfaces that can accommodate any type of household object. → Shelving with Douglas fir base and face frames and painted plywood dividers. Six decades after Boligens Byggeskabe was designed, the system remains absolutely useful and imbues a room with a warm character.

By the end of 1956, Meyer and Mogensen had given up their initial goal of providing space-saving storage for new low-cost apartment buildings, in the knowledge that their cabinets would never satisfy the budget. No matter the builder, it would always be less expensive to have a carpenter erect two partitions with a few shelves and a closet rod. As a result, the two architects signed a contract with the furniture dealers Curt and Kirsten (Larsen) Danel, owners of the furniture shop C. Danel, in the Frederiksberg section of Copenhagen.[16] That contract granted the Danels exclusive rights to produce and sell Boligens Byggeskabe, on the condition that the parts were manufactured at C.M. Madsens Fabrikker, on the island of Funen, which also made Mogensen's storage furniture for FDB.

During the early 1960s, with the Danels' backing, Meyer and Morgensen extended Boligens Byggeskabe beyond clothing storage and adjustable shelving to include shelving units with folding writing surfaces, built-in beds and all manner of shelving and dividers for libraries, offices and schools. In 1960, the Danels opened a dedicated showroom for Boligens Byggeskabe, not far from their original shop, to demonstrate the vast range of possible applications.[17] The price of the cabinets included assembly and installation by a carpenter. Two years later, they opened a shop in Aarhus, in Jutland, to promote Meyer and Mogensen's cabinets along with Mogensen's other designs. Sales of Boligens Byggeskabe would rise over the 1960s and finally plateau in the mid 1970s.

In 1973, Grethe Meyer was invited to exhibit her industrial designs at the offices of the Danish Association of Arts and Crafts and Industrial Design.[18] Her passing remark about the storage system that she designed with Børge Mogensen, who died in 1972, has been reprinted in several books, as if to condemn Boligens Byggeskabe for the fact that it was never the cheapest storage solution on the market. In fact, it could be quite expensive due to the optional pieces and inserts that allowed customized solutions. As she exclaimed,

"Naturally, Boligens Byggeskabe is lovely to live with, but unfortunately, it has also become quite expensive — and therefore too exclusive for the young. I guess I've dreamed of also making another Boligens Byggeskabe with totally different requirements. Their function should be maintained, but would the materials need to be so precious? Would it all have to be so thoroughly detailed? Couldn't we just give young people a practical design solution that was also inexpensive?"[19]

In a bedroom, the wall of cabinets with sliding doors in Douglas fir conceals clothing for two people and, in doing so, promotes a restful atmosphere. / Elsewhere, shelving units with folding writing surfaces makes it possible to conceal the debris of daily life. → A wall of shelving in a dining room accommodates a complete range of items for cooking and serving. The combination of open and closed upper cabinets provide storage for odds and ends as well as an assortment of prized objects. The contents of the dining room wall include the Stub glasses that Grethe Meyer designed with Ibi Trier Mørch and parts of her own Hvidpot porcelain service.

Meyer was pandering to the press, in an era when truly cheap and essentially disposable furniture (along with many other consumer products) was seen as a vehicle of individual freedom, and the conservation of resources was a fringe concern. She knew better than anyone that the cost of the cabinets was not a function of the materials but of the flexibility and durability of the system. Eliminating the details would undermine the practical character of the cabinets. And she ignored the fact that Ikea was already providing inexpensive storage furniture to people of every age, at the large store on the outskirts of Copenhagen that opened in 1969.

Boligens Byggeskabe proved to be a commercial success in both Denmark and Sweden and remained in production for about twenty-five years. During 1963–68, Mogensen's Swedish production partner Karl Andersson & Söner produced Bostadens Byggeskåp in the version with Douglas fir veneer, and a painted version that was entirely gray. In Denmark, production ended in the early 1980s, under the onslaught of less expensive options, a few years before the Danels closed their business and retired in 1988. Over the decades, so many cabinets were produced, for shelving and closets, that it is relatively easy to locate vintage examples through online sources and second-hand shops. While the shelves, drawers, and fiberboard elements can be repainted, the veneered doors and solid wood edges can be refinished.

Meyer and Mogensen's collaboration on Boligens Byggeskabe led to an exchange of creative practices that had a lasting impact on their individual work. As a student of Kaare Klint, Mogensen was accustomed to using geometry to solve design problems.

Børge Morgensen and Grethe Meyer, 1959. While the Boligens Byggeskabe series of cabinets was essentially completed in 1957, the two architects continued to design inserts into the early 1960s. Their close relationship continued until the end of his life, in 1972.

However, Meyer's systematic approach rekindled his fascination with the power of numbers to unite a universe of factors within a simple framework that was suited to mass production. So inspired by their collaboration, Mogensen quickly developed the Øresund storage system for Karl Andersson & Söner, which was introduced in 1955, in a choice of teak, Douglas fir or oak veneer. As the system was based on the same data that informed Boligens Byggeskabe, Meyer was credited as the co-designer and received a portion of the royalties.[20]

For Meyer's part, the collaboration marked her transition from statistician to industrial designer whose forms were grounded in data. In the process, she absorbed the affinity for subtle colors and natural materials that constitute the aesthetic hallmarks of the Klint School. Indeed, we can understand her work with gray faience, white porcelain and unglazed stoneware (Blåkant, Hvidpot and Ildpot) as extensions of her work on Boligens Byggeskabe. As seen in her glassware and ceramics, Meyer designed tableware that reduced the cost to the consumer and allowed for compact storage in small apartments. But she drifted away from the idea that her diligence might improve the lives of social housing residents, based on the realization that economic factors superseded all other concerns.

In retrospect, Boligens Byggeskabe can be seen as an antidote to a culture of disposable consumer goods, which are (at least from an environmental standpoint) a remnant of a bygone era and now obsolete. Grethe Meyer and Børge Mogensen's cabinets remain completely contemporary, but the Ikea effect makes it unlikely that they will ever to return to production. While few people today own sewing machines and televisions are often too large to fit into even the widest shelving unit (135.3 cm), our household storage needs have expanded dramatically since 1957, due to increased incomes, leisure time and more diverse interests. And so, Boligens Byggeskabe provides further evidence that the archetypes of Danish design are as useful as ever and in some cases even more so.

Børge Mogensen's adjustable lounge chair is a masterpiece of industrial design that provides comfort in a range of positions by actively engaging the body. Moreover, an examination of the structure reveals the essence of his work as a designer of factory-made furniture. Mogensen's adjustable chair with a sliding seat represented a new phase in his work, as he moved beyond the traditional examples that were the basis of his work for FDB in the 1940s (p. 188). Rather than adapt models rooted in handicraft to machinery, he designed new models specifically for factory production. By aligning design and technique, he hoped to create more comfortable furniture that could be constructed at a lower cost than traditional models through savings on labor and material.

Historically, most wooden furniture has been constructed using small pieces of material that could be shaped with hand tools. On many lightweight chairs, including every single one of Mogensen's upright chairs for FDB, the legs are connected with horizontal pieces (stretchers) that provide bracing and reduce the stress on the connections to the seat. Locating the stretchers closer to the floor increases the stiffness of the legs but also creates a tripping hazard. As Mogensen designed truly industrial furniture, he created a simple structural model by eliminating legs and lowering the customary stretchers to the floor, where they function like runners on a sled. In doing so, he created extremely rigid frames that could be assembled using slender, standardized pieces of wood and machine-made joints.

The simplest example of Mogensen's "runner" series is the lightweight oak armchair with rattan panels for seat and backrest that was first produced by the P. Lauritsen & Søn factory, in 1957. The same factory produced two sideboards and a chest of drawers with runner frames of solid oak or teak, which were filled with veneered panels and fitted with brass hardware. On the sideboards, double-hinged doors reduce the clearance required to access the contents. With the adjustable lounge chair eventually labeled **Fredericia 2254**, Mogensen applied his runner model to a more complex type of furniture, while incorporating lessons from at least two historical models.

Børge Mogensen. BM 62 armchair, 1957. Oak and cane. / BM 57 sideboard and BM 59 chest of drawers, 1957. Solid rosewood and veneer, brass hardware. P. Lauritsen & Søn. → Børge Mogensen. Fredericia 2254, 1957. Oak with foam rubber cushions. 1:1 scale. The notable detail is the contoured armrest that ends in finger joints at the corners of the side frames, which provide decoration derived from the construction.

BØRGE MOGENSEN 1956–63

Fredericia 2254

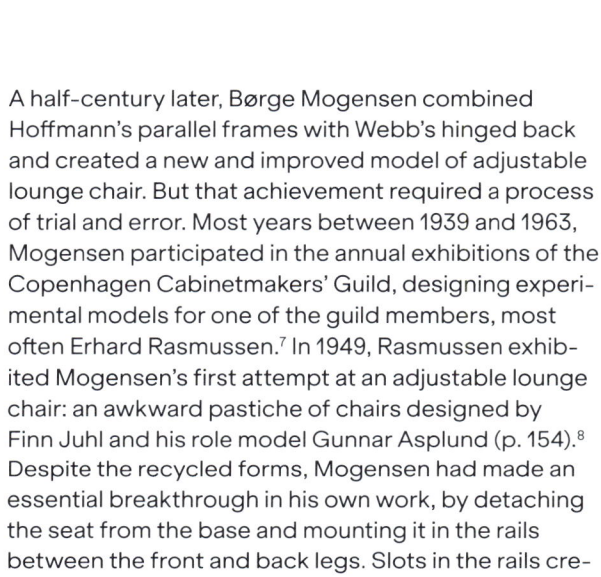

As a result of his years working with Mogens Koch and Kaare Klint, Mogensen had a wide knowledge of furniture history. Klint was particularly fascinated with the furniture of the British Arts and Crafts movement, the circle of architects and designers that coalesced around the author and designer William Morris, circa 1860.[1] Their common project of reviving traditional crafts and creating new models based on vernacular examples anticipated much of Klint's own work. He found a partial model for his wooden armchair with a rush seat in the Sussex armchair that architect Philip Webb designed for Morris's home, the Red House. Webb's other designs included an upholstered lounge chair with a hinged back, which could be adjusted by inserting a loose metal rod through the holes of the extended armrests.[2] Many examples of the chair were upholstered with Morris's patterned fabrics, creating a union of furniture and textiles that would inspire both Klint and Mogensen.

Around 1900, as industrialization in Europe altered nearly every aspect of life, many artists and architects searched for a new decorative style that could provide a cultural anchor in an era of unprecedented change.[3] In Denmark, the organic designs of Morris and his circle contributed to the development of "Skønvirke," an artistic movement rooted in native crafts and landscape.[4] In Austria, the British movement inspired the founding of the Wiener Werkstätte, by the artist Koloman Moser and the architect Josef Hoffmann.[5] As Hoffmann designed the furniture for his Purkersdorf Sanatorium, in 1905, he adapted Webb's example of an adjustable lounge chair to a lightweight structure of stained plywood and steam-bent beech, which he referred to as the "machine for sitting."[6] Despite Hoffmann's good intentions, the horizontal seat made even an upright sitting position uncomfortable.

A half-century later, Børge Mogensen combined Hoffmann's parallel frames with Webb's hinged back and created a new and improved model of adjustable lounge chair. But that achievement required a process of trial and error. Most years between 1939 and 1963, Mogensen participated in the annual exhibitions of the Copenhagen Cabinetmakers' Guild, designing experimental models for one of the guild members, most often Erhard Rasmussen.[7] In 1949, Rasmussen exhibited Mogensen's first attempt at an adjustable lounge chair: an awkward pastiche of chairs designed by Finn Juhl and his role model Gunnar Asplund (p. 154).[8] Despite the recycled forms, Mogensen had made an essential breakthrough in his own work, by detaching the seat from the base and mounting it in the rails between the front and back legs. Slots in the rails created a sliding seat that worked in tandem with the hinged back and accommodated a range of postures.

By 1956, Mogensen had fully embraced industrial design methods and developed his structural model of parallel frames on runners. In the autumn, Erhard Rasmussen presented Mogensen's second version of an adjustable lounge chair at the annual exhibition of the Copenhagen Cabinetmakers' Guild, made of teak with woven rattan panels for seat and back, with loose cushions covered in solid-colored linen.[9] The curved frames that support the body were made of steam-molded bentwood, while the box-like base was constructed of straight lengths of natural wood. As with so many other designs presented at the guild exhibitions, Mogensen's handcrafted specimen was a prototype for factory production. In 1957, the Fredericia Stole- og Polstermøbelfabrik (hereafter Fredericia), introduced the chair as **Fredericia 244**, with an oak frame that included teak runners for durability and a more elaborate version of the rattan panels.

Børge Mogensen. Adjustable armchair with suspended neck cushion, 1949. Solid and laminated oak or ash with teak armrest and feet. Executed by Erhard Rasmussen for the 1949 exhibition of the Copenhagen Cabinetmakers' Guild. / Børge Mogensen. Fredericia 244, 1957. Oak with teak runners, woven cane panels, foam rubber cushions. ← Philip Webb. Adjustable-back armchair, circa 1869. Ebonized oak with brass casters. Upholstered in William Morris's "Bird" pattern (1878). Chair adapted from vernacular model of late Georgian period, circa 1810. / Josef Hoffmann. "Sitzmaschine", 1905. Jacob & Josef Kohn, model 670. Stained plywood and steam-bent beech with mahogany details and brass rod. Upholstered in beige suede (later). Hoffmann's "Sitting Machine" was also known as the "Morris armchair."

Wooden structure with woven rattan backrest.
→ Detail of sliding mechanism on underside of rails.
/ View of independent seating element and base.

The woven rattan backrest on Fredericia 244 displayed Mogensen's lingering attachment to handicraft, even as the wooden structure revealed his maturity as an industrial designer. The two-part structure promoted an efficient workflow at the factory by separating the curved frames of molded wood from the box-like base of natural wood. While the seat and backrest were molded under pressure, carpenters would assemble the base of the chair from straight pieces of lumber. After the two parts were fabricated, they were joined with metal clips that slide along the underside of the rails and guide the sliding seat. Beyond the divisions of material and labor, the curved and straight frames reconcile the conflict between human anatomy, which requires complex forms, and industrial production, which favors standardized parts and simple assemblies.

As Mogensen balanced anatomy and industry, he arrived at an extremely strong and elegant design that emphasizes the precise carpentry and natural character of the wood. In addition to simplifying production, the two-part structure reduces stress on the box-like base of the chair. Because the two curved elements are independent of the base and merely supported on the horizontal rails, the parallel frames on either side of the base are not subjected to the direct weight of a person sitting in the chair. As a result, those frames could be constructed with simple connections (finger joints) that display the wood grain from two directions and have a decorative character.

Fredericia 244 was a delicate union of industrial and artisanal techniques that remains a high point of Mogensen's collaboration with Fredericia. Prior to the joining of the curved frames, skilled basket weavers used long strands of rattan to wrap the edges of the backrest and create a dense pattern known as a box-weave.

By varying the tension in the fibers — with the vertical strands slightly looser than the horizontal strands — the artisans created woven panels that followed the curvature of the frame and ensured continuous support to the back. Mogensen incorporated the weaving into the woodwork by milling vertical slots into the sides of the frame. As a result, the rattan wrapped along that portion of the frame does not come in contact with the horizontal rail that carries the backrest, avoiding friction that would damage the strands.

Despite the careful details and care taken to protect the rattan, Mogensen's design was undermined by the fragility of the material. Some early examples of Fredericia 244 included rattan seats, but that was quickly curtailed in favor of linen webbing and finally fiberglass cloth. Moreover, the chairs were too delicate to be installed in public spaces. By the early 1960s, Mogensen had embraced a more robust aesthetic that emphasized the strength of the wood. At the same time, Andreas Graversen, the owner of Fredericia, was rationalizing the production and moving away from handicraft. As a result, they agreed to eliminate the handwoven rattan backrest on 2254.[10] Mogensen's new solution not only provided a more durable chair but also a more comfortable chair.

Fredericia 2254, 1963. Oak with foam rubber cushions.
→ Time-lapse view with two seating positions. The front edge of the seat is only 35 cm above the ground, so that a person's feet remain in contact with the floor, even in a reclining position. Despite the low seating height, the long armrests provide sufficient leverage that it is easy to settle into and exit the chair.

In January 1963, Mogensen revised the backrest on Fredericia 244 by replacing box-woven rattan with molded oak slats that followed the curvature of the frame. The substitution increased support to the lumbar region at the base of the spine, which includes five crucial vertebrae. As before, foam rubber cushions were attached to the hinged seat-and-backrest with leather straps that are sewn into the zippered slipcovers and fastened to brass studs. The ingenious method of attachment simplified assembly of the chair, while also protecting the textile from wear and tear. Any stress on the cushions due to a person's movement is transferred to the leather straps, which are much stronger than the woven material. The refined design was renumbered **Fredericia 2254** and became a popular fixture in Danish living rooms during the 1960s and '70s.

The ultimate result of Mogensen's extended design process, which began with the awkward exhibition model of 1949, was a lounge chair that provides comfort by engaging a range of muscles from knees to neck. The excellent lumbar support provided by the curved wooden staves makes it easier to shift positions, which prevents muscle fatigue over extended periods of time.

As the backrest reclines, it supports a larger share of the body's weight, which decreases pressure on the thighs and makes it easier to slide forward in the seat. As the seat slides forward, the diaphragm of a person sitting in the chair expands and promotes the deep breathing necessary for relaxation.

Fredericia 2254 realized Mogensen's ambition to design furniture for the factory that would equal handcrafted models in terms of comfort but required minimal handwork. In traditional lounge chairs, including Philip Webb's adjustable model, comfort is a function of the upholstery that includes layers of padding and hand-tied springs. Mogensen's design replaced upholstery with foam rubber cushions and molded wooden elements that follow the shape of the body and provide resistance where it is most needed. And yet, the character of the chair is defined by the natural properties of wood and leather. In his mind, industrial design did not require the use of artificial substances, such as steel and plastic, but could be usefully applied to natural materials that include wool and cotton.

Børge Mogensen's pursuit of simple structures encompassed the woven materials that completed his furniture. While many architects regard textiles as decorative accessories, he regarded them as fundamental to the character of a chair or sofa. Whether woven by hand or machine, most textiles have a geometric structure in which two sets of fibers (warp and weft) intersect at a right angle. Mogensen's artistic ideal was a union of rigid and pliable structures — wood and fiber — that correspond visually and create a complete object. He was particularly concerned with neat transitions at the seams, where the cloth changes direction and wraps around the cushion. Those transitions are much easier to accomplish with simple geometric designs such as checks, plaids and stripes.

Mogensen found his ideal creative partner in Lis Ahlmann, a handweaver and expert on historic Danish peasant textiles.[11] The two artisans had first met at Kaare Klint's office in the late 1930s, when Ahlmann wove the coverings for several pieces of Klint's furniture. Their shared ambition was to extend Danish craft traditions by adapting those practices to industrial production. After Ahlmann was hired as a design consultant at C. Olesen A/S, Denmark's largest textile producer, in 1953, her work included a vast range of furniture fabrics (p. 258). Many of those patterns were created in consultation with Mogensen and with his furniture in mind, such that she often credited him as co-designer. Her simple patterns corresponded to the straight lines and right angles of his structures, while her palette of subtle colors rooted in natural pigments complemented the oak and beech that he favored for his furniture. As Mogensen declared,

"Lis's textiles are a union of the rational and the painterly. If clothes make the man, then it seems my furniture had found its perfect wardrobe."[12]

The best-known example of their collaboration is the plaid pattern that provided the standard covering for a number of Børge Mogensen's models, Cotil 863/53932, which is illustrated on these pages. Ahlmann initially created the pattern in 1941, in cotton, to cover a wing-back lounge chair designed by Kaare Klint.[13] While Klint's chair was a refinement of an eighteenth-century English example, Ahlmann based her plaid on a traditional peasant weave from her native northern Jutland. In 1954, as Ahlmann adapted the pattern to mass production, she created a more durable material by blending cotton and wool. In doing so, she not only created a handsome upholstery fabric but also preserved a fragment of Danish cultural history and demonstrated its value to contemporary life.

Armchair 2254 and footstool 2248, 1963, upholstered in Cotil 863/55803. ← Kaare Klint. Armchair, 1941. Teak with cotton/wool upholstery. Rud. Rasmussens Snedkerier model 6212. Lis Ahlmann's wool and cotton upholstery fabric Cotil 863/55803 is based on the linen original that she wove for the first example of the chair, which was presented in the 1942 exhibition *Danskt Konsthantverk* (p. 207).

Mogensen complemented his high-backed lounge chair with a low-backed model that was not adjustable. As with the high-backed model, the low chair was introduced in 1957 with woven rattan on the backrest (Fredericia 246) and altered in 1963 to include curved staves (Fredericia 2256). The footstool that served both models was initially produced with rubber webbing (Fredericia 245), which was later replaced with wooden slats (Fredericia 2248). Models 2254 and 2256 were among Mogensen's most popular designs for Fredericia and 2254 remained in production until 2012, when the company relocated to a new factory and discontinued several low-selling models. Vintage examples of both models are readily available and are easily refurbished, due to the high quality of the wood and the durable construction.

On account of Mogensen's early work for FDB, which was designed to be as inexpensive as practical, he has often been described as a "democratic designer."[14] Nearly as often, the authors struggle to explain his more expensive later works, such as Boligens Byggeskabe (p. 218) and the leather-covered sofas of the early 1960s. Fredericia 2254 supports a more nuanced view of Mogensen as a craftsman turned designer who recognized the necessity of industrial production, if the principles he had absorbed from Kaare Klint were going to survive. Mogensen's fundamental goal was not inexpensive furniture but excellent furniture that required the least amount of handicraft, so that it would be commercially viable. As a result, he devoted himself to balancing the requirements of the human body with the demands of the factory, which prioritizes economy.

Fredericia 2254 embodies that balance of competing factors, with a curved cradle for the human body that is suspended in a simple and economical framework that is ideal for the factory. While Mogensen's runner (or sled) series was rooted in his concern for economy, the starting point for the design of the lounge chair was the hypothetical occupant. There were certainly less expensive ways of constructing the seat and backrest than molding wood into curved frames but none so accommodating to the curvature of the spine. The curved staves that were added in 1963 enhanced the comfort of the chair, but they did not reduce the price. As such, the structure of Mogensen's adjustable lounge chair reveals his overarching priority as a designer of factory-made furniture: the comfort of those who would incorporate his work into their daily lives.

Having discovered both the starting point and the ultimate result of Mogensen's work on Fredericia 2254, we can describe him as a humanist whose commitment to providing people with excellent furniture led him to design models for a wide range of income levels. While the more costly products of his later career include the leather-covered sofas that make simple interpretations of Mogensen's career unreliable, the less costly products include the folding deck chair SM 50 (p. 3049) that he designed by incorporating lessons from Fredericia 2254.

Frederica Furniture Fair, 1958. View of Fredericia stand including low-back lounge chair Model 246 and daybed on runners Model 311. ← Fredericia 2254. Detail with backrest with adjustable bridle leather straps for neck cushion.

Over the course of his career, Mogens Koch designed perhaps thirty models of furniture under his own name. Each one of those models is decidedly unconventional, because he ignored the standard practices of furniture design. Rather than design models for specific types of rooms, he created simplified versions of general types — bookcase, armchair, sofa — that might be used anywhere. Rejecting the symbolic role of furniture, to convey wealth and social status, he conceived each model as an unpretentious piece of equipment that would serve its purpose as simply as possible. In place of personal expression, he emphasized the properties of the materials and used geometry to create anonymous forms.

Koch's ideal was a durable, well-made object that can be used by many people in a variety of settings according to their individual needs, which may change over time.[1] In the case of his wooden shelving units, a square box can simply be rotated 90° to accommodate books and other items of varied heights (p. 16). For more complex functions, he developed folding mechanisms that are easy to use and require minimal storage space. The emblematic example is the low folding table that was prototyped in 1938, forgotten for two decades and rediscovered in 1959. As with each of Koch's models, the unique character of **MK-49** is only truly revealed in use.

Kaare Klint. Folding table, 1938. Mahogany. Model 4701, Rud. Rasmussens Snedkerier. / Mogens Koch. MK-49 folding table, 1938/1960. Beech with pear veneer. 1:1 scale.

MOGENS KOCH 1938/1960
MK-49

Koch was a devoted student of history whose many fascinations included the collapsible furniture developed in nineteenth-century Britain for military campaigns, expeditions and excursions into the countryside. As he explained,

"There is a group of furniture for which the functional aspects are so influential on the design that style and ornamentation become secondary, and the furniture takes on the character of a tool."[2]

That group of furniture included a folding table with a split top that was originally designed to fit into a horse-drawn coach or carriage. In 1933, Kaare Klint designed his version of a "coaching table" to accompany the folding deck chair he designed the same year. Like the British model, it could not be flattened.[3] Five years later, Mogens Koch designed a table of roughly the same size and height that can be folded into a thin slab.

In 1938, master cabinetmaker N. C. Jensen Kjær presented a prototype of Koch's folding table at the annual exhibition of the Copenhagen Cabinetmakers' Guild, alongside four prototypes of a folding armchair that Koch had designed in 1933 (p. 292). Those ingenious inventions were completely overshadowed by the other two models that Koch and Jensen Kjær presented: a Cuban mahogany desk with pigskin top and a matching armchair with woven leather straps for seat and back.

The mahogany models were hailed as masterpieces of handicraft and soon acquired by the Danish Museum of Applied Art (now Designmuseum Danmark), but it seems that the collapsible models were not even photographed for posterity.[4] Koch and Jensen Kjær's flimsy contraptions must have seemed like prototypes for industrial production, which was precisely the case.

Twenty-one years later, Koch's folding table was resurrected by happy accident. In early 1959, he received a call from Axel Thygesen, the co-founder of a small furniture producer dedicated to unorthodox designs: Interna A/S.[5] Paging through an old issue of an architectural journal, Thygesen had come across a drawing of Koch's folding armchair and hoped to put it into production. Koch agreed and asked if Interna might also be interested in the folding table that had been exhibited with the armchair. Despite the fact that no drawings of the table had ever been published and the design was completely unknown to him, Thygesen accepted the offer sight unseen. As Koch prepared the working drawing for the factory, he replaced the solid wood planks of the initial design with a flush plywood plate, to eliminate a slight overhang and emphasize the compact form of the folded slab.

247

In March 1960, Interna introduced Koch's folding table with a solid beech structure and a plywood top with pearwood veneer, which provided a contrast to the beech and emphasized the proportions of the top. The table was initially designated MK-19 but later relabeled as MK-49, following the introduction of a mahogany version, and is still produced with that model number.

As described below, Koch's design has the self-contained logic of a mathematical equation, but it was rooted in two human factors. The first was the comfortable height for a low table used alongside chairs and sofas, which is in the range of 40–50 cm. The second factor, which is even more reflective of the human scale, is the widest comfortable distance between two hands when carrying an object, which (depending on the weight of the object) is in the range of 55–75 cm.

As every cabinetmaker knows, a pair of intersecting frames provides more stability than four legs, because the bottom rails of the frames are self-leveling. To that end, Koch designed a base of pivoting frames that unfold to 45° — a neutral angle that is equally stable in both directions — and outline a square with sides of 48 cm, which has a diagonal proportion of √2. Because the folded frames are stored beneath the tabletop, their length (√2 x 48 cm) determined its length: 68 cm.

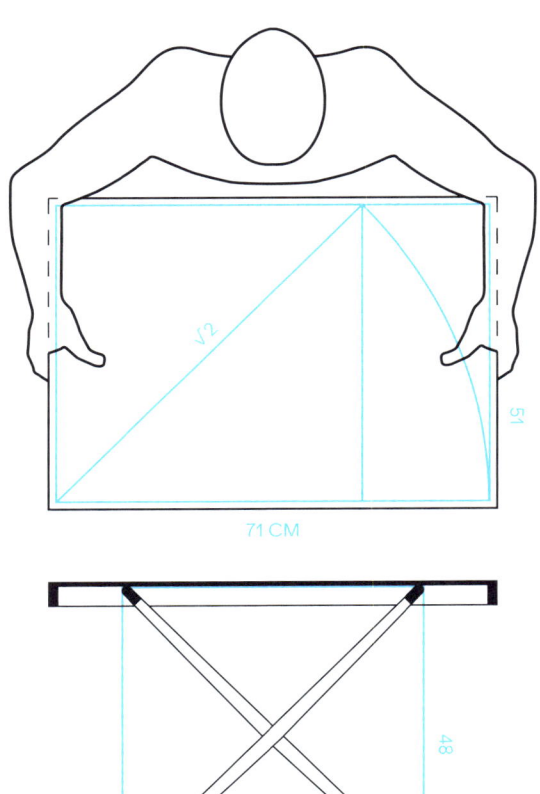

Overhead view with dimensions. The width of the table was based on a comfortable distance between two hands. Mathematics determined the other two dimensions. / MK-49 at standard height of 48 cm.
→ Folding action seen from below.

Because a cube is equally stable in all three directions, the width of the base matches the height and length of 48 cm. The width of the base determined the width of the tabletop. Adding the thickness of the apron that frames the top, Koch arrived at a table that is 71 x 51 x 48 cm, which can be folded into a slab with a thickness of 4 cm. For ease of storage, he attached a leather strap at one end of the apron, which allows the folded table to be hung on a wall using a special brass stud.

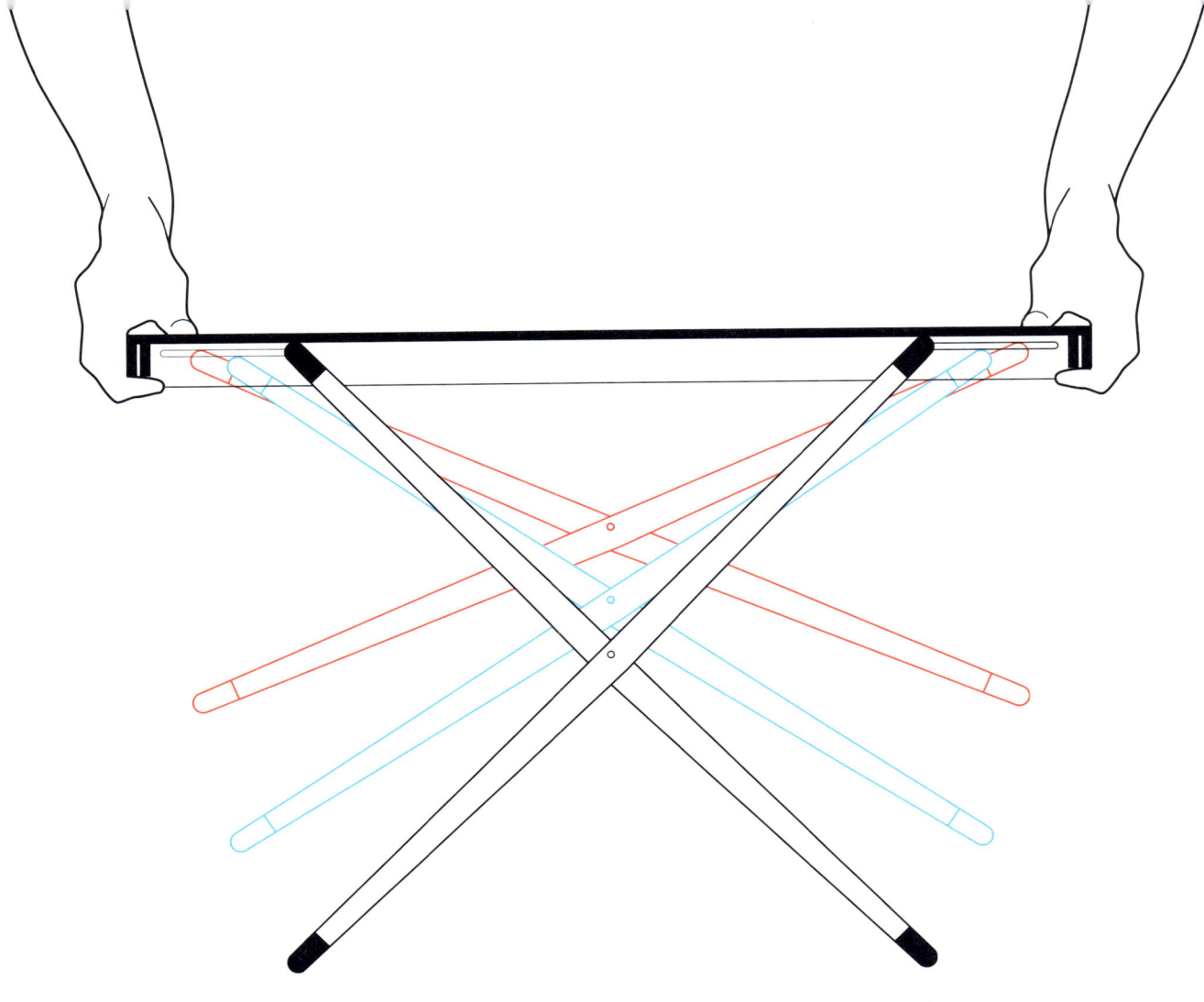

The operation of Koch's folding table will be familiar to anyone who has used a collapsible ironing board, but the mechanism he devised seems to have been unprecedented. As with his other collapsible models, he used as few moving parts as possible in order to limit possible malfunctions. For ease of use, the operation would be intuitive and powered by gravity, as the structure unfolded under its own weight. Folding structures are governed by geometric equations that determine lines of travel and angles of rotation. In fact, the branch of mechanics that preoccupied Koch (kinematics) has been described as the "geometry of motion". Plotting the movements of the pivoting frames that support the tabletop was elementary for Koch. His actual challenge was to devise a manually operated, self-locking mechanism that would hold the frames in place when they were folded or unfolded, for convenience and safety.

Koch found his solution in the two-part apron that frames the tabletop, with a fixed outer layer and a loose inner layer. Both layers contain slots that guide the movement of the folding frames, via metal pins at the ends of the top rails. While the inner slots are horizontal, the outer slots are diagonal and shaped like a check mark. When the ends of the inner and outer slots overlap, they hold the pivoting frames in an open or closed position.

Koch's mechanism is operated by handles cut into both ends of the apron. When the frames are folded, their weight bears on the loose inner layer of the apron and holds the metal pins in place. [A] Grasping the handles and squeezing both layers of the apron — as illustrated above — alleviates that weight and frees the metal pins to travel. As the pins travel along both slots at the same time and the frames unfold, the inner layer of the apron is pulled out of alignment with the outer layer. [B] When the metal pins reach the lowest point of the diagonal slots, a gentle squeeze on the handles will force the inner and outer layers of the apron back into alignment. As the layers align, the metal pins travel to the top of the diagonal slots, which locks the base in the open position. [C] The operation is reversed by compressing both layers of the apron, which allows the pins to travel backwards along the inner and outer slots, folding the base and locking the two frames in place.

Unfolding of table to height of 48 cm.
→ Detail of two-part apron with folded (A) and unfolding (B/C) frames. / Underside of table with loose inner frame during unfolding.

A

B

C

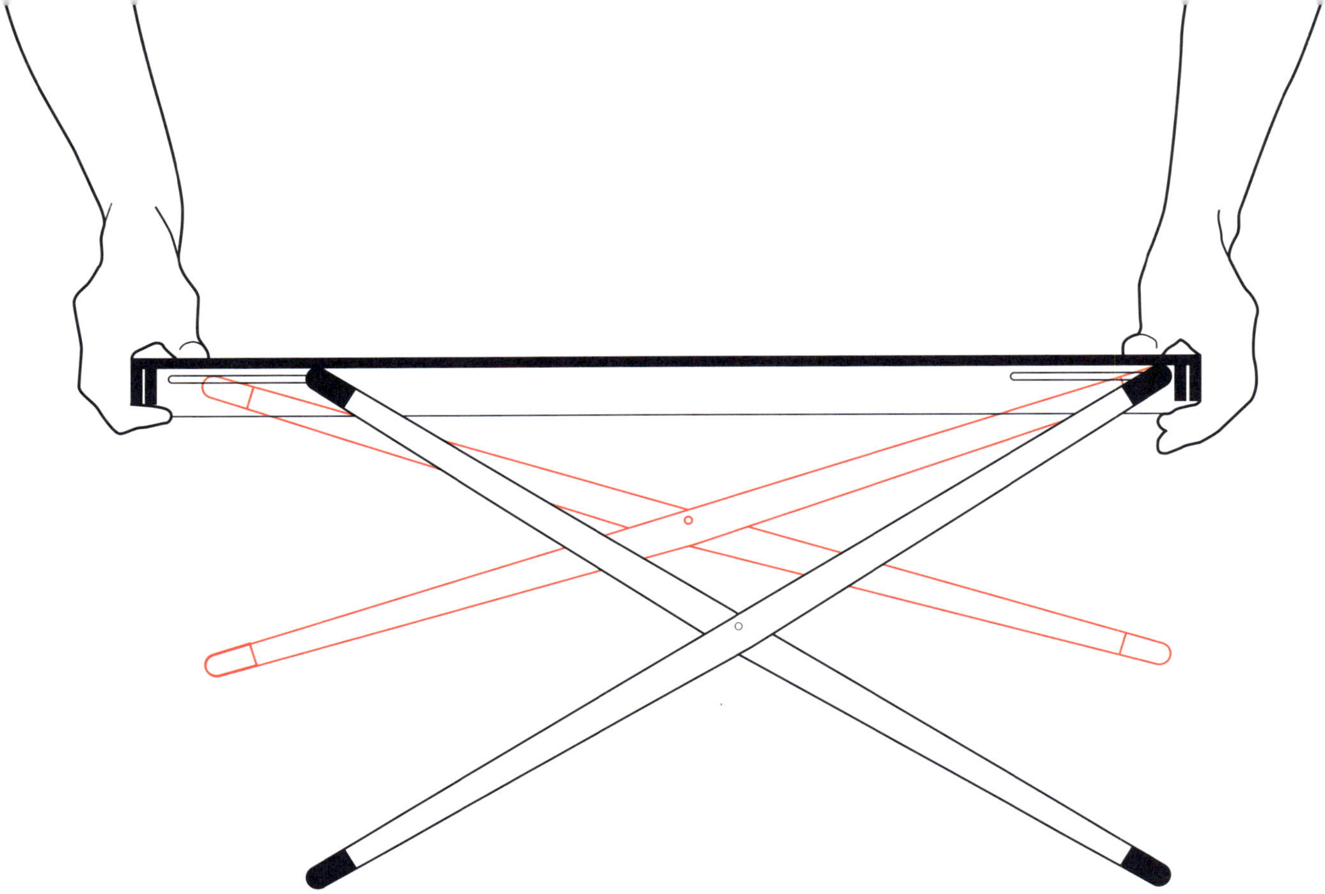

252

MK-49 has a second height that was never promoted by Interna, or any of the later producers, and has not previously been described. Because the two pivoting frames intersect at their midpoints, the rotation of one frame is mirrored by the rotation of the other. When one end of the apron is compressed, and the other end is not — as illustrated above — only one of the frames is free to travel along the slots in the apron. As the traveling frame moves sideways and rotates, it pulls the other frame into action. Because that other frame rotates in a fixed position, both frames are limited to an angle of 30°. The resulting height of 36 cm (12 cm lower than advertised) expands the useful character of Koch's folding structure, to such a degree that it provides the owner with a second type of table. The decision not to advertise the second height was undoubtedly made by the designer and rooted in his devotion to simple shapes: Koch simply preferred the table with a symmetrical structure and cubic base. But that decision, which was unusual for Koch because of his commitment to practical concerns, has obscured the extraordinary utility of his mechanical marvel.

The ability to unfold at two different heights transforms MK-49 from an elegant convenience into a uniquely versatile piece of furniture that promotes individualized interiors. Depending on the height, the table is useful in a living room, dining room, bedroom or bathroom, or anywhere else a low table is needed for a day, a week or a year. The temporary character of the table provides yet another example of Koch's unconventional approach to furniture design. Moreover, the bare wooden structure is free of stylistic associations and comfortably coexists with almost any other sort of furniture. Furniture that is independent of any specific setting or particular style is also free of social conventions and corresponding notions of good taste and decorum. Perhaps the most liberating aspect of MK-49 is the ability to remove it altogether and use the space for other purposes, without taking up space elsewhere for storage. From that perspective, the leather strap and brass wall stud are integral features of the table.

Underside of table with folded frame and double apron. Beech. ← Unfolding of table to height of 36 cm. / Tables at heights of 36 and 48 cm. Beech with pear veneer/mahogany.

MK-49 has been in production for more than sixty years, with a minor variation along the edge of the tabletop. In the original design, the top and upper edge of the apron were aligned, so that two or more tables could be combined to create a continuous surface. [**A**] That alignment required the plywood top to be recessed into the solid wood apron, which entailed some risk: If a plywood plate warped, due to weak glue or excess humidity, it would split the edge of the apron.[6] In 1964, Koch revised the design, so that plywood and solid wood were separated by a narrow piece of trim that could absorb any movement. That same year, Interna introduced the table in mahogany, the dense hardwood that Koch prized for its straight grain and rich luster. [**B**] The beech/pearwood and all-mahogany versions of the table remained in production until 1973, when Interna declared bankruptcy.

During 1978–2016, MK-49 was produced by Rud. Rasmussens Snedkerier, the cabinetmaking workshop that had been making Koch's modular bookcases since 1930. For the sake of consistency, the workshop altered the trim on the edge of the tabletop to match the profiled edge on the bookcase.[7] [**C**] Alongside the beech and mahogany tables, the workshop introduced a version made of ash with matching veneer, which can be identified by the distinctive, highly figured grain. [**D**] After Rud. Rasmussens Snedkerier closed, Carl Hansen & Søn restored the edge of the tabletop to Koch's original design and produced the table until 2020, in oak and walnut with matching veneers. Since 2022, Getama A/S has produced MK-49 using the original detail, in beech or oak with matching veneers or a laminate top that eliminates the risk of rings and stains. [**E**]

Mogens Koch worked within a cultural tradition that dates to the Renaissance, in which art and science were intertwined and advances in one field informed the other. Driven by curiosity and searching for harmony, he mastered complex subjects that included geometry, mechanics, optics and myriad forms of handicraft, and used his knowledge to develop apparently natural and seemingly artless solutions for everyday life. His ambition was to create at least a few things that possess the quintessential character he admired in certain historical artifacts, produced by societies as varied as the ancient Greeks, eighteenth-century French and Inuit of Greenland.[8] He succeeded in that ambition and, in doing so, forged new links in a chain of cultural development that extends back into the ancient world and forward into our own time. The clearest expression of Koch's evolutionary approach is the folding armchair that he exhibited alongside the folding table in 1938, which incorporated lessons from a three-thousand-year-old Egyptian model and provides the subject for a later chapter.

Top views of MK-49 in beech and mahogany.
← Evolution of the edge. Bottom to top:
A. Beech/pear veneer with flush edge, 1960.
B. Mahogany/mahogany with raised edge, 1964.
C. Beech/beech with raised edge, 1978.
D. Ash/ash with raised edge, 1980s.
E. Beech/laminate with flush edge, 2023.

Based on the decoration of her own very small apartment, weaver Kim Naver created a multipurpose textile that makes it possible to cover windows, walls, tables and beds with the same simple design and create a sense of harmony throughout the home. In place of a pattern, Naver employed a wide band of color that becomes a defining element in the room and makes it possible to adjust the atmosphere based on the color of daylight and of the surrounding surfaces. Designed for industrial production, **Cotil 1828** was produced in three combinations of colors that can be used uniformly or combined according to taste. While Naver's design was rooted in the Danish weaving tradition, her muted shades were inspired by early Renaissance paintings that she encountered as a child, on cultural journeys organized by her father, publisher Rasmus Naver.[1]

Castle by a Lake. Attributed to Sassetta (Stefano di Giovanni), circa 1425. (Also attributed to Ambrogio Lorenzetti, circa 1340, and Simone Martini, circa 1310.) Tempera on wood panel, 23 x 39 cm. Pinacoteca Nazionale, Siena, Italy.
→ Kim Naver. Cotil 1828/3, 1967–68. Cotton and linen. 1:1 scale.

Between the ages of nine and twelve, Kim Naver enjoyed an annual trip with her parents and a group of their artistic friends, for pleasure and to advance their understanding of visual art. In Italy, she found herself fascinated by the works of masters such as Piero della Francesca, Fra Angelico, Ambrogio Lorenzetti and Sassetta.[2] Decades later, the painters' collective palette of warm, mineral-based colors remained lodged in her memory and preserved in the collection of postcards that she accumulated during her travels. That collection contains several reproductions of Sienese paintings from the early 1400s, including the mysterious *Castle by the Lake* that has provided Naver with a creative touchstone for many decades.

Like Naver's sensitivity to color, her interest in textiles was formed at an early age.[3] After finishing high school in 1959, she moved to Paris and spent a year studying art history at the École du Louvre. Returning to Denmark, she enrolled at the School for Interior Design but found the courses uninspiring and left after one year. Five years earlier, at the age of sixteen, she had painted simple designs on lengths of cloth and sold them at a consignment shop, along with the necklaces and tote bags that she made with her boyfriend. Leaving the academic path behind, she returned to her formative experience with textiles and decided to take up the loom. In 1962, she began an apprenticeship with Lis Ahlmann, the stubborn guardian of the Danish weaving tradition, who sustained that tradition by embracing industrial production.

KIM NAVER 1967–69
Cotil 1828

Lis Ahlmann. Selection of upholstery fabrics for the Cotil collection, 1953–58. / Dronningensgade 13, Copenhagen. Floor plan illustrating Kim Naver's use of a single textile for multiple purposes, 1964. 1:100 scale. / Cotil trademark. → Sample of Naver's 1964 multi-purpose textile. 1:1 scale. / Vibeke Klint. Handwoven carpet, early 1960s. Wool, 220 x 145 cm.

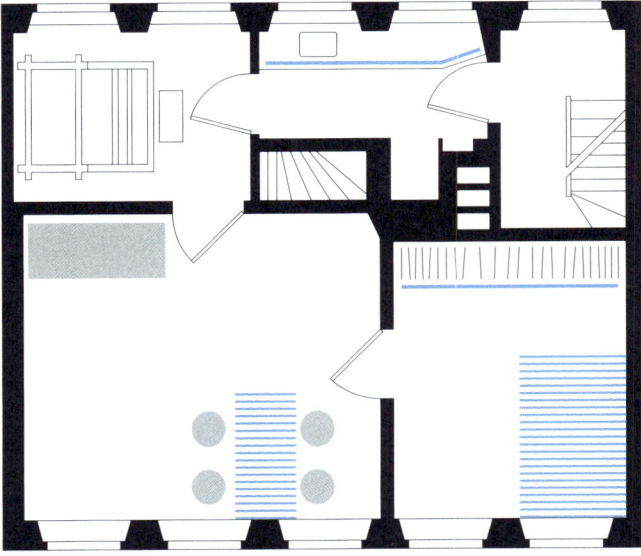

In addition to operating her workshop, Lis Ahlmann designed textiles for C. Olesen A/S. Founded in 1892, by the eponymous Carl Olesen, the company quickly grew from an importer to a manufacturer with a large factory in Kastrup. By the founder's death in 1927, C. Olesen was the largest textile wholesaler in Scandinavia. That same year, Gerda (Heydorn) Henning established a weaving school within the Danish Museum of Applied Art (now Designmuseum Danmark) and accepted Ahlmann as her first student.[4] She completed her training in 1929 and spent the next five years in Henning's workshop, where her labors included carpets jointly designed by Kaare Klint and Mogens Koch. In the process, she absorbed Klint's dictum that mastery of material and technique are the prerequisites to individual artistic expression.[5]

After Ahlmann established her own workshop, in 1934, Klint encouraged her to travel and find inspiration in traditional patterns, in Denmark and abroad.[6] During the late 1930s, she made repeated journeys across the Danish countryside and collected pieces of traditional peasant weaves. At her suggestion, the Danish Museum of Applied Art staged the three-part exhibition *Folkelig vævning i Danmark* (Folk Weaving in Denmark) during 1940–41, which was based on her fieldwork.[7] By 1944, Mogens Koch was actively campaigning for Ahlmann's employment in the textile industry.[8] In 1953, C. Olesen director Jørgen Anthon hired her to create designs for his factory, with a focus on furniture coverings. That position provided Ahlmann financial security and allowed her to maintain the workshop where she would later train Kim Naver.

In 1956, Jørgen Anthon established Cotil — **C. O**lesen tek**stil** — a collection of modern fabrics for the home, which would include carpets, curtains and upholstery fabrics.[9] To ensure a high artistic standard, a committee composed of Koch, Mogensen, Ahlmann and the director of the Danish Association of Arts and Crafts, Bent Salicath, reviewed submissions and selected the designs. As the program was an extension of Ahlmann's work for C. Olesen, the Cotil collection naturally included many of her designs, which were often co-credited to Mogensen, and Koch contributed a design for a carpet. At the same time, the committee selected a great many designs by an eclectic group of weavers and fabric printers, whose artistic impulses extended well beyond the muted colors and simple patterns favored by Koch, Ahlmann and Mogensen.[10]

In 1964, a newly married Kim Naver and her husband moved into a 32-square-meter apartment in Christianshavn, a charming section of Copenhagen crisscrossed with canals.[11] Their compact dwelling included a bedroom, living room, galley kitchen and a tiny chamber that barely accommodated Naver's loom. She understood that a mix of textiles in a few small rooms could easily become overwhelming, due to clashing colors and patterns. Intent on harmony, she decided to use a single textile throughout the apartment, which would also make the interior seem more spacious. After visiting a discount fabric store and buying some meters of the blue-and-white striped cotton fabric used to cover mattresses, Naver made curtains for the kitchen shelves and an improvised closet in the bedroom as well as a bedspread and tablecloth.

Two years into her apprenticeship, Naver gave birth to her first child and took a yearlong break from her training. During that hiatus, Ahlmann suggested that Naver spend the final year of her apprenticeship in another workshop, to broaden her range of weaving techniques.[12] With her mentor's assistance, Naver secured a place with Vibeke (Nielsen) Klint, who was three decades younger than Ahlmann but had also been trained by Gerda Henning, and later married the landscape architect Morten Klint, a son of Kaare Klint. In 1966, Naver completed her training by weaving a double-woven plaid blanket of undyed Faroese wool. After Ahlmann showed the piece to Jørgen Anthon, he hired Naver as a textile designer with a monthly salary of 325 Danish kroner (around 500 U.S. dollars in today's money) as an advance against future royalties.[13]

Kim Naver. Wrapping samples for multi-purpose textile, 1967. The various knots of colored thread record her progress toward the final combination. → Cotil 1828 in three colorways. 52% cotton and 48% linen, 150 cm wide. Top to bottom: 1828/1, 1828/2, 1828/3.

Naver's earliest designs for the Cotil collection were plaid blankets that resembled her apprenticeship testpiece, but she conceived a more ambitious project by the end of 1967. On the strength of her experience in Christianshavn, she imagined a multipurpose textile with a large and simple motif that would occupy an intermediate scale between architecture and furniture and promote tranquility within and between rooms.[14] That textile would be equally attractive flat or gathered and suitable for both horizontal and vertical uses, including but not limited to curtains and Roman shades, bedspreads and tablecloths and furniture slipcovers. The idea was rooted in Naver's use of a ready-made pattern, but her design would reflect her sensitivity to color and establish her own artistic direction, quite apart from the plaid and diagonal motifs favored by her two former teachers.

Her fundamental decision was to abandon any sort of pattern or overall motif in favor of a symmetrical composition centered on a wide band of color framed by narrower bands of undyed fibers. On either side of the central band, a pair of colored lines softens the boundary between the bands of artificial and natural colors and introduces an accent color provides a grace note.

Similarly to the blue-and-white mattress cloth that Naver employed in Christianshavn, her own design includes narrow areas of undyed fibers that appear as a second set of stripes. As the eye shifts back and forth between the two sets of narrow stripes that frame the wide band of color, the distinction between foreground and background is blurred. The resulting sense of flatness anchors Naver's colors in the weave and has a calming effect.

As Naver searched for her ideal colors, she used the weaver's traditional method of wrapping threads around a piece of cardboard to determine the width of the two sets of stripes and the number of threads per centimeter. After settling on three combinations of major and minor colors, Naver wove a cotton sample of the orange colorway and presented it to the Cotil committee for consideration.[15] In 1968, C. Olesen introduced Naver's multipurpose textile with the model number Cotil 1828 in a blend of cotton, which provides rich color, and linen, which imparts structure and strength. While the width of the cloth (150 cm) corresponded to the size of the loom at the factory, the width of the colored band (98 cm) was determined by Naver's sensitivity to the optical weight of the various colors and her delicate sense of proportions.

Kim Naver's textile designs are rooted in a creative principle that she had inherited from Kaare Klint, by way of her apprenticeship with Lis Ahlmann and Vibeke Klint. According to that principle, artistic expression in woven materials is indivisible from material and technique.[16] Natural fibers — wool, cotton and linen — have specific properties that include weight, texture and ability to hold color. Whether woven by hand or machine, textiles have a geometric structure in which two sets of fibers (warp and weft) intersect, typically at a right angle. When a design is based on the weaving process and the properties of the materials, it is intrinsic to the finished piece of cloth. Absent those factors, the design is imposed on the textile, like paint on canvas, and the result is a personal work of art rather than the product of cultural tradition.

Weavers of the Klint School worked within the limitations imposed by their technique and created geometric designs that emphasized the properties of their raw materials. In doing so, they created variations on a few simple themes while maintaining the distinction between woven materials for daily use and fiber art. As a matter of fact, that limited approach is capable of yielding nearly endless variations. The immediate example is Lis Ahlmann's upholstery fabrics for the Cotil collection (previous spread), in which she used both wrap and weft to vary the size and density of her plaid patterns. Designing Cotil 1828, Kim Naver used the longer fibers (warp) as vehicles for color, while limiting the crossways fibers (weft) to threads of undyed linen. As the linen crosses the strands of dyed cotton, the brightness of the colors is muted and the pigments are absorbed into the woven structure.

In 1970, when asked to describe the lessons of her apprenticeship, Naver also discussed the difference between art and industrial design,

"Above all, a heightened sense of quality and a better grasp of materials and their possibilities and compositions based on a limited range of colors with the capacity to 'stay fresh' in the long term, i.e., resist fleeting shifts in fashion. These are basic requirements for being able to work with industry. By the way, it is strange that so many people seek to disparage any engagement with industry … it is seen as less 'noble', and in fact, in Denmark, very few of us work directly with industry … most [weavers] seek the freedom of 'free textiles'. My end-goal is not necessarily this 'free' expression … my freedom lies mainly in being allowed to develop without artificially accelerating my pace."[17]

There are no photographs or other evidence that any of C. Olesen's customers ever employed Cotil 1828 to its full potential and realized Naver's vision of a single textile that could be used throughout the home. Nonetheless, it is possible to create the effect by employing vintage rolls of fabric in the designer's apartment. The first impression is one of intimacy, as the eye is drawn to the bands of color and visually connects the horizontal and vertical surfaces. Moreover, the borders of undyed fibers are revealed as essential elements in Naver's composition, because they isolate the central bands of color from the floor and walls. As a result, the colored bands appear to be independent elements that float in the room and provide a simple context for all of the objects in the room.

Kim Naver at her loom, 1969.
→ Interior with Cotil 1828/1. 2023.

Naver's inspired use of color created a woven instrument of interior design. It is widely recognized that the character of daylight varies with the orientation of the room. Rooms that receive direct light have a warmer tone, while north-facing rooms that receive light reflected from the dome of the sky have a cooler tone. In the Nordic countries, daylight arrives at a low angle for most of the year and has a bluish tone, because water-laden clouds absorb red wavelengths of light. As a result, the ability to adjust the color tone of a room is a pressing concern, no matter the orientation. In Cotil 1828, the width of the colored band makes it possible to use that color as a defining element in a room, with the precise color determined by the materials on the floor, walls and ceiling, the color of natural light and individual preference.

Regardless of the colorway, Naver's design of Cotil 1828 encapsulates her concern for those who would live with her designs. She hoped that her anonymous design would allow people to enjoy her work for decades, freed from worries about whether the curtains or tablecloth had fallen out of fashion. The elimination of pattern in favor of parallel bands was one element of that strategy. Another element was the use of distinctly unfashionable colors that were inspired by painting of the 1400s and would — in her words — "stay fresh" over time. Mindful of the fact that choosing colors is a distinctly personal matter (as seen in Naver's own, esoteric palette), she blended yellow with either red or blue to create complex shades of orange or green that respond to changes in ambient light and selected a deep blue that becomes luminous in dim light.

During the 1970s, Kim Naver's designs were as important to the Cotil collection as Lis Ahlmann's designs had been during the 1950s and '60s. Over the course of the decade, Naver created hundreds of designs for curtains, upholstery fabrics and carpets. On occasion, she collaborated with Vibeke Klint, with Klint determining the weave and Naver developing the palette of colors.[18] Naver's work for C. Olesen continued until 1981, when the company collapsed under pressure from low-cost imports and the debt incurred constructing a new factory on the edge of Copenhagen. By that point, her handwoven textiles had been featured in several exhibitions, and she had received her first public commissions for decorative tapestries and carpets.

> Interior of Naver's apartment, 2023. In the bedroom that receives north light, the cork floor warms the atmosphere and provides a rich foil for the warm blue tone of Cotil 1828/3. In fact, cool colors are more easily perceived in dim light, so that the curtain will glow at dusk.
> → Cotil 1828/1 / As an alternative to identical colors, the contrasting tones of Cotil 1828/3 at the windows and Cotil 1828/2 on the table increase the apparent depth of the room. The similar tones of tablecloth, floor and bookcases emphasize the blue bolt of the curtains.

Kim Naver's most important public work is the set of five large tapestries that she designed for the headquarters of the National Bank of Denmark, in Copenhagen's historic core, which were installed in 1978. The building was designed by Arne Jacobsen during the 1960s and completed after his death in 1971 by his successors, Hans Dissing and Otto Weitling. In 1976, they invited Naver to submit her ideas for decorating the spectacular lobby, with its 20-meter-high ceiling, at the south end of the building.[19] Located along a skewed street — Havnegade — the wedge-shaped lobby is 4 meters wide at the entrance and 14 meters wide at the opposite end. Naver's commission was to design textiles that would fill the shallow niches along the skewed wall and reinforce the special character of the room. She did so by emphasizing the quality of daylight.

Naver based her work on the fact that the lobby is brightest at the wide end, due to the increased size of the space and corresponding reflections of daylight.[20] She designed the tapestries using diagonal bands of colors that create a forced perspective, in which the bands appear consistent to someone standing at the entrance. As that person walks from the entrance towards the wide end of the room, the dominant color of the tapestries shifts from red to orange to yellow as the room grows brighter. In that way, the tapestries are experienced as integral features of the lobby that reveal an essential feature of the space through movement. While the diagonal compositions are site-specific, the rich colors and optical device of a forced perspective both recall the Renaissance paintings that captivated Naver as a child.

The contemporary character of Cotil 1828, which Kim Naver designed in 1968 based on a creative principle codified in the 1920s, is at once a tribute to her artistic sensibility and to the enduring value of the weaving tradition in which she was trained. More generally, Cotil 1828 embodies the historical arc of Danish design during the twentieth century — from the workshop to the factory — as certainly as Kay Bojesen's steel flatware (p. 24) and Børge Mogensen's furniture after 1950. Like the silversmith's utensils and the cabinetmaker's tables and chairs, Naver's industrial textile was an extension of her artisanal practice, in which she applied the virtues of handicraft to mass production. In doing so, she created a useful item for daily life that preserves the ideals of an earlier era and remains a source of wonder and inspiration.

> National Bank of Denmark, Arne Jacobsen (1961–71) and Dissing+Weitling (1971–78). Interior of lobby with three of Kim Naver's five site-specific tapestries, 1977–78. Wool and linen, 2.3 x 3 m. ← Kim Naver. Curtain fabric for the Cotil collection in three colorways, circa 1977. Cotton and linen.

During most of his career, Knud Holscher maintained parallel practices in architecture and industrial design, while attempting to erase the distinction between the two fields. In both fields, his ideal was a flexible system composed of a very few parts that could be rearranged as needs changed.[1] Among Holscher's industrial designs, the outstanding example of his open-ended, systematic approach is a series of twelve lamps that employ a single lighting element: **String-line**. He based the series on a now-obsolete incandescent bulb, but String-line has been restored to utility by recent advances in lighting technology. As a result, this lighting series from the 1970s is once again a contemporary design that provides the ageless benefit of excellent illumination.

Holscher's work as an industrial designer was rooted in his frustration as an architect. In 1955, he graduated from the School of Architecture at the Royal Danish Academy and held several positions prior to 1958, when he joined Arne Jacobsen's office.[2] The following year, Jacobsen assigned him the role of project architect for St Catherine's College at the University of Oxford, in England. Holscher and his family lived in Oxford during 1962–64, while he supervised the construction. As the college neared completion, Holscher found that no manufacturer could supply all of the necessary pieces of hardware for doors, windows and other applications, which forced him to combine pieces from a variety of sources.[3] In 1964, he established a design practice with architect Allan Tye, one of his colleagues on the college, and they began work on a comprehensive hardware system.

Holscher & Tye's **Modric** (modular metric) system of aluminum hardware reached the market in 1966 and was an immediate success.[4] That same year, Holscher joined the Danish architectural practice Krohn & Hartvig Rasmussen with the proviso that he would become a partner, if he won the competition to design the new university in Odense, in central Denmark, which he did.[5] With the university in mind, Holscher designed a system of hardware for the Carl F. Pedersen A/S factory — **d-line** — that was introduced in 1971, was extended over two decades and remains in production.[6]

Working with a few diameters of stainless steel rod, Holscher and his assistants developed a limited number of elements that can be combined to suit almost any application, while providing a sense of unity within rooms and between buildings.

In 1973, Holscher & Tye were contacted by H.F. Belysning A/S, a small producer of household lighting seeking ideas for new products.[7] Holscher seized the opportunity and designed a series of light fixtures that are based on a single element: a cylindrical tube that combines bulb, shade and switch. As with d-line, the fixtures were made of stainless steel, which is immensely strong and extremely durable. Similarly to the hardware, the fixtures can be combined according to individual need in a wide range of settings. No matter the combination, the uniform lighting element ensures harmony among groups of different fixtures. Holscher selected Jens Rølling, his primary assistant on d-line, to handle the research and drawings and named the system after the narrow pieces of curved steel tubing or rod that support the lighting element on all of the fixtures.

Knud Holscher. d-line hardware system, since 1971.
→ Knud Holscher. String-line, 1976. Detail of worktable lamp. 1:1 scale.

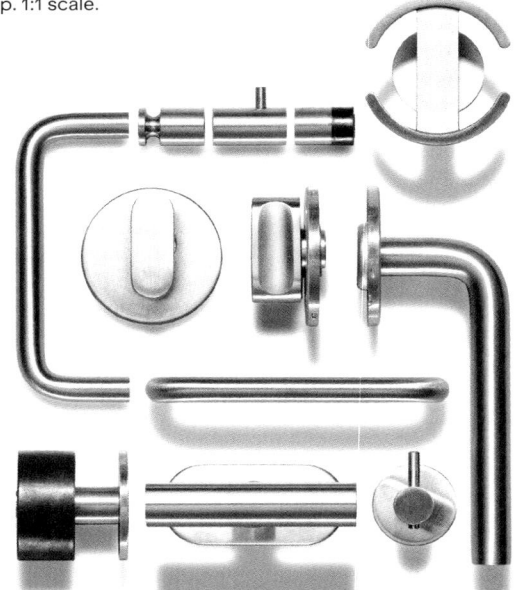

KNUD HOLSCHER 1973–76/1981–82
String-line

An assortment of partial models for String-line. Left to right: Arne Jacobsen. Oxford table lamp, 1964. Louis Poulsen A/S. Jo Hammerborg. Trombone pendant, table lamp and floor lamp, 1966. Fog & Mørup/Warm Nordic. Verner Panton. Flower Pot table lamp, 1968. Louis Poulsen A/S. Achille Castiglioni/Pio Manzù. Parentesi lamp, 1971. Flos.

As Knud Holscher and Jens Rølling developed String-line, they incorporated ideas and mechanisms from a number of existing fixtures. The obvious example is Arne Jacobsen's Oxford table lamp of 1964, which is based on a built-in fixture at St Catherine's College.[8] As Jacobsen revised the design for factory production, he adopted the circular base of metal tubing with an integral cord that Kaare Klint devised for his 1944 convertible wall/table lamp (p. 12). The three Trombone fixtures that Jo Hammerborg designed in 1966 demonstrated the appeal of a single lighting element across a variety of fixtures and included stands of parallel tubes that allow the element to pivot.[9]

In 1968, Verner Panton combined the circular base of Jacobsen's Oxford lamp and the parallel structure of Hammerborg's table lamp to create the stand for his Flower Pot table lamp.[10] The closed loop of steel rod terminates in a curved tip that allows adjustment of the hemispherical lighting element. Three years later, Achille Castiglioni (working from sketches by Pio Manzù) designed the Parentesi lamp, a new type of light fixture that employs a steel cable stretched between ceiling and floor.[11] The pivoting bulb is suspended on a length of bent steel tubing that is held in place by friction between tubing and cable and can be adjusted vertically.

Ultimately, Holscher combined aspects of these varied models and created a cohesive series of new fixtures that constitutes a unique achievement in lighting design.

40 W silver-reflector bulb that served as the basis for String-line. / Clip-on shade with welded spring steel clips. → Model 1. Pendant based on String-line lighting element. / Floor lamp with stainless steel tubes and cast iron base.

Knud Holscher based the design of String-line on a 40-watt reflector bulb that provides focused illumination for concentrated tasks, such as reading and cooking, and is also useful for accent lighting. His plan was to combine the bulb with a stainless steel tube and create a standard lighting element that could be used across the entire series. Locating that tube would require an industrial scavenger hunt. H.F. Belysning was unwilling to spend money on tools and dies. As a result, Holscher and Rølling were forced to search for ready-made parts that could be assembled to provide the lighting element.[12] Sourcing sockets and switches would be straightforward; the manufacturer had a warehouse filled with components. The architects' challenge would be finding a stainless steel tube with the required diameter and wall thickness.

Eventually, Rølling found a tube that was widely used in the dairy industry and developed what Holscher described as "a typically Danish solution: practical and inexpensive."[13] The tube was normally used for milking cows but could easily be converted into a lamp by drilling holes and cutting a slot for the switch. A segment of a slightly wider tube was fitted with flexible steel clips, to create a shade that snaps onto the end of the bulb and prevents glare. The resulting element was labeled Model 1 and used as a pendant for illuminating countertops. By 1976, when String-line reached the market, the series included eight models that provided twelve different fixtures. Aside from the pendant, all of the fixtures featured a pivoting element and five of them made it possible to adjust the element horizontally.

The floor lamp (Model 7) contains the typical features of the series and demonstrates the interplay of aesthetic and practical concerns that characterizes String-line. As on most of the other fixtures, the lighting element on the floor lamp rotates on rubber disks that are held in place by parallel lengths of steel tubing. Similarly to the table lamp (Model 5) and working lamp (Model 6), the electrical cord is contained in the tubing and long enough to allow for adjustment of the lighting element. The combination of rigid tubing and flexible cord imbues those fixtures with the character of kinetic sculpture, as though an artist had created lines in space using lengths of rope — or string. As the lighting element is moved, the electrical cord assumes a new form, and the composition of lines is reconfigured.

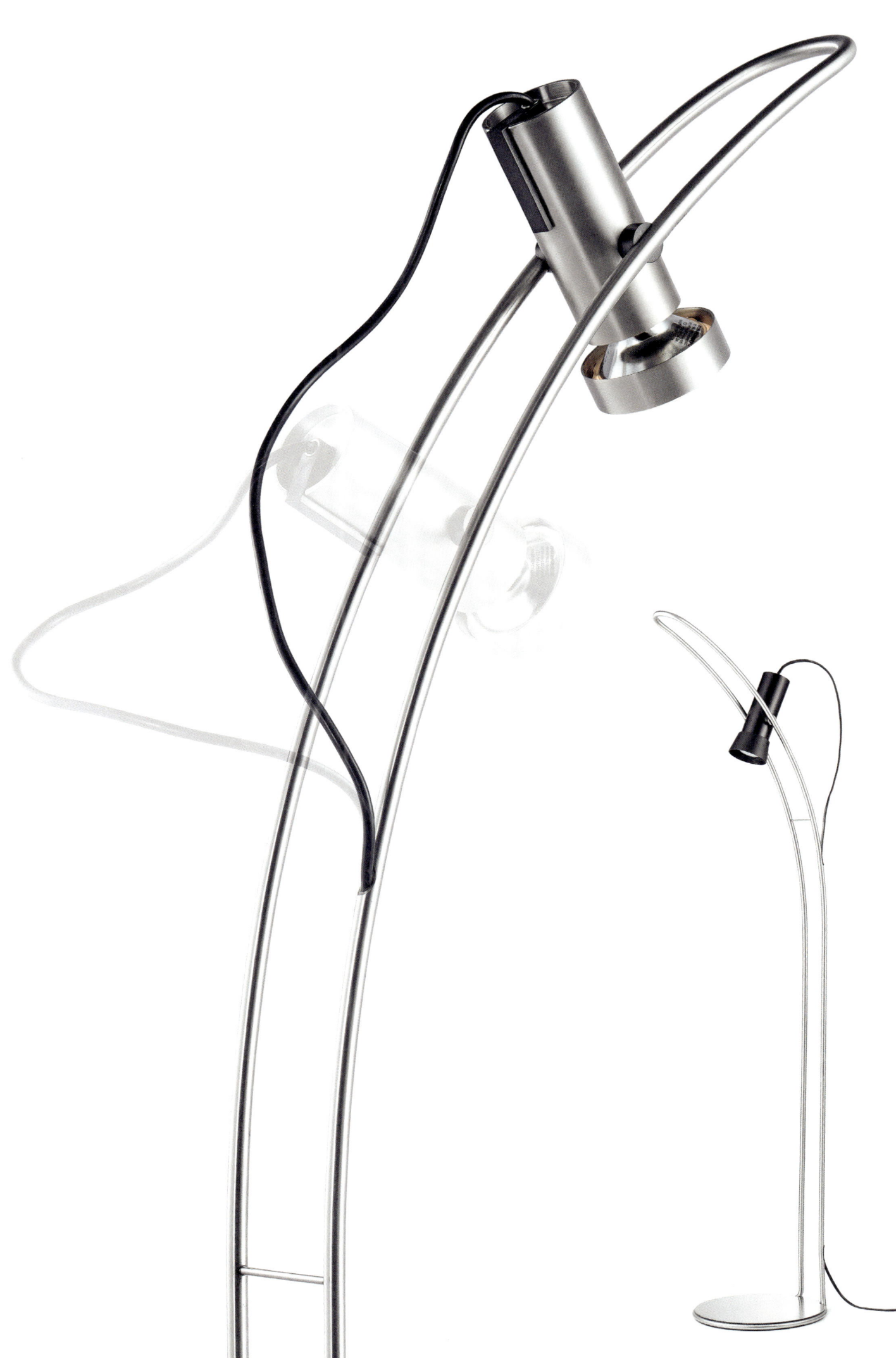

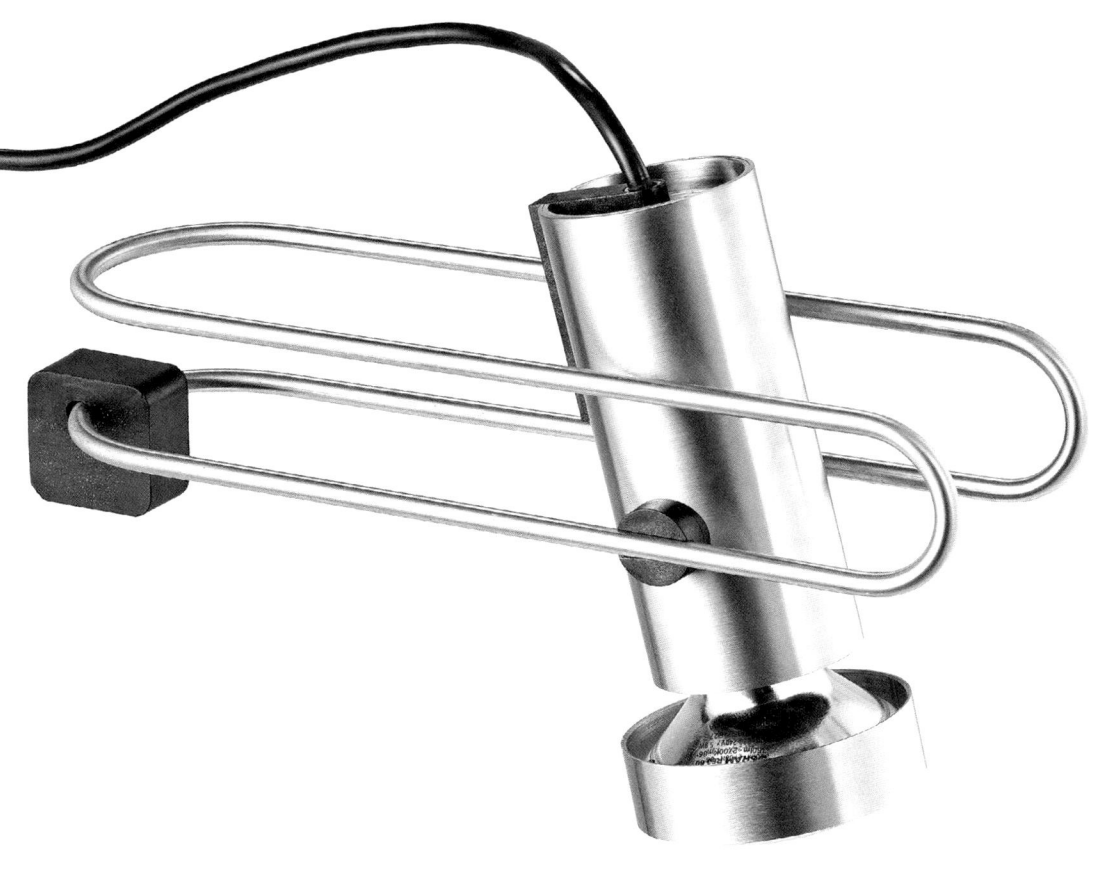

Model 4. Clamping lamp with rotating rubber block for shelves of varied thickness.

Untangling the similarities between String-line and Arne Jacobsen's Cylinda-line of hollowware (p. 76) in material, form and name advances our understanding of both series. In the context of Danish design culture of the 1960s and '70s, it becomes clear that Jacobsen and Holscher were working within an aesthetic movement led by architects and designers born in the 1930s and '40s. While Holscher was a member of that generation, Jacobsen (always attuned to the latest developments) was an outlier. Holscher and his cohort had turned away from the refined artistic ideals promoted by mentors such as Jacobsen, in favor of a plainly industrial approach.[14] Rather than create unique objects and interiors, they designed consumer products that included prefabricated fireplaces (p. 74) and outdoor cooking equipment (p. 316), with the goal of creating standard models for mass production.

In the service of that goal, Holscher and his peers adopted an aesthetic approach based on raw materials and repetitive elements that signaled the authentic and apparently artless character of their designs. Their preferred material was steel, which is extremely versatile and relatively inexpensive, at least in its basic form. Stainless steel was ideal because it did not require a coating and was genuine.

And so, we can recognize a Steel Age of Danish design that began around 1952, when Magnus L. Stephensen designed his first steel hollowware (p. 79) and ended around 1977, when Ole Palsby finished the original version of Eva Trio (p. 132). While the new generation of architect-designers rejected the manner of their predecessors, they were unable to abandon their inherited fascinations with fine materials and delicate details.

With String-line, Holscher's inventive use of materials reached a peak in the bookshelf lamp (Model 4) that is simply held in place by compression. The lighting element is carried by a welded loop of steel rod that was doubled to create a U-shaped bracket. At the open end of the bracket, a rotating rubber block compresses the edge of the shelf against the upper end of the loop. As the point of rotation is not located in the center of the rubber block, the vertical distance between the two ends of the loop can be adjusted by rotating the block. The combination of resilient steel and flexible rubber makes it possible to attach the fixture to shelves of different thickness: 12, 18, 22 and 28 mm, even as the lighting element slides along the U-shaped bracket.

Several parts of String-line include self-guiding clamps that make it easier to attach the fixtures to a shelf or table and also secures them in place. While Model 4 is relatively short and lightweight, the longer and heavier fixtures with stems of steel tubing (Models 2b and 3b) require rigid attachments to prevent them from twisting on the shelf. To make that possible, Holscher and Rølling designed a C-clamp with a notched plate and a vertical post that guides the plate as the clamp is tightened. While the rectangular plate provides an ample surface area against the underside of a shelf or table, the post prevents the plate (and thus the fixture) from rotating if and when the fixture is bumped.

Further development of the self-guiding clamp made it possible to adjust the height of the working lamp (Model 6) while it is attached to the table. Similarly to the lamps for shelves, the clamp on Model 6 includes a rectangular plate that ensures sufficient compression against the underside of the table. The innovative feature is the two-part assembly of nested segments, which compresses the stem from opposite directions. As a result, it is possible to loosen the clamp and then slide the stem up and down without dismantling the entire apparatus. Moreover, compression from opposite directions holds the stem upright when the fixture is raised to its maximum height.

Model 6. Detail of worktable lamp with self-tightening clamp. As the clamp is tightened, the steel tubing that carries the lighting element also guides the plate and prevents it from rotating. → Model 3b. Bookshelf lamp with self-tightening clamp. / Self-tightening clamps for Model 3b and Model 6.

A trio of adjustable lamps. Left to right: Model 6 worktable lamp. Model 5 table lamp. Model 8 wire-lamp.

A trio of fixtures displays the harmony produced by Holscher's uniform lighting element, as well as the DIY (Do It Yourself) impulse that inspired him to design the series. In pursuit of multi-functional fixtures, he rejected the classical ideal of a complete and fixed object that is embodied by Arne Jacobsen's Oxford table lamp (p. 272). While Jacobsen's lamp is beautiful and provides enchanting illumination, it cannot be adjusted and directs light in a single direction. Rather than design a series of ideal lighting fixtures, Holscher designed an ideal lighting element and used it to create adjustable fixtures that people can use as they see fit. The contrast between the classical and DIY approaches is most apparent in Holscher's table lamp with a circular base (Model 5), which is based on Jacobsen's Oxford lamp but has a pivoting lighting element that slides along the steel tubing.

Holscher's ideal of dynamic fixtures led him to design a lamp suspended on a vertical cable (Model 8) that employs the same principle as the Parentesi lamp (p. 273). On Model 8, the lighting element is held in compression by a length of bent steel tubing, which can slide along the cable that is attached to the ceiling and weighted at the floor. The tubing is held in place by friction with the cable that holds the lamp, but a slight tug on the cable reduces the friction and makes it possible to adjust the height of the tubing. As a result, the lighting element can move vertically and horizontally, even as it pivots in the typical manner. The family resemblance between Model 8 and the Parentesi lamp led to a dispute that illuminates Holscher's achievement with the entire series.

Multiples of Model 8 can be combined to provide direct and indirect illumination.
→ Model 8. Detail of wire-lamp with lighting element and armature that allows adjustment vertically and horizontally.

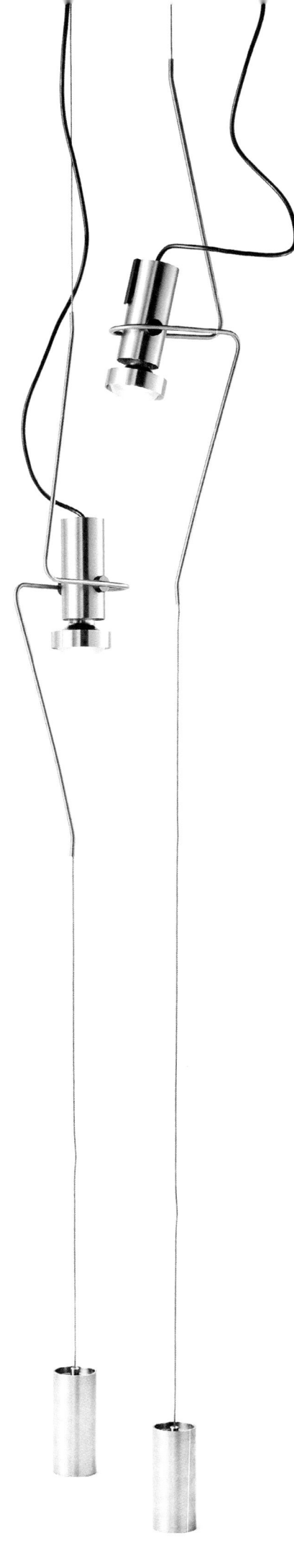

There is no possibility of mistaking Knud Holscher's Model 8 for Achille Castiglioni and Pio Manzù's Parentesi lamp, nor is there any doubt that Model 8 was inspired by their inventive mechanism. In 1971, the Italian lamp established a new paradigm for lighting fixtures, which can be compared in importance to the first cantilevered chair made of steel tubing in the 1920s. Much as Marcel Breuer and Alvar Aalto created new chairs based on Mart Stam's prototype (p. 152), Holscher created a new lamp that offers several improvements on the original example. By bending the steel tubing into a complex form with horizontal sections and a half-round loop, he increased the contact between tubing and cable, which also increased the friction and made it easier to control the height of the element. Moreover, the idea of suspending the lamp within the steel tubing, which allows it to slide horizontally or be removed and inverted for uplighting, was unprecedented.

Despite Holscher's several innovations, the manufacturer of the Parentesi lamp, Flos S.p.A., adopted the position that its copyright extended beyond the design, to include the underlying idea of a lamp suspended on a steel wire by friction. A year or so after String-line was introduced in 1976, Flos's lawyers contacted H.F. Belysning and threatened legal action if Model 8 remained in production.[15] Their argument was akin to Louis Poulsen A/S threatening a lawsuit because the stand on the String-line floor lamp recalls Verner Panton's Flower Pot table lamp. As a matter of fact, none of the String-line fixtures copied an existing design. Holscher had collected a series of general ideas and incorporated them into a series of new designs. Nonetheless, the threat of a lawsuit prompted H.F. Belysning to discontinue Model 8 after one year of production. As a result, it is one of the rarities of the series. But indeed all of the fixtures are rare.

By 1978, it had become apparent that String-line would not be a commercial success.[16] One of the factors was the relatively high price of the fixtures in a market accustomed to inexpensive constructions of plastic and painted sheet metal. The stainless steel tubes were not especially expensive, but the intricate details and cost of bending steel tubing into different shapes for relatively small numbers of fixtures resulted in higher prices than the market would bear. Another factor is that the heat produced by the incandescent bulbs caused the stainless steel tubes to become so hot that it was painful to turn off the switch after prolonged use. As a result of those two factors, 1978 was the final year of production for the first generation of String-line fixtures.

Unwilling to abandon his concept of varied fixtures based on a single element, Holscher directed his associate Jens Christian Larsen to address the problems of high cost and overheated elements that had undermined String-line.[17] Larsen solved both problems simultaneously by replacing stainless steel with aluminum, which is at once less expensive, easier to machine and dissipates heat more rapidly. As before, the lighting element was designed for a reflector bulb, but the shade would be a tapered acrylic ring that snapped onto the end of the aluminum tube. In pursuit of economy, Holscher and Larsen reduced the series to a handful of models with curved stems and stands of aluminum tubing, which were inspired by the first-generation floor lamp.

String-line second-generation pendant, 1982. Aluminum and acrylic. / Second-generation bookshelf lamp with adjustable clamp. → Jens Christian Larsen. Concept sketch for second-generation fixtures, 1981.

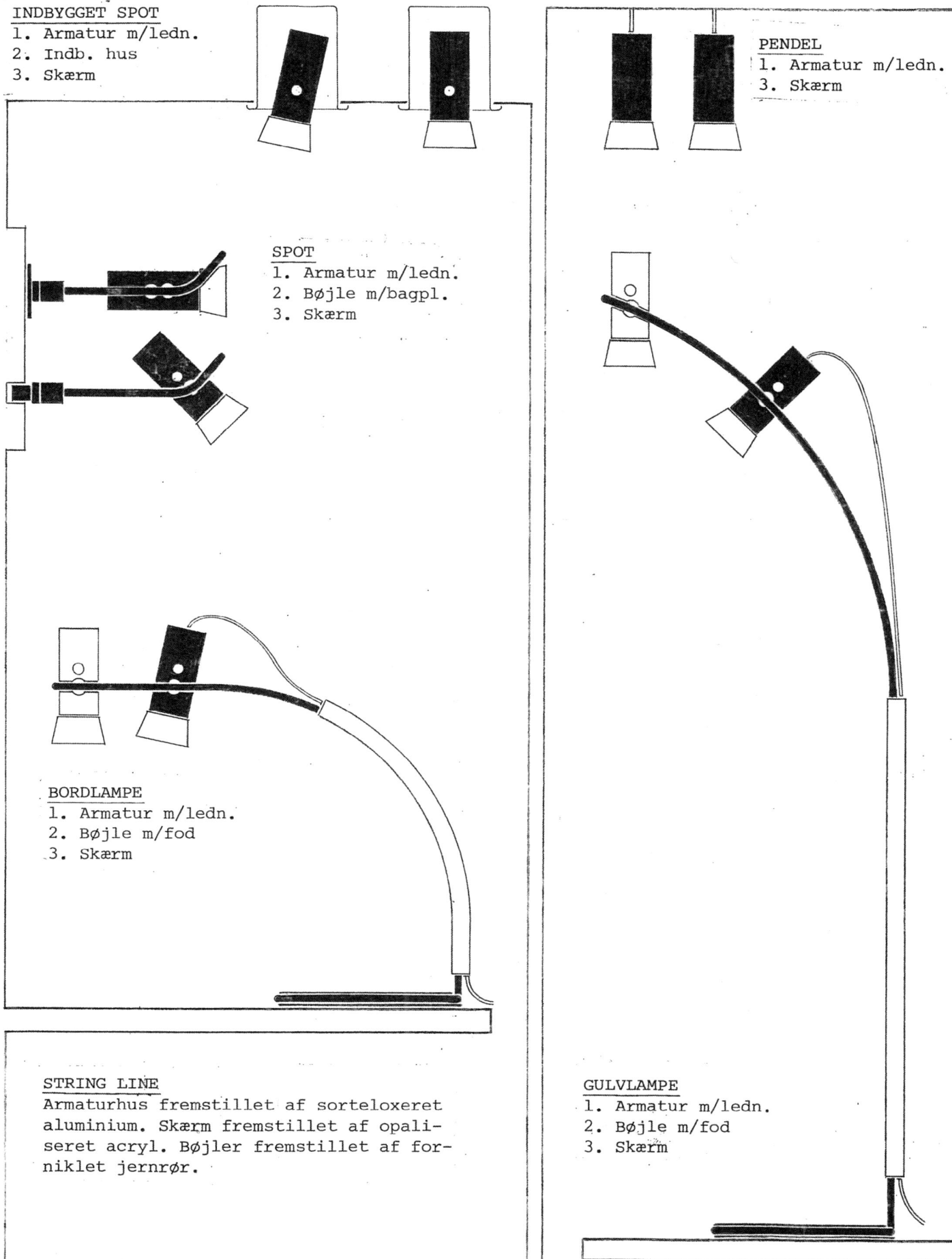

INDBYGGET SPOT
1. Armatur m/ledn.
2. Indb. hus
3. Skærm

SPOT
1. Armatur m/ledn.
2. Bøjle m/bagpl.
3. Skærm

BORDLAMPE
1. Armatur m/ledn.
2. Bøjle m/fod
3. Skærm

PENDEL
1. Armatur m/ledn.
3. Skærm

GULVLAMPE
1. Armatur m/ledn.
2. Bøjle m/fod
3. Skærm

STRING LINE
Armaturhus fremstillet af sorteloxeret aluminium. Skærm fremstillet af opaliseret acryl. Bøjler fremstillet af forniklet jernrør.

design: Knud Holscher/industrial design
v/Jens Chr. Larsen

Nordisk Solar Compagni A/S

Second-generation table lamp with curved stand of aluminum tubing.
→ Detail of second-generation floor lamp.

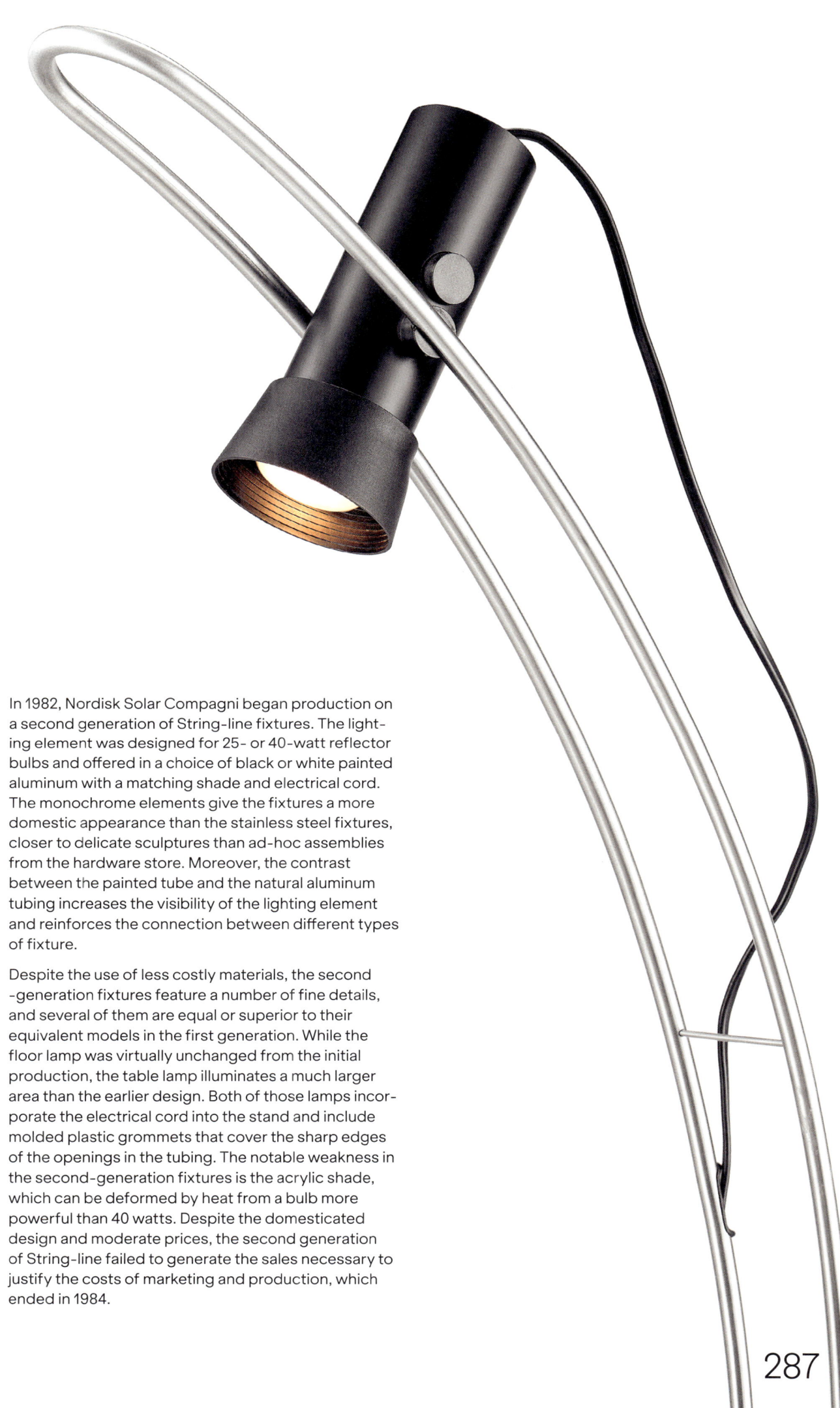

In 1982, Nordisk Solar Compagni began production on a second generation of String-line fixtures. The lighting element was designed for 25- or 40-watt reflector bulbs and offered in a choice of black or white painted aluminum with a matching shade and electrical cord. The monochrome elements give the fixtures a more domestic appearance than the stainless steel fixtures, closer to delicate sculptures than ad-hoc assemblies from the hardware store. Moreover, the contrast between the painted tube and the natural aluminum tubing increases the visibility of the lighting element and reinforces the connection between different types of fixture.

Despite the use of less costly materials, the second-generation fixtures feature a number of fine details, and several of them are equal or superior to their equivalent models in the first generation. While the floor lamp was virtually unchanged from the initial production, the table lamp illuminates a much larger area than the earlier design. Both of those lamps incorporate the electrical cord into the stand and include molded plastic grommets that cover the sharp edges of the openings in the tubing. The notable weakness in the second-generation fixtures is the acrylic shade, which can be deformed by heat from a bulb more powerful than 40 watts. Despite the domesticated design and moderate prices, the second generation of String-line failed to generate the sales necessary to justify the costs of marketing and production, which ended in 1984.

In the 1970s, the useful character of String-line was undermined by the inefficiency of incandescent light bulbs, which convert most of the power consumed into heat. With the advent of energy-efficient LED bulbs, technology has caught up to Holscher's visionary lighting concept, and String-line is once again a contemporary design. In 2008, the design brand Sorø Møbler made plans to revive several of the first-generation fixtures for use with LED bulbs. In order to allow a variety of bulbs, the steel ring-shade was independent of the bulb and fastened to the lighting element by three steel pins.[18] The following year, Sorø tested the market with the pendant (Model 1), which is the least expensive and also the most generic part of String-line. Isolated from other fixtures that would demonstrate the harmonic effect of the series, the pendant failed to sell and was discontinued after a year.

Given the beauty and practical benefits of String-line, it is possible that some of the fixtures will return to production, perhaps in a hybrid series that combines the best parts of the two generations. That series would surely include the first-generation wire lamp, which encapsulated Holscher's ideal of a dynamic fixture; the second-generation table lamp, which provides superior illumination; and the floor lamp produced in both generations.

The use of stainless steel would ensure that the fixtures last for a lifetime or longer. In the meantime, vintage String-line fixtures can be used with LED reflector bulbs. While filaments have been retired, the E-type bases named for Thomas Edison remain the standard method of mounting a bulb in a lamp. The stainless steel fixtures accept bulbs with an E27 base and the aluminum fixtures accept bulbs with an E14 base.

Whether or not String-line ever returns to production, it will remain a defining work of Knud Holscher's career. His systematic approach to design allowed him to create solutions to problems that most other designers could not recognize. And yet, he did not err on the side of standardization. Instead, he designed systems of objects that can be configured by the people who use them and then reconfigured, in an ongoing process without end. With String-line, a uniform lighting element provides the harmony required for calm and comfort, even as the range of fixtures provides the flexibility required for true utility. In that elusive combination of order and variety lies a working model for both architecture and industrial design that illuminates Holscher's attempts to unify the two fields in the pursuit of harmony.

> Knud Holscher, circa 1976.
> → Graphic overview of String-line first-generation fixtures, 1976.

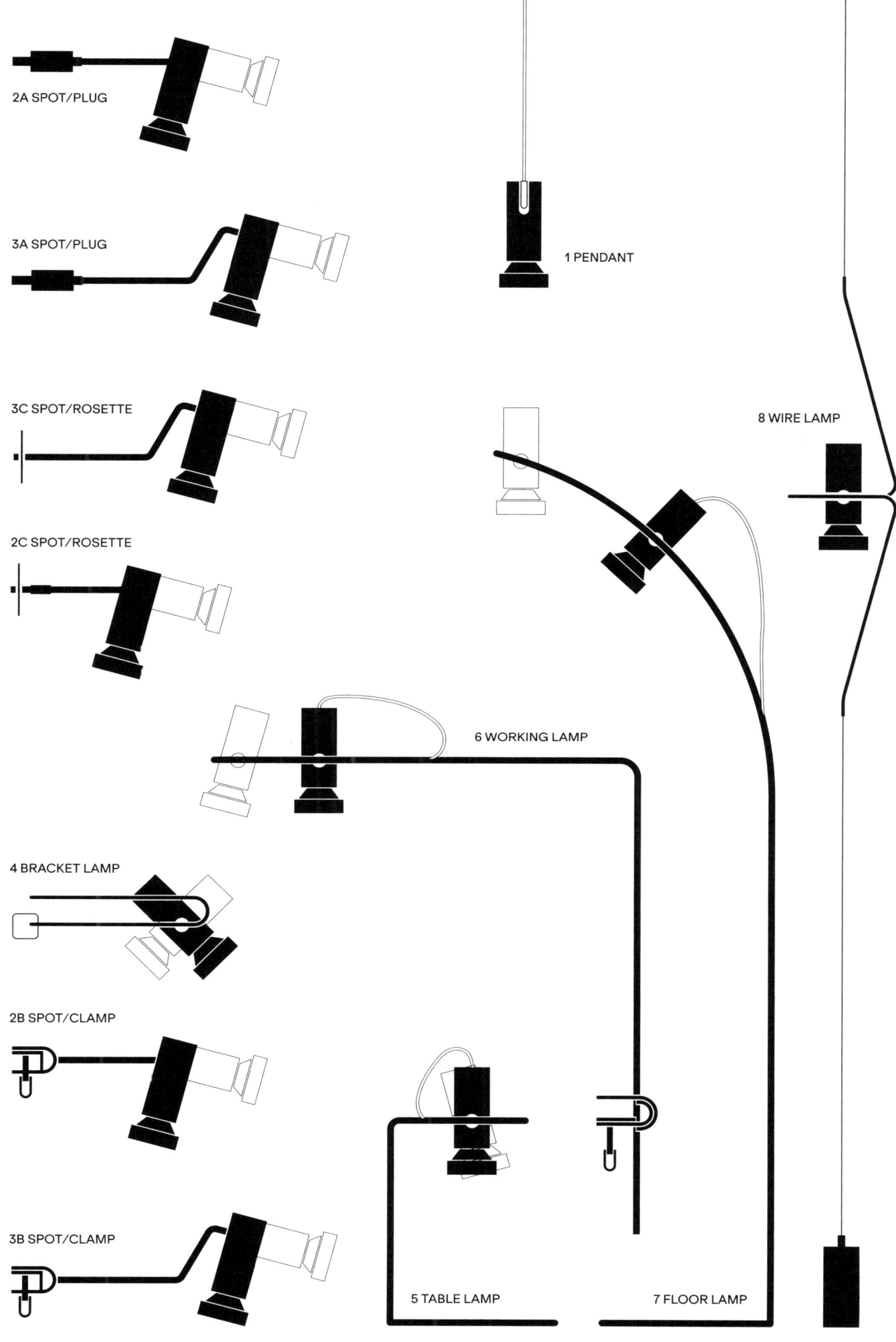

Terrace and

Garden

In 1933, Mogens Koch designed an armchair that condensed more than 3,000 years of furniture history into a lightweight, collapsible structure that erases the distinction between indoor and outdoor seating. Despite its ancient pedigree, the chair was so far ahead of its time that it would take a quarter-century of indifference, disaster and rejection before the chair was finally put into production. As with Koch's square bookcase, which is described in the introduction, the design of the folding chair began at home. In 1927, he and his wife, the weaver Ea (Varming) Koch, moved into a small row house in Brønshøj, on the edge of Copenhagen. The following spring, he went to a hardware store and purchased a pair of inexpensive folding armchairs for the terrace, which had been made in Italy with wooden frames, pivoting metal braces and canvas for seat and back.[1]

Over the next several years, Koch and his family became quite familiar with the shortcomings of their Italian folding chairs, which included flimsy steel braces that often malfunctioned, heavy wooden armrests that often crushed fingers, and four legs that caused the chairs to wobble on the paved terrace.[2] In December 1932, the Society for Ecclesiastical Art published a notice in the journal *Arkitekten* (The Architect) announcing a design competition for church furnishings, with a deadline six weeks later.[3] The categories included textiles and ritual articles as well as a folding chair that could be used for temporary seating. Considering the tight schedule, it becomes clear that Koch had been contemplating an improved version of the chairs on his terrace for some time. By the end of January 1933, he had resolved the mathematics and submitted a drawing to the competition, along with designs for several other items.

In March 1933, the competition jury awarded cash prizes to a dozen artisans and architects, among them Mogens Koch, who was recognized for his designs of an altar cloth and the carpet used for covering a catafalque. Evidently, the jurors were not impressed by his proposal for a folding armchair. Fortunately, the editorial board of *Arkitekten* had a different opinion as well as a more general appreciation of his talent. The issue of the weekly edition published on 15 April 1933 featured a report of the competition results with three illustrations: a small drawing of Koch's folding chair, a segment of his prize-winning carpet design (which also appeared on the front cover) and the proposal for altar wares that Koch and Kaare Klint had submitted together.[4] If not for that coverage, it is entirely possible that Koch's folding armchair would never have entered production.

Italian folding chair purchased by Mogens and Eva Koch, 1928. → Mogens Koch. Folding armchair MK-16, 1960. Oak, canvas and leather with brass hardware. 1:1 scale.

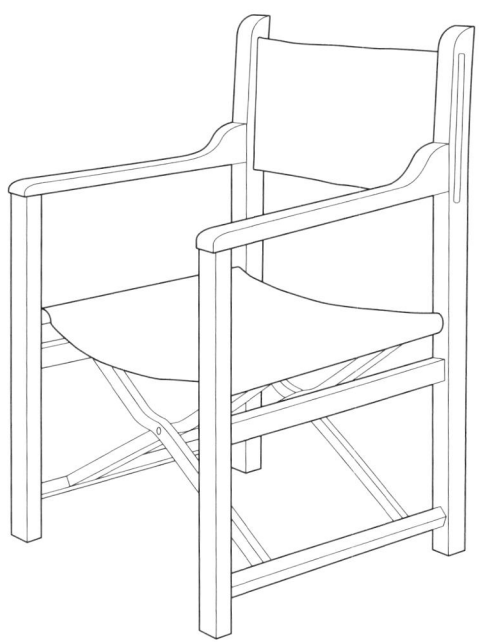

MOGENS KOCH 1933/1938/1960
MK-16

However flawed, the folding armchairs that Mogens Koch purchased in 1928 were the products of an evolutionary process that extends back into antiquity.[5] During the Renaissance, Italian craftsmen developed a folding armchair with a removable seat and back that became known as the *Savonarola* chair. The gentle curves of the pivoting wooden slats made it possible to extend them and provide comfortable armrests. The pivoting slats can be traced to the medieval *faldstool* that was found across Europe from the 1100s but constructed of straight lengths of wood that made armrests impractical.[6] That medieval model was rooted in a bronze stool from ancient Rome, which can be traced back to a folding wooden structure developed as early as 1400 BC in several parts of the world, notably Egypt.[7] Most often, the horizontal rails on those folding stools projected beyond the sides of the frames for increased stability.

By the mid 1700s, craftsmen across Europe were constructing lightweight folding chairs that could be easily transported. One of the best-known examples is the campaign chair made for Napoleon Bonaparte, circa 1800, with a beech frame and leather seat and back.[8] In Britain, the Napoleonic Wars spurred the development of the collapsible furniture that Kaare Klint and Mogens Koch regarded as shining examples of unpretentious, functional design. Their favored models included the folding Douro lounge chair, which became popular during the Peninsular War (1808–14), and its descendent, the knock-down Roorkhee chair, which was developed in the 1890s and named after the headquarters of the British Army's Bengal Engineer Group.[9] Both chairs employed leather straps for armrests, which made them easier to fold or dismantle.

The design for a folding armchair that Mogens Koch submitted to the Society for Ecclesiastical Art combined parts drawn from several models, which included the chairs on his terrace. His leap of imagination was to combine the ancient model of a folding stool with the four uprights from his terrace chairs, the leather seat and back of Napoleon's campaign chair, and the leather armrests found on British campaign furniture. Through that astonishing act of creative synthesis, Koch arrived at a new type of structure that would surpass any earlier example of a folding armchair for durability and ease of operation. Moreover, it was designed using simple wooden elements that were suited to industrial production; all that Koch needed was a willing factory owner.

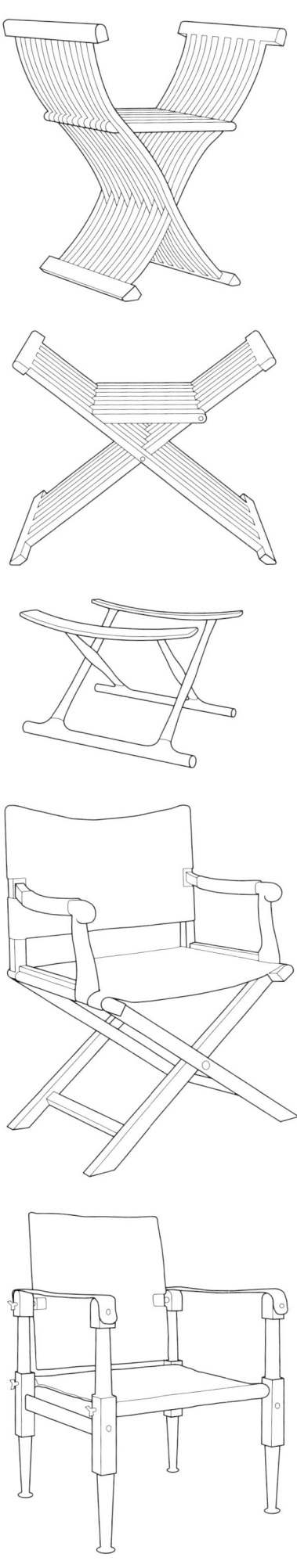

Drawings reproduced in *Arkitekten*, 1933. 1:20 scale. Folding stool. Egyptian, 1500–1300 B.C. / Faldstool. Germany, circa 1400. / Savonarola chair. Italy, circa 1500. / Folding camp chair. France, 1810. / Roorkhee chair. India, circa 1895. → Mogens Koch. 1938 beech prototype of folding chair with canvas armrests, seat and back.

In 1938, master cabinetmaker N. C. Jensen Kjær produced four prototypes of the armchair for the annual exhibition of the Copenhagen Cabinetmakers' Guild.[10] To lower the cost of materials, Koch replaced the leather seat, back and armrests with canvas and introduced a detail that would become a permanent feature of the chair:[11] Worried that canvas armrests might stretch over time, he placed a hole through each post at the appropriate height. Heavy cords running along the edges of the armrests were threaded through the holes and tied outside the posts. If the armrests became slack over time, the cords could be untied and pulled taut. To prevent the knotted cords from slipping on the posts, the holes were recessed in a groove. As previously described, the prototypes were completely ignored at the exhibition (p. 246). Afterwards, Koch took them home and used them on his terrace.

Over the next twenty years, Koch's former assistant Børge Mogensen tried to shepherd his mentor's folding armchair into production at least twice. In 1943, Mogensen decided to include the chair in his furniture program for FDB, the Danish Consumers Cooperative Society, alongside Koch's book box and children's bed/playpen (p. 19).[12] To that end, one of the four prototypes was shipped to FDB's main chair factory, Tarm Stole- og Møbelfabrik. But it disappeared after the factory was blown up in 1944, by members of the Schalburg Corps, Danish sympathizers of the Nazi regime that occupied Denmark during 1940–45. After Mogensen began his collaboration with Fredericia Stole- og Polstermøbelfabrik (now Fredericia Furniture), in 1956, he advised the owner Andreas Graversen to produce Koch's folding chair. Graversen rejected that advice, on the grounds that he was not running "a matchstick factory."[13]

In December 1958, Axel Thygesen, the co-owner of the small furniture company Interna A/S, was paging through an issue of *Arkitekten* from April 1933 and came across the drawing of Mogens Koch's folding armchair.[14] Recognizing a design that matched his vision of unconventional, multi-purpose furniture, he contacted Koch and asked for permission to produce the chair, which was granted.

As Koch revised the design for production, he restored the leather armrests of his initial design and specified top-grain cowhide for maximum strength. To avoid holes in the leather that would weaken the material, the ends of the armrests would be folded over rectangular brass loops and sewn with heavyweight thread. As Koch attached the armrests to the posts, he preserved the grooves and holes that were added in 1938, but rotated the holes by 90° and used them to anchor the brass loops. Finally, he fastened the canvas seat to the wooden frame with copper nails that would resist corrosion when the chair was used outdoors. In 1960, Koch's folding chair entered production as Interna model **MK-16**, with a beech structure, leather armrests, and seat and back of unbleached canvas.

Side view and diagram of folding action. 1:5 scale.
→ MK-16. Beech and canvas.

Aside from the canvas seat and backrest and the attachment of the armrests, the production model of Koch's folding chair was virtually unchanged from his original design. In 1933, Koch had based his design on a comfortable seating height of 45 cm and a simple mechanism that would prevent crushed fingers. When the chair is folded, a gentle tug on the posts activates the pivoting frames and the seat unfolds automatically. As a person settles into the chair, the canvas seat transmits their weight to the pivoting frames, which transforms the loose assembly of parts into a rigid structure. When the seat is no longer occupied, a slight tug on the posts activates the pivoting base, and the folding operation is reversed.

Koch's mastery of geometry would have impressed the Renaissance artisans who constructed the Savonarola chairs. By lowering the intersection of the pivoting frames to a point *just* below their midpoints, he created a tapered base (wider at the seat than the floor) that skews the four posts by +/- 4°. As a result of that skew, the pivoting frames and upright posts follow different arcs as they rotate, which allows the chair to be flattened and stand upright. The base of the chair tapers in both directions, so that it is equally stable from front-to-back and side-to-side. As a result, the 4° angles of the skewed posts also govern the construction of the pivoting frames. Folding and unfolding are dependent on loose connections between posts and frames, and — by extension — the two pieces of brass hardware that Koch designed to create those connections.

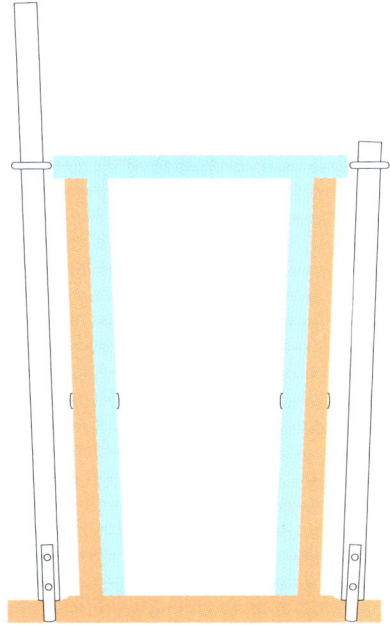
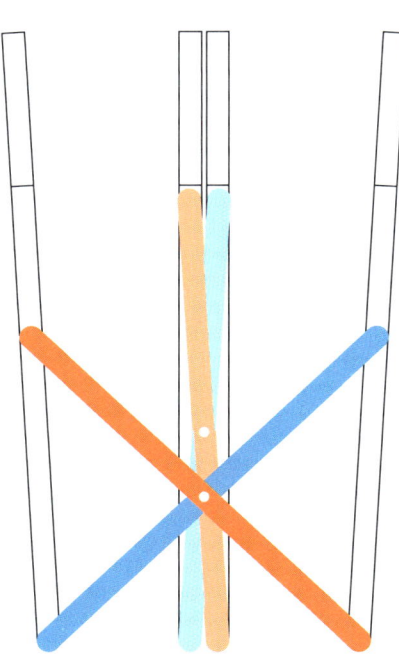

Koch designed his folding chair for industrial production, but he treated the pieces of wood with a cabinetmaker's attention to detail. He worked from the bottom up, in the knowledge that the floors in old churches are rarely level. As such, the bottom rails of the pivoting frames are rounded on the underside, to provide more contact with the floor and prevent wobbling. The rounding of the bottom rails is mirrored on the top rails, where the absence of a sharp edge reduces stress on the canvas seat. Both sets of rails are cut at a right angle to the diagonal parts of the frames, to provide flat surfaces and enable strong joints. As a grace note, the inside corners of the diagonal parts are cut at a 45° angle along their upper ends, to avoid pinching the canvas when the chair is folded.

Koch's entire design is based on two pieces of brass hardware — a ring and a U-shaped bracket — that provide loose connections between the posts and the pivoting frames. Fixed connections would have made the chair impossible, because the width and height of the base change in the course of folding and unfolding, from 50 x 45 cm to 10 x 75 cm. As those dimensions change, the angles between posts and frames also change. Due to the changing angles, the posts must be able to rotate on the bottom rails of the frames.

Brass ring and rotating bracket. / Time-lapse image of folding action. → Beech structure with profiled elements and brass hardware.

To make that possible, Koch designed a U-shaped bracket that is fitted over each end of the bottom rails and fastened to the post with screws. Prior to assembly, the ends of the rails are turned on a lathe to reduce the diameter and accommodate the thickness of the bracket. As a result, the post-and-bracket can rotate without touching the floor.

While the connections between posts and bottom rails must rotate, they are located at the floor and stationary. In contrast, the connections between posts and top rails must vary in both angle *and* height, as they travel up and down the posts. To that end, Koch designed a thick brass ring that is slightly larger than the diameter of the posts, which is attached to the ends of the top rails by a threaded bolt that allows rotation.

Koch's flexible joints are subtle, but the folding structure they enable is simply based on a pair of triangles, which meet at the intersection of the frames and vary in size during operation. That combination of simplicity and virtuosity is typical of his designs, in which everything arbitrary has been eliminated, without reducing the object to a banal husk that offers little in the way of aesthetic pleasure or signs of imagination. Indeed, one of the pleasures of encountering Koch's geometric structures, whether a lantern, table or chair, is recognizing the astonishing level of ingenuity that informed the design.

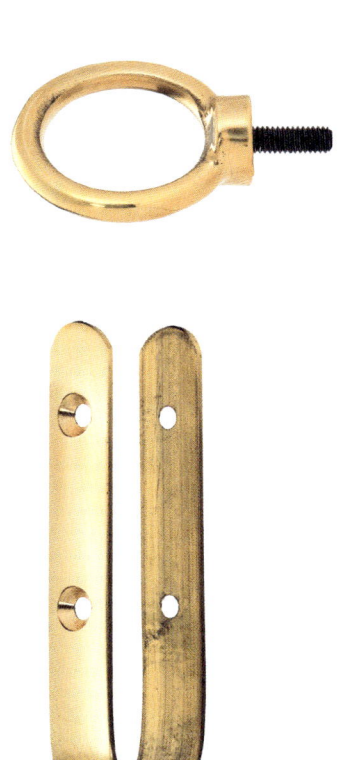

Having finally seen his MK-16 folding chair into mass production, Mogens Koch was faced with the question of storage, but he would be preoccupied with the design of other folding models for several years.[15] One of his tasks was a folding stool that would be lighter and less expensive than his folding armchair. Determined to develop a new model that would be specific to the task, Koch rejected the idea of simply reusing the base from MK-16. Instead, he reduced the pivoting frames to a minimum dimension and folded the seat through double rails at the top of each frame, to avoid holes in the material. As with the folding table MK-49 (p. 246), a leather strap allows the folded stool to be hung on the wall.

In 1964, Interna launched the stool as MK-30, with a beech frame and a seat of canvas or natural leather. A deluxe version was constructed of rosewood with a black leather seat and designated MK-40. By that point, Axel Thygesen had expanded the options for Koch's folding armchair, producing a beech structure with seat, back and armrests of natural leather (MK-16s) and a rosewood structure with black leather fittings (MK-41). Meanwhile, Koch had designed a child-sized version of the folding armchair, following the example of the small Italian model that he had purchased for his children, circa 1930, but did not allow them to operate, for their own safety. Designated MK-28, the little chair was produced in beech and canvas, or beech and natural leather. While the overall size is 2/3 of the adult model, the pieces of wood are 3/4 of the original dimensions, to maintain the proportions and prevent them from appearing flimsy. In 1965, Koch finally designed a beech storage rack (MK-75) that holds six adult-sized chairs and can be folded flat for storage.

Axel Thygesen was a visionary, but he struggled to find customers for Interna's unconventional models in a market dominated by furniture that symbolized good taste and decorum. By 1973, Interna was insolvent, and the production rights for MK-16 were sold to Poul Cadovius, a successful furniture designer who had shifted to manufacturing. That sale required Koch's approval, which he granted out of loyalty to Thygesen but soon came to regret.[16] During 1974–80, Cado A/S produced the chair using a lesser grade of canvas for the seat and back, while the leather armrests were riveted instead of sewn.

Following Cadovius's bankruptcy, production moved to Rud. Rasmussens Snedkerier, the cabinetry workshop that had been making Koch's modular bookcases for a half-century, and his folding table since 1978. Over the next thirty years, the beech-and-canvas model was produced in both adult and child-sized versions, using wooden elements from the same subcontractor that had supplied Interna and Cado. The adult model was also produced in mahogany with vegetable-dyed Niger goatskin or several shades of dyed cowhide for seat, back and armrests. In the process, Jørgen Rudolf Rasmussen introduced a seat cushion that ensures comfort for a wide range of body types. During 2016–20, Carl Hansen & Søn produced the adult model of the folding armchair in beech or oak, with the standard canvas and leather fittings.

Child's chair MK-28. Beech and canvas. → Folding rack MK-75 for six chairs. Beech. / Folding stool MK-30. Beech and canvas.

Since 2022, the Danish manufacturer Getama A/S has produced MK-16 alongside the low folding table, the modular bookcase and most of Mogens Koch's other furniture designs, using the original model numbers. In a reversal of the normal progression, in which the quality of the materials and construction decline over time, MK-16 is now produced to a higher standard than any previous edition.[17] To prevent stretching, the seat and back are made of two layers of canvas, which are preshrunk to tighten the weave. Moreover, the leather armrests are sewn along their entire length, to stiffen the edges and prevent curling. At the same time, the brass hardware that makes the chair possible is still produced by the small factory on the outskirts of Copenhagen that has supplied all of the previous producers. The folding armchair MK-16, folding rack MK-75 and folding stool MK-30 are now produced in beech or oak with natural canvas and leather fittings and the option of dyed leather for seat, back and armrests.

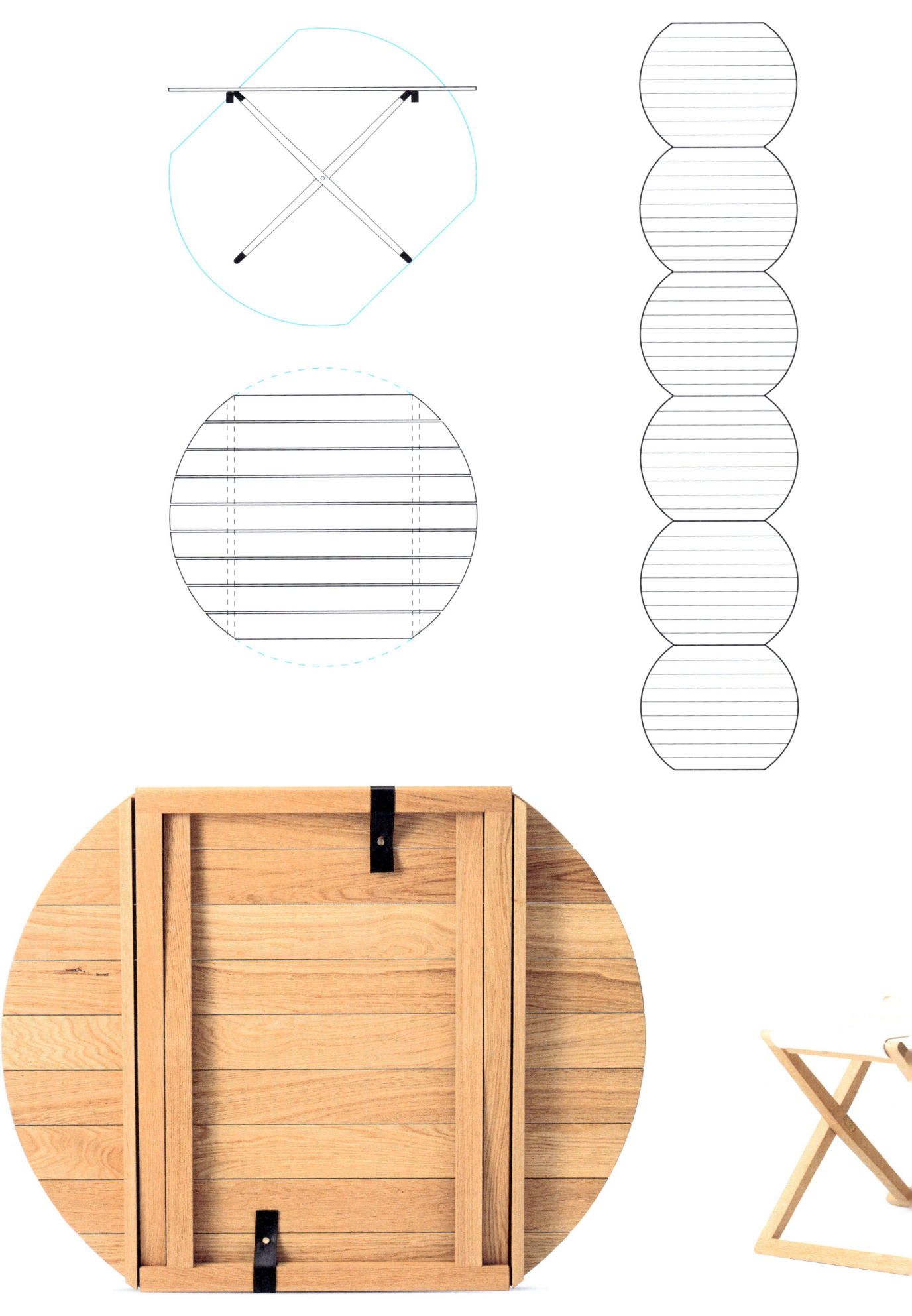

As part of the new production, Getama revived the folding table that Koch designed in 1960. The catalyst for the design was Finn Juhl's furnishing program for the new Danish embassy in Washington, D.C. After Juhl selected MK-16 for the terrace, he asked Koch to recommend a suitable table.[18] Koch quickly produced a drawing of a folding table for four people, which is constructed with a base of pivoting frames and a rounded top with straight sides, allowing several tables to be joined for parties. Top and base are independent, for ease of handling and storage, but can be fastened together using leather straps and the brass studs mounted on the underside of the top. During 1960–70, Interna produced MK-23 (also known as the "Embassy Table") with a beech frame and teak slats. The current production of MK-23 includes the original version in beech/teak and an all-oak version.

The genesis of the Embassy Table illustrates the peculiar journey of Mogens Koch's folding chair, which was initially inspired by a piece of outdoor furniture and designed for the interiors of churches, but migrated back to the open air. The chair is entirely suitable for indoor use, but it is a special treasure for terrace and balcony, because Koch solved the fundamental problem of outdoor furniture, which is exposure to the elements.

Seating group in oak: MK-30, MK-23, MK-16.
← MK-23 plan and elevation. Multiple tabletops.
∕ MK-16 (Embassy Table). Oak and leather. Underside with folded base.

Most pieces of outdoor furniture are constructed to withstand rain, snow and prolonged exposure to ultraviolet light, because they are too bulky to be brought inside and must remain outdoors in every kind of weather. By creating a collapsible chair that can be brought inside at the first sign of a shower, Koch made it possible to avoid massive structures of wood or synthetic materials that imitate wood or rattan. In the process, he created a universal chair that can be used virtually anywhere.

Ultimately, Koch succeeded in his ambition to create furniture for the ages: by designing a chair that embodies the development of Western furniture every bit as much as the historical models that informed his work. By incorporating lessons from a range of past cultures, from ancient Egypt to Victorian Britain, independently of their social models and decorative styles, Koch created a chair that remains contemporary nearly a century after he began calculating the triangulated wooden structure. In place of artistic gestures, he distilled his design to the character of the materials and an effortless mechanism made possible by his mastery of mathematics. The unpretentious tool for sitting that resulted from Koch's modest approach embodies the ethos of Klint School described in the introduction, which employed historical knowledge to create treasures for modern life that are essentially ageless.

Børge Mogensen's final masterpiece was a folding deck chair designed for compact storage that embodies his creative process during 1942–72. That is to say that his industrial design was rooted in one of Kaare Klint's handmade models, informed by his own knowledge of furniture history and perfected by virtue of his training as a cabinetmaker. Indeed, Mogensen would not have developed the innovative, slightly flexible structure without the deep understanding of wood that he had acquired in the workshop during the 1930s. Through a union of example and expertise, he surpassed his mentor's model and created a new type of folding chair that provides comfortable seating over extended periods. Similarly to Mogens Koch's folding armchair (p. 292), the genesis of Mogensen's dynamic structure began at home.

In 1956, Børge and Alice (Krohn) Mogensen purchased a narrow lot on a steep slope in Gentofte, north of Copenhagen, where they would build a house for themselves and their two young sons. The couple asked architect Erling Zeuthen Nielsen, one of Børge Mogensen's collaborators, to design a compact, one-story brick house with a basement that would include Mogensen's design studio, which was completed in 1958.[1]

Four years later, the couple hired their friend Arne Karlsen and his associate Allan Jessen to extend the house at both ends, with a glass-enclosed terrace to the south and an elevated deck to the north that would provide a view of the nearby forest. By the end of 1964, the additions were finished, and Mogensen was sketching a deck chair for the new outdoor sitting areas, which would eventually be produced by Søborg Møbelfabrik: **SM 50**.

The design of that chair would be one of the more complex projects of Mogensen's career. In addition to the usual challenge of ensuring comfort, which is always a daunting task, he was determined to create a chair that could be folded flat for compact and convenient storage, akin to Mogens Koch's folding table MK-49 (p. 246). To realize that goal, he combined knowledge from multiple sources and employed his handicraft training to solve the problems of comfort and compact storage simultaneously. In the process, he created a new type of structure with a potential for further development that was never realized. By examining Mogensen's sources and retracing the development of his most subtle chair, we gain a deeper understanding of his apparently modest masterpiece and, by extension, his singular place in the history of Danish furniture.

Børge Mogensen. Initial sketch for folding deck chair, December 1964. → SM 50 deck chair, 1964–69. Detail of beech armrest. 1:1 scale.

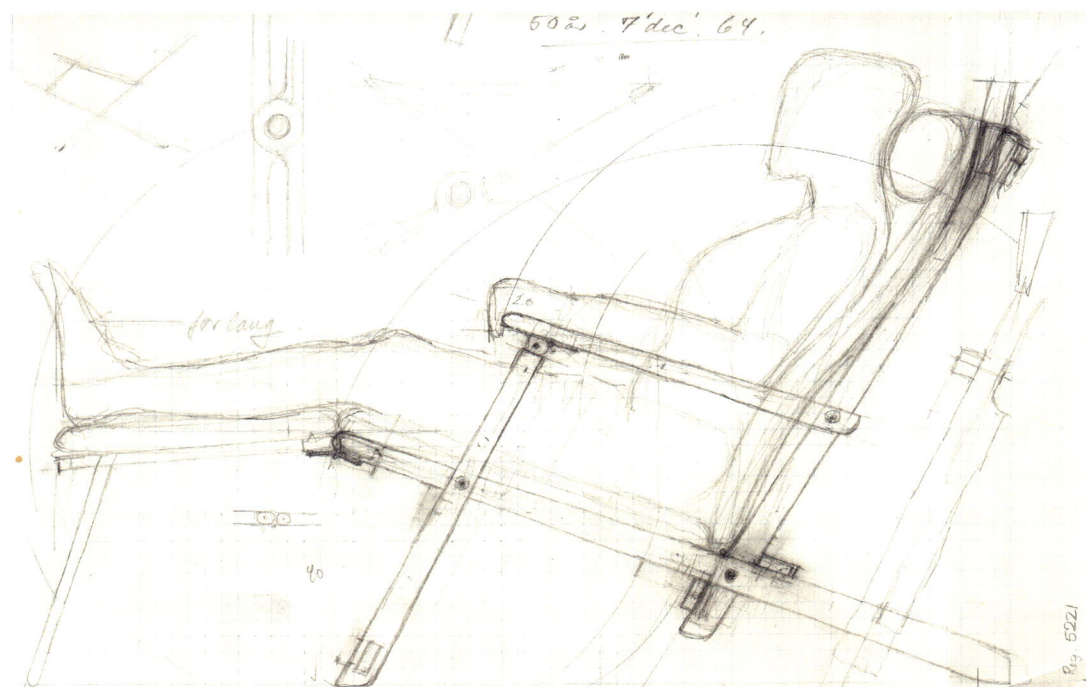

BØRGE MOGENSEN 1964–69
SM 50

As Mogensen sketched his new lounge chair, he used Kaare Klint's deck chair of 1933 as a model and grappled with two problems that his mentor had left unsolved. Dissatisfied with the folding deck chairs commonly used on ocean liners, Klint decided to create an improved version.[2] To that end, he designed a set of pivoting frames, armrests and legs that were based on the same curve, which made it possible for all of the parts to be folded into a compact unit. While the wooden parts were made of solid teak, which resists sea air and saltwater, the frames were filled with woven cane panels that provide the seat and backrest. The continuous cushion and adjustable neck pillow were made of Pomeranian linen and filled with a natural fiber (kapok) that is both waterproof and buoyant. The result was an exquisite piece of handicraft that was based on functional concerns, but undermined in its function by the curve that Klint used to ensure compact folding.

The fundamental problem with Klint's deck chair is the inadequate lumbar support, due to the curved backrest that is based on a segment of a circle, rather than the S-curve of the spine. Klint recognized that flaw and tinkered with the design as late as 1951–52, when he assigned two of his students at the Royal Danish Academy to investigate possible solutions.[3] As Arne Karlsen pointed out, "The chair is an example of how the furniture designer will often be forced to disregard one functional requirement in order to meet another."[4] The other problem with Klint's design, which he ignored in pursuit of an ideal mathematical solution, is that curved objects require more storage space than flat objects. Furthermore, they tend to slide sideways when stacked. Mogensen was determined to solve both of those problems in the simplest ways possible, without compromising either solution.

By 1965, Mogensen had arrived at a working design, and a prototype had been constructed at C.M. Madsens Fabrikker, the producer of the *Boligens Byggeskabe* cabinet system (p. 218). Four years would pass before a revised version of the deck chair entered production, but Mogensen had already solved the problems of lumbar support and compact storage by drawing lessons from two partial models. One of those models was his adjustable lounge chair, Fredericia 2254, which employs curved staves to support the lower back (p. 234). However, he could not use those staves on his folding deck chair, because their deep curves would make it impossible to fold the chair into a flat unit. Mogensen required a folding structure that combined flat frames and curved back supports. Surveying the history of furniture design, he found another partial model in an especially uncomfortable folding chair from the medieval era.

Børge Mogensen. Fredericia 2254, 1963. Oak structure with webbing seat and canvas. ← Kaare Klint. Deck chair, 1938. Mahogany with kapok cushion covered in Pomeranian canvas. / Børge Mogensen. Prototype deck chair, 1965. C.M. Madsens Fabrikker. Beech with foam rubber cushions covered in canvas.

Mogensen was certainly familiar with the variations on a *faldstool*, the portable chair of interlocking wooden slats that was developed in medieval Europe for traveling priests and magistrates. He would have encountered the basic model during his years with Kaare Klint and Mogens Koch, due to their joint obsession with folding furniture. Indeed, the medieval folding chair was a link in the historical chain of solutions that eventually led to Koch's MK-16 (p. 292). Mogensen could also rely on articles and books written by Ole Wanscher, the furniture designer and historian, whose scholarly specialty was the evolution of folding stools and chairs.[5] The medieval chairs were notable for the ingenuity of their construction and for the hard, flat surfaces of the seat and back.

Despite its lack of comfort, the faldstool provided Mogensen with a useful example of a folding chair that could be collapsed into a minimal thickness. Because the wooden slats are arranged in alternating rows, they can be folded together to occupy the same space without obstructing each other. Moreover, the rows of slats could be oriented in different directions, to construct a simple chair without arms or the armchair that served as the model for the Renaissance Savonarola chair (p. 294). Inspired by the principle of offset rows, Mogensen employed alternating strips of wood for the seat and backrest of his deck chair. By adopting the pivoting front legs and armrests that Klint had employed in 1933, Mogensen created a collapsible chair that can be folded into a thin slab.

Time-lapse view of folding action.
← Faldstool. Switzerland, circa 1600.
╱ SM 50 deck chair, 1968. Beech with galvanized steel hardware.

Mogensen's imaginative use of wood allowed him to resolve the conflict between a collapsible chair and a comfortable chair. Most folding structures are based on sets of points and lines that form triangles, as seen in Mogens Koch's armchair MK-16 and his table MK-49. However, our bodies are made up of bones and soft tissues that do not correspond to simple geometric shapes. With MK-16, Koch resolved that conflict by using thin flexible materials (canvas and leather) that adapt to the human form and hold it in suspension, as in a hammock. But that method will not provide a comfortable lounge chair, because a reclining body requires continuous support with varying degrees of resistance. To provide that support within a folding framework, Mogensen exploited the natural character of wood to create a hybrid of flexible and rigid elements.

That hybrid structure was a radical departure from standard practice. In the interests of economy and stability, most wooden chairs are constructed entirely of rigid elements, often at the expense of comfort as seen in the faldstool. Mogensen's lounge chair Fredericia 2254 provides a more comfortable example of rigid construction, in that the curved staves provide excellent lumbar support. Those staves were produced by softening lengths of wood with steam and drying them in curved molds, to overcome the strength of the wood along the natural grain and create the necessary curves. With that in mind, Mogensen realized that he could use flexible wooden strips to provide the seat and backrest on his deck chair, if they were attached to rigid crossbars that would impart the subtle curves required for comfort.

Folded structure. → Cross-sections illustrate Børge Mogensen's use of wooden strips with different thicknesses for seat (blue) and backrest (red). / Unfolded structure.

Mogensen enhanced the comfort of his flexible seat and backrest by varying the thickness of the wooden strips. As the seat carries the greater share of a person's weight, it is constructed of 4-mm strips that are at once extremely strong and slightly pliable. On the backrests, the strips are only 3 mm thick, which makes them more responsive as a person shifts their weight, turns or twists and so promotes relaxation. The result is an interactive structure that can respond to the changes in posture necessary for comfort over extended periods. It is also an excellent design for industrial production, because the entire chair is constructed of straight lengths of wood that are assembled with screws. And yet, Mogensen's brilliant industrial design was based on the intuitive understanding of wood that he had acquired as a teenage apprentice.

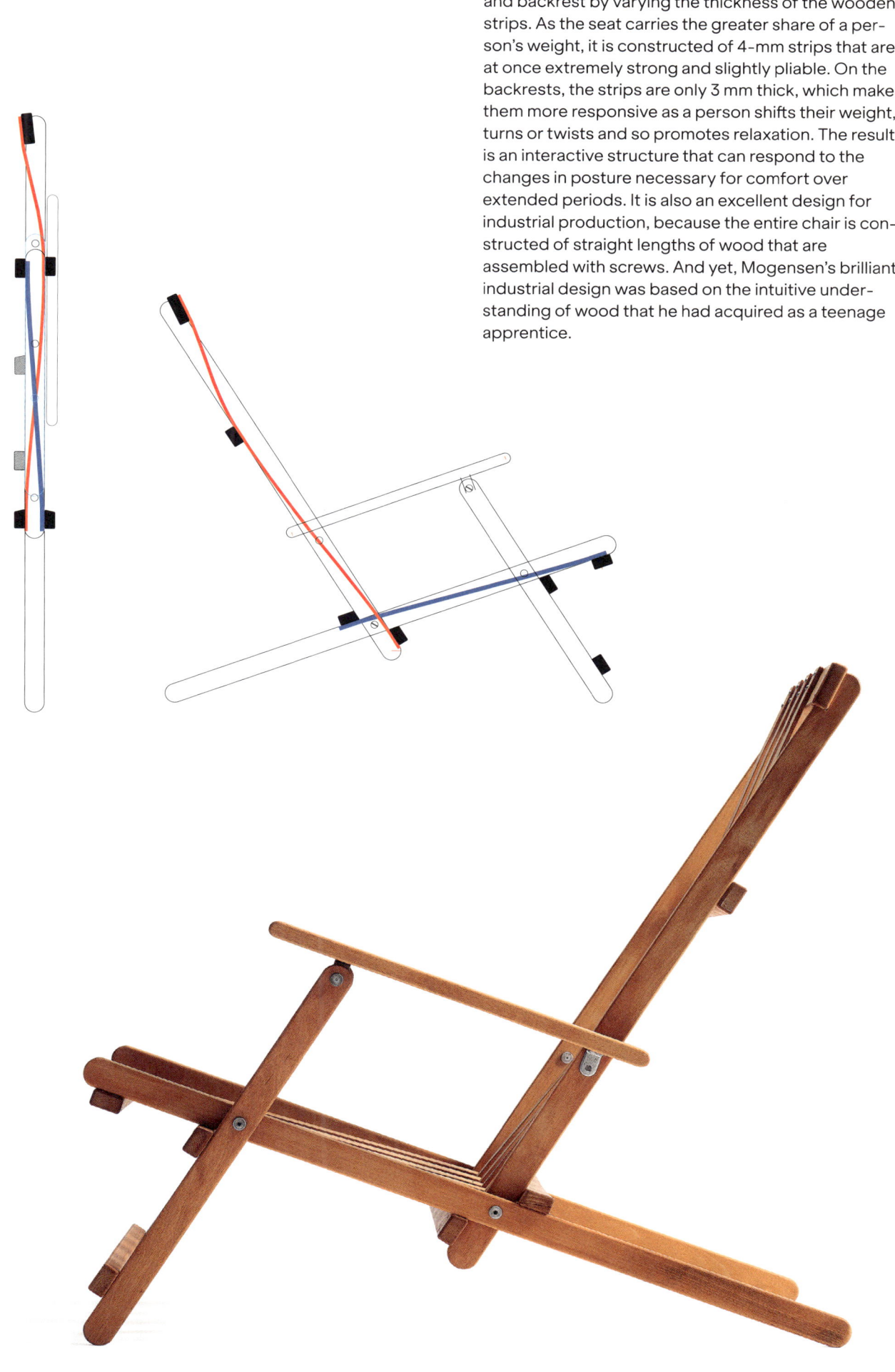

Following the construction of his 1965 prototype, Mogensen put the deck chair aside for several years, for unknown reasons that likely included an enormous workload. In 1968, he returned to the project and reached a production agreement with Søborg Møbelfabrik. Refining the design for production, he simplified the armrests and eliminated the footrest that appeared on the prototype. As a replacement, he designed a folding stool that could double as a footstool. The segmented cushion was filled with polyester granules that are more responsive to movement than foam rubber. To simplify attachment, the cushion includes generous loops that fit the corners of the seat and backrest. Designated model no. 50, or SM 50, the chair was produced in unfinished beech that weathers to a light gray, although many customers would oil the wood to preserve the warm color.

As was his habit, Mogensen pursued a union of furniture and textile by selecting standard coverings for the cushion that would complement the wooden structure. The clearest example is the design of light-colored Pomeranian linen with dark brown stripes that correspond to the slats of the seat and backrest, as illustrated on these pages. The same material, which both Klint and Mogensen prized for its durability, was also available in unbleached versions, either plain or checked. The two options in cotton included a pattern of blue stripes that recalls the work of weaver and designer Lis Ahlmann, although there is no reason to believe that she designed the pattern. But as she and Mogensen collaborated so closely on other textiles for his furniture (p. 242), he undoubtedly consulted her on the options for SM 50 and sought her approval.

SM 50 with folding stool SM 51.
← Standard cushion fabrics. Pomeranian canvas or cotton. 1:1 scale. / SM 50. Beech with polygranulate cushions covered in canvas.

SM 50 provided the centerpiece for an entire series of folding outdoor furniture. While the other parts of the series are much simpler than the deck chair, they nonetheless exhibit Mogensen's concern for utility and durability. In addition to the folding stool, which can be paired with a tray to create a low table, he designed a simple chair, two tables suitable for meals, a bench and a cot. He completed the series with pegboards that allow the folded pieces to be hung on a wall for storage, a final tribute to the furniture of the American sect known as the Shakers, which had inspired him since the early 1940s (p. 192). In 1970, Søborg Møbelfabrik began selling Mogensen's outdoor series in brown paper bags that expressed his goal of creating excellent furniture with the unpretentious character of high-quality gardening tools.

Mogensen's outdoor furniture was a commercial success during the 1970s, as standardized "type houses" were constructed across Denmark and several hundred thousand people moved into suburban homes that provided them with a garden. As a result, vintage examples of Mogensen's deck chair can be found and refurbished. In later decades, sales were hindered by a lack of promotion, as Søborg Møbelfabrik's fortunes gradually declined. In 2017, Carl Hansen & Søn purchased the factory's production rights for the express purpose of reviving Mogensen's outdoor furniture and established a new factory in Vietnam to produce the series. Two years later, the series was relaunched in sustainable, plantation-grown teak and now includes the deck chair with integral footrest that Mogensen imagined in 1965.

Folding chairs (beech) and table (teak). → Garden furniture with pegboards for storage, 1970.

In late 1970, Børge Mogensen was diagnosed with the neurological disease that ended his life, in October 1972, at the age of fifty-eight. After thirty years of intense work, his legacy includes every common type of furniture, from chairs and tables for every purpose to sofas and beds, a vast array of cabinets and a series of built-in storage systems that includes Boligens Byggeskabe, which he designed together with Grethe Meyer (p. 218). Indeed, Mogensen was so versatile that it is possible to furnish an entire home with his furniture, without it being apparent that all the items are the work of a single designer. By leaving personal expression to others and focusing on materials, dimensions and construction, he created models that are distinguished by their fitness to purpose and durability, rather than the signature of the designer.

While some of Mogensen's models have remained in production since they were introduced, others have been discontinued due to changes in popular taste and then later revived; a pattern that will almost certainly continue. As a result of his prolific output and the popularity of so many of his models, Denmark is a virtual warehouse of Mogensen's furniture, which makes it possible to purchase many of his models second-hand. In all of these ways, Mogensen's work lives on, such that we can recognize him as one of the most important furniture talents of his time and our own.

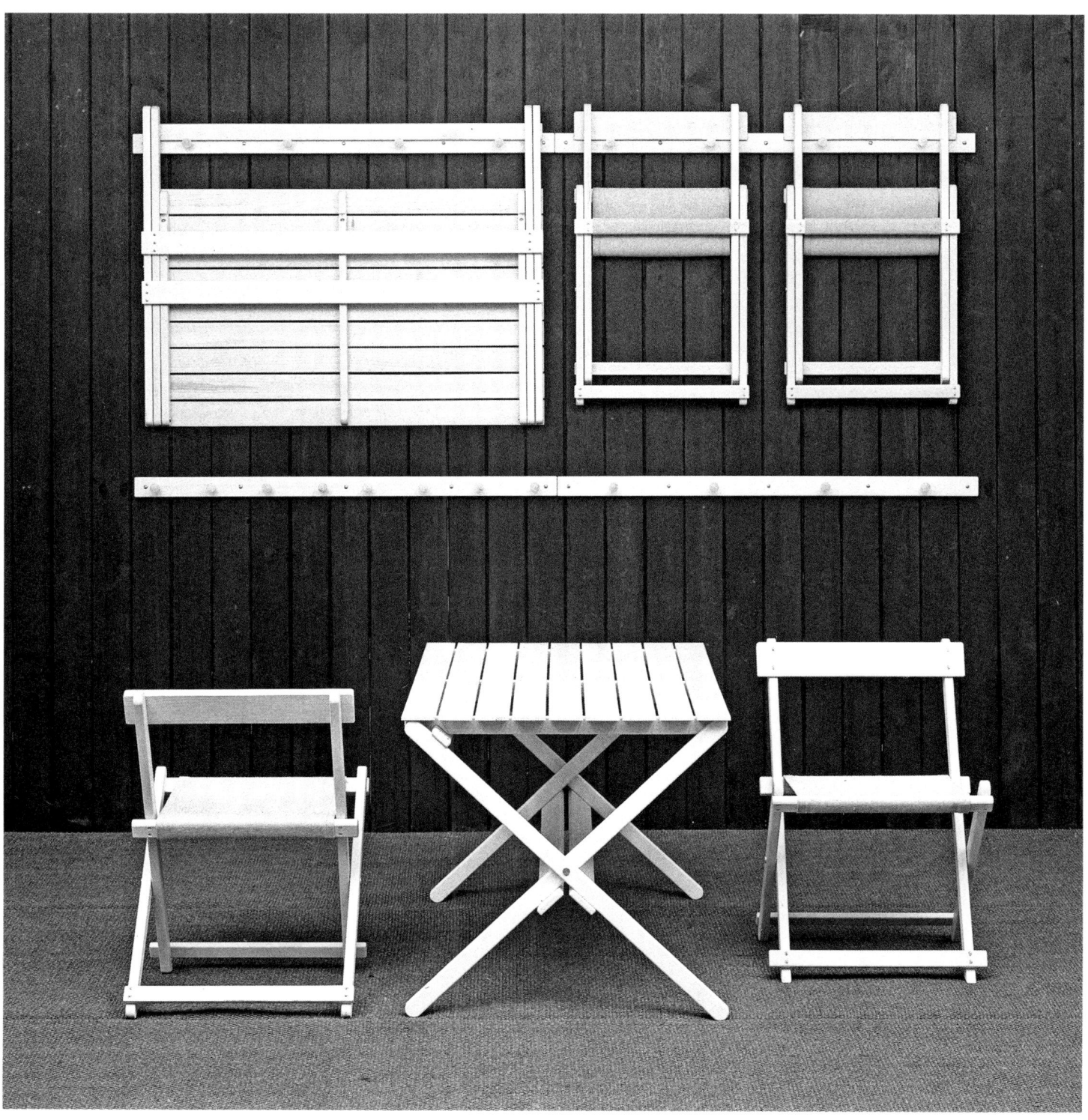

As they employed industrial materials to artisanal ends, Karsten Ravn and Lars Lundquist created grills and cooking tools that have the precise character of machine parts, modernized an ancient culinary technique, and created a system for constructing inexpensive outdoor kitchens that can be tailored to the setting. The results of their brief partnership constitute one of the outstanding chapters in the history of Danish design, but have been out of production for decades and are now nearly forgotten.

Ravn and Lundquist first met in 1966, as they were beginning their studies at the School of Architecture within the Royal Danish Academy.[1] By 1969, the two friends were pursuing advanced studies in the Department of Industrial Design and both were newly married. They and their spouses enjoyed meeting for grilled dinners but their meals were repeatedly spoiled by the miserable quality of the cooking equipment. While the clumsy designs made it difficult to regulate the heat, the grates consisted of narrow wires — "like knitting needles" — that were too thin to transfer heat to the food.[2] Frustrated by their encounters with useless grills, Ravn and Lundquist decided to design an improved model as a parallel to their studies at the Academy. They based their design on the knowledge that cooking with fire encompasses a range of techniques.

The familiar technique of grilling (often known as *barbeque*) involves cooking food on a grate or grill directly above a fire, which is an excellent technique for quickly preparing small or relatively thin pieces of food.[3] Steaks, burgers and sausages all benefit from being seared on a hot grate, which seals the surface and preserves the juices. Moreover, the heat catalyzes the so-called Maillard reaction and produces the browned surfaces and complex aromatic flavors that we associate with baked or roasted foods.

With careful control of the heat, grilling can also be used to prepare more delicate fare, such as fish and vegetables; that will satisfy every palate. No matter the menu, it is important to prevent fats and fluids from dripping into the fire, because the resulting flare-ups include particles that are certainly distasteful and possibly hazardous.

Until the late 1800s, when enclosed iron ovens became common, roasting generally involved slowly cooking food on a rotating spit, either above an open fire or in front of it. That technique (also known as rotisserie) makes it possible to cook whole birds and fishes on the fire and is unsurpassed for cooking large pieces of meat.[4] However, spit-roasting above a fire leads to the same problems with dripping fats and flare-ups that often occur when grilling. A far better technique is to roast the food in front of the fire, with the spit rotating away from the heat. As the food turns, gravity carries the juices from the warmer portion to the cooler portion that is rising towards the heat. While meat cooks in its own juices, the drippings can be collected for basting or making sauces. Moreover, the risk of flare-ups is eliminated.

On the basis of their own grilling mishaps and a close study of historical roasting practices, Ravn and Lundquist developed a compact and portable piece of equipment that provides excellent conditions for both types of cooking. In doing so, they made a quantum leap in grill design while liberating spit-roasting from the restaurant and making the benefits of rotisserie available to any home cook with a square meter of outdoor space.

Karsten Ravn and Lars Lundquist. RL Grill Series, 1969–73. Adjustable hardware for spits: bracket for basic spit and counterweight for basic and clamping spits. Brass and steel.
→ Detail of Reversible Grill. Cast iron. 1:1 scale.

KARSTEN RAVN / LARS LUNDQUIST 1969–73
RL Grill Series

Ravn and Lundquist were not alone in their dismay with the grills available in Denmark during the 1960s, nor were they the first Danish designers to imagine an alternative. In 1966, architect Nils Fagerholt designed a precisely detailed and extremely durable apparatus based on the understanding that grilled food is cooked by heat transferred from the grate. To that end, the welded steel frame supports two hinged grates of cast iron, which can be opened with a hook when the fire is burning. To protect the area beneath the grill from scorching, the firebox is suspended on steel clips; a layer of sand can be used to vary the distance between the fire and grates. After the fire has died, the sheet metal firebox can be lifted off the frame and emptied. The frame itself was constructed of steel angles and resembles a piece of furniture, as though Fagerholt had designed an altar for a temple of gastronomy.

Fagerholt's massive grill is excellent for cooking thin pieces of meat quickly and evenly, but the fixed height of the grates makes it difficult to regulate the heat. Writing in *Berlingske Tidende*, the chef and restaurateur Conrad Bjerre-Christensen praised Fagerholt for designing a first-class piece of cooking equipment and then provided a description of his ideal grill that neatly summarizes Ravn and Lundquist's approach two years later:

"There is nothing to prevent you from cooking geese, ducks, turkeys and other large items on a grill, but that type of grill is not normally available to us. The grill that I am describing, which allows for slow-roasting, has the embers placed vertically behind a grate. The spits can be moved closer to or further from the heat source, so that you can grill even very large pieces of meat, for example a whole suckling pig or a lamb. Of course, it requires a very special technique to work in that way, and the methods tried so far, such as placing chickens and other pieces on a rotating spit over a normal grill, do not lead to a happy result. In that case, all the juices drip into the charcoal and cause minor fires that burn the meat."[5]

Ravn and Lundquist began their design project by researching historical cooking techniques. As both of them were conversant in French, they studied the writings of Auguste Escoffier, the renowned chef whose early positions included that of *rôtisseur*, as well a variety of roasting manuals and cookbooks by lesser-known authors.[6] While Fagerholt's gastronomic altar provided a model of durable construction, and French texts introduced the two young men to the intricacies of spit-roasting, the evolution of European clocks provided Ravn and Lundquist with a portable solution to the age-old problem of rotating the spit.

Historically, the task of rotating the spit most often fell on children, but running dogs in wooden drums were also employed, as were geese.[7] In Europe, the solution to that cruel practice arrived in the early 1300s, with weight-driven spit-jacks derived from the clockworks on church towers. A century later, the need for portable clocks led to the invention of the mainspring, a coiled strip of metal that slowly unwinds and transfers its energy to a cone-shaped pulley (fusee).[8] By the mid 1500s, mechanics in Italy had developed spring-driven spit jacks that could be placed over or next to a fire.[9] Mainsprings in clocks and watches were finally rendered obsolete by batteries around 1920. Nonetheless, spring-driven mechanisms remained popular throughout the twentieth century, for inexpensive devices such as alarm clocks, wind-up toys and small rotisserie motors.

"Roasting mill with three spits." Plate XVIII from Bartolomeo Scappi, *Opera di Bartolomeo Scappi divisa in sei libri* (Venice: Michele Tramezzino, 1570). Scappi (1500–77) was the chef to the papal court in Rome and published one of the first illustrated cookery books. The twenty-seven woodcuts depict a range of cooking tools and techniques as well as the earliest published of picture of a fork. His magnum opus went through at least seven editions and remained in print through 1643. ← Nils Fagerholt. Grill, 1966. Cast iron, 5 mm steel angle and sheet metal. Grate 45 x 60 cm. Weight unknown.

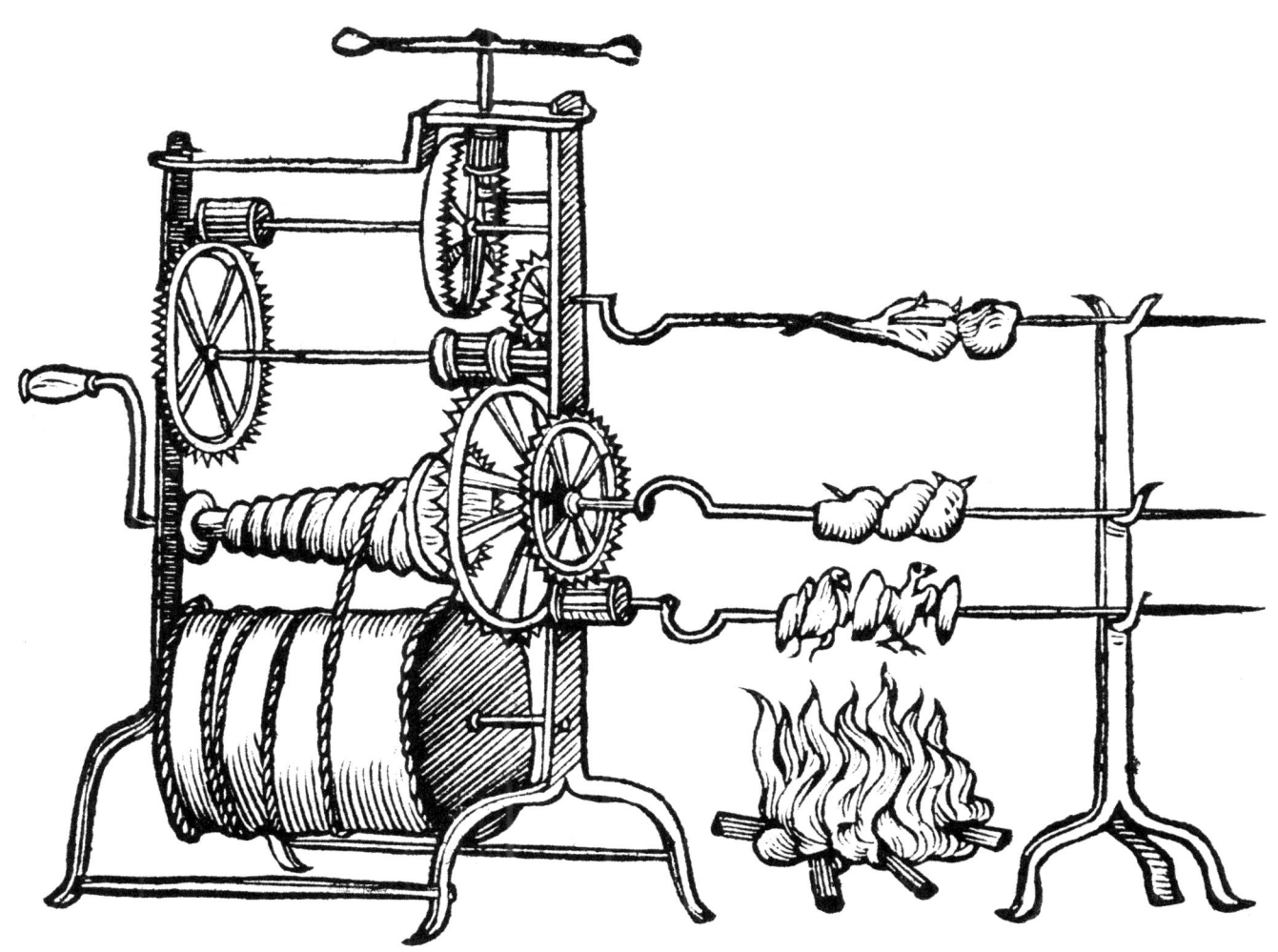

During 1970, Karsten Ravn and Lars Lundquist spent most of their free time in a blacksmith's shop north of Copenhagen, inspecting a series of prototypes and testing the wind-up motor for a spit that they had located in Sweden.[10] In early 1971, they visited Ole Palsby in his kitchenware shop on Læderstræde (p. 134), bearing a working prototype of their multi-purpose grill and designs for other grills and accessories.[11] Palsby recognized a successor to Fagerholt's grill, which he had sold in his design showroom on Hovedvagtsgade and represented on the wholesale market, alongside Fagerholt's fireplaces and Hanne Valeur's K-60 kitchen system (p. 58). In short order, Palsby offered Ravn and Lundquist a contract to produce and sell all of their designs and initiated a brief period of creative and commercial success that would come to an absurd end, as history repeated itself.

Ravn and Lundquist's first principle of grill design was the use of durable materials that would withstand high temperatures and promote even cooking.[12] With that in mind, they designed a shell of 4-mm steel plate that was bent and welded into the form of a double cube — 60 x 30 x 30 cm — with two open sides. At either end of the shell, a series of slots makes it possible to raise and lower the grate or vary the distance between spit and fire, depending on the orientation of the shell.

The grate was constructed of 9-mm steel rods, which are excellent for transferring heat to food and nearly indestructible. The same steel rods were used to create the handle at each end of the shell used for rotating the apparatus, as well as the handle on the pivoting panel that allows the firebox to be emptied. The result is a heavy-duty assembly that weighs about 20 kg, but is easily transported by removing the grate.

When the shell is used for grilling, the grate is surrounded on three sides by steel plates that block wind and promote a constant cooking temperature, while also reflecting heat back towards the food. Because the grate can be set at five different heights, it is possible to regulate the heat according to the thickness of the food and at and each stage of cooking, from searing and tending to resting and keeping the food warm. On the underside of the shell, narrow steel ribs elevate the grill above the supporting surface and ensure a steady air supply to the holes in the bottom of the firebox.

Ravn and Lundquist. Reversible Grill. Grate 60 x 30 cm. Weight 20 kg. Grilling position. → Roasting position. / Detail of cork handle on motor.

When the shell is used for roasting, the spit is protected from wind on three sides, while the bottom of the shell provides a surface for a plate or drip pan. After the spit has been loaded, it is inserted into the central slots on the two ends of the shell, which contain notches that hold the spit in place as it rotates. The two sets of notches allow the cook to vary the distance between spit and fire, in a similar manner to the adjustment of the grate. Behind the fire, the pattern of 3-mm holes on the outside of the firebox continues to supply oxygen to the fire, for even combustion and efficient use of fuel.

The speed of rotation is a fundamental concern when spit-roasting, because a lower speed reduces the loss of fluids. With that in mind, the architects searched for a heavy-duty motor that would make one revolution per minute. After locating their Swedish model, Ravn and Lundquist designed a black aluminum casing that includes an on-off switch and added a round cork handle that provides insulation from the hot metal. Turning the handle and winding the spring to maximum tension provides enough power to rotate the spit for about thirty minutes; roasting an average-sized chicken requires 90–120 minutes. The architects named their dual-purpose cooking machine the **Reversible Grill** and completed their invention with a series of ingenious implements and hand tools.

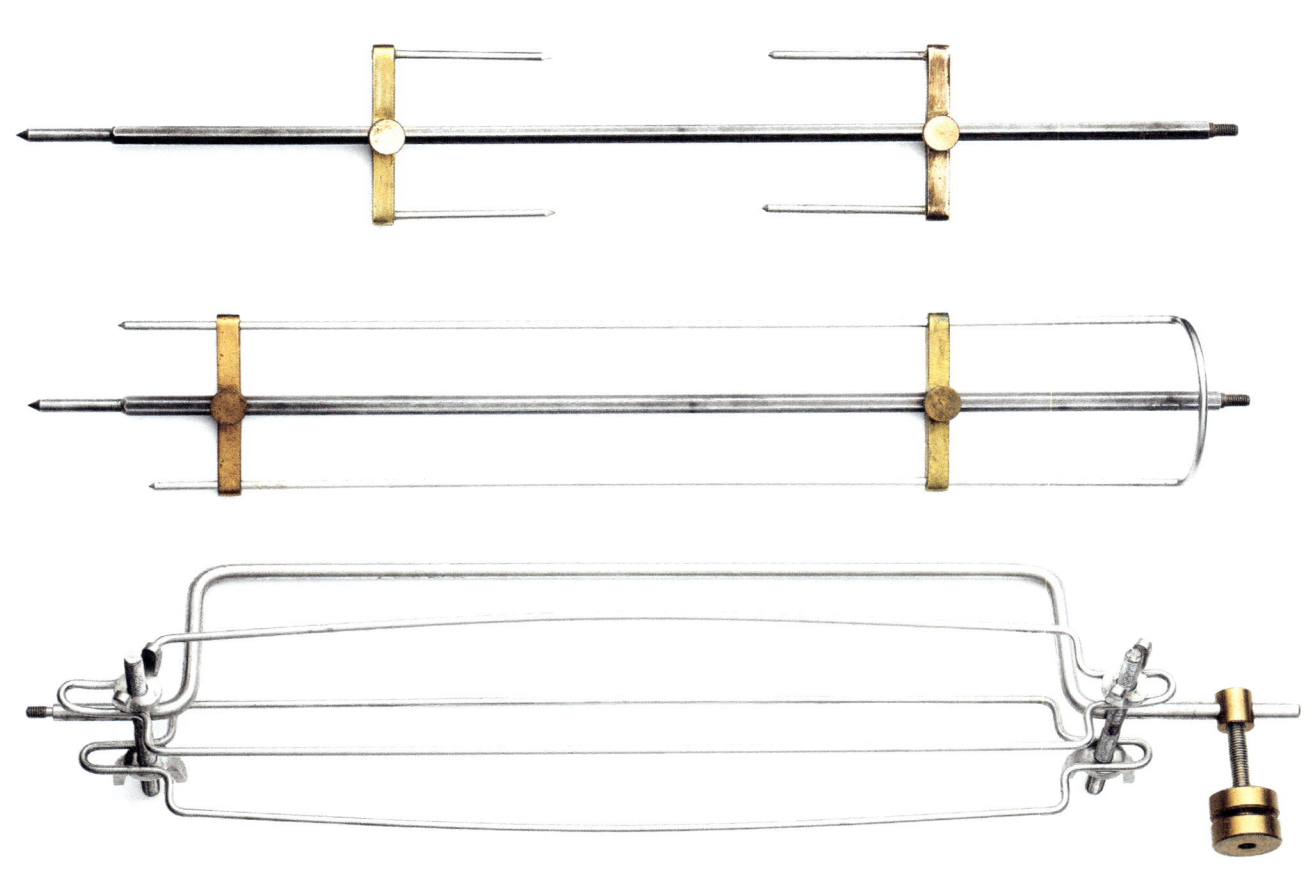

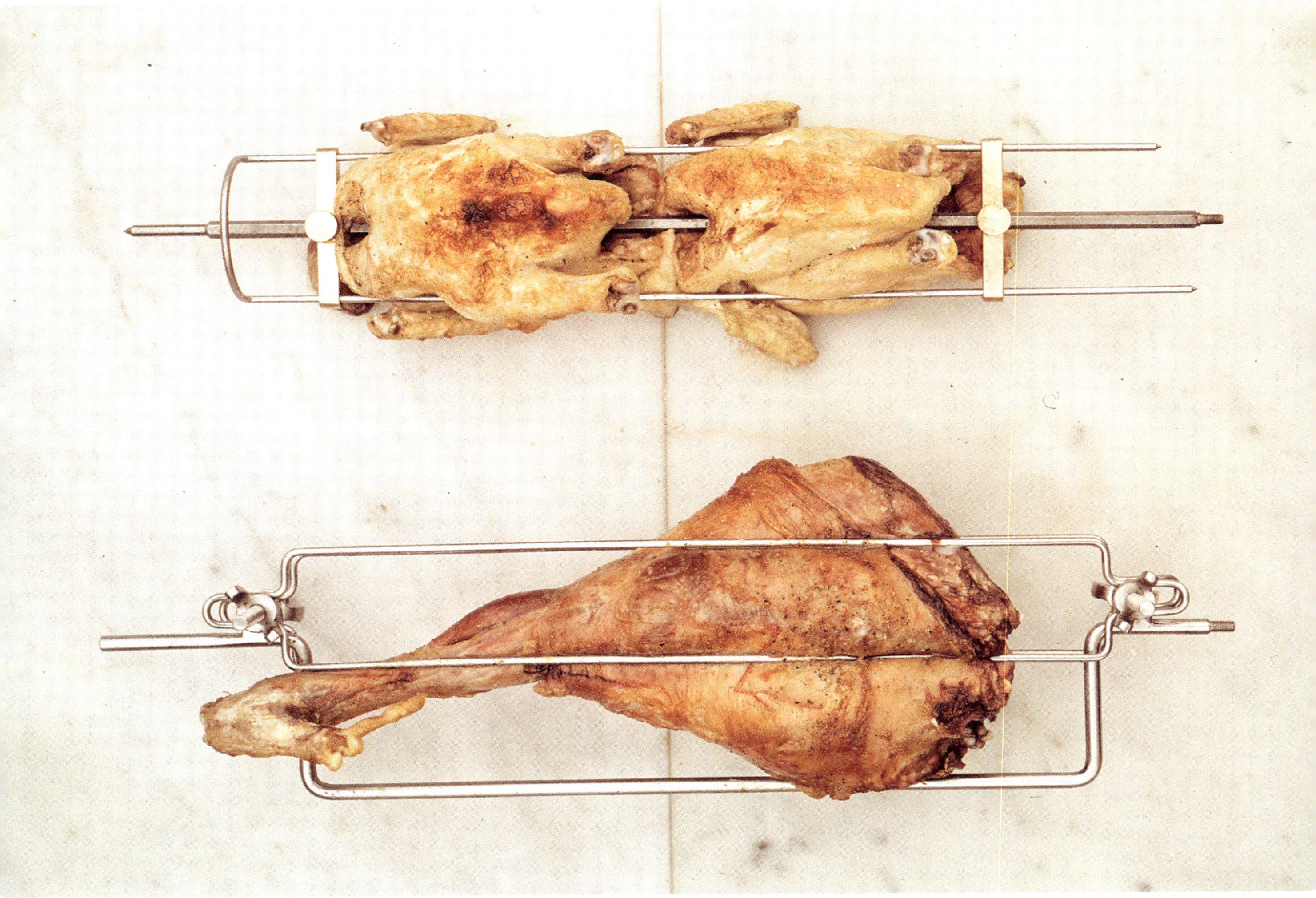

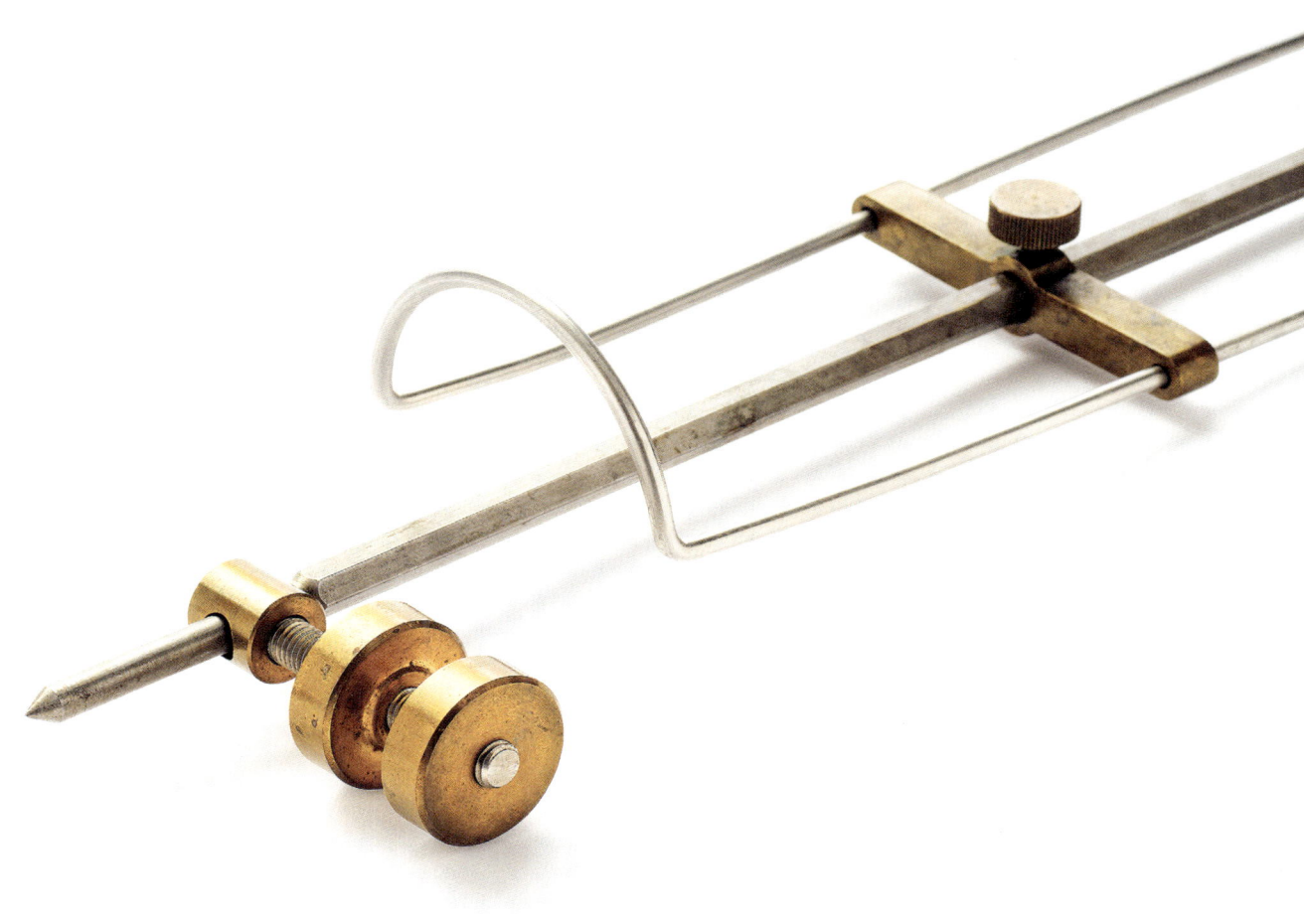

Detail of basic spit with wire skewers and adjustable counterweight. ← Three options for spitting food. Top to bottom: basic spit with adjustable brackets and spikes. Basic spit with adjustable brackets and wire skewers. Clamping spit with adjustable counterweight. Stainless steel and brass. / Basic spit and Clamping spit with roasted victuals.

The essential accessories for the Reversible Grill are the two spits that convert the shell into a rotisserie. The basic model is a hexagonal steel rod with round ends that ensure smooth rotation as they rest in the notches on the steel shell. A pair of adjustable brass brackets that recall early scientific instruments can be fitted with attachments that will prevent food from turning on the spit as it rotates. They include threaded steel spikes that can be screwed into the brackets, to hold a chunk of meat in the center of the spit. For thicker roasts and more eccentric loads, a bent steel wire with pointed ends can be threaded through the brackets, to provide additional skewers and compress the meat against the spit. The heavy-duty 'clamping spit' will accommodate a very large roast or a leg of lamb without piercing it and so conserve the juices. Because the wire clamps and bent rod are fastened together with wing nuts, the tension in the clamps can be adjusted to suit the size and shape of the meat.

One of the secrets of successful rotisserie is the even distribution of weight on the spit. If the load is heavier on one side, the spit will rotate at an irregular speed, leaving part of the food undercooked and the other part overcooked. While a fish or beef loin is more or less symmetrical around its length, most large pieces of meat have an irregular mass; the obvious example is a leg of lamb. To ensure smooth rotation for eccentric loads, Ravn and Lundquist developed an ingenious counterweight with solid brass disks that works on both types of spit. When an unevenly loaded spit is slotted into the steel shell, it will rotate towards its natural center of gravity. Fastening the counterweight to the end of the spit — at 180° from the direction of the meat — and moving the brass disks along the threaded rod — until the meat rotates 90° — will shift the center of gravity and ensure a constant speed of rotation.

Ravn and Lundquist complemented their dual-purpose grill with the hand tools they designed to protect food from being lost or damaged on the grate. To protect the cook, all of the tools have the same cork handle used on the wind-up motor for the spit. The low density of cork not only provides excellent insulation but also makes it flameproof. While cork can scorch and turn black, it will not burst into flame.

To ensure even cooking and prevent losses to the fire, the two friends designed a double skewer on the model of the Italian *il spiedo doppio*. A single piece of 2.5-mm stainless steel wire continues through the handle and provides a loop for hanging on a hook. While the parallel lengths of wire prevent food from rotating when the skewer is turned, the narrow gauge minimizes the holes and reduces dripping. The duo also designed a fork and spatula made of flexible stainless steel that makes it possible to remove food from the grate, even when it sticks. On both utensils, a curved neck between handle and implement imparts a slight spring to the tool, making it easier to lift the food without breaking the surface. The steel shank continues through the handle for maximum strength and ends in a rounded tab with a hole for hanging.

Detail of double skewer with hanging loop. 2.5-mm stainless steel wire and cork. / Grill steel fork and spatula. 1 mm stainless steel sheet with cork handles. Length 29 cm. → Standard box of six double skewers. Length 48 cm.

RL Grill Series. Autumn Exhibition of the Association of Arts and Crafts and Industrial Design, Charlottenborg, Copenhagen, 1974. Front to back: RL concrete elements, Element Grill; Reversible Grill; Element Grill and RL Hibachi. On the elements in the foreground: teak salad bowl designed by Søren Georg Jensen and Stub glassware designed by Grethe Meyer and Ibi Trier Mørch. / Garden table. 120 x 180 or 240 x 66 cm. 1:10 scale.

Alongside the Reversible Grill, Ravn and Lundquist designed a quartet of less elaborate grills that are portable to varying degrees and suited for many locations, from courtyards and gardens to the landscape and coastline. Moreover, the prices of those grills varied widely and included options for those who did not require or could not afford Ravn and Lundquist's convertible wonder. While the four grills vary in size and sophistication, they were all constructed to the same standard of quality as the Reversible Grill, using heavy-duty materials. None of them were produced in the same quantity as the Reversible Grill, and they are rare. However, photographs from the 1970s document the designers' talent for creating elegant tools through a careful study of practical concerns.

The inventive duo also designed a reinforced concrete block for supporting the grills and constructing outdoor kitchens and furnishings, which they referred to as an element. A single element is at once small enough (60 x 30 x 15 cm) and light enough (20 kg) to be moved and stacked by hand. One person can erect a variety of platforms, shelving and benches that are easily reconfigured and can be left outside all year round, as with the planters formed by turning units on their edges. The elements could also be stacked to create a dining table with a wooden top of pressure-treated pine, which was produced in three sizes. On either side of the stacked elements, deeper pieces of pine held the tabletop in place.

Ravn and Lundquist's do-it-yourself furniture system is emblematic of their work across the entire grill series, in the sense that they used industrial materials without a hint of nostalgia for a lost era of handicraft. Rather than decorate the concrete or deny its raw character, the designers treated the material as simply as possible and dimensioned the blocks to provide the greatest number of useful combinations, based on the scale of the human body.

Anodized aluminum stacking trays (natural, red and black). 24 or 48 x 28 x 4 or 8.5 cm.
→ Detail of Element Grill with grill fork.
/ Element Grill. Grate 60 x 30 x 15 cm. Weight 20 kg. / Concrete elements 60 x 30 x 15 cm. Weight 20 kg.

The same industrial impulse guided the design of the stacking metal trays that complement the concrete furniture and can likewise withstand the elements. Rather than create a pattern, the duo selected ready-made sheets of perforated aluminum that could be cut and bent to create lightweight rigid containers. The heights of the trays were determined by the diameter of the holes that allow for drainage and make it easy to grasp the trays from any angle. On the underside of each tray, rubber disks set into the holes at the corners prevent stacked trays from sliding sideways.

Ravn and Lundquist's system of outdoor furnishings inspired them to design the **Element Grill**, which was dimensioned to fit the cavity of their concrete element. Within the cavity, the firebox is raised on narrow ribs that ensure airflow to the perforated bottom, as on the Reversible Grill. An adjustable plate within the firebox makes it possible to maintain two fires for cooking different types of food or simply contain a small fire. The loose frame of steel angles carries a 50 x 30-cm grate and rests on the ends of the concrete element. The resulting gap between frame and firebox supplies the fire with oxygen and promotes a high cooking temperature on the grate.

The indispensable tool for the Element Grill is the flexible steel fork that Ravn and Lundquist designed for use on all of the steel grates in the grill series. As anyone with a whit of grilling experience is aware, food that sticks to the grate is easily damaged when turned. To prevent that common mishap, the gaps between the tines of the fork are slightly wider than the steel rods on the grate. As a result, the cook is able to insert the fork beneath the food and gently work it loose if necessary, rather than scrape it off the grate. Recalling the spoiled meals with their spouses, Ravn and Lundquist worked to provide a satisfying experience that would be memorable for the quality of the food, rather than the performance of the equipment.

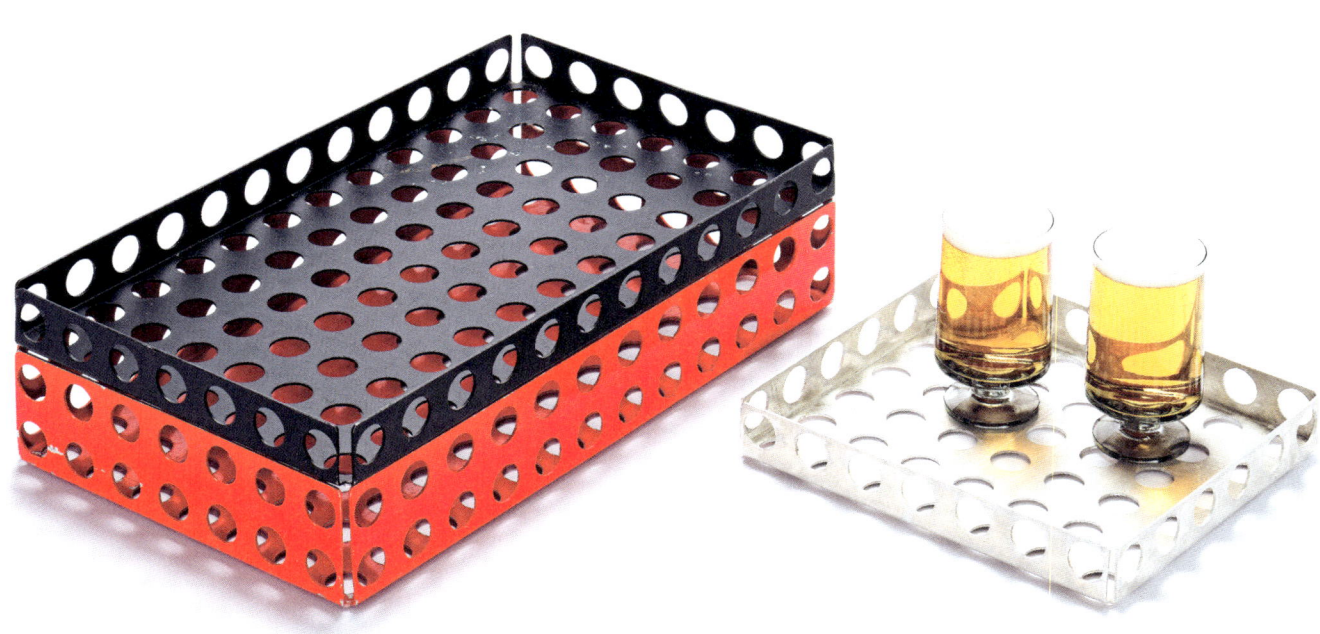

Despite the careful design, the grate on the Element Grill has a fixed height that makes it difficult to regulate the heat. Furthermore, there is no protection from wind, which can lower the cooking temperature. The **Standing Grill** addressed both of those concerns with a fully adjustable apparatus that works equally well in a garden or open landscape. The separate firebox and fence are attached to the steel pipe with rotating handles that include set screws and hold the two parts in place. While both parts are easily moved up and down the pipe, the fence includes slots for adjusting the height of the 50 x 50-cm grate. Finally, the entire grill can be rotated according to the position of the sun and prevailing winds.

Imagining picnics or excursions into the countryside, the designers created a demountable appliance that they labeled the **Camping Grill**. The cooking element is a cast-iron grate roughly the size of an A3 sheet of paper, which is mounted on a steel pipe that can be driven into the ground and then easily removed. Similarly to the Standing Grill, the grate is attached to the pipe with a handle that makes it possible to adjust the height for different cooking temperatures. With a weight of less than 5 kg, the two-piece grill was sold in a burlap bag that could be strapped to a bicycle or thrown in the trunk of a Volkswagen Beetle.

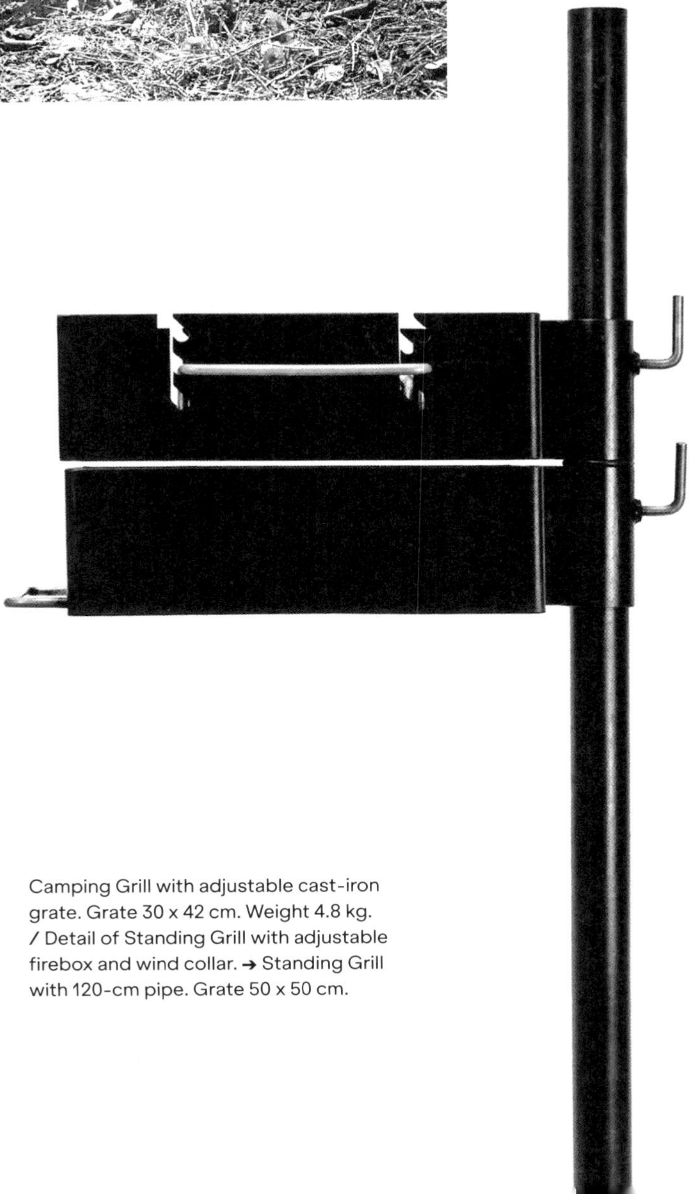

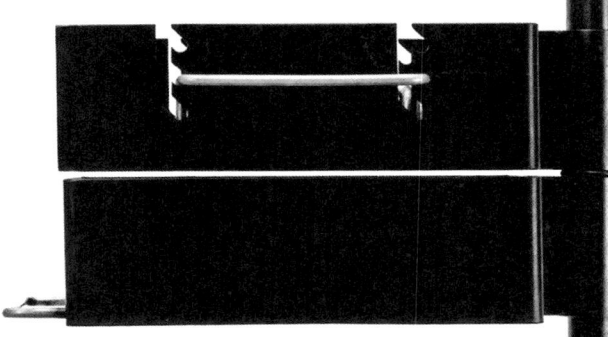

Camping Grill with adjustable cast-iron grate. Grate 30 x 42 cm. Weight 4.8 kg. / Detail of Standing Grill with adjustable firebox and wind collar. → Standing Grill with 120-cm pipe. Grate 50 x 50 cm.

The final model in Ravn and Lundquist's 1971 grill series was also the smallest and most portable part of the series. The **Hand Grill** was constructed entirely of 9-mm steel rods and provided a grate about the size of an A4 sheet of paper, for use in a fireplace or outdoors. Together, the small grill and the firebox that was sold as an accessory created a self-contained unit for cooking sausages in the forest or making coffee at the beach. Five years later, Ole Palsby employed the looped handle on the grill for the pans and lids on his Eva Trio cookware (p. 132).

In 1972, Ravn and Lundquist designed a simple structure inspired by the Reversible Grill that can be used in a fireplace and, in doing so, restored roasting to its traditional place in the home. As the fire is already contained, the **Fireplace Grill** consists of two steel brackets with two sets of holes, which are connected by a 60 x 30-cm grate of standard rods with wing nuts. Attaching the grate at the front set of holes provides a simple grill for small cuts and kebabs. When roasting, the grate is moved to the second set of holes and rotated to contain the fire. In that case, the spit can be mounted in the first set of holes or supported on the brackets, which makes it simple to adjust the distance from the fire.

The architects also designed an enlarged version of the Fireplace Grill that was roughly 90 cm wide, with a rotating firebox 60 cm deep and a massive spit that could carry an entire lamb. The one example of this apparently Renaissance-inspired machine that is known to have been constructed was kept at Ole Palsby's cookware shop on Læderstræde and rented out for parties at a price of 125 Danish kroner per evening.[13]

Hand Grill with steel firebox. Grate 30 x 42 cm. Weight 2.4 kg.
→ Fireplace Grill. Grate 60 x 30 cm. Weight 5.3 kg.

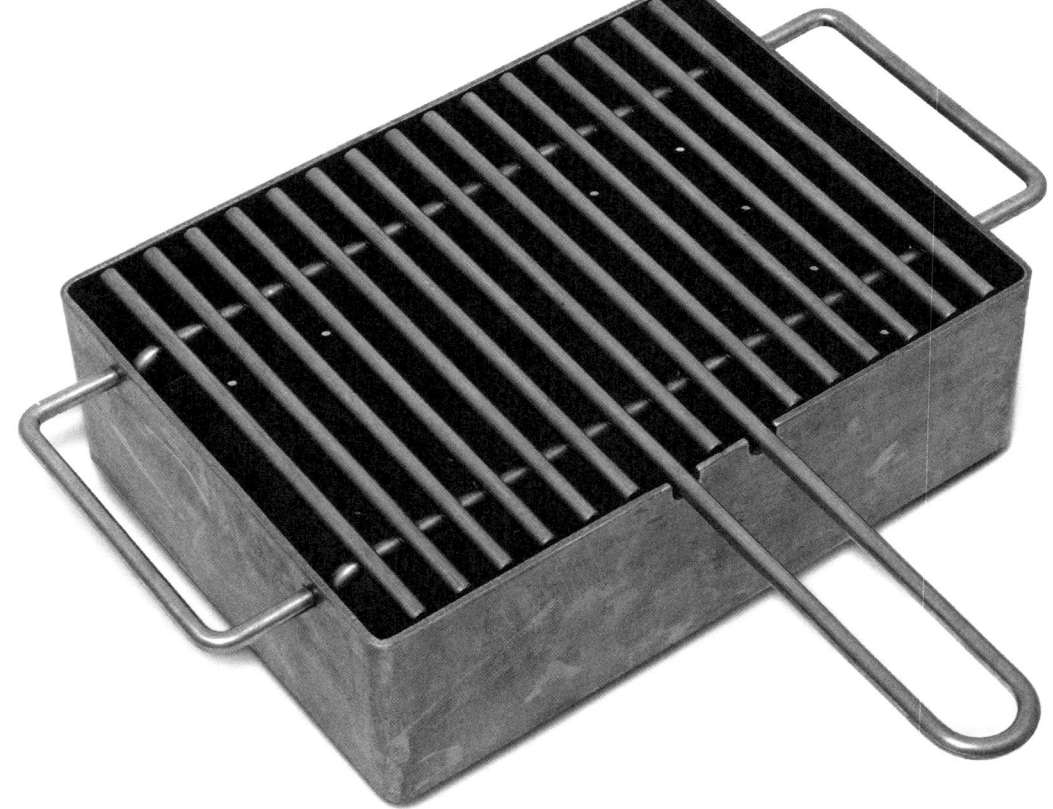

Smoking oven, 1973. Cement board with steel hatch. 28 x 48 x 117 cm. Weight 30 kg.
→ Lars Lundquist. Portable rotating grill with hinged grates, circa 1976.

In 1971, Karsten Ravn and Lars Lundquist were awarded the annual ID Prize from the Danish Design Council, in recognition of their five grills and concrete building element. Two years later, they completed their final design for Ole Palsby: an oven for smoking food that reflected the growing popularity of traditional preservation techniques. By then, sales of their grills were collapsing due to cheaper imitations from a number of Danish manufacturers.[14] As with the K-60 kitchen system, Palsby found his business undermined by plagiarism. After the leading plagiarist made the rounds of Palsby's wholesale customers, his sales for 1974 dropped by 500,000 kroner.[15]

Palsby planned to seek an injunction that would prohibit production of the pirated design, but doing so would have required him to deposit up to 200,000 Danish kroner into an escrow account.[16] He was unable to make that deposit due to the loss of income caused by the very design that Palsby hoped to prohibit. By the end of August 1975, Palsby was unable to pay his suppliers, and he declared bankruptcy three months later. As a result, production rights for Ravn and Lundquist's grill series reverted to the designers. During the next decade, most parts of the series were produced in small numbers, by the blacksmiths Kay Dideriksen and later Carsten Fagerholt (Nils Fagerholt's brother).[17] By 1986, Fagerholt's production had dwindled to a pair of grills, a single spit and the concrete block, and soon came to an end.

In 1972, Ravn and Lundquist graduated from the Royal Academy's School of Architecture, after presenting their portable shelter for victims of natural disasters and the grill series. By 1975, as Palsby's business collapsed, the two architects' paths had diverged.[18] Ravn was working in product development at the Georg Jensen A/S, which had recently been purchased by the Royal Copenhagen Porcelain Factory. In time, he became design director at Royal Scandinavia A/S, the corporate successor to Royal Copenhagen. In retirement, he has often served as an expert witness in copyright lawsuits. Lundquist operated his own design practice and created a string of works that included cast-iron cookware and furniture made from the wood produced for shipping pallets.[19] In later years, he taught and lectured in industrial design, in Denmark and overseas.

The **RL Grill Series** was a product of its time that was created at the beginning of the culinary era in which we live, now more than ever concerned with the origins and quality of our food. Paradoxically, Ravn and Lundquist's industrial designs provide us with tools to resist the industrial food chain promoted under the twin banners of economy and convenience. Indeed, there are few cooking techniques less convenient than roasting in front of an open fire, which is not a method for daily meals but a wholesome alternative to the norm. The RL series supports an approach to food that requires time and attention but is also rewarding in ways that transcend nutrition. Given those benefits, it would not be surprising if parts of the series return to production, their meaning and value only increased by the passage of time.

Among the archetypes of Danish design, even the smallest and simplest examples embody the underlying ideals of modest forms and adaptability to different purposes. And so, the selection of objects featured in this book concludes with the **Hyggelampe** (Cozy Lamp) designed by Per Lütken, the artistic director at Holmegaard Glassworks during 1942–98.[1] Initially trained as an illustrator, Lütken specialized in soft forms that preserved the fluid character of the molten material, as seen in his glassware services Copenhagen (1953), Canada (1955) and Skotland (1961). Due to concerns about overproduction and excess inventory, Holmegaard never completely mechanized its production of table glass. As a result, Lütken was able to work with master glassblowers wielding iron pipes and enjoyed complete artistic freedom.

During 1956–66, Lütken's work reached a peak of refinement, as he combined an intuitive feeling for his material with a restrained approach to form. In 1964, he turned his hand to a traditional type of enclosed candleholder modeled on the "hurricane" oil lamps that were used on ships during the 1800s. Working towards a design that would be equally useful indoors and outdoors, he created a low cup of molded, smoke-colored glass that is sufficiently heavy to resist wind. Moreover, the massive base will not crack if the candle burns all the way down. To create an atmospheric effect, the mouth-blown chimney was made of tinted glass in a variety of colors that suit different moods and color preferences. The result is a simple source of light that embodies the flexible character of the selected archetypes.

Per Lütken's lamp is a charming example of the mix-and-match ethos that informed the designs of the selected objects in this book. In decades past, it was a commonly held ideal that the furniture in a room should match and that propriety required a respectable household to collect complete sets of tableware or flatware, no matter how infrequently the olive fork was used. Uniform place settings promote harmony around the table, and the urge to collect is an innate human trait. But the ideal of the complete set is rooted in displays of wealth that can be traced to Versailles, where Louis XIV established enduring standards of décor and presentation. Thankfully, that type of social pressure has also faded into history and no longer afflicts most people. Indeed, flexibility and the ability to combine items of different series and types are inherent in the archetypes.

The designers of the selected objects rejected traditional notions of propriety and "good taste" at a time when they were still in full force. Instead, they designed things that have the character of useful tools or pieces of equipment. They did so in the belief that people should be able to buy only what they wanted, based on actual needs. Grethe Meyer's Hvidpot porcelain, which she hoped would be combined with parts of other services, is only the most pronounced example. Kay Bojesen designed a set of flatware with thirty-eight parts that includes an oyster knife and a marmalade spoon, so that people could consume those foods in a graceful manner rather than emulate a vanished aristocracy. Ole Palsby's Eva Trio cookware provided vessels suited to individual habits that could be covered with interchangeable lids. In every case, the series is a resource rather than an obligation.

The designers also resisted the notion of a rigid arrangement or static interior and created adjustable furniture and lighting that can be used wherever and however it is needed. Mogens Koch's folding furniture was conceived for absolute convenience and portability, even as the chairs designed by Arne Jacobsen and Vilhelm Wohlert provide temporary seating that is easily moved and can be stacked for compact storage. Grethe Meyer and Børge Mogensen designed their storage system so that it could be customized, reconfigured and then moved if needed. Knud Holscher's system of lamps was based on the idea of adjustable lighting, and the rotating grill designed by Karsten Ravn and Lars Lundquist could be adapted to different cooking techniques and placed on concrete elements that were easily reconfigured.

> Per Lütken. Hyggelampe, 1963. Molded and mouthblown glass with red chimney. 1:1 scale.

EPILOGUE

Design for Life

The objects presented in this book were not designed in the conventional sense of the term, as symbols of social status or personal statements by the designer, but instead developed on the basis of real life. In many cases, the design of the object was rooted in personal experience, whether Poul Henningsen's formative years in the glow of kerosene lamps, Kim Naver's decoration of a tiny apartment or the years spent living in close quarters that led Grethe Meyer to focus on compact storage. While the folding chairs designed by Børge Mogensen and Mogens Koch were initially conceived for their makers' own homes, Karsten Ravn and Lars Lundquist grills were inspired by their ill-fated encounters with conventional models.

In each case, the object or series was designed with other people in mind and a profound concern for their comfort. The most literal and poignant example of that concern is the armchair that Arne Jacobsen designed as an interactive assembly of industrial materials, but we recognize the same priority in Børge Mogensen's adjustable lounge chair and folding deck chair. The human touch was the essential factor in Kay Bojesen's designs for steel flatware, Grethe Meyer and Ibi Trier Mørch's glassware and Meyer's designs for ceramic plates, platters and cookware. While the key that serves as a door handle on Boligens Byggeskabe was designed for operation with fingertips, the handles on Eva Trio were designed to minimize contact with the metal, and the handles on Ravn and Lundquist's grill tools provide natural insulation.

We can trace the designers' intense focus on the human touch to the handicraft tradition that provided each of them with a standard of quality, even as they conceived their designs for industrial production. Nowhere is that legacy more pronounced than in the works of artisans Kay Bojesen, Børge Mogensen and Kim Naver, as they attempted to sustain traditional values by transferring them from the workshop to the factory. And yet, that impulse was not limited to the trained craftspeople, as Arne Jacobsen created the industrial equivalent of silver hollowware, and Ole Palsby distilled his knowledge of traditional cookware into mass-produced tools. While Hanne Valeur's K-60 kitchen was initially handcrafted by cabinetmakers, it was conceived for the factory and produced in hundreds of thousands of examples, albeit by others.

The creators of the archetypes have left us industrial equivalents to handcrafted items, which were designed for daily use and have not been improved upon over the intervening decades. These archetypal examples of Danish design occupy a wrinkle in time: neither truly old-fashioned, due to their excellent functions and modest forms, nor truly new, due to their vintage. Historians will insist that no thing is timeless, because every thing is a product of its time and culture, which is entirely correct.

However, some activities are so basic and so essential to well-being that they can be regarded as essentially timeless: cooking and eating, sitting down and relaxing, lighting and decorating a room, arranging and storing possessions. And so, too, the vintage things that serve those needs with such excellence and grace that they remain contemporary can be regarded as *nearly* timeless.

These archetypal objects embody a design culture that flourished in Denmark through an intersection of traditional values and industrial production. As such, they provide a standard to which future industrial designers might aspire. Moreover, they promote cultural sustainability at a time when digital technology threatens to erase national and local distinctions in the service of profit. The environmental sustainability of these objects is self-evident, because they present alternatives to the disposable goods that have become the norm. Some of the objects are inexpensive, and some require an investment, but all of them will last a lifetime with a modicum of care, and some far longer. Ultimately, the archetypes presented in this publication embody our ability to use technology in the service of human well-being, and so, their meaning extends far beyond their excellent service and graceful forms.

Hyggelampe in standard colors of green, light green, blue and grey at the top.

Notes

Bibliography

Index

Credits

Acknowledgments

PROLOGUE / LIVING HISTORY

1 Grete Jalk (ed.), *40 Years of Danish Furniture Design: The Copenhagen Cabinet-makers' Guild Exhibitions 1927–1966 = Dansk Møbelkunst Gennem 40 År: Københavns Snedkerlaugs Møbeludstillinger 1927–1966*, vol. 2 (Høje Tastrup: Teknologisk Instituts Forlag, 1987, reprinted in 2017 by Lindhardt og Ringhof / Forlaget Carlsen), 54–55. **2** *Blåkant catalog* (Copenhagen: Royal Copenhagen Porcelain Manufactory, 1971), 3. **3** The notable exception was the simple wooden chair that Klint designed in 1938 to furnish his Bethlehem Church, which was put into standard production by Fritz Hansen, as the Church Chair, with or without arms. **4** Michael Sheridan, *Klint + Kjærholm* (Copenhagen: Dansk Møbelkunst, 2010). **5** Esbjørn Hiort, trans. Martha Gaber Abrahamsen, *Finn Juhl: Furniture, Architecture, Applied Art: A Biography* (Copenhagen: Danish Architectural Press, 1990), 138–139. As the author explained, "But Finn Juhl was in principle an opponent of 'schools' because in his view they adopt a certain idiom and limit creativity." **6** For a panoramic overview of Wegner's creative output, see Christian Holmsted Olesen, trans. Mark Mussari, *Wegner: Just One Good Chair* (Copenhagen: Strandberg Publishing, 2014). **7** Notable examples include Ib Kofod, Illum Wikkelsø, Hans Olsen and Kai Kristiansen. **8** See Claire Selkurt, "Design for a democracy: Scandinavian design in postwar America" in Widar Halén and Kerstin Wickman (eds.), *Scandinavian Design Beyond the Myth: Fifty Years of Design from the Nordic Countries* (Stockholm: Arvinus Förlag/Form Förlag, 2003). Elizabeth Gordon, the editor of the monthly magazine *House Beautiful*, regarded mainstream European modernism (the Bauhaus) as an instrument of creeping collectivism (i.e. Communism). As an alternative, she promoted Danish and, more generally, Nordic design culture as an appropriate style for a democratic society. As part of that effort, Gordon and her cohort coined the terms Scandinavian Modern and Danish Modern, based on the vogue for "Swedish Modern" that originated in the Swedish pavilion at the 1939 World's Fair in New York City. **9** See, for example, Stig Guldberg, *Jens Quistgaard: The Sculpting Designer* (London: Phaidon, 2023). Henning Koppel is not yet the subject of a lavish monograph. For well-illustrated coverage, see *Mobilia*, no. 273, April 1958, and Viggo Sten Møller, *Henning Koppel* (Copenhagen: Rhodos, 1965). **10** Gorm Harkær, *Kaare Klint,* vol. 1 (Copenhagen: Klintiana, 2010), 77–90. **11** Ibid., 291–302. **12** Mogens Koch, *Moderne Dansk Kunsthåndværk* (Copenhagen: Thaning & Appel, 1948), [2]. **13** Arne Karlsen, trans. Martha Gaber Abrahamsen, *Danish Furniture Design in the 20th Century*, vol. 2 (Copenhagen: Christian Ejlers' Forlag/Dansk Møbelkunst, 2007), 16–17, 48–50. **14** Mogens Koch, "reoler," in *Nyt Tidsskrift for Kunstindustri*, vol. 13, no. 7, 1940, 111.

KAY BOJESEN / GRAND PRIX, 1938/1951–53

1 Viggo Sten Møller and Henrik Sten Møller, *Kay Bojesen: Kunstner og Haandværker: Den Legende Mand* (Copenhagen: Christian Ejlers' Forlag, 1983). Henrik Sten Møller's childhood memories of Kay Bojesen presenting him with toys established the template for many later descriptions of Bojesen's work. **2** As Bojesen explained to the American merchant Stanley Marcus, "I only make toys for a smile. And there's money in a smile." Kay Bojesen, Scrapbook 13, 1 May – 3 August 1955. Special Collections of the Royal Danish Library. **3** Erik Lassen, "Kay Bojesen. I anledning af hans udstilling," in *Dansk Kunsthaandværk*, vol. 23, no. 1, 1950, 7–9. **4** Mirjam Gelfer-Jørgensen, "Georg Jensen: A Man of His Time," in David A. Taylor (ed.), *Georg Jensen Jewelry* (New York: Bard Graduate Center, 2005), 43–63. **5** Kay Bojesen, Scrapbook 1, 19 June – 12 December 1931. Special Collections of the Royal Danish Library. **6** Lars Hedebo Olsen, *Kay Bojesen*, in the series *Danske Designere*, Poul Erik Tøjner (ed.) (Copenhagen: Aschehoug/Louisiana Museum of Modern Art, 2007), 39–41. As well: Pierre Lübecker, trans. Mary Fulfold, *Applied Art by Kay Bojesen* (Copenhagen: National Association of Danish Handicrafts, 1955). **7** Kay Bojesen, "Det hamrede sølv," in *Berlingske Tidende*, 23 July 1928. Reprinted as "Hammerslag," in *Nyt Tidsskrift for Kunstindustri*, vol. 1, no. 7, 1928, 143–144. **8** Ibid. **9** Kay Bojesen, "Hen til kommoden og tilbav's igen: Sølvet på Kunsthaandværkets forårsudstilling," in *Dansk Kunsthaandværk*, vol. 25, no. 5, 1952, 74–77. **10** Bojesen's breakthrough in flatware design is commonly dated to 1929, when it was included in the exhibition for the 500th anniversary of the Copenhagen Goldsmiths' Guild. However, the fork and spoon were both presented at the 1928 Autumn Exhibition of the Arts and Crafts Association, at the Danish Museum of Applied Art (now Designmuseum Danmark), as published in *Nyt Tidsskrift for Kunstindustri*, vol. 1, no. 1, 1928, 203. Despite the misunderstanding, Pierre Lübecker correctly noted the connection between Bojesen's utensils of 1928 and 1938, in his previously cited book. **11** See Erik Lassen, *Ske, Kniv og Gaffel = Knives Forks & Spoons* (Copenhagen: Høst & Søn, 1960). Lassen's survey of the flatware collection at the Danish Museum of Applied Art included many examples of English work from the 1700s that influenced Bojesen's work toward distilled forms. The book includes an informative historical essay, and almost all of the examples are reproduced at a 1:1 scale. **12** Frederik Sieck, *Danish Arts and Crafts 1931–81: Illustrated Through Glimpses of the History of Den Permanente* (Copenhagen: Den Permanente A/S, 1981), 7–11. **13** Kay Bojesen, "Thus 'Den Permanente' was established: One of the founders narrating ...," in *Dansk Kunsthaandværk*, vol. 29, no. 8–9, 1956, 163–65. **14** Notice in *Børsen*, 31 January 1930. **15** Kay Bojesen, Scrapbook 1 includes an outline of his plans to renovate the Bing & Grøndahl flagship store on Amagertorv, in central Copenhagen, and renew the company's product lines. His plans included contributions by Mogens Koch, Kaare Klint, Poul Henningsen and a number of visual artists. Kaare Klint's design for a serving cart is reproduced in Gorm Harkær, *Kaare Klint*, vol. 2 (Copenhagen: Klintiana, 2010), 66–67. Following his departure from Bing & Grøndahl, Bojesen suffered a nervous breakdown and took a recuperative trip to Africa, where he encountered several of the exotic animals that inspired his wooden toys of the 1950s. In 1936, Bojesen published and distributed a pamphlet that includes his correspondence with Bing & Grøndahl, in order to protect his reputation. See Kay Bojesen, *En "Misforstaaelse": Blade af en Dansk Kunsthaandværkers Dagbog* (self-published, 1936), 1–8. Special Collections of the Royal Danish Library. **16** Bojesen and his colleague Ejnar Dragsted developed a curriculum for the Technical School that would convey the fundamentals of jewelry and flatware production. Moreover, Bojesen designed a set of standard silverware for the Danish Goldsmith's Silverware Factory, which is published in *Nyt Tidsskrift for Kunstindustri*, vol. 4, no. 10, 1931, and a number of Danish newspapers. Both items: Kay Bojesen, Scrapbook 1. **17** Kay Bojesen, "Sølvets Anvendelighed," in *Nyt Tidsskrift for Kunstindustri*, vol. 5, no. 3, 1932, 38. **18** Kay Bojesen, "Kay Bojesen Udstilling," in *Nyt Tidsskrift for Kunstindustri*, vol. 11, no. 11, 1938, 195. **19** Kay Bojesen, "Lidt om vort spiseværktøj," in *Dansk Kunsthaandværk*, vol. 29, no. 3–4, 1956, 63. **20** Lise Funder, *Dansk Sølv: 20. Århundrede* (Copenhagen: Nyt Nordisk Forlag Arnold Busck, 1999), 129. Funder describes the multi-piece serving tray that Kay Bojesen produced by melting down several older pieces of hollowware to obtain the 3.9 kg of silver that he required for the piece. **21** Bojesen, "Lidt om vort spiseværktøj," 66 (see note 19). **22** "Dansk Kunsthaandværk i dag – og i fremtiden," in *Nyt Tidsskrift for Kunstindustri*, vol. 11, no. 10, 1938, 177. **23** Kay Bojesen, "En ny dansk knivfabrik," in *Dansk Kunsthaandværk*, vol. 22, no. 4, 1949, 52–55. **24** Lübecker, *Applied Art by Kay Bojesen*, 31 (see note 6). **25** Headlines from the second week of December 1953 included "Rostfritt med dansk charm" and "Svensk rostfritt i dansk silvermodell." Kay Bojesen, Scrapbook 10, 1953, Special Collections of the Royal Danish Library. **26** "Just nu," in *Dagens Nyheter*, 21 November 1953. **27** For the histories of flatware and discussions of metals, see Margaret Visser, *The Rituals of Dinner* (New York: Grove, 1991), 183–196; and Bee Wilson, *Consider the Fork: A History of How We Cook and Eat* (New York: Basic Books, 2012), 181–195. **28** Bojesen, "Lidt om vort spiseværktøj," 63 (see note 19). **29** Henrik Sten Møller, "Kay Bojesen," in *Mobilia*, no. 185, December 1970, unpaginated.

Notes

GRETHE MEYER / IBI TRIER MØRCH / STUB, 1957–59

1 Both women were fiercely independent and committed to self-determination, and both were proud single mothers in an era when that was not generally considered an acceptable course in life. While it was widely known that Grethe Meyer's former classmate Bent Salicath had fathered her child, Ibi Trier Mørch refused to publicly identify the father of her two children, on the grounds that it was an entirely personal matter. Meyer's attitudes and personal life are chronicled in great detail in Christina B. Kjeldsen and Isabel Bernadette Brammer, *Grethe Meyer: Arkitekten, Der Revolutionerede Middagsbordet* (Copenhagen: Gyldendal, 2024). **2** Poul Kjærgaard, "Byggebogen: Et samleværk for byggeriets data," in *Arkitekten. Ugehæfte*, vol. 47, no. 25–26, 1945, 105–111. **3** Ibi Trier Mørch's son, Andreas Trier Mørch, compiled a book of pictures and text chronicling his mother's life. It includes several photographs from her years in Sweden, where she worked on the design of standardized kitchens during 1937–40. Her place(s) of employment are unknown, but she almost certainly spent some time in the architectural office of Hyresgästernas Sparkasse- och Byggnadsförening (the Tenants' Savings and Building Society), which had been developing standard kitchens since 1925. **4** Anker Tiedemann and Arne Karlsen, "Samtale med Ibi Trier Mørch," in *Spatium*, vol. 1, no. 3, 1963, iii–iv. Ibi Trier Mørch was referring to the ideal of the subsistence dwelling that gained popularity among modernist architects in Germany during the 1920s and was codified at the 1929 exhibition *Die Wohnung für das Existenzminimum* (The Dwelling for Minimal Existence) in Frankfurt. That model gained widespread acceptance in Sweden in the 1930s and provided the framework for Trier Mørch's work on kitchen designs during 1937–40. Those efforts informed her work with Meyer on the kitchen survey, which extended to the resulting publication: *Køkkenundersøgelse* (Copenhagen: Fællesudvalget for Boligundersøgelser, 1949), 30–31. **5** "Danskt Konsthantverk: Kvinnlig byggnadsarkitekt blev känd som sølvsmed," in *Sundvalls Tidning*, 23 May 1953. (See Kay Bojesen, Scrapbook 9, 1 January – 21 August 1953. Special Collections of the Royal Danish Library.) Trier Mørch's silver hollowware is relatively rare but widely known and often appears in books focused on female architects and designers. **6** For a capsule biography of this relatively mysterious figure, see Søren Sass, "Ibi Trier Mørch," https://kvindebiografiskleksikon.lex.dk/Ibi_Trier_Mørch (accessed 9 October 2024). **7** Poul Erik Skriver, "Kvinde og Hjem: Danske kvinders udstilling for rationel husførelse i Forum 1.-17. september 1950," in *Arkitekten. Ugehæfte*, vol. 52, no. 44, 1950, 213–215. **8** "Resultatet af køkkenkonkurrencen," in *Arkitekten. Ugehæfte*, vol. 53, no. 11, 1951, 49–52. As well: "Forslag af arkitekt Grethe Meyer i samarbejde med arkitekt Emanuel Johansen, Tildelt 1. præmie i gruppe A," in *Boligen*, no. 8, 179–183, 1951. **9** Susanne Outzen and Mette Bielefeldt Bruun, "Jacob Eiler Bang: Danish idealism based on reality," in *Journal of Glass Studies*, vol. 62, 2020, 229–244. Bang outlined his approach to table glass in Jacob Eiler Bang, "Glas: Orientering ved begyndelsen af en ny produktion," in *Nyt Tidsskrift for Kunstindustri*, vol. 1, no. 10, 1928, 189–200. **10** Susann Vihma and Tapio Yli-Viikari, "Kaj Franck at Wärtsilä," in Marianne Aav (ed.), *Kaj Franck: Universal Forms* (Helsinki: Designmuseo, 2011), 54–59. **11** Ibid., 10–34. Marianne Aav describes Franck's education and early professional experiences in the chapter "Towards universal forms." **12** Oppi Untracht, *Saara Hopea: Life and Work* (Helsinki: Werner Söderström Osakeyhtiö, 1988), 86–87, 165. **13** Notice in *Dansk Kunsthaandværk*, vol. 30, no. 6, 1957, unpaginated. The competition was announced in June with a submittal deadline of 20 January 1958. **14** "A/S Kastrup Glasværk: Resultatet af konkurrence om forslag til nye glas," in *Dansk Kunsthaandværk*, vol. 31, no. 1, 1958, 23. **15** Esbjørn Hiort, "Nye glas fra Kastrup Glasværk: En konkurrence og dens resultater," in *Dansk Kunsthaandværk*, vol. 32, no. 6, 1959, 112–116. **16** Ibid. **17** Svend Erik Møller, "Glasmenageri med mange, rige løfter," in *Politiken*, 10 June 1959; "Glas, der har laant himlens farver," in *Berlingske Tidende*, 12 June 1959; Kirsten Brøndsted, "Stor konkurrence med fint resultat," in *Hjemmet*, 18 August 1959; "Glas til bruk," in *Bo Nytt*, no. 2, February 1960, unpaginated. **18** Hiort, "Nye glas fra Kastrup Glasværk," 112–116 (see note 15). **19** Historically, much of the white wine consumed in northern Europe was produced in Germany and unfiltered. As a result, it became common to serve white wine in green glassware that concealed the slightly cloudy appearance. **20** "Taarne af drikkeglas skabt af arkitekter," in *Berlingske Tidende*, 9 June 1959; "Glas i stabler," in *Dagens Nyheder*, 10 June 1959; "Glassene kan stables," in *Politiken*, 16 June 1959; Poul Erik Skriver, "Glasparade," *Arkitektur*, vol. 3, no. 4, 152–155. Skriver singled out Stub and recommended that it be put into production. **21** Grethe Meyer's typewritten notes are dated March–May 1959 and included among her papers in the Danish Design Archive, Designmuseum Danmark. **22** Meyer alluded to this scenario in an interview with a Swedish journalist, when pressed on the resemblance between the Stamme champagne glass and a test tube. After declaring her allegiance to "simple shapes," she explained "Since you don't use a champagne glass very often, Grethe Meyer thinks that, well, you can defend a little silliness at that point." See note 20, *Dagens Nyheder*. **23** See "Kastrup og Holmegaards Glasværker A/S 1965-1975" in Erik Lassen and Mogens Schlüter, *Dansk Glas 1925–85* (Copenhagen: Nyt Nordisk Forlag/Arnold Busck, 2002), 41–47. **24** Retired Holmegaard employee Verner Hansen, email to the author, July 2014. **25** In 1985, investment managers from the Carlsberg Group bought a controlling stake in Royal Copenhagen, which owned Georg Jensen and Holmegaard and soon took over the Bing & Grøndahl porcelain company. Following the purchase of the Swedish glassworks Orrefors Kosta Boda, in 1997, the company changed its name to Royal Scandinavia A/S. That multi-brand corporation proved to be unprofitable, and the various companies were sold to new owners. Holmegaard ended up in the hands of speculators who hoped to create an entertainment complex at the old glassworks. After that project failed, the glassworks was shuttered, and the design rights were separated from the property rights. Today, the old glassworks is an enchanting branch of Museum Sydøstdanmark. **26** In the early 1970s, as dishwashing machines became increasingly popular in Denmark, Holmegaard was inundated with complaints about chemical etching of the glassware in the machines. The chemists traced the problem to silica in the detergent and excessively hot water. In response, the glassworks developed a new recipe for soda glass and began distributing tips for safe mechanical washing of glassware. The number one recommendation, which remains in effect today, is limiting the water temperature to 60° C, which is also the threshold for killing bacteria. **27** See note 3.

HANNE VALEUR / K-60, 1962

1 Hanne Valeur in conversation with the author, August 2019. **2** Malene Lytken, "The Danish School of Interior Architecture: A visionary functionalist, a visionary aesthete, and their women students," in *Journal of Interior Design*, 38, no. 3, 2013, 1–19. Lytken traces the origin and evolution of the school and emphasizes the shift towards an artistic focus that occurred after Finn Juhl became director in 1948. **3** Hanne Valeur in conversation with the author, August 2019. **4** Børge Mogensen and Arne Karlsen, "Brugskunst på afveje," in *Arkitekten*, no. 1, 1962, 1–11. **5** Svend Erik Møller, "Kritik på afveje," in *Politiken*, January 1962. **6** Børge Mogensen and Arne Karlsen, "Tradition og fornyelse," in *Spatium: Tidsskrift for Rumindretning og Brugskunst*, vol. 1, no. 1, 1963, 1–8. **7** Hanne Valeur in conversation with the author, August 2019. **8** Antonia Surmann, "The evolution of kitchen design: A yearning for a modern Stone Age cave," in Nicolaj van der Meulen and Jörg Wessel (eds.), *Culinary Turn: Aesthetic Practice of Cookery* (Bielefeld: Transcript Verlag, 2017), 47–56. **9** In 1925, painter and Bauhaus master Georg Muche expressed the prevailing sentiment among the German avant-garde when he declared, "The kitchen should be the workspace, the laboratory for the housewife, in which every superfluous bit of space and every inconvenient arrangement of the fixtures creates additional work in the long run. It must be a mechanism, an instrument." **10** Maria Perers, "Bygge och Bo," in *Scandinavian Journal of Design History*, no. 11, 2001, 74–97. **11** Jannie Rosenberg Bendsen, Svava Riesto and Henriette Steiner, trans. René Lauritsen, *Untold Stories: On Women, Gender and Architecture in Denmark* (Copenhagen: Strandberg Publishing, 2023), 69. **12** Following the establishment of the Danish Ministry of Housing, in 1947, a vast infrastructure was put in place to rationalize building standards, which included the National Building Research Institute (SBI). Modeled on Swedish efforts, notably Hemmens Forskningsinstitut, SBI absorbed the *Byggebogen* project founded by Poul Kjærgaard at the Royal Danish Academy and continued his efforts to arrive at construction standards on a much larger scale. As part of that incorporation, Grethe Meyer and Børge Kjær found themselves working for SBI. **13** Leif Leer Sørensen, *Edvard Heiberg og Dansk Funktionalisme: En Arkitekt og Hans Samtid* (Copenhagen: Arkitektens Forlag, 2000), 297–306. **14** Edvard Heiberg, "Om køkkener," in *Arkitekten. Ugehæfte*, vol. 1, no. 10–11, 1948, 37–40. **15** The results of the kitchen survey that Grethe Meyer and Ibi Trier Mørch were involved in were distilled into Edvard Heiberg, Eske Kristensen and Bent Salicath, "Planlægning af køkkener i etagehuse" (Copenhagen: Fællesorganisationen af almennyttige danske boligselskaber, 1950). In an attempt to develop new standards for kitchen cabinets, on the Swedish model, the Joint Organization sponsored a design competition. While Grethe Meyer won the category for kitchen planning, Christian Hage won the category for cabinets. After Hage's entry was deemed lacking, Heiberg, Kristensen and Salicath created their own design, which became known as the Esto Kitchen and was renamed the Tectum Kitchen, in 1960. **16** Edvard Heiberg, "Elementkøkkener: De første erfaringer," in *Arkitekten. Ugehæfte*, vol. 8, no. 44, 1955, 361–366. **17** The Esto Kitchen designed by Heiberg, Kristensen and Salicath was advertised in the FDB member's magazine, *Samvirke*, as early as 1955. See *Samvirke*, 1 June 1955, 3. **18** Poul Erik Skriver, "Slotsparken i Kolding", in *Arkitektur*, vol. 7, no. 4, 1963, 155–160. **19** See Bo Gunnar Lindgren (ed.), *Kök: Planering, Inredning* (Stockholm: Hemmens Forskningsinstitut, 1952). As well: Cecilia Björk, *Tidstypiska Kök & Bad 1880-2000* (Stockholm: Svensk Byggtjänst, 2020), 113–157. **20** Mogensen and Karlsen, "Tradition og fornyelse," 1–8 (see note 6). **21** Børge Nissen in conversation with the author, April 2024. Nissen did the drawing for the pull with Henning Jensen's supervision. **22** Hanne Valeur, descriptive text from K-60 Køkkenelementer brochure. **23** Rigmor Jessen, "Super-køkken," in *B.T.*, 25 September 1962. As well: "Ikke et laboratorium, men et menneskeligt Køkken," in *Jyllands-Posten*, 22 September 1962. Additional clippings can be found in the library of Designmuseum Danmark. **24** Finn Juhl, "Det er ikke nok at Kaare Klint til konge," in *Berlingske Tidende*, 8 October 1962. **25** Christian Enevoldsen, "Køkkenelementer K-60," in *Spatium: Tidsskrift for Rumindretning og Brugskunst*, vol. 1, no. 1, 1963, 8–10. **26** For a brief account, see Michael Sheridan, *Louisiana: Architecture and Landscape* (Humlebæk: Louisiana Museum of Modern Art, 2017), 176–177. For coverage of the Palsby house and the seven houses at Piniehøj, see Poul Erik Skriver, "Arbejder af Jørgen Bo og Vilhelm Wohlert," in *Arkitektur*, vol. 7, no. 5, 1963, 161–200. **27** Ole Palsby established his company to market K-60 while still employed in his father's stock brokerage, where he set up a model kitchen in a back room. The first brochure for K-60 locates Palsby's company at Bredgade 33, where Palle Palsby had his office. **28** Henrik Sten Møller, "Et nyt samarbejde omkring boligen," in *Politiken*, 2 December 1965; Christian Enevoldsen, "Et udstillingslokale," in *Arkitektur*, vol. 9, no. 4, 1966, 174–176. **29** For a brief account, see Michael Sheridan, *Landmarks: The Modern House in Denmark* (Ostfildern: Hatje Cantz, 2014), 68–72. **30** Jørgen Bo possessed an affinity for nature that was rare among architects of his generation and was mentored by the eminent landscape architect C. Th. Sørensen. See Sheridan, *Louisiana*, 47–52 (see note 26.) **31** "Første hus færdigt i Kristineparken," in *Frederiksborgs Amts Avis*, 28 February 1965. "Fryd for øjet," in *B.T.*, 27 February 1965, and "Moderne luksuskædehus," in *Aktuelt*, 28 February 1965. **32** Røn., "3 danske køkkener," in *Berlingske Aftenavis*, 14 November 1967. **33** "Nyt dansk køkkensæt," in *Bo Bedre*, November 1968, 23. The article provides a brief history of Dansk Køkkensæt and a detailed account of the Tectum Kitchen. Børge Kjær was the first student employed on *Byggebogen* in the 1940s and managed the project between 1948 and 1956. During 1959–64, he created type-house designs for the Joint Organization. Developing a copy of K-60 was simply his next assignment for the organization. **34** Røn., "3 danske køkkener" (see note 32). **35** "Det bedste danske elementkøkken," *Samvirke*, no. 2, 15 January 1962, 21. **36** *Dansk Køkkensæt* (Copenhagen: Fællesorganisationen af almennyttige danske boligselskaber, 1967). **37** Esbjørn Hiort was quite familiar with K-60 and included it in his review of the exhibition: "Fornyelse og Tradition: En anmeldelse af Københavns Snedkerlaugs 36. udstilling," in *Arkitekten*, vol. 64, no. 23, 1962, 433–437. For his discussion of the Tectum Kitchen, in 1967, see Esbjørn Hiort, "Køkken i Forum," in *Arkitekten*, vol. 70, no. 2, 1968, 43–45. **38** Røn., "3 danske køkkener" (see note 32). **39** "Palsby søn også konkurs," in *Ekstra Bladet*, 16 February 1968. **40** "Run på Palsby-villa," in *Berlingske Tidende*, 22 February 1968. Jørgen Mouritzen, "Ole Palsby: Jeg er ikke slået: Jeg sælger ud," in *B.T.*, 27 March 1968. **41** See note 33. **42** Hanne Valeur in conversation with the author, August 2019. **43** For example, see the section "Om plagiat og retsbeskyttelse" in Åke Huldt (ed.), *Skrevet af Bent Salicath* (Copenhagen: Foreningen Dansk Kunsthaandværk og Industriel Design, 1974), 38–49. **44** Ole Eichen, the current owner of Tectum Køkkenet, has estimated that an average of 2,000 kitchens per month were sold during 1966–82, with an additional 70–80,000 sold since then. Ole Eichen, email to the author, 6 March 2024. **45** Klaus Meedom, "Tectum Inventar," in *Mobilia*, no. 214, May 1973, unpaginated.

ARNE JACOBSEN / CYLINDA-LINE, 1964–67

1 Michael Sheridan, *Room 606: The SAS House and the Work of Arne Jacobsen* (Copenhagen: Strandberg Publishing, 2023), 86–123, 182–203. **2** Sheridan, *Room 606* (see note 1). For an encyclopedic record of Arne Jacobsen's work, see Carsten Thau and Kjeld Vindum, *Arne Jacobsen*, trans. Martha Gaber Abrahamsen (Copenhagen: Danish Architectural Press, 2001). **3** Peter Holmblad recounted his ruse in an email to the author, February 2015. **4** Sheridan, *Room 606*, 296–299 (see note 1). **5** Erik Christian Sørensen and Elisabeth Jensen (eds.), *Søren Georg Jensen* (Copenhagen: Christian Ejlers' Forlag, 1997), 113–115. **6** The working relationship between Kay Bojesen and Magnus L. Stephensen is well-known, thinly documented and awaits deeper investigation. The silversmith and the architect were working together by 1938, when Stephensen designed Bojesen's exhibition at the Danish Museum of Applied Art (now Designmuseum Danmark). The exhibition included their joint design for children's furniture, which initiated their collaboration on hollowware. The two men remained close friends, and Stephensen continued to design Bojesen's exhibitions even after he began designing silver for Georg Jensen. **7** Ulrike Müller, *Bauhaus Women: Art, Handicraft, Design* (Paris: Flammarion, 2009), 118–125. As well: Libby Sellers, *Women Design* (London: Frances Lincoln, 2017), 48–50. **8** Leah Dickerman, "Bauhaus Fundaments," in Barry Bergdoll and Leah Dickerman (eds.), *Bauhaus 1919–1933: Workshops for Modernity* (New York: Museum of Modern Art 2009), 14–39. **9** Christina Lodder, "Searching for Utopia" in Christopher Wilk (ed.), *Modernism: Designing a New World 1914-1939* (London: V&A Publications, 2006), 22–69. For a summary relative to Arne Jacobsen's work, see notes 1, 12–16. **10** Valerie J. Fletcher, *Dreams and Nightmares: Utopian Visions in Modern Art* (Washington, D. C.: Smithsonian Institution Press, 1983), 90–95. For Arne Jacobsen's preoccupation with technology, see Sheridan, *Room 606*, 28–31, 318–322 (see note 1). **11** Poul Erik Tøjner and Kjeld Vindum, *Arne Jacobsen: Architect & Designer = Arne Jacobsen: Arkitekt & Designer*, trans. Ida Mackintosh (Copenhagen: Danish Design Centre, 1991), 111. **12** Frank C. Motzkus, *Stelton* (Copenhagen: Stelton A/S, 2010), 62. The genesis of Jacobsen's hollowware is described in the chapter "Cylinda-line and Arne Jacobsen, 1964–76," in ibid., 47–85. **13** Peter Holmblad, email to the author, February 2015. **14** Sheridan, *Room 606*, 314–317 (see note 1). **15** Thau and Vindum, *Arne Jacobsen*, 193–201, 508–521 (see note 2). **16** Motzkus, *Stelton* (see note 12).

GRETHE MEYER / HVIDPOT, 1966–71

1 *Dansk Kunsthaandværk*, vol. 32, no. 6, 1959, 128. **2** A curriculm vitae documenting Grethe Meyer's early work history and resulting letters of recommendation are preserved among her papers within the Danish Design Archive, Designmuseum Danmark. **3** Kaj Franck, "Kauneutta etsimässää", in *Kaunis koti*, no. 3, 1949. See Leena Maunula, "Smash the Services," trans. Michael Wynne-Ellis, in Kay Kalin (ed.), *Kaj Franck: muotoilija = formgivare = designer* (Helsinki: Taideteollisuusmuseo/Werner Söderström Osakeyhtiö, 1992), 47–48. **4** F.G., "Der blæser en frisk vind," in *Berlingske Tidende*, 29 January 1953. **5** Gösta Arvidsson, *Gustavsberg: Form och Funktion i Folkhemmet* (Lund: Historiska Media, 2015), 141–143. As well: Praktika catalog (Stockholm: Gustavsberg AB, 1933). A copy can be found in the Gustavsberg Archive, Nationalmuseum, Stockholm. **6** Nils Palmgren, *Wilhelm Kåge: Konstnår och Hantverkare* (Stockholm: Nordisk Rotogravyr, 1955), 148–150. **7** "Nye porcelænsservicer: Porcelænsfabriken 'Danmark's konkurrence afgjort," in *Dansk Kunsthaandværk*, vol. 32, no. 10, 1959, 208–209. **8** Souris, "Ingen sovs paa undersiden," in *Berlingske Aftenavis*, 24 November 1959. **9** Leif Lautrup-Larsen, *Stentøj: Den Kongelige Porcelainsfabrik* (Copenhagen: Nyt Nordisk Forlag, 2007), 263–267. **10** Ibid., 263. **11** Leif Lautrup-Larsen in conversation with the author, December 2013. **12** Ibid. **13** Ibid. **14** Christina B. Kjeldsen and Isabel Bernadette Brammer, *Grethe Meyer: Arkitekten, Der Revolutionerede Middagsbordet* (Copenhagen: Gyldendal, 2024), 155. **15** Leif Lautrup-Larsen, *Stentøj: Den Kongelige Porcelainsfabrik*, 2007. **16** "Servicet skal ikke være fremtrædende," in *Aarhus Stiftstidende*, 21 August 1965. **17** "Et nyt spisestel tegnet af Grethe Meyer," in *Arkitekten*, vol. 67, no. 9, 1965, 180–181. **18** Blondie, "En klassiker. Et nyt, smukt og gennemarbejdet fajance-service, der også vil være tiltalende år 2000," in *B.T.*, 20 March 1965. **19** Former Royal Copenhagen production engineer, email to the author, January 2024. **20** Lautrup-Larsen, Stentøj (see note 15). **21** Isabel Bernadette Brammer, email to the author, 26 October 2021. **22** "Mange års forskning ligger bag spisestellene Blåkant og Hvidpot," in *Jyllands-Posten*, unknown date, 1973. The clipping is located among Grethe Meyer's papers, Danish Design Archive, Designmuseum Danmark. **23** Grethe Meyer Papers (see note 22). **24** See note 3. **25** Hvidpot catalog (Copenhagen: Royal Copenhagen Porcelain Manufactory, 1971), 3. **26** Kjeldsen and Brammer, *Grethe Meyer*, 2024, 273–275, 283–286 (see note 14). **27** Former Royal Copenhagen production engineer, email to the author, November 2021. **28** Ibid. **29** Ibid. **30** The exhibition: *Grethe Meyer. Inventar, glas, fajance, porcelæn.* 28 May – 28 July. Sankt Annæ Plads 10B. The prize was bestowed upon Meyer by the national associations of applied art and design in Denmark, Sweden, Norway and Finland. **31** Axel Thygesen, "Brugskunst med kultur = Industrial art with a touch of culture," in *Mobilia*, no. 218, September 1973, unpaginated.

GRETHE MEYER / ILDPOT, 1970–76

1 Leif Lautrup-Larsen, *Stentøj: Den Kongelige Porcelainsfabrik* (Copenhagen: Nyt Nordisk Forlag, 2007), 265–267. **2** Colin Clair, "The evolution of the kitchen," in *Kitchen and Table: A Bedside History of Eating in the Western World* (London: Abelard-Schuman, 1964), 54–118. Clair provides accounts of serving and dining practices during the medieval, Renaissance and English Tudor periods. In addition, he describes the evolution of the kitchen on pages 194–215. **3** Lucy Creagh, Helena Kåberg and Barbara Miller Lane, *Modern Swedish Design: Three Founding Texts* (New York: Museum of Modern Art, 2008). The contents include Ellen Key's 1889 essay "Beauty in the home" and Gregor Paulsson's 1919 statement "Better things for everyday life," which adapted Key's ideals to an industrial era and established the ethos for many of the objects featured in this book. **4** Gösta Arvidsson, *Gustavsberg: Form och Funktion i Folkhemmet* (Lund: Historiska Media, 2015), 127. **5** Ibid., 185–186. **6** Magnus Palm (ed.), *Stora Boken om Stig Lindberg: Porslin, Keramik, Industridesign, Textil* (Malmö: Egmont, 2016), 36–37. **7** Ibid., 38. **8** Outstanding examples include vitroporcelain pots and pans produced by Lyngby Porcelæn as part of the "Dan-ild" service, designed by Axel Brüel (1956); Royal Copenhagen's "Patella" collection of porcelain dishes and accessories, designed by Magnus Stephensen (1957) and Aluminia's "Pyrolin" line of "flint porcelain" covered dishes, designed by Ingvar Olsen (1959). **9** A handwritten note located among Grethe Meyer's papers in the Danish Design Archive, Designmuseum Denmark, refers to Mrs. E. Jespersen. She was referring to civil engineer Ebba (Grue) Jespersen, who was the head of that department at the Danish Technical College (DtH), the forerunner to the Technical University of Denmark. What little is known about her can be found in her husband's biographical summary: https://biografiskleksikon.lex.dk/Aage_Jespersen (accessed 11 October). **10** James Beard, Milton Glaser and Burton Wolf (eds.), *The Cooks' Catalogue: A Critical Selection of the Best, the Necessary, and the Special in Kitchen Equipment and Utensils* (New York: Harper & Row, 1975). **11** Ibid. **12** Former Royal Copenhagen production engineer, email to the author, January 2024. **13** Ildpot catalog (Copenhagen: Royal Copenhagen Porcelain Manufactory, 1984), unpaginated. **14** Former Royal Copenhagen production engineer, email to the author, January 2024. **15** Lautrup-Larsen, *Stentøj* (see note 1). **16** Former Royal Copenhagen production engineer, email to the author, November 2021. **17** Ibid. **18** Blåkant catalog (Copenhagen: Royal Copenhagen Porcelain Manufactory, 1971), 3.

OLE PALSBY / EVA TRIO, 1976–77

1 Hanne Valeur in conversation with the author, August 2021. A number of Palsby's friends invested 5,000 or 10,000 Danish kroner and became shareholders in Ole Palsby Studio A/S, which owned and operated first one shop and then another. **2** Artemis Cooper describes the development and reception of David's first three books in *Writing at the Kitchen Table: The Authorized Biography of Elizabeth David* (London: Michael Joseph; New York: Penguin Putnam, 1999). **3** Ibid. See Cooper's chapter "The shop" on pages 237–255. **4** George Kringelbach, "Det skete med Ole Palsby," in *Politiken*, 7 February 1976. **5** Palsby published at least two tabloid-sized catalogs (in December 1972 and May 1973) that combined descriptions of his products with practical cooking tips and the occasional in-joke about Auguste Escoffier. **6** "Butik med idé," in *Politiken*, 23 July 1974. **7** Malin Lindgren, "Plagiater truer dansk design," *Berlinske Tidende*, 8 February 1976. **8** Kringelbach, "Det skete med Ole Palsby" (see note 5). **9** George Kringelbach, "Godt køkkengrej," in *Politiken*, 17 December 1977. **10** Tin is the traditional lining of choice for French copper cookware, due to its relatively low cost and low melting point (230° C). However, it is also a relatively soft metal and gradually erodes. As a result, pans lined with tin and subject to frequent use require periodic retinning, typically every 10–20 years. Silver has a much higher melting point (900° C) and is harder than tin, so that a silver lining will last for many decades if treated with a minimum of care, which includes avoiding the use of metal spoons and spatulas. Due to its extraordinary rate of heat transfer, it is the ideal material for lining copper pans, except for the cost. **11** Ole Palsby and Nils Fagerholt's project is preserved among Fagerholt's architectural drawing in the Royal Danish Library. According to Troels Hasner, Fagerholt's assistant at the time, Palsby would sit next to Fagerholt at the drawing board and instruct him as to the useful sizes of things and the most practical details. Troels Hasner in conversation with the author, May 2018. **12** Fritz Togo, *Fra Fog og Mangor til Eva Denmark A/S* (Frederiksberg: Fiskers Forlag, 2001). Togo's chapter "Eva-Trio: Start og udvikling" (98–107) provides a detailed account of the introduction of Palsby's cookware, changing product lines and the use of various metals during 1977–2000. **13** Karsten Ravn in conversation with the author, January 2022. **14** Børge Nissen, email to the author, December 2014. **15** Togo, *Fra Fog og Mangor til Eva Denmark A/S*, 99–101 (see note 12). **16** Kringelbach, "Godt køkkengrej" (see note 9). **17** Togo, *Fra Fog og Mangor til Eva Denmark A/S*, 101 (see note 12). **18** David Kamp, *The United States of Arugula: How we became a gourmet nation* (New York: Broadway Books, 2006). See Chapters 3 and 4, "The food establishment part I" and "The food establishment part II," along with Chapters 5 and 6, "Radical notions" and "Righteous and crunchy." **19** During September 1979–March 1980, a trio of unscrupulous brothers from Texas: Nelson Bunker Hunt, William Herbert Hunt and Lamar Hunt, attempted to control the world market in silver and manipulate the price to increase the value of their immense holdings of the metal. Their scheme collapsed in March 1980, but they had already ensured instability in the market for months to come. In 1985, they were indicted by the United States government for financial chicanery and paid significant fines but unfortunately did not go to prison. **20** Togo, *Fra Fog og Mangor til Eva Denmark A/S*, 102–103 (see note 12). **21** Ibid., 103–107.

ARNE JACOBSEN / FH 3207, 1954–55

1 Michael Sheridan, *Room 606: The SAS House and the Work of Arne Jacobsen* (Copenhagen: Strandberg Publishing, 2023), 8–31. **2** Carsten Thau and Kjeld Vindum, *Arne Jacobsen*, trans. Martha Gaber Abrahamsen (Copenhagen: Danish Architectural Press, 2001), 219. **3** Bård Henriksen, "Arne Jacobsen and His Laminated Chairs," in *Scandinavian Journal of Design History*, vol. 7, 1997, 7–10. The author was employed at Fritz Hansen from 1954 and served as design manager for several decades. **4** Sheridan, *Room 606*, 268–271 (see note 1). **5** Per Mollerup, "The Cantilever Chair," *Mobilia*, no. 315/316, 1983, 63–65. **6** Göran Schildt (ed.), *Alvar Aalto, Sketches* (Cambridge, MA: The M.I.T. Press, 1978), 30. **7** Kaarina Mikonranta, "Alvar Aalto: Master of variation," in Pirkko Tuukkannen (ed.), *Alvar Aalto: Designer* (Jyväskyla: Alvar Aalto Foundation/Alvar Aalto Museum, 2002), 80–103. **8** David G. de Long, "Rediscovering Eero Saarinen," in David G. de Long, C. Ford Peatross (eds.), *Eero Saarinen: Buildings from the Balthazar Korab Archive* (New York: W.W. Norton, 2008), 10–12. **9** Witold Rybczynski, *Now I Sit Me Down: From Klismos to Plastic Chair: A Natural History* (New York: Farrar, Straus and Giroux, 2017), 130–131. **10** The competition "Organic Design in Home Furnishings" was sponsored by the Museum of Modern Art in New York and announced in October 1940. The results were published as Eliot F. Noyes, *Organic Design in Home Furnishings* (New York: The Museum of Modern Art, 1941). **11** John Neuhardt, Ray Eames and Marilyn Neuhardt, *Eames Design: The Work of the Office of Charles and Ray Eames* (New York: Abrams, 1989), 26–43, 56–80. The ultimate resource on the work of Charles and Ray Eames and their associates. **12** Michael Sheridan, "No. 6000/AX Chair," in Mateo Kries, Jochen Eisenbrand (eds.), *Atlas of Furniture Design* (Weil am Rhein: Vitra Design Museum, 2019), 542. **13** Sheridan, *Room 606*, 274–277 (see note 1). **14** E. v. Z, "Hur dansken bor", *Dagens Nyheter*, 8 March 1953. The clipping can be found in the Fritz Hansen scrapbook collection. See Bård Henriksen's notes in the article that is described in note 2. Jacobsen recounted the genesis of the Ant chair in an interview that appears in *Information*, 9 February 1953. **15** For a comprehensive history of Asplund's work on the building, see Claes Caldenby and Caroline Losman, *Göteborgs Rådhus = Gothenburg Court House* (Stockholm: Arkitektur Förlag, 2014). **16** Kerstin Wickman, "A democratic aesthetic," in Claes Caldenby (ed.), *Tiden, platsen, arkitekturen: Asplunds rådhus i Göteborg = Asplund's Law Court Extension in Gothenburg* (Stockholm: Arkitekturmuseet, 2010), 87–117. Asplund's chair for the judges is discussed on 104–105. For a discussion of Arne Jacobsen's city halls in Aarhus and Søllerød, see notes 1 and 2. **17** H55 received a great deal of coverage in the Swedish press and a great many Danish visitors, but it has not received sustained attention comparable to the 1930 Stockholm Exhibition. For a detailed account, see Ulrika Hübinette, *Reconstruction of the Recent Past: Focus on the Modern Movement and "H55"* (Gothenborg: Göteborgs Universitet, 1999). **18** Bård Henriksen, "Arne Jacobsen and his laminated chairs," 1997, 17. **19** Arne Jacobsen, "Über Form und Gestaltung in der Gegenwart" (acceptance speech for Fritz Schumacher Prize, 6 December 1963), translated from the German manuscript by Dorte H. Silver. Reprinted as "Contemporary form and design," trans. Layla Dawson, in Michael Asgaard Andersen (ed.), *Nordic Architects Write* (New York: Routledge, 2008). This citation appears on page 68. Jacobsen provided a more detailed description of his youthful travels to Germany and longstanding admiration of Mies van der Rohe's work in *Bauen + Wohnen*, no. 5, 190 f. 1966. A brief excerpt appears in Thau and Vindum, *Arne Jacobsen*, 165 (see note 2).

VILHELM WOHLERT / LOUISIANA CHAIR, 1957–58

1 See Michael Sheridan, "A home for art: 1956–58," in *Louisiana: Architecture and Landscape* (Humlebæk: Louisiana Museum of Modern Art, 2017), 78–135. **2** Ibid., 24–26. **3** Ibid., 39. As Knud W. Jensen noted, "It was obvious I had to keep this lovely name. I could hardly call the place the Humlebæk Museum of Art or Jensen's Museum — people would die laughing." **4** Ibid., 42–46. **5** The full extent of Juhl's artistic approach to design can be seen in Christian Bundegaard, *Finn Juhl: Life, Work, World*, transl. Max Minden Ribeiro (Copenhagen: Strandberg Publishing, 2018), which concludes with a comprehensive graphic index of his work as a designer of furniture, exhibitions and objects during 1930–82. **6** For a discussion of Wegner's youth and prodigal talent, see Christian Holmsted Olesen, *Wegner: Just One Good Chair* (Copenhagen: Strandberg Publishing, 2014), 18–21. The remainder of the book displays his fundamentally artistic treatment of wood. **7** Sheridan, *Louisiana*, 62–67 (see note 1). **8** The type appears in most of Ole Wanscher's scholarly works, from *Møbeltyper* (Copenhagen: Nyt Nordisk Forlag Arnold Busck, 1932), 25–26, 50, to *Møblets Æstetik* (Copenhagen: Arkitektens Forlag, 1985), 57, 59, 62. **9** Sheridan, "A home for art," 118 (see note 1). **10** Ibid., 122. **11** Ibid., 146. **12** The exception can be found in Lars Dybdahl, trans. Dorte Herholdt Silver, *Furniture Boom: Mid-century Modern Danish Furniture 1945–75* (Copenhagen: Strandberg Publishing, 2018), 149–151. **13** Sheridan, "A home for art," 182–202, 270–287, 300–315 (see note 1).

POUL HENNINGSEN / PH 5, 1955–58

1 Notably: Paul Hammerich, *Lysmageren: En krønike om Poul Henningsen* (Copenhagen: Gyldendal, 1986); Hans Hertel, *PH: En Biografi* (Copenhagen: Gyldendal, 2012); Mogens Voltelen, "En elskers død: Poul Henningsen 1894-1967," *Arkitekten*, no. 5, 1967, 109–111; Hans Hertel (ed.), *Poul Henningsen Dengang og Nu: Lysmageren i Nyt Lys: En Debatbog* (Copenhagen: Gyldendal, 2012). **2** There are two essential resources for the study of Poul Henningsen's light fixtures, both of which have been essential to the development of this chapter. One is the collection of Henningsen's writings about light during 1926–60, which was compiled by four of his former associates: Ebbe Christensen, Sophus Frandsen, Steen Jørgensen and Mogens Voltelen (eds.), *PH Om Lys* (Copenhagen: Rhodos, 1974). The standard reference work on the lamps is Tina Jørstian and Poul Erik Munk Nielsen (eds.), *Light Years Ahead: The Story of the PH Lamp*, trans. Tam McTurk (Copenhagen: Louis Poulsen, 1994). **3** Jørstian and Nielsen (eds.), *Light Years Ahead*, 76–86 (see note 2). **4** Ibid., 102–116. **5** Ibid., 120–130. **6** Poul Henningsen, "Hjemmets belysning." Originally published in the Norwegian architectural journal *Byggekunst* in February, March and April 1928. Reprinted in Christensen et al. (eds.), *PH Om Lys*, 15–30 (see note 2). **7** Ibid. **8** Jørstian and Nielsen (eds.), *Light Years Ahead*, 120–122 (see note 2). **9** Ibid., 300. **10** Ibid., 139–150. **11** Ibid., 139–141, 166–170, 301. **12** Ibid., 240–243. **13** Hammerich, *Lysmageren*, 293–297 (see note 1); Hertel, *PH*, 215–229 (see note 1). **14** Nils Koppel and Poul Henningsen, "Langeliniepavillonens belysning," *Nyt* 196 (Easter 1958), 1570–1574. As well: *Mobilia*, no. 33, April 1958, 30–38. **15** Jørstian and Nielsen (eds.), *Light Years Ahead*, 269–270 (see note 2). As well: *Mobilia*, no. 33, April 1958, 35. **16** Johan Pedersen, "Glas, lys og farver," in *Dansk Kunsthaandværk*, vol. 31, no. 4, 1958, 65–69. **17** Poul Henningsen, "En omvendelse," in *Nyt* 196 (Easter 1958), 1564. Reprinted in *Mobilia*, no. 33, April 1958, 23–25. **18** Poul Henningsen, "Indstillingen," in *Nyt* 196 (Easter 1958), 1565. **19** Allan de Waal, "From filament to fluorescence: PH: Child of the incandescent bulb era," in *Nyt*, 1994, unnumbered issue titled *PH 100*, 16–19. **20** Ibid., 16. **21** Poul Henningsen, "Farven," in *Nyt* 196 (Easter 1958), 1567–1569. **22** Jørstian and Nielsen (eds.), *Light Years Ahead*, 274 (see note 2). PH 5 receives an abbreviated discussion on pages 272–274.

BØRGE MOGENSEN / FREDERICIA 6286, 1964–66

1 The best source of biographical information on Børge Mogensen was written by his son and dwells on his at times grim upbringing in Aalborg: Thomas Mogensen, *Et Fuldt Møbleret liv: En Bog om Børge Mogensen* (Copenhagen: Gyldendal, 2004). **2** Fællesforeningen for Danmarks Brugsforeninger (The Joint Association of Danish Cooperative Societies; FDB) was established in 1896, with the goal of strengthening the purchasing power of local cooperative groups across Denmark. Eventually, FDB opened a chain of grocery stores and then multiple chains, making it a dominant force in Danish food retail. In 2013, the name of the organization was changed to Coop Danmark. **3** Gorm Harkær, *Kaare Klint*, vol. 1 (Copenhagen: Klintiana, 2010), 634–644. **4** Grete Jalk (ed.), *40 Years of Danish Furniture Design: The Copenhagen Cabinetmakers' Guild Exhibitions 1927–1966 = Dansk Møbelkunst Gennem 40 År: Københavns Snedkerlaugs Møbeludstillinger 1927–1966*, vol. 4 (Høje Tastrup: Teknologisk Instituts Forlag, 1987, reprinted in 2017 by Lindhardt og Ringhof / Forlaget Carlsen), 106–107, 124–127. **5** Claus Bjørn, "Frederik Nielsen," https://biografiskleksikon.lex.dk/Frederik_Nielsen_-_direktør (accessed 11 October). **6** The single best description of Frederik Nielsen's goals and the development of the FDB furniture program is found in Arne Karlsen, *Danish Furniture Design in the 20th Century*, vol. 1 (Copenhagen: Christian Eljers' Forlag/Dansk Møbelkunst, 2007), 167–179. **7** Mogensen, *Et fuldt møbleret liv*, 48 (see note 1). **8** Karlsen, *Danish Furniture Design in the 20th Century* (see note 6). **9** Mogensen, *Et fuldt møbleret liv*, 48 (see note 1). **10** See note 6. **11** Børge Mogensen, "FDB Møbler," in *Nyt Tidsskrift for Kunstindustri*, vol. 27, no. 12, 1944, 165–73. **12** Edward Deming Andrews and Faith Andrews, *Shaker Furniture: The Craftsmanship of an American Communal Sect* (New Haven, CT: Yale University Press; London: H. Milford; Oxford: Oxford University Press, 1937). **13** Ibid., 11–13, 23–24. As well: Thomas Merton's "Introduction" to Edward Deming Andrews and Faith Andrews: *Religion in Wood: A Book of Shaker Furniture* (Bloomington, IN: Indiana University Press, 1966). **14** Andrews and Andrews, *Shaker Furniture* (see note 12). As well: Alan Gowans, "Shakerne og deres møbelkunst," in *Dansk Kunsthaandværk*, vol. 33, no. 9, 1960, 192–197. **15** Gorm Harkær placed the Andrews' book in the library of the Danish Museum of Applied Art (now Designmuseum Danmark) in 1941. Klint's office was in the same building complex, and the book was probably ordered at his request. See Harkær's authoritative *Kaare Klint*, vol. 1, 637 (see note 3). **16** Arne Karlsen, *Furniture Designed by Børge Mogensen: Selected and Described by Arne Karlsen = Møbler Tegnet af Børge Mogensen: Udvalgt og Beskrevet af Arne Karlsen* (Copenhagen: Arkitektens Forlag, 1968), 28–29. **17** At one point during the 1950s, Mogensen was simultaneously working with Søborg Møbelfabrik, P. Lauritsen & Søn, C.M. Madsens Fabrikker, Karl Andersson & Söner and Fredericia Stolefabrik. **18** Mogensen, *Et fuldt møbleret liv*, 207 (see note 1). **19** Erik Berglund, *Bord för Måltider och Arbete i Hemmet* (Stockholm: Svenska Slöjdföreningen, 1957). Børge Mogensen and Arne Karlsen used one of Berglund's drawings in their article "Illusion og realitet: Betragtninger over Snedkerlaugets Møbeludstilling 1959," in *Dansk Kunsthaandværk*, vol. 32, no. 8–9, 1959, 165. Karlsen pointed out the importance of Berglund's research on Mogensen's work in his pamphlet describing Boligens Byggeskabe: Arne Karlsen, *Fra Enkeltmøbler til Fast Inventar* (Copenhagen: C. Danel, 1967). **20** They include Model 141, a round table in which the leaves are stored beneath the top; the rectangular Model 181, with a sliding top for leaves; the rectangular Model 183, with a hinged and rotating top; and Model 103, the library table with a hinged flap at either end. Models numbers from Karl Andersson & Söner catalog, 1964. **21** Dimensions provided by Børge Mogensens Tegnestue. **22** Rasmus Graversen, email to the author, August 2024. **23** Per H. Hansen, *En Lys og Lykkelig Fremtid: Historien om FDB-møbler* (Albertslund: Samvirke, 2014), 233–238. **24** The company was founded, in 1911, as Fredericia Stole- og Polstermøbelfabrik and later appeared under the name Fredericia Stolefabrik. Today, the name is Fredericia Furniture. **25** Mogensen, *Et fuldt møbleret liv*, 49 (see note 1).

MOGENS KOCH / LE KLINT 105, 1942

1 Peter Koch, "Fætter Mogens," in Axel Thygesen (ed.), *Tilegnet Mogens Koch* (Copenhagen: Nyt Nordisk Forlag Arnold Busck, 1968), 326. **2** Anker Tiedemann, "'Kokhans' leger: Hans H. Koch's syvklodspil og julekar." in *Dansk Kunsthaandværk*, vol. 32, no. 10, 1959, 198–201. **3** Koch, "Fætter Mogens," 327 (see note 1). **4** See Chapter 4, "Carl Petersen's assistant," in Gorm Harkær, *Kaare Klint*, vol. 1 (Copenhagen: Klintiana, 2010), 77–90. As well: Anders V. Munch, "Faaborgstolen: Ikon og inventar," in Gertrud Hvidberg-Hansen and Gry Hedin (eds.), *I Skøn Forening: Faaborg Museum 1915* (Copenhagen: Strandberg Publishing, 2015), 120–133. The ten essays by selected scholars provide a comprehensive description of the museum. This author's contribution, "Fra guldalder til modernisme: Carl Petersen og nordisk arkitektur", provides biographical material. A number of the essays were translated into English and reprinted: Gry Hedin and Gertrud Hvidberg-Hansen (eds.), *Faaborg Museum and the Artists' Colony* (Aarhus: Aarhus University Press, 2019). **5** References to Mogens Koch's work with Kaare Klint are sprinkled throughout both volumes of Harkær's *Kaare Klint* (see note 4); for example, see vol. 2, 14–18. As well: Arne Karlsen, trans. Martha Gaber Abrahamsen, *Danish Furniture Design in the 20th Century* (Copenhagen: Christian Eljers' Forlag/Dansk Møbelkunst, 2007). **6** Koch, "Fætter Mogens," 330 (see note 3). **7** Grete Jalk (ed.), *40 years of Danish Furniture Design: The Copenhagen Cabinet-makers' Guild Exhibitions 1927–1966 = Dansk Møbelkunst Gennem 40 År: Københavns Snedkerlaugs Møbeludstillinger 1927–1966*, vol. 2 (Høje Tastrup: Teknologisk Instituts Forlag, 1987, reprinted in 2017 by Lindhardt og Ringhof / Forlaget Carlsen), see the years 1933–38. **8** Koch, in *Tilegnet Mogens Koch*, 332 (see note 1). **9** Torsten Nothin, "Hälsning till Danmark," in *Form*, vol. 40, no. 8, 1944, 129–130. **10** Vilhelm Slomann (ed.), *Dansk Kunsthaandværk: Udstillet i Nationalmuseet, Stockholm Oktober-November 1942* (Copenhagen: Det Danske Kunstindustrimuseum, 1942), 92–93. See also Harkær, *Kaare Klint*, 404–405 (see note 4). **11** Gregor Paulsson, "Utställningen i Stockholm av danskt konsthantverk," in *Nyt Tidsskrift for Kunstindustri*, vol. 15, no. 12, 1942, 185–188. Gotthard Johansson's review for *Svenska Dagbladet*, reprinted in same issue, 188–191. **12** To sample the outrage, see the protests collected in "Om udstillinger i udlandet," in *Nyt Tidsskrift for Kunstindustri*, vol. 15, no. 12, 1942, 177–180. Gorm Harkær describes this episode in *Kaare Klint*, 405 (see note 4), along with Steen Eiler Rasmussen's public defense of Koch. As Rasmussen pointed out, "clique" is a pejorative term for what will later be regarded as a School, and so it was. See *Politiken*, 8 November 1942. **13** Transcript of lecture delivered at the Royal Danish Academy, 7 December 1942. Reprinted in the student journal *A5 Meningsblad for unge arkitekter*, vol. 1, no. 1, 12–22. As Koch referred to the controversy swirling around the exhibition, he explained "It has been strongly criticized that the selection was placed in the hands of a single man, and I was also promised that the work would be hell. Well, it certainly wasn't boring." Koch's small book *Moderne Dansk Kunsthaandværk* (Copenhagen: Thaning & Appel, 1948) contains captioned photographs of 36 objects and recalls his work on the Stockholm exhibition. **14** Åke Stavenow, "Danskt konsthantverk," in *Form*, vol. 40, no. 9, 1944, 157–158. **15** The outrage continued after the exhibition was installed in Copenhagen. One headline read "The unretouched misunderstanding." See *Politiken* 18 January 1943, or any of the other major Copenhagen newspapers that week. **16** Kaare Klint described his family history of making pleated lampshades in the first catalog for Le Klint Lampeskærme, October 1943, unpaginated. **17** Harkær, *Kaare Klint*, 237–241 (see note 4). **18** Ibid., 60–61, 68–71 (see note 4). **19** Steen Eiler Rasmussen, "Bauhaus og den danske brugskunst," in *Dansk Kunsthaandværk*, vol. 33, no. 7–8, 1960, 142–149. **20** (Lise) Le Klint, *Erindringstråde* (Valby: Vindrose, 1998), 34–36. **21** Albrecht Dürer, *Underweysung der Messung mit dem Zirckel und Richtscheyt in Linien, Ebenen unnd gantzen Corporen* (Nuremburg: 1525). An English-language translation was published using the full title. See Albrecht Dürer, *The Painter's Manual: A Manual of Measurement of Lines, Areas, and Solids by Means of Compass and Ruler Assembled by Albrecht Dürer for the Use of All Lovers of Art with Appropriate Illustrations Arranged to be Printed in the Year MDXXV*, trans. and commentary by Walter L. Strauss (New York: Abaris Books, 1977). **22** Klint, *Erindringstråde*, 50–51 (see note 20). **23** Kaare Klint, "Butik for Le Klints

Lampeskærme," in *Arkitekten Ugehæfte*, vol. 47, no. 51, 21 December 1945, 224–225. **24** Klint, *Erindringstråde*, 54–56 (see note 20). **25** Harkær, *Kaare Klint*, 586–595; ibid. vol. 2, 74–75 (see note 4). **26** Paul Hammerich, *Lysmageren: En Krønike om Poul Henningsen* (Copenhagen: Gyldendal, 1986), 328–331. As well: Johan Pedersen, "Wall-paper and lamp-shades: A new Danish artistic paper industry," in *Dansk Kunsthaandværk*, vol. 21, no. 5, 1948, 84–85. **27** Tina Jørstian and Poul Erik Munk Nielsen (eds.), *Light Years Ahead: The Story of the PH Lamp*, trans. Tam McTurk (Copenhagen: Louis Poulsen, 1994), 262–263. **28** Mette Strømgaard Dalby, *Le Klint: Design – Håndværk – Historie* (Odense: KreativGrafisk Forlag, 2008), 34. **29** Dansk Patent no. 73486. The first lamp to be produced in the new material was model 109, a round lantern designed by Esben Klint, who was a son of Kaare Klint and an especially skilled designer of pleated shades.

GRETHE MEYER / BØRGE MOGENSEN / BOLIGENS BYGGESKABE, 1952–57

1 Christina B. Kjeldsen and Isabel Bernadette Brammer, *Grethe Meyer: Arkitekten, Der Revolutionerede Middagsbordet* (Copenhagen: Gyldendal, 2024), 104. **2** Ibid. **3** Like so many other Danish architects with a strong social-political inclination, Poul Kjærgaard was deeply inspired by Swedish efforts to standardize constructions practices and, by extension, residential buildings, starting with the kitchen. According to Morten Kjærgaard, his father conceived *Byggebogen* in 1940 for an imagined post-Second World War housing boom, in the hope that the perennial housing shortage would finally be solved through government intervention. Conversation with the author August 2021. See Poul Kjærgaard, "Byggebogen: Et samleværk for byggeriets data," in *Arkitekten. Ugehæfte*, vol. 47, no. 25–26, 1945, 105–111. **4** Grethe Meyer and Børge Mogensen, "Byggeskabe til fast anbringelse i boligen," in *Boligen*, vol. 23, no. 4, 1955, 106–111. **5** Ibid., 107–108. **6** Ibid. **7** Ibid., 109. **8** Ibid., 111. **9** Arne Karlsen, *Danish Furniture Design in the 20th Century*, vol. 1 (Copenhagen: Christian Eljers' Forlag/Dansk Møbelkunst, 2007), 72. **10** Arne Karlsen, *Furniture Designed by Børge Mogensen: Selected and Described by Arne Karlsen = Møbler Tegnet af Børge Mogensen: Udvalgt og Beskrevet af Arne Karlsen* (Copenhagen: The Danish Architectural Press, 1968), 55. **11** Arne Karlsen and Anker Tiedemann, *Made in Denmark: A Picture-book about Modern Danish Arts and Crafts* (Copenhagen: Gjellerup, 1960), 104–109. **12** Ibid., 108. **13** Ole Dybbroe, "Boligens Byggeskabe," in *Dansk Kunsthaandværk*, vol. 30, no. 10, 1957, 191–194. **14** Agner Christoffersen, "Udstilling af svenske byggemøbler," in *Arkitekten. Ugehæfte*, vol. 47, no. 37, 1945, 160. **15** Dybbroe, "Boligens Byggeskabe" (see note 13). **16** Kjeldsen and Brammer, *Grethe Meyer*, 114–116 (see note 1). **17** Poul Erik Skriver, "Udstillingslokale for Boligens Byggeskabe," in *Arkitektur*, vol. 4, no. 2, 1960, 78–80. **18** The exhibition *Grethe Meyer: Inventar, Glas, Fajance, Porcelæn.* 28 May–28 July 1973. Sankt Annæ Plads 10B. See Axel Thygesen, "Brugskunst med kultur = Industrial art with a touch of culture," in *Mobilia*, no. 218, September 1973, unpaginated. **19** Henrik Sten Møller, "Grethe Meyer: Brugskunst og industriel design," in *Brugskunst og industriel design*, vol. 44, no. 5/6, 1973, 35. **20** Kjeldsen and Brammer, *Grethe Meyer*, 121 (see note 1).

BØRGE MOGENSEN / FREDERICIA 2254, 1956–63

1 Rosalind P. Blakesley, *The Arts and Crafts Movement* (London: Phaidon, 2006) explores the development of the movement in Britain and traces its diffusion across Europe. **2** For a detailed description of Webb's adjustable armchair, which was based on a vernacular model from Sussex, see the object listing on the Victoria and Albert Museum's website: https://collections.vam. ac.uk/item/O372099/armchair-webb-philip-speakman. **3** Wendy Kaplan (ed.), *The Arts and Crafts Movement in Europe & America: Design for the Modern World* (London: Thames & Hudson, 2004). Kaplan's catalog for her exhibition at the Los Angeles County Museum of Art includes specialist essays that trace the influence of the British movement on much of Europe and the Nordic countries. **4** See "A kaleidoscopic period: European movements in relation to Denmark," in Mirjam Gelfer-Jørgensen's authoritative *The Joining of the Arts: Danish Art and Design 1880-1910*, trans. René Lauritsen (Copenhagen: Strandberg Publishing, 2020), 39–81. **5** Christian Witt-Dörring, "From art object to standard product: The Wiener Werkstätte 1903–1918," in Christoph Thun-Hohenstein et al. (eds.), *Josef Hoffmann 1870–1956: Progress Through Beauty: The Guide to His Oeuvre* (Basel: Birkhäuser, 2021),101–107. **6** Anne-Katrin Rossberg, "No. 670 / Sitzmaschine," in Mateo Kries and Jochen Eisenbrand (eds.), *Atlas of Furniture Design* (Weil am Rhein: Vitra Design Museum, 2019), 104–105. **7** For an illustrated record of their collaborations, see Grete Jalk (ed.), *40 Years of Danish Furniture Design: The Copenhagen Cabinet-makers' Guild Exhibitions 1927–1966 = Dansk Møbelkunst Gennem 40 År: Københavns Snedkerlaugs Møbeludstillinger 1927–1966* (Høje Tastrup: Teknologisk Instituts Forlag, 1987, reprinted in 2017 by Lindhardt og Ringhof / Forlaget Carlsen). **8** The influence of Swedish architect Erik Gunnar Asplund on the work of Finn Juhl has generally been overlooked. Asplund's furniture and interiors for the Gothenburg District Court, completed in 1937, provided the basis for the interiors that Juhl designed while employed in the office of Vilhelm Lauritzen during 1937–45, notably the Danish Radio House and the first building at Copenhagen Airport. Moreover, Asplund's sensuous treatment of wood emboldened Juhl to treat the material in a sculptural manner that became increasingly pronounced during the late 1940s. **9** Jalk (ed.), *40 years of Danish Furniture Design*, vol. 3, 386–387 (see note 7). **10** Rasmus Graversen, email to the author, September 2024. **11** For a description of Ahlmann's methods and principles, see Thomas Mogensen, *Lis Ahlmann: Tekstiler* (Copenhagen: Christian Ejlers' Forlag, 1974), 5–24. **12** Thomas Mogensen, *Et Fuldt Møbleret Liv: En Bog om Børge Mogensen.* (Copenhagen: Gyldendal, 2004), 70. **13** Gorm Harkær, *Kaare Klint*, vol. 1 (Copenhagen: Klintiana, 2010), 406; Ibid., vol. 2, 84. **14** Much as Kay Bojesen has been caricatured as a jolly toy designer akin to Santa Claus, Børge Mogensen is typically described as a sort of social worker who designed "the people's chair" and became "furniture designer for the Danes." In fact, Mogensen was a highly complex figure whose multi-faceted career still awaits the nuanced, book-length treatment that it deserves.

MOGENS KOCH / MK-49, 1938/1960

1 Mogens Koch published two seminal texts that offer fundamental insights into his thoughts on design. The first was his introduction to a collection of outstanding examples that he selected: Mogens Koch, *Moderne Dansk Kunsthaandværk* (Copenhagen: Thaning & Appel, 1948). The second was the transcript of a lecture that he presented in 1954, *Møbelkunst* (Furniture Art), which actually encompasses a wide range of useful articles and is cited below. **2** Mogens Koch, "Møbelkunst" in *Dansk Kunsthaandværk*, vol. 27, no. 7, 1954, 114. **3** Gorm Harkær, *Kaare Klint*, vol. 1 (Copenhagen: Klintiana, 2010) 356; Ibid., vol. 2, 69. **4** Grete Jalk (ed.), *40 Years of Danish Furniture Design: The Copenhagen Cabinet-makers' Guild Exhibitions 1927–1966 = Dansk Møbelkunst Gennem 40 År: Københavns Snedkerlaugs Møbeludstillinger 1927–1966*, vol. 2 (Høje Tastrup: Teknologisk Instituts Forlag, 1987, reprinted in 2017 by Lindhardt og Ringhof / Forlaget Carlsen), 54–55. **5** Erling and Axel Thygesen, "Interna A/S," in *Mobilia*, no. 65, December 1960, 43–56. **6** Mogens S. Koch in conversation with the author, January 2024. **7** Ibid. **8** Koch, "Møbelkunst," 113–114 (see note 2).

KIM NAVER / COTIL 1828, 1967–69

1 The publisher Rasmus Naver, who specialized in art, literature and poetry, was the first to publish the work of Tove Ditlevsen. See Godfred Hartmann, "Rasmus Naver," https://biografiskleksikon.lex.dk/Rasmus_Naver (accessed 10 October 2024). **2** Kim Naver, email to the author, 19 June 2019. **3** Ibid. **4** Charlotte Paludan, "Gerda Henning," https://biografiskleksikon.lex.dk/Gerda_Henning (accessed 10 October 2024). **5** Charlotte Paludan, *The Art of Weaving: Danish Hand Weaving in the 20th Century* (Copenhagen: Danish Museum of Decorative Art, 2004), 19–21. Thomas Mogensen, a former apprentice of Lis Ahlmann, described Kaare Klint's impact on her work in Thomas Mogensen, *Lis Ahlmann: Tekstiler* (Copenhagen: Christian Ejlers' Forlag, 1974), 9–10. **6** Lisbeth Tolstrup, "Lis Ahlmann," https://kvindebiografiskleksikon.lex.dk/Lis_Ahlmann (accessed 10 October 2024). **7** The exhibition was shown in three stages that focused on different regions of Denmark and spawned a catalog: Ellen Andersen and Elisabeth Budde-Lund, *Folkelig Vævning i Danmark* (Copenhagen: Berlingske

Forlag, 1941). The library of Designmuseum Denmark contains a scrapbook with an extensive collection of newspaper clippings that occasionally mention Lis Ahlmann. **8** Mogens Koch, "Lis Ahlmanns vævning," in *Nyt Tidsskrift for Kunsthaandværk*, vol. 17, no. 5, 1944, 65–67. **9** E. Zeuthen Nielsen, "Nyt udstillingslokale for boligtextiler," in *Arkitekten. Ugehæfte*, vol. 58, no. 49–50, 1956, 383–385. As well: Jørgen Anthon, "Boligtekstil på markedet," in *Dansk Kunsthaandværk*, no. 1, 1964, 16–18. **10** As seen in monthly advertisements that appeared in *Bo Bedre* during the 1960s, designers for the Cotil collection included weavers Annie Fisker, Lisbeth Have, Paula Trock, Birthe Ziebe, fabric printers Marie Gudme Leth and Dorte Raaschou, and architect Arne Jacobsen. **11** Kim Naver, email to the author, 19 June 2019. **12** Kim Naver in conversation with the author, March 2019. **13** Kim Naver, email to the author, 19 June 2019. **14** Ibid. **15** Paludan, *The Art of Weaving*, 184 (see note 5). **16** See note 5. **17** Torben Schmidt, "Kunsthåndværkeren som industridesigner: Et interview fra Form med Kim Naver," in *Dansk Brugskunst*, vol. 42, no. 3–4, 1971, 88. As well: Mogens Koch, "Kim Naver," in *Dansk Brugskunst*, vol. 42, no. 3–4, 1971, 79–82. **18** The library of Designmuseum Danmark holds at least three ring binders with samples of Cotil fabrics from the early 1970s. **19** Kim Naver in conversation with the author, March 2024. Hans Dissing and Otto Weitling approached Naver following her 1975 exhibition at the Danish Museum of Applied Art (now Designmuseum Danmark). **20** Kim Naver, "Forslag til udsmykning af forhal i Danmarks Nationalbank," unpublished typewritten manuscript.

KNUD HOLSCHER / STRING-LINE, 1973–76/1981–82

1 Maija Kärkkäinen, "Knud Holscher: An architectural autobiography = En arkitektonisk autobiografi," in Marja-Ritta Norri and Maija Kärkkäinen (eds.), *Knud Holscher & KHR A/S: A Universal Aesthetic Experience = En altomfattende æstetiske oplevelse* (Helsinki: Museum of Finnish Architecture, 1992), 45–51. **2** Ibid. **3** Knud Holscher in conversation with the author, September 2014. **4** Ibid. **5** Ibid. **6** Ibid. **7** Ibid. **8** Michael Sheridan, *Room 606: The SAS House and the Work of Arne Jacobsen* (Copenhagen: Strandberg Publishing, 2023), 160–162. **9** Malene Lytken, *Danish Lights: 1920 to Now* (Copenhagen: Strandberg Publishing, 2019), 102. **10** Ibid., 106. **11** Alberto Bassi, *Italian Lighting Design 1945–2000* (Milan: Electa, 2004), 145. As well: Sergio Polano, *Achille Castiglioni: Complete Works* (Milan: Electa, 2006). **12** Knud Holscher in conversation with the author, September 2014. **13** Ibid. **14** In addition to the figures examined in this book – Knud Holscher, Arne Jacobsen, Karsten Ravn and Lars Lundquist, and Nils Fagerholt – the leading actors include Poul Kjærholm, Jørgen Kastholm and Preben Fabricius, Erik Magnussen, Verner Panton, Poul Gammelgaard, and Niels Jørgen Haugesen. For a discussion of designs not included in the book, see Lars Dybdahl, trans. Dorte H. Silver, *Furniture Boom: Mid-century Modern Danish Furniture 1945–75* (Copenhagen: Strandberg Publishing, 2018), 268–294. **15** Knud Holscher in conversation with the author, September 2014. **16** Jens Christian Larsen, email to the author, October 2015. **17** Ibid. **18** Ibid.

MOGENS KOCH / MK-16, 1933/1938/1960

1 Per Mollerup, "Koch's Collapsible," in *Mobilia*, no. 319, 1983, 25–33. **2** Ibid. **3** "Selskabet for Kirkelig Kunst," *Arkitekten. Ugehæfte*, vol. 34, no. 52, 30 December 1932, 220. **4** "Kirkelig kunst," *Arkitekten. Ugehæfte*, vol. 35, no. 15, 13 April 1933, 71–72. **5** For a detailed and lavishly illustrated overview, see Florence de Dampierre, *Chairs: A History* (New York: Abrams, 2006). For a historic summary based on furniture types, see Ole Wanscher, *The Art of Furniture: 5000 Years of Furniture and Interiors*, trans. David Hohnen (London: Allen & Unwin, 1968). **6** Wanscher, *The Art of Furniture*, 87–88 (see note 5). **7** Ibid., 12, 42-47. **8** Ibid., 408, 410. **9** Nicholas A. Brawer, *British Campaign Furniture: Elegance under Canvas, 1740–1914* (New York: Abrams, 2001), 61, 66, 70–72. **10** The exhibition is described in Grete Jalk's encyclopedic, four-volume compendium of the annual exhibitions and illustrated using a contemporary photograph of the folding chair. Grete Jalk (ed.), *40 years of Danish furniture design: the Copenhagen Cabinet-makers' Guild exhibitions 1927–1966 = Dansk Møbelkunst Gennem 40 År: Københavns Snedkerlaugs Møbeludstillinger 1927–1966*, vol. 2 (Høje Tastrup: Teknologisk Instituts Forlag, 1987, reprinted in 2017 by Lindhardt og Ringhof / Forlaget Carlsen), 54–55. **11** Mogens S. Koch in conversation with the author, March 2024. **12** Ibid. **13** Ibid. **14** Erling and Axel Thygesen, "Interna A/S," in *Mobilia*, no. 65, December 1960, 43–56. **15** The descriptions of individual models are drawn from the 1964 Interna catalog. **16** Mogens S. Koch in conversation with the author, March 2024. **17** Ibid. **18** See note 15.

BØRGE MOGENSEN / SM 50, 1964–69

1 Poul Erik Skriver, "Børge Mogensens hus," in *Arkitektur*, vol. 9, no. 3, 1965, 108–118. **2** Rigmor Anderson, *Kaare Klint Møbler* (Copenhagen: Kunstakademiet, 1979), 48. As well: Gorm Harkær, *Kaare Klint*, vol. 1 (Copenhagen: Klintiana, 2010), 348–356; Ibid., vol. 2, 32. **3** Harkær, *Kaare Klint*, vol. 2, 48 (see note 2). **4** Arne Karlsen and Børge Mogensen, "Illusion og realitet: Betragtninger over Snedkerlaugets Møbeludstilling 1959," in *Dansk Kunsthaandværk*, vol. 32, no. 8–9, 1959, 162–177. The cited quotation is found on page 165. The article was a precursor to the same authors' article "Brugskunst på afveje" (Applied Art Gone Astray), which initiated the chain of events that led Hanne Valeur to design the K-60 kitchen system, described in Chapter 3 of this book. **5** Ole Wanscher, *Sella Curulis: The Folding Stool: An Ancient Symbol of Dignity* (Copenhagen: Rosenkilde & Bagger, 1980), see Chapter VIII: "Faldestoel. Faldestorium," 191–262.

KARSTEN RAVN / LARS LUNDQUIST / RL GRILL SERIES, 1969–73

1 Karsten Ravn in conversation with the author, October 2019. **2** Ibid. **3** The familiar term "barbeque" is derived from the Spanish word barbacoa. Early explorers to the New World adopted the term from Indigenous peoples around the Caribbean, who used a framework of branches to suspend meat over a fire. The English terms "grill" and "roast" are both derived from old French terms that gained currency in the British isles following the Norman Conquest. While "grill", "gridiron" and "griddle" are all derived from greil or gredile, the French terms rostir (to roast), *rôtissoir* (the equipment for doing so) and *rotisseur* (the place where meat is roasted) spawned the roast, so beloved in the UK, and the universal rotisserie. **4** For an introduction to roasting, see Bee Wilson, *Consider the Fork: A History of How We Cook and Eat* (New York: Basic Books, 2012), 73–89. Wilson discusses the gradual development of the enclosed kitchen oven on pages 89–93. Colin Clair covers the same topic on pages 201–215 of his charming tome *Kitchen and Table* (see note 7). **5** Conrad Bjerre-Christensen, "Grill og havegrill," in *Berlingske Tidende*, 17 September 1967. **6** Karsten Ravn in conversation with the author, January 2020. **7** Colin Clair, "The evolution of the kitchen," in *Kitchen and Table: A Bedside History of Eating in the Western World* (London: Abelard-Schuman, 1964), 194–200. Clair also provides a summary of Bartolomeo Scappi's groundbreaking cookery book on pages 245–246. As well: Lawrence Wright, *Home Fires Burning: The History of Domestic Heating and Cooking* (London: Routledge & Kegan Paul, 1964), 41–57. **8** Carlo M. Cipolla, *Clocks and Culture: 1300–1700* (New York: Norton, 1967), 47–58. **9** Ivan Day, "The clockwork cook: A brief History of the English spring-jack," in Ivan Day (ed.), *Over a Red-hot Stove: Essays in Early Cooking Technology.* (The Leeds Symposium on Food History Series "Food and Society") (London: Prospect Books, 2009), 99–124. **10** Karsten Ravn in conversation with the author, January 2020. **11** Ibid. **12** The descriptions of the grills and tools are taken from Ole Palsby's printed advertisements and seasonal catalogs. **13** *Eva*, May 1972, 59. **14** George Kringelbach, "Det skete med Ole Palsby," in *Politiken*, 7 February 1976. **15** Malin Lindgren, "Plagiater truer dansk design," in *Berlinske Tidende*, 8 February 1976. **16** Ibid. **17** Product brochures issued by Kay Dideriksen and Carsten Fagerholt, which are currently in the possession of Karsten Ravn. **18** Karsten Ravn in conversation with the author, July 2023. **19** Frederik Sieck, "Lars Lundquist," in *Mobilia*, no. 276, 1978, 18–25.

EPILOGUE / DESIGN FOR LIFE

1 Per Lütken, *Glass is Life* (Copenhagen: Nyt Nordisk Forlag, 1986).

SELECTED BIBLIOGRAPHY

- Berglund, Erik. *Bord för Måltider och Arbete i Hemmet*. Stockholm: Svenska Slöjdföreningen, 1957.
- Bruun, Vibeke, Esbjørn Hiort, Richard Kjærgård and John Vedel-Rieper, eds. *Dansk Kunsthåndværkerleksikon: Kunsthåndværkere og Designere Siden 1925*. Vols. 1–2. Copenhagen: Rhodos, 1979.
- Caldenby, Claes, ed. *Tiden, Platsen, Arkitekturen: Asplunds Rådhus i Göteborg = Asplund's Law Court Extension in Gothenburg*. Stockholm: Arkitekturmuseet, 2010.
- Enevoldsen, Christian. "Køkkenelementer K-60." *Spatium*, 1963, vol. 1, no. 1: 8–10.
- Gelfer-Jørgensen, Mirjam. *The Joining of the Arts: Danish Art and Design 1880–1910*. Copenhagen: Strandberg Publishing, 2020.
- Harkær, Gorm. *Kaare Klint*. Copenhagen: Klintiana, 2010.
- Jalk, Grete, ed. *40 Years of Danish Furniture Design: The Copenhagen Cabinet-makers' Guild Exhibitions 1927–1966 = Dansk Møbelkunst Gennem 40 År: Københavns Snedkerlaugs Møbeludstillinger 1927-1966*. Høje Tastrup: Teknologisk Instituts Forlag, 1987. Reprinted 2017 by Lindhardt og Ringhof / Forlaget Carlsen.
- Jørstian, Tina and Poul Erik Munk Nielsen, eds. *Light Years Ahead: The Story of the PH Lamp*. Trans. Tam McTurk. Copenhagen: Louis Poulsen, 1994.
- Karlsen, Arne. *Danish Furniture Design in the 20th Century*. Trans. Martha Gaber Abrahamsen. Copenhagen: Christian Ejlers' Forlag/Dansk Møbelkunst, 2007.
- Karlsen, Arne. *En Linie i Dansk Arkitektur og Brugskunst*. Aarhus: Arkitektskolen Aarhus, 1985. Reprinted in: Karlsen, Arne. *Krydsklip i en arkitekts dagbog 1950-2000*. Copenhagen: Christian Ejlers' Forlag, 2002.
- Karlsen, Arne. *Furniture Designed by Børge Mogensen = Møbler Tegnet af Børge Mogensen*. Copenhagen: Danish Architectural Press, 1968.
- Karlsen, Arne. "Om Mogens Kochs arbejder." *Dansk Kunsthaandværk*, 1963, vol. 36, no. 9–10: 157–196.
- Klint, Kaare. "Om møbeltegning." *Arkitekten Maanedshæfte*, 1930, vol. 32, no. 10: 193–224.
- Koch, Mogens. *Moderne Dansk Kunsthaandværk*. Copenhagen: Thaning & Appel, 1948.
- Koch, Mogens. "Møbelkunst." *Dansk Kunsthaandværk*, 1954, vol. 27, no. 7: 108–116.
- Mogensen, Børge and Arne Karlsen. "Tradition og fornyelse." *Spatium*, 1963, vol. 1, no. 1: 1–8.
- Mogensen, Børge and Arne Karlsen. "Brugskunst på afveje." *Arkitekten*, 1962, no. 1: 1–11.
- Mogensen, Børge and Arne Karlsen. "Illusion og realitet: Betragtninger over Snedkerlaugets Møbeludstilling 1959." *Dansk Kunsthaandværk*, 1959, vol. 32, no. 8–9: 162–177.
- Mogensen, Thomas. *Lis Ahlmann: Tekstiler*. Copenhagen: Christian Ejlers' Forlag, 1974.
- Paludan, Charlotte. *The Art of Weaving: Danish Hand Weaving in the 20th Century*. Copenhagen: Danish Museum of Decorative Art, 2004.
- Sheridan, Michael. *Room 606: The SAS House and the Work of Arne Jacobsen*. Copenhagen: Strandberg Publishing, 2023.
- Sheridan, Michael. *Louisiana: Architecture and Landscape*. Humlebæk: Louisiana Museum of Modern Art, 2017.
- Sheridan, Michael. *Landmarks: The Modern in Denmark*. Ostfildern: Hatje Cantz, 2014.
- Thau, Carsten, and Kjeld Vindum. *Arne Jacobsen*. Trans. Martha Gaber Abrahamsen. Copenhagen: Danish Architectural Press, 2001.

SUGGESTED READING

- Beard, James, et al., eds. *The Cooks' Catalogue: A Critical Selection of the Best, the Necessary, and the Special in Kitchen Equipment and Utensils*. New York: Harper & Row, 1975.
- Clair, Colin. *Kitchen and Table: A Bedside History of Eating in the Western World*. London: Abelard-Schuman, 1964.
- Kamp, David. *The United States of Arugula: How We Became a Gourmet Nation*. New York: Broadway Books, 2006.
- Kjeldsen, Christina B. and Isabel Bernadette Brammer. *Grethe Meyer: Arkitekten, der revolutionerede middagsbordet*. Copenhagen: Gyldendal, 2024.
- Koch, Mogens. *Moderne Dansk Kunsthaandværk*. Copenhagen: Thaning & Appel, 1948.
- Lassen, Erik. *Ske, Kniv og Gaffel = Knives, Forks & Spoons*. Copenhagen: Høst & Søn, 1960.
- Lasssen, Erik and Mogens Schlüter. *Dansk Glas 1925-85*. Copenhagen: Nyt Nordisk Forlag, 2002.
- Lübecker, Pierre. *Applied Art by Kay Bojesen*. Trans. Mary Fulfold. Copenhagen: National Association of Danish Handicrafts, 1955.
- Brandt Poulsen, Mogens, Bo Karlsen, Poul Østergaard and Erik Nygaard. *Arne Karlsen: Arkitekt og skribent*. Aarhus: Arkitektskolen Aarhus, 1997.
- Salicath, Bent and Arne Karlsen. *Modern Danish Textiles*. Trans. Birthe Andersen. Copenhagen: Danish Society of Arts and Crafts and Industrial Design, 1959.
- Skak-Nielsen, Luise. *Det påklædte hjem: Tekstiler og boligkultur i Danmark gennem 300 år*. Nørre Alslev: Historismus, 2017.
- Visser, Margaret. *The Rituals of Dinner*. New York: Grove, 1991.
- Wilson, Bee. *Consider the Fork: A History of How We Cook and Eat*. New York: Basic Books, 2012.

A

Aalto, Aino 152
Aalto, Alvar 69, 74, 150–152, 158, 282
Ahlmann, Lis 13, 242–243, 256–259, 262, 265, 313
Andersen, Rigmor 6, 62
Angelico, Fra 256
Anthon, Jørgen 259
Asplund, Erik Gunnar 154, 158, 236

B

Bækmark, Jørgen 201
Bang, Jacob E. (Eiler) 47–48, 51, 178
Baumann, Povl 204
Beckman, Alice 97
Bentsen, Ivar 204
Berglund, Erik 193–194
Biilmann-Petersen, Gunnar 24, 26, 206
Bjerre-Christensen, Conrad 318
Bo, Jørgen 62, 68–69, 72, 136, 162, 167, 172
Bojesen, Erna 40
Bojesen, Ernst 24
Bojesen, Kay 24–34, 37–41, 48, 55–57, 78, 85, 140, 145, 269, 336–338
Bojesen, Otto 24
Bojesen, Thyra 24
Bonaparte, Napoleon 294
Bonfils, Bo 69, 132–136
Brandt, Marianne 78, 82, 86
Breuer, Marcel 69, 82, 152, 282
Brüel, Axel 97
Brun, Alexander 162
Brun, Louise 162

C

Cadovius, Poul 300
Castiglioni, Achille 272–273, 282
Child, Julia 143
Christensen, E. (Ejvind) Kold 11

D

Danel, Curt 228, 233
Danel, Kirsten 228, 233
David, Elizabeth 132, 138, 143
Dideriksen, Kay 335
Dissing, Hans 269
Ditzel, Jørgen 48, 136
Ditzel, Nanna 48
Dürer, Albrecht 210
Dybbroe, Ole 226

E

Eames, Charles 152, 158
Eames, Ray 152, 158
Enevoldsen, Christian 67
Escoffier, Auguste 318

F

Fagerholt, Carsten 335
Fagerholt, Nils 69–71, 74, 132, 136, 318–319, 335
Falkentorp, Ole 204
Fisker, Kay 206
Francesca, Piero della 256
Franck, Kaj 47–48, 51, 94, 97, 100, 106–110, 118, 128
Frandsen, Erik 47–48

G

George I, King of Great Britain 26
Grauballe, Christian 27
Graversen, Andreas 193, 239, 295

H

Hammerborg, Jo 272–273
Hansen, Christian E. (Eduard) 150
Hansen, Fritz 150–152, 158
Hansen, Poul 150
Hansen, Søren 150
Hansen, Victor 72
Heiberg, Edvard 60–61, 71, 218
Helmer-Petersen, Keld 132
Henning, Gerda 258–259
Henningsen, Poul 62–63, 174–187, 206–208, 215, 338
Henriksen, Hans H. 47, 51
Herløw, Erik 44–47, 51, 78, 97, 99
Hiort, Esbjørn 47, 72, 97
Hoffmann, Josef 236–237
Holmblad, Peter 76, 84, 87
Holscher, Knud 270, 273–284, 288, 336
Hopea, Saara 47, 50–51
Hvidt, Peter 152

J

Jacobsen, Arne 14, 76–87, 97, 109, 132, 140, 150–161, 172, 206, 269–276, 281, 336–338
Jalk, Grete 167
Jensen-Klint, Peder Vilhelm 12, 208
Jensen, Børge 71
Jensen, Georg 24, 26, 78
Jensen, Henning 58, 61–63, 66–68, 74, 132
Jensen, Knud W. 162, 167, 170
Jensen, Søren Georg 69, 78, 327
Jeppesen, Poul 167–168, 172
Jespersen, Ebba 119
Jessen, Allan 304
Johansen, Svend 178
Johansen, Viggo 180
Johansson, Ejvind A. 201
Juhl, Finn 6, 9, 32, 58, 67, 71, 157, 164, 170, 236, 303
Jung, Carl 6

K

Kåge, Wilhelm 94, 97, 100, 116, 118, 128
Karlsen, Arne 58, 62, 67, 75, 304, 307
Key, Ellen 116
Kindt-Larsen, Edvard 47
Kindt-Larsen, Tove 47
Kjær, Børge 44, 71, 75
Kjær, N.C. Jensen 247, 295
Kjærgaard, Poul 44, 92, 218
Kjærholm, Poul 8, 11, 69, 136, 172
Klint, Kaare 6–16, 19, 27, 58, 62, 75, 162–164, 167, 170, 188–190, 193, 204–208, 212, 214–215, 218, 224, 233, 236, 242–247, 258–259, 262, 273, 292–294, 304, 307–309, 313
Klint, Lise Le Charlotte 214–215
Klint, Morten Le 259
Klint, Tage 206–208, 212, 215
Klint, Vibeke 258–259, 262, 265
Knudsen, Jørgen 84
Koch, Ea 9, 16, 58, 204, 292
Koch, Hans 204, 208, 210, 215
Koch, Mogens 6–9, 12, 14–19, 58, 62, 75, 188, 204–217, 236, 246–255, 258–259, 292–304, 309–310, 336, 338
Kofod-Larsen, Ib 48, 58
Koppel, Henning 10, 48, 136
Koppel, Niels 32, 178
Kringelbach, George 134, 140, 143
Kristensen, Svenn Eske 61, 218

Index

L

Lannik, Poul 140
Larsen, Jens Christian 284
Lauritzen, Vilhelm 206
Lautrup-Larsen, Leif 99
Lindberg, Stig 118, 128
Lindgren, Erik 97, 99, 102, 104
Lorenzetti, Ambrogio 256
Louis XIV, King of France 336
Lundquist, Lars 132–138, 316–328, 332–338
Lütken, Per 336
Lyager, Marianne 97

M

Mangor, Erik 134–140
Manzù, Pio 272–273, 282
Markelius, Sven 60
Meyer, Grethe 8, 44–55, 57, 60, 75, 84, 92–113, 116–128, 188, 201, 218–233, 315, 327, 336, 338
Michelsen, A. (Anton) 45
Mogensen, Alice 304
Mogensen, Børge 6, 16, 19–20, 45, 50, 58, 62–63, 67, 75, 128, 188–201, 218–228, 233–245, 259, 269, 295, 304–315, 336, 338
Moholy-Nagy, László 82
Mølgaard-Nielsen, Orla 6, 152, 188
Møller-Jensen, Jens 12
Mørch, Ibi Trier 44–51, 57, 60, 84, 92–102, 128, 229, 327, 338
Morris, William 236–237
Moser, Koloman 236

N

Naver, Kim 256–269, 338
Naver, Rasmus 256
Nielsen, Erling Zeuthen 304
Nielsen, Frederik 190, 201

O

Olesen, Carl 258

P

Palsby, Ole 67–75, 132–146, 276, 320, 332, 335–336, 338
Palsby, Palle 67, 72
Panton, Verner 272–273, 282
Paulsson, Gregor 116
Petersen, Carl 12, 204, 208, 210
Plato 6

Q

Quistgaard, Jens Harald 10–11, 58

R

Rams, Dieter 69
Rasmussen, Erhard 62, 236–237
Rasmussen, Jørgen Rudolf 300
Rasmussen, Steen Eiler 190, 206
Ravn, Karsten 132–138, 316–328, 332, 335–338
Rohde, Johan 12
Rosenkvist, Sus Bojesen 40
Rølling, Jens 270, 273–274, 278

S

Saarinen, Eero 152, 158
Salicath, Bent 44, 60–61, 75, 97, 218, 259
Sandgaard, Svend 84
Sass, Elisabeth 47, 97
Sass, Søren 97
Scappi, Bartolomeo 319
Schrader, Åse Voss 47
Schütte-Lihotzky, Margarete 60
Slomann, Vilhelm 206
Stam, Mart 282
Stephensen, Magnus L. (Læssøe) 32, 78, 276
Suenson, Palle 58
Svedberg, Elias 226

T

Thygesen, Axel 113, 247, 296, 300
Tye, Allan 270

U

Utzon, Jørn 214–215
Utzon, Lis 215

V

Valeur, Hanne 58–71, 74–75, 132, 320, 338
Valeur, Torben 58, 62–63, 66–68, 74, 132
Vasegaard, Gertrud 97–99
Vestergaard, V. (Viggo) Wismar 97
Vodder, Knud 97
Vodder, Niels 164
Volther, Poul M. 201

W

Waal, Allan de 180
Wanscher, Ole 6, 167, 309
Webb, Philip 236–237, 241
Wegner, Hans J. (Jørgensen) 6, 9, 16, 164, 170
Weitling, Otto 269
Weylandt, Teit 86
Windeleff, Aage 188
Wohlert, Vilhelm 62, 68–69, 72, 78, 136, 162–172, 215, 336

Z

Zachariassen, Hans 71
Zachariassen, Inger 71

Unless otherwise noted, all drawings:
© Michael Sheridan

All images: © Mikkel Jul Hvilshøj
with the exception of:

Anders Sune Berg: 263–264, 267; Anker Tiedemann: 86; Courtesy Arne Jacobsen Design I/S: 150; Courtesy of Bruun Rasmussen Auctioneers: 9–10, 12–13, 31, 33b, 41t, 234r; Børge Mogensens Tegnestue: 63, 191, 192b, 221, 237t, 245, 306b; Børge Mogensens Tegnestue/Erik Hansen: 226b; Børge Mogensens Tegnestue/Jesper Høm: 62b, 225t; Børge Mogensens Tegnestue/Mogens S. Koch: 21; Børge Mogensens Tegnestue/Photo: Aage Strüwing, © Jørgen Strüwing: 222–223; Brahl Fotografi/Louis Schnakenburg: 326, 329b, 330t, 331; Dansk Møbelkunst ApS: 16, 18; Designmuseo Finland/Pietinen: 94r; Designmuseum Danmark/Jesper Høm: 178, 179b; Designmuseum Danmark/Pernille Klemp: 11b; Designmuseum Danmark/Sisse Jarner: 262; Still photo from PH lys, instruktør Ole Roos, 1964. © Det Danske Filminstituts arkiv: 187; © Dorotheum Vienna: 236r; FDB Møbler: 19m; Courtesy Jakob Bonfils: 322, 329t, 330b, 332–335; From Spatium no. 1, 1963: 64–65, 67; Courtesy Svenskt Tenn: 215; Grethe Meyer Design: 50, 92, 96–97, 116; Hanne Valeur: 66; Heart Museum of Contemporary Art: 11t; Jens Markus Lindhe: 59, 69–75; Keld Helmer-Petersen by courtesy of Jan Helmer-Petersen: 68b, 318; Kim Naver: 269; Knud Holscher Design: 288; Le Klint: 214l, 216t; Louisiana Museum of Modern Art/Jesper Høm: 162, 172; Louisiana Museum of Modern Art/Wolfgang Etzold: 167; Mikkel Palsby: 134–135, 137, 139br; Mogens Koch Design: 7, 15, 206; Mogens S. Koch: 19t and b, 41b, 201, 233, 315; Nationalmuseum – Sweden's Museum of Art and Design: 95, 118, 207; Photo Scala, Florence – Courtesy of the Ministero Beni e Att. Culturali e del Turismo: 256; Rauner Special Collections Library, Dartmouth College: 319; © Royal Danish Library – The Art Library: 8, 14–15, 153b, 208, 209r, 306t; Ryland, Peters & Small: 129; SMK Photo/Jakob Skou-Hansen: 181; Swedish Centre for Architecture and Design/Sune Sundahl: 60b; Digital image, The Museum of Modern Art, New York/Scala, Florence: 94tl, 94bl; Thomas Mikkelsen: 35b; Victoria and Albert Museum: 236l; Winterthur Museum, Garden & Library/William F. Winter: 192t.

The editors have made every effort to find all licenses with regard to printed illustrations. Should any be missing, the license holder is welcome to contact Strandberg Publishing, who will honor the license in question as if an agreement had been reached previously.

Credits

A book such as this requires the assistance of many people, and I am grateful to each and every one of them, including any that I might inadvertently omit from this lengthy list. Researching the book, it was my privilege to spend time with Knud Holscher, Kim Naver, Ole Palsby, Karsten Ravn, Hanne Valeur and Vilhelm Wohlert. Their willingness to explain their designs to me provided the spark that lit the fire. Beyond the designers, I am deeply indebted to the heirs who provided me with facts and access to objects, archival photographs and drawings: Mogens S. Koch and Susanne Havning; Sus Bojesen Rosenqvist; Peter Mogensen, Thomas Mogensen and Sarah A. Moutouh; Dorte Salicath; Isabel Bernadette Brammer; Peter Holmblad; Mikkel Palsby and Caroline Palsby; and Andreas Trier Mørch.

The research and writing of this book were assisted by Jenny Phan, image archivist at Nationalmuseum in Stockholm; Sara Fruelund and Morten Langkilde of the library at Designmuseum Danmark; Steen Søndergaard Thomsen and his colleagues at the Art Library of the Royal Danish Library; and the staff of the Miriam and Ira D. Wallach Division of Art, Prints and Photographs at the New York Public Library. Thanks also to Christian Holmsted Olesen, Designmuseum Danmark; Helle Crenzien, Louisiana Museum of Modern Art; and Susanne Outzen, Museum Sydøstdanmark. I am especially indebted to Jens Christian Larsen, Fritz Togo, Peter Poulsen, Børge Nissen, Troels Hasner, Michael von Essen, Morten Kjærgaard, Michael Asgaard Andersen and Ole Eichen, for their replies to my repeated inquiries and detailed questions.

The wealth of images in this book would not have been possible without the cooperation of Jørgen Strüwing, Jan Helmer-Petersen, Jakob Bonfils, Dorte Værno and Ole Høstbo, Dansk Møbelkunst ApS; Per Mollerup; Per Ahldén, Svenskt Tenn; Kristian Harsted-Simonsen; Camilla Streton, Bruun Rasmussen Kunstauktioner A/S; Marianne Lewis, Kirsten Strømstad and Ida Præstegaard. Special thanks to Ragnhild Wibe Nielsen and Sigve Sletnes Madsen for each lending a helping hand. Further thanks to the owners and custodians of rare objects who allowed them to be photographed for this publication: Caspar Koch, Birgit Lyngbye Pedersen, Poul Himmelstrup, Vagn Henriksen, Susanne and Henrik Olesen as well as Ida Heiberg Bøttiger, Georg Jensen A/S.

The new photographs include objects that were borrowed from a number of current producers. As such, I extend my thanks to their employees past and present: Sinja Svarrer Damkjær, Le Klint A/S; Mia Sacks and Sidsel Faaberg Lensbjerg, Eva Solo A/S; Marie-Louise Høstbo, Ida Leisner, Christian Andresen and Sanne Lund Hansen, Fritz Hansen A/S; Rasmus Graversen, Fredericia Furniture; Jesper Temp and Leif Jensen, Getama A/S; Vendela Johansson, d line A/S; Annemette Thybo Madsen, Warm Nordic ApS; Louise Abildlund, &Tradition A/S; and Anne Dorthe Staggemeier, FLOS Scandinavia A/S.

I have been enormously fortunate to work with a team of creative talents that includes the photographers Jens Markus Lindhe, Anders Sune Berg and Thomas Mikkelsen. The vast majority of the new images were taken by Mikkel Jul Hvilshøj, who has captured the objects in their very best light and been an ideal working partner. Once again, and for the fifth time, my essential collaborator Michael Jensen has designed a book that embodies the ideals of the project and has only grown more beautiful by virtue of his skill and insight. The totality of these efforts was transformed into printed matter by a team of dedicated professionals, starting with Lars Erik Strandberg. I am especially grateful to my esteemed editor, Pernille Gøtze Johansson, gifted copy editor, Dorte Herholdt Silver, resourceful production manager, Morten Ommestrup and the irreplaceable Claudia Juul Kassentoft. None of the above efforts would have been possible without the support and encouragement of Rikke Ravn, Lars Christiansen, Annette Sletnes and Torben Madsen.

This book is dedicated to Annette and Torben, Vilma and Sigve.

Acknowledgments

Archetypes
ESSENTIAL WORKS OF DANISH DESIGN

© 2024 Michael Sheridan and Strandberg Publishing

Editor: Pernille Gøtze Johansson
Copy editor and proofreader: Dorte Herholdt Silver
Design and cover: Michael Jensen
Art director: Michael Sheridan
Editorial assistants: Markus Gehlert
and Sofie Ulrich Elisiussen
Cover photos: Mikkel Jul Hvilshøj

Typeset in Klarheit Grotesk
Paper: 130g Munken Polar
Image processing: Garn Grafisk
Printing and binding: Livonia Print
Printed in Latvia 2024
1st edition, 1st printing
ISBN 978-87-94102-88-9

Copying from this book may only take place at institutions that have entered into an agreement with Copydan and only within the terms and conditions set down in said agreement.

Strandberg Publishing A/S
Gammel Mønt 14
DK-1117 Copenhagen
www.strandbergpublishing.dk

Published with generous support from:

Arne V. Schleschs Fond

Bestles Fond

 DREYERSFOND

Lemvigh-Müller Fonden

NY CARLSBERG FONDET
NEW CARLSBERG FOUNDATION

POLITIKEN-FONDEN

Dr. arch. **Michael Sheridan** is an American architect and an internationally recognized scholar of twentieth-century Danish architecture and design. His previous books on those subjects include *Landmarks: The Modern House in Denmark* (2014), *Louisiana: Architecture and Landscape* (2017) and *Room 606: The SAS House and the Work of Arne Jacobsen* (2023). He currently divides his time between New York and Copenhagen.